The Secret War

The Secret War

Treason, Espionage, and Modern Fiction

Eva Horn
Translated from the German
and with an Introduction by
Geoffrey Winthrop-Young

Northwestern University Press
Evanston, Illinois

Northwestern University Press
www.nupress.northwestern.edu

Printed in the United States of America

10 9 8 7 6 5 4 3 2 1

Library of Congress Cataloging-in-Publication Data

Horn, Eva.
[Geheime Krieg. English]
The secret war : treason, espionage, and modern fiction / Eva Horn ; translated from the German and with an introduction by Geoffrey Winthrop-Young.
p. cm.
"Originally published in German as Der geheime Krieg: Verrat, Spionage und moderne Fiktion in 2007 by S. Fischer Verlag GmbH, Frankfurt am Main."
Includes bibliographical references and index.
ISBN 978-0-8101-2763-0 (pbk. : alk. paper)
1. Spy stories, English—History and criticism. 2. Spy stories, German—History and criticism. 3. Espionage in literature. 4. Spies in literature. I. Winthrop-Young, Geoffrey, 1960– II. Title.
PR830.S65H6713 2013
823'.087209—dc23

2012050887

The paper used in this publication meets the minimum requirements of the American National Standard for Information Sciences—Permanence of Paper for Printed Library Materials, ANSI Z39.48-1992.

CONTENTS

ACKNOWLEDGMENTS

The years in which I wrote this book were exciting, demanding, and full of new encounters with texts, films, and people. As may be glimpsed from my selection of texts and themes, large parts of the manuscript were written in the United States. The places I stayed in—New York, Berlin, Los Angeles, and finally Basel and Zurich—left their mark on my work and were as indispensable to me as the conversations with friends and colleagues. Happily, not all these talks revolved around treason, espionage, and secrets.

I would like to thank the late Friedrich Kittler and Joseph Vogl for an early, encouraging exchange about espionage in Buenos Aires that provided the initial spark for the project; Annette Bitsch for her astute insights into the comedy of the sexes in the spy world; Bernhard Siegert for his suggestion to include Rudyard Kipling (followed), Erskine Childers (followed), and John Buchan (not followed); Marcus Coelen for discussions of holy wars and the ethics of treason; Frank Berberich for publishing my first essay on the topic in *Lettre International;* Wolbert Smith for long and highly instructive talks about the reality of the intelligence world and for incisive critique of the manuscript from the point of view of an intelligence practitioner; Eva Geulen for her New York hospitality and her comments on the first chapters; Michèle Lowrie for conversations about Tacitus, Irenaeus, and Roman *arcana* while swimming in New York and hiking in Tannersville; Tricia Dailey for a tour of Big Sur, sushi in Malibu, and parties in Hollywood, as well as for her wisdom and art of living; Lena Kugler for her perfect listening skills; my mother, who in the final stage of this book asked me whether I would ever finish my studies; Larry and Beth Horowitz for their Upper East Side apartment, which became the site of the final revisions; Peter Krapp for Internet theory and practice in Konstanz, Montauk, Berlin, and Irvine; Catherine Liu for teaching me how to pronounce Sun Tzu; Anson Rabinbach for insisting on the Rosenbergs and for many joint conspiracies; Stefan Andriopoulos for suggesting DeLillo; Felicity Scott and Branden Joseph for their confidence in my essays for *Grey Room;* Claus Pias for insights into game theory and war gaming; Juliane Rebentisch for holding the fort in Frankfurt/Oder; Albert Koschorke for years of encouragement and support; Karl Schlögel for his insightful reader's report; Beate Fricke for her refreshing interest and enthusiasm; and last but not least Alexander Roesler, my editor, who was hesitant at first but then increasingly excited and helpful.

For this translation, which is an updated version of my book of 2007, I first and foremost must thank Geoffrey Winthrop-Young, who not only converted my tortuous German prose into elegant English but also discussed arguments, requested precise details, checked facts, and suggested updates—which made the translation process the most interesting and helpful discussion I ever had on this book. Martina Süess and Marion Mang did a fantastic job helping me edit the manuscript. My editors at Northwestern University Press, Henry L. Carrigan Jr. and Peter Raccuglia, provided all technical help necessary.

This translation was financed by the Geisteswissenschaften International Prize, awarded to the German original of *The Secret War* by the Fritz Thyssen Foundation. I am truly grateful for this wonderful form of support to the international dissemination of German humanities research. Without it, a translation of this size would not have been possible.

In addition, I am indebted to several institutions whose generous support enabled the research for this book: the Alexander von Humboldt Foundation for sixteen months as a Feodor Lynen research fellow in New York; the Department of German at New York University for its hospitality and excellent research facilities; the Junge Akademie of the Berlin-Brandenburg Academy of Sciences and Humanities for financing several research trips; the Graduiertenkolleg "Representation-Rhetoric-Knowledge" for inspiring discussions; and the Faculty of Social and Cultural Studies at the Europa University Viadrina in Frankfurt/Oder for its collegial atmosphere.

I especially want to thank my teacher, colleague, and friend Anselm Haverkamp, without whose generosity, brilliance, and unwavering confidence I would not have been able to complete this book, and Jacques Hadad, who was with me during the most intense writing periods and helped me to understand the secret war.

The Secret War

Translating Betrayal: Signpost for *The Secret War*

Geoffrey Winthrop-Young

A secret's worth depends on the people from whom it must be kept.
—Carlos Ruiz Zafón, *The Shadow of the Wind* (2001)

The Structure of Treason

Traduttore, traditore, the Italians claim: translators are traitors. According to academic legend the saying is rooted in Italian dismay over early French translations of Dante but it has long since become a widely acknowledged proverb. Its popularity is due to a fertile mix of rhetorical opposites: it is both trite and touchy, an emotionally fraught truism as volatile as it is banal.

On the one hand *traduttore, traditore* points to the disturbing fact—yes, it is a fact, not just a possibility—that some translators deliberately alter texts. There are many motives, ranging from the malicious to the merely misguided: I, the translator, hate this book and will therefore engage in willful distortion. Or maybe I believe that I am more familiar with the subject than the author, so I will help things along by improving the argument. Granted, there are worse crimes. Disfiguring a text is not the same as disfiguring a person. But the basic structure of the misdemeanor is identical with that of more serious acts of treason. Authors need and trust translators because they cannot write in the language of the readers; readers need and trust translators because they cannot read the language of the author. Deliberate mistranslation is therefore, first, a breach of trust that affects a community and, second, an act of deception that abuses a position of privilege. Exploiting their expert knowledge and privileged access to the original text and sometimes even to the author, translators can be to authors what Judas was to Jesus, Brutus to Caesar, and Kim Philby to MI6. That is the dark side of *traduttore, traditore.* Dante, who knew a thing or two about treason, reserved the deepest pit of hell for traitors and stuck Judas, Brutus, and Cassius straight into the mouths of Satan. One can imagine his Italian readers praying that his French translators end up there as well.

On the other hand, matters are obvious and not worth the fuss. Translators are neither angels nor superconductors. They cannot relay messages across time, space, and languages without loss of signal strength or free of distortion. Since any switching of codes involves an admixture of noise that affects the original message, a translator can no more prevent a change of meaning than a waiter can prevent a change of temperature when pouring coffee from a pot into a cup. Take the most important word in *The Secret War.* German does not distinguish between "treason" and "betrayal"; both are *Verrat.* Each time it occurs in the original, the translator must decide which of the two English words comes closer. Since neither matches the semantic bandwidth of *Verrat,* all the treasons and betrayals in this translation are autologies: the words themselves constitute acts of treason or betrayal of the German original. But then, to believe in faithful, nontreacherous translations is to believe in a world devoid of noise and friction—a very boring world (formerly known as paradise, now called entropy) in which the concept of treason, indeed of difference itself, has no meaning. However, if faulty translations are said to be the result of deliberate deviation *and* the unavoidable effect of switching from one language into another, then this form of "treason" is both intentional and ineluctable, artificial and natural. And with that we are right in the middle of Horn's description of a modern world in which *treason is as infamous as it is inevitable.*

But why this inflation of treason? *The Secret War* offers an explanation, but unlike many other attempts it is neither sociological, psychological, ethical, nor moral but rather structural, discursive, and media-technological. Horn's analysis consists, in essence, of a diachronic study of the variable components that together make up the changing configurations of treason in the twentieth century. Things will soon get complex, so let us start with a deceptively simple model. Treason involves passing on something that should not be passed on to a third party who should not be in possession of it. That something can be anything or anybody: an artifact, a piece of information, or a person. Espionage, in turn, involves the symmetrical operation of obtaining something one should not possess from someone unwilling to share it. In short, treason involves the *communication* of a secret *to* an enemy, espionage the *extraction* of a secret *from* an enemy. To repeat, this is not a definition but a structure, which means that two (once again, deceptively simple) points have to be kept in mind—indeed, they have to be on readers' minds throughout Horn's book:

1. A structure assigns positions but does not predetermine who will occupy which position. Think of the Shannon-Weaver model of communication featuring sender, receiver, source, channel, and noise. Reversing the flow of communication does not affect the structure itself, but those who were the receivers are now the senders, and vice versa. If an agent is "turned" and begins to communicate false intelligence or "chicken feed" to his (former) masters, the basic structure of the treacherous transaction remains the same, but the former beneficiaries are now the duped party. Structural properties, therefore, are not to be taken as the innate properties of those occupying a position. You are not a traitor to begin with; you *become* a traitor (or the betrayed, the interested third, or maybe even the channel) by occupying a certain position.

2. The properties of the structural components are mutually constitutive. Change one and all the others will be affected. If—to anticipate the next sections—a government decides to classify hitherto unclassified knowledge in the interest of state security, it thereby expands the realm of state secrets and thus expands the potential sphere of treason. If (as first happened in England under Edward III) merely imagining the king's death is legally defined as treason, if words and thoughts can be as criminal as acts, there is a vast increase of potential treachery. Likewise, if there is a leap in the technological ability to detect treason or to engineer leaks, the realm of potential enemies is expanded. If—as Horn details in her section on 9/11—the shape of the enemy changes, it automatically affects the shape and media of the intelligence necessary for identifying the enemy. In short, it is misleading to discuss treason on its own; it is always already part of a structure comprising *sovereignty, secrecy,* and *enmity* as well as the *media* involved. This structure is subject to change because there has hardly been a period in history in which not at least one of the main components changed. And no period has witnessed more change than the twentieth century.

Here we are at the center of Horn's study. Following theoretical and methodological introductions that lay out the key problematic, *The Secret War* devotes a set of chronologically arranged parts, chapters, and sections to the most important epochs in the changing history of modern treason and secrecy: the early conceptualization of space and intelligence in the lead-up to the First World War; the rise of professional intelligence agencies in and after World War I; the introduction of female agents (as a result of which the war between the sexes is superimposed on those between nations); the internationalization of the enemy in the shape of the Comintern agent fighting for a "World Revolution"; the mirror-imaging showdown of the Cold War; the "state paranoia" of McCarthyism; the reconfiguration of the paradigm of clues following the Kennedy assassination; the emergence (in all the old and new meanings of the word) of new shapes of enmity and (state) terror in the wake of 9/11. In each segment, Horn scrutinizes and deconstructs the prevailing ideas of treason, espionage, and/or enmity by analyzing fictional and nonfictional texts. She then explains how these texts either reveal or attempt to gloss over the period's specific configuration of sovereignty and secrecy to its epistemic, discursive, and technological conditions. As a result she emphasizes how epochs differ from one another. The doomed Comintern agents of the late 1920s may be fighting for the same enemy as the supposedly rational upper-echelon Soviet military cooked up in NATO war games of the late 1950s, just as the conspiracy theories surrounding JFK may look like those spawned by 9/11, but Horn shows that the conditions underlying the conceptualization of friends and enemies, secrecy and treason, have changed in such a way as to preclude convenient narratives of continuity. The treason and secrets of 1925 are not those of 1955; the conspiracies and invisible governments of 1961 are not those of 2001. As we shall see, this procedure is indebted to a prominent current in contemporary German theory, the most conspicuous feature of which is a highly effective fusion of discourse analysis, narratology, and media theory informed and tempered by a resolutely historicist approach. With the latter, *The Secret War* is also heir to the grand tradition of German historicism: each epoch has its very own form of treason and has to be understood accordingly.

However, on a basic level there is little to "betray" about Horn's book. *The Secret War* does not hide (or pretend to hide) any secrets. First, large parts explore material that will be more familiar to Anglo-American readers than it was to the original German audience: from Erskine Childers to Graham Greene, Don DeLillo, and John le Carré; from the Great Game of Rudyard Kipling's *Kim* to the Great Shame of T. E. Lawrence's *Seven Pillars of Wisdom;* from November 22, 1963, in Dallas, to September 11, 2001, in New York. Like sex and money, treason is too big and tempting a topic to be monopolized by any one nation or language, but apart from the biographical fact that Horn spent a lot of time researching *The Secret War* in Anglophone countries, there may be deeper reasons for the high profile of Britain and the United States in her book. Starting with an important cameo performance by Tacitus, supreme pathologist of the Roman Principate, there is an imperial subtext running through *The Secret War.* Empires, including their British and American variants, are the privileged playground of treason because attempts to increase and defend control over large heterogeneous territories call for deeper descents into the murkiness of political and administrative secrecy. In the case of Britain, matters were exacerbated by internal differentiations along class lines (which do much to explain the Philby case); in the case of the United States, matters are and continue to be exacerbated by the politics of exceptionalism (and Horn will show the degree to which the existence and deployment of state secrets amount to an ongoing *state of exception*).

Second, *The Secret War* is a very upfront book, written with great clarity, interest, and even enthusiasm (not all of which, hopefully, was lost or betrayed in the translation). But its joys are its dangers: it is easy to lose sight of the prevailing themes, especially when discussing a topic on which we are so quick to judge and slow to question our judgment. The following remarks therefore aim to provide a few historical and conceptual signposts to help readers navigate the changing structure of the landscape of treason. But for all the satisfaction that comes with reading an interesting book, it will be a *descensus ad infernos*—in literary terms, from the happy regions of Kiplingshire through the ambivalent expanse of the Lawrentian desert down into the moral twilight of Greeneland and the murky depths of Lecarrénia.

Nurturing Treason: Assumptions of Sovereignty

Treason—pardon the cheap pun—is a treacherous topic. It is even more slippery than pornography. According to Justice Potter Stewart's famous assessment it is impossible to define the latter, but you know it when you see it. The same applies to treason: it is difficult to define (and as we shall see, there are good reasons not to define it well), yet we appear to recognize it on sight. But then again, the closer you look, the more it dissolves into something else.

Some frequently discussed difficulties are misleading because they are not on the level of the issue. Introductions to treason and espionage like to highlight problems of perspective. Just as one person's terrorist is another person's freedom fighter, one person's traitor is another person's hero. The Soviet Union put Kim Philby on a stamp, an honor he is unlikely to receive in Britain. Whether you consider Benedict Arnold a traitor depends on which side of the Atlantic (or the Forty-Ninth Parallel) you live. Whether you consider Daniel Ellsberg and Julian Assange heroes of free speech depends on where you draw the line—discussed in great detail by Horn—between the public's right to know and the state's need to keep certain things secret. Was the former FBI source Ronald Reagan—"the most powerful ex-informer in history" (Hewitt 2010, 72)—a concerned patriot or a deluded snitch? Then there is the related problem that what counts as treason today may well be something very different tomorrow, especially if it turns out to be a success. At the time, the British viewed the American Revolution, defended by its perpetrators as a God-given right to secede and create a new government, as an act of treason. It is highly unlikely that there are many Britons around today who still consider the United States a seditious rogue state. Tobias Kelly and Sharika Thiranagama are right to point out that "treason is at the heart of the processes through which modern states are made" (2010, 3), but the insight comes with certain taboos on revisiting history. Like major banks that have accumulated spectacular debt, victorious treason is too big and powerful to fail or to be labeled criminal. To quote John Harington (seasoned Elizabethan courtier and inventor of the first British flush toilet): "Treason doth never prosper: what's the reason? / Why, if it prosper, none dare call it treason."

Or in the even pithier words of Talleyrand, who betrayed more masters than he could count: treason is a matter of date. For Horn, these discussions are of little help because they focus on the political, ideological, or moral observations of the act rather than on the structure sketched earlier. Nonetheless, it is necessary to add a historical sketch to understand the basic dynamics of change.

Let us begin with the Romans, to whom we owe so much in the overlapping arts of law, war, and murder. In the beginning, enshrined in the Roman Republic's Twelve Tablets of the Law (Leges Duodecim Tabularum) from the mid-fifth century B.C.E., there was a crime defined as *perduellio*. *Perduellis* was the old term for enemy, though it soon came to denote the "inner" enemy, as opposed to *hostis*, the "outer" enemy. The name and the examples used to describe it indicate that the crime was associated with the military domain. If you act "as an enemy," if you deliver a citizen or a city to those at war with Rome, you have in effect crossed over to the other side, and you will be hung, crucified, or cast from the Tarpeian Rock; your name will be consigned to oblivion or survive in infamy; and nobody, not even your family, will be allowed to mourn you.

At the turn from the second to the first century B.C.E., when the Republic (now big enough to become its own worst enemy) began its fatal descent into decades of civil unrest, a second, related law was added.

Political rather than military in nature, it referred less to treasonous acts committed in complicity with an outside enemy than to what these acts threatened: *maiestas*—the majesty or sovereignty of the Roman people. The specific circumstances that gave rise to this law—in essence, a volatile political feedback involving military crises and the desire to exert greater control over military and administrative elites—need not concern us. Suffice it to say that the law was successful for the same reason that humans are such a successful species: it was nonspecialized, highly adaptable, and very helpful when it came to pursuing personal interests under the guise of serving a higher purpose. For what exactly was *maiestas*? Nobody really knew, though as in the case of pornography (at which the Romans excelled as well) everybody claimed to recognize it on sight. Not even the Roman legal establishment, with its centuries' worth of accumulated sophistry, was able to furnish a binding definition. However, it was precisely the vagueness of *maiestas* that now made it possible to denounce as treason acts outside the purview of *perduellio*. Matters were exacerbated when with the fall of the Republic the concept was assimilated to the person of the emperor. Two professions, after all, profit more than any other from imprecise legislation—lawyers and dictators. The latter use legal vagary to extend their power; the former use it either to support dictators or to defend their clients by accusing the state of misapplying the law. The advocates on both sides would therefore offer their definitions of *maiestas* on the lines of "he diminishes *maiestas* who . . ." (Harries 2007, 74). Who says we have progressed beyond Rome?

Something similar happened in the course of the slow, frequently acrimonious emergence of the nation-state that began in the late Middle Ages. To defend and extend the sovereignty of the king, the crown made increasing use of the Roman *crimen maiestas;* and just like the Roman emperors of old, the new kings used the law as "a most important legal justification with which to anticipate charges of arbitrary repression or personal vengeance" (Cuttler 1981, 238). A significant portion of modern political and cultural theory revolves around the evaluation of this development. Did the sacralized centralization, with its successful conquest of municipal, feudal, and ecclesiastical jurisdictions, prepare the grounds for an equality before the law and thus for modern democracy? Or is it a nefarious power game in the course of which we attain formal equality only under the condition of being controlled by that which grants us what little nominal justice we enjoy? To sound a grim Foucauldian note, at the end of the development that leads from the Roman inception of *maiestas* to its early modern recursions, the sovereign state is poised to occupy a position similar to that of God in the book of Job: an entity so beyond reach that it cannot be held accountable because the very idea of accountability presupposes the blasphemous notion of a level judicial playing field accommodating both sovereign deity and lowly subject. God does not waste any time on self-defense or quibbling; he bluntly informs his presumptuous interlocutor that he cannot presume to question his creator because he, Job, is unable to draw a hook through Leviathan's nose. We, facing off against the modern Leviathan, are equally inadequate—we are always already on the brink of treason.

A closely related second aspect: as mentioned above, in the ongoing attempt to enshrine the king's sovereignty it was deemed that *imagining* the king's death constituted an act of treason. This has momentous consequences, for once treason moves from a physical to a mental action, "trying a person for the crime would mean discovering or constructing an inward truth as it was manifest in the character and words of the accused" (Cunningham 2002, 2). Just as there is a direct feedback between the growth of state sovereignty and the potential for treason, there is one between the growth of state sovereignty and subjectivity. Here we have another Foucauldian inflection that will occasionally emerge in *The Secret War*. The state extends its grip by probing our inner secrets (which obviously implies our construction as beings capable of harboring clandestine secrets that need to be divulged), yet in doing so it creates precisely that which it is looking for—an inwardness that proceeds to confirm the state's suspicions by having us develop the skills to remove ourselves and our secrets from the prying orders to make us speak and confess. The penetrating sovereign gaze is recast as a subject—an inner sovereign—that takes control of itself and thereby breaks with that which gave rise to it. "This is a call to treason: to imagine that the self is the agent of the events in one's life" (Cunningham 2002, 143).

At this point it is helpful to consider an alternate take on treason. In chapter 1 in part 2 (both the most German and the most theoretical), Horn introduces a lineup of German theorists of treason including Carl Schmitt and Margret Boveri. Schmitt, with his injunction not to unnecessarily politicize the functionality of the state apparatus and its "trade secrets," and, more important, his well-known diagnosis that the formation of a political collective is linked to the presence of a perceived common enemy, is the most important theorist working in the wings of *The Secret War*. However, let us address Boveri, whose four-volume *Treason in the Twentieth Century* has done much to enshrine the twentieth century as one big "landscape of treason." At the end of the fourth volume (titled *Treason as Epidemic: America*), after hundreds of pages of historical case studies, Boveri claims that it is "easy" to define treason:

> On a personal level treason is present if I create the impression of being something: a friend, a disciple, a democrat, a nationalist, a communist, a loyal citizen, a fellow campaigner for an idea, an obedient soldier, a member of a sect—and if I then think and act contrary to this by handing over the friend, denying the prophet, working against the ideological leader, harming democracy, the nation, communism, supporting the enemy of the state, or adopting a different belief. (Boveri 1960, 275)

Note that there is little talk about plots, secrets, or conspiracies, and that the traitor's allegiance to an "enemy" comes almost as an afterthought. The focus is on disguise and dissimulation. Treason is pretending to be something you are not with the intention of harming those you are deceiving. The arch-traitor, then, is neither Judas nor Brutus; it is the ever-scheming Iago, who is never on the outside what he is on the inside: "I am not what I am." In other words, treason (not to mention espionage) is fundamentally related to *acting*—a link that Horn explores in a detailed analysis of Bertolt Brecht's most controversial play, *The Measures Taken.*

Boveri claims that treason has become endemic because, to quote her somewhat scriptural phrase, in our day and age "man is not one thing alone"—*der Mensch ist nicht eines allein* (Boveri 1960, 275). Her prime example is J. Robert Oppenheimer, who was so much more than one thing: Jew, scientist, one-time Communist sympathizer, creator and critic of the atomic bomb, intellectual, administrative power broker, bearer of secrets, security risk. Moving between these professional and existential spheres, he never fully belonged to any of them. As in the case of translating a text from one language to another, every move involved some breach of loyalty:

> Almost all of [Oppenheimer's] actions and convictions were by one party or another construed as treason or transgression. Antifascism, support of Spanish-aid committees, and friendship with communists all amount to a betrayal of Americanism . . . The development of the bomb equals genocide. The refusal to name [Haakon] Chevalier: putting national security at risk. The naming of Chevalier: betraying a friend. Lack of support for the hydrogen bomb: another security risk. Later support of the hydrogen bomb: abetting genocide. (Boveri 1960, 276)

As Horn points out, Boveri contrasts this fracturing of ties and sense of self with a bygone age characterized by an all-encompassing, identity-supporting allegiance to sovereign lords (fathers, chieftains, leaders, kings), that is, by personal ties that were eroded by modernity's depersonalization of sovereignty. Boveri is in effect arguing for a correlation between the clarity of loyalty and identity. Honesty and a sense of rounded identity on the one hand and deception and treason on the other are opposites. Or, in the words of one of John le Carré's optimistically deluded protagonists: "I *am*, therefore I don't spy" (le Carré 2010, 88).

It is easy to dismiss this as antimodernist resentment. Boveri is lamenting what sociologists like Niklas Luhmann call functional differentiation. Modern societies with their disconcerting Oppenheimer plurality are comprised of autonomous systems such as law, science, politics, art, or education, each of which processes its environment (which includes all the other systems) by means of its very own code. And while Luhmann admits that the maintenance, indeed the very feasibility, of a self-identical subject moving through these systems poses a quandary, he insists that the success of modern societies depends precisely on the degree to which these systems are closed off from one another. Ideally, religion should not impose its coding system on politics; law should be immune to the aesthetic codes of art; the code of the system of economics should not run education.

Boveri's point about bygone personal loyalties appears to be worse than reactionary: it is romantic—a myopic idealization of premodern times when everybody "belonged." But let us take a closer look at it in light of the aforementioned recursion of *maiestas*. As sketched earlier, the Roman development went from *perduellio,* based on a logic of exclusion in which the "inner" enemy is always already the "outer" enemy, to *maiestas,* based on a logic of reentry that redrew the external divide between Rome and its enemies *within* Rome by delineating an even more "inner" or true domain of representative "Romanness" (*maiestas populi Romani*). The corresponding point of departure in the gradually consolidating European nation-states is not *perduellio* but precisely what Boveri had in mind: a feudal concept of fidelity to one's lord. This loyalty (*fides*), however,

> was not absolute and unconditional, but had become the expression of a voluntary, bilateral contract of vassalage cemented by a personal bond. Should a vassal feel grieved, he could seek justice through rebellion by offering formal defiance (*diffidatio, défi*), which meant literally a withdrawal of loyalty. Thus the vassal who resorted to war in defence of what he perceived as his rights could not be guilty of treason. (Cuttler 1981, 5)

This possibility of a legitimized withdrawal of fidelity, not to mention the recourse to legitimized rebellion, was incompatible with the growing notion of royal sovereignty. To implement the latter, it was necessary to ensure that only the king had the right to wage war and that he was beyond the feudal mechanisms of *diffidatio*. There is no nontreasonous way to break with the king. This new conceptualization of treason and lèse-majesté invoked the Roman notion of *maiestas* and modeled the king on the Roman emperor. Just as the sovereign (and later the state) was able to hide personal or partisan agendas behind the appeal to divine powers, the public good, or national security, acting against the sovereign "was no longer a form of personal betrayal but an act of disloyalty to the official order" (Kelly and Thiranagama 2010, 4). Vassals were turned into subjects—and subjects are those who gain the right and ability to discover that they cannot opt out of their subjection. It is therefore less the increased fracturing and abstraction of loyalty that results in "epidemic" treason than the expansion of sovereign state power. There is, simply put, more to guard and thus more to betray. An increasing domain of sovereignty increases the need for secrecy, and both create a greater potential of enmity and betrayability—that is, the opportunity or likelihood to betray and be betrayed, whether deliberately or unknowingly. The arts of treason and statesmanship develop in synergy:

> Treason is not simply . . . a foreign emergency or a violent oppositional force. Rather, by viewing treason as a threat defined in and through law, one that expands and contracts, and is both dangerous to the state and self-serving, we are then better able to analyze the interdependence of sovereignty and treason law. (Lemon 2006, 163)

There is a second, related point that sheds light on the murky nether regions explored by Horn. The Middle Ages tend to be great deal more subtle than those who idealize them. There is no shortage of texts from that time which shed light on the potential for violence inherent in personal oaths of loyalty (and which Boveri leaves unmentioned). No better example can be found than the alleged German national epic, the *Nibelungenlied*. Leaving aside the question of whether the designation "German" makes sense, it contains the greatest act of betrayal in German culture, Hagen's murder of Siegfried. But pernicious as it may be, it is also an act of realpolitik, something that was necessary in the interest of dynastic security because Siegfried's big biceps and (his wife's) bigger mouth posed a threat to the sovereignty of the kings of Burgundy. To use Joseph Fouché's infamously pragmatic description of Napoleon's seizure and execution of the Duke d'Enghien, the murder of Siegfried was worse than a crime; it was a mistake. What is deplorable is not the killing itself but the fact that the act and the identity of the perpetrators became public knowledge. Like the involvement of Emperor Tiberius in the assassination of one of his competitors (a historical case recorded by Tacitus and used by Horn to introduce the important concept of *arcana imperii*), the disposal of Siegfried at the hands of members of the Burgundian royal household should have remained a Burgundian state secret—a blond skeleton in the closet of power.

But it is the epic's second half that reveals the murderous dimension of unquestioned personal loyalty. Siegfried's widow Kriemhild, now married to Hunnish King Etzel, invites the Burgundians to the Hunnish court, where she engineers one of world literature's greatest massacres. In a brilliant analysis the medievalist Jan-Dirk Müller has shown how appeals from both sides to loyalty and honor (in this early feudal world, you are only as honorable as you are loyal) ensure that one bystander after another is drawn into a maelstrom of violence. Etzel's court becomes the anti-Camelot: the whole delicate balance of loyalty and sovereignty defused by the Round Table here reveals its dark underside as the volatile identity of honor and loyalty spirals out of control. Precisely those personal ties idealized by Boveri and others turn out to be "rules for the endgame" (Müller 2007) leading to a carnage of near-genocidal proportions.

The epic's most tragic figure is Rüdiger von Bechelaren. An old friend of the Burgundians, he hosts them on their doomed passage east and gives his daughter's hand in marriage to one of their kings. He is, however, also a vassal of King Etzel and has sworn a personal oath of loyalty to Kriemhild, who now calls on him to take up arms against his friends, guests, and in-laws. Whichever side he chooses, he will commit a breach of faith. Remaining neutral is also out of the question: he can neither refuse to fight nor accept the offer of the Burgundians not to fight him, since both would incur unforgivable dishonor. Rüdiger has been called the first modern figure of German literature because he displays the first signs of a modern subjective interiority. He is the first Graham Greene hero insofar as there is a clear correlation between self-understanding and the anguished contemplation of conflicting loyalties; and he is also the first le Carré hero because there is no way out. Indeed, Rüdiger's fate shows that Boveri got it right by getting it wrong. There is a clear connection between self-identity and loyalty. However, self-identity is not destroyed by the inescapable conflict of loyalties; the latter (just like the sovereign gaze sketched earlier) serve to *create* subjectivity in the first place. Luhmann said much the same when referring to the subject as an artifact of ascription, an address that appears to remain unchanged as people traverse the systems. The subject compensates for the instability of self-identity in functional differentiation; it both covers up and reveals the inevitability of treason in much the same way that the alleged stability of meaning both reveals and counteracts the inevitable betrayal of meaning in all acts of communication, including translation. I am, I develop my unmistakable identity because I am forced to ponder what kind of traitor I will be. This, no doubt, is one of the grimmest aspects of the shadowy world of war and treachery depicted by Horn: that subjects come into being only to realize their own impossibility.

Media Determine Our Treason

Given the content of Horn's book, the most important event to have occurred since its original publication in 2007 is Cablegate, the "leaking" of tens of thousands of diplomatic cables on the WikiLeaks website. Horn has updated her study by critiquing the simple and biased binary put forward by Julian Assange between total openness (good) and any governmental attempt to keep things secret (bad)—a binary, incidentally, that is reminiscent of Jean-Jacques Rousseau's politically troublesome fetish for transparency (see Starobinski 1988). Horn's more functional approach comes close to the concept of "pragmatic sovereignty" developed in Rebecca Lemon's incisive study of treason in Shakespeare. It is a sovereignty that has learned the tricks of the treacherous trade necessary for its survival. Lemon's prime exhibit is *Macbeth,* the story of good but hapless King Duncan, who is murdered by the cunning traitor Macbeth. Macbeth, in turn, is deposed by Duncan's son Malcolm, who rises to power because he has learned to act more like his father's murderer than his father: "Malcolm adopts the villainous characteristics of Macbeth's own reign, employing the deceptive mechanisms alleged of traitors to rule his kingdom effectively" (Lemon 2006, 87).

However, Horn also deals with the frequently overlooked technological aspect. With Cablegate and WikiLeaks in mind, the always quotable William Gibson has sounded a note of warning to those in power:

> In the age of the leak and the blog, of evidence extraction and link discovery, truths will either out or be outed, later if not sooner. This is something I would bring to the attention of every diplomat, politician and corporate leader. The future, eventually, will find you out. The future, wielding unimaginable tools of transparency, will have its way with you. In the end, you will be seen to have done that which you did. (Gibson 2012, 170)

This is a form of electronically enhanced eschatology. The divine books to be opened at the end of times to judge the living and the dead are replaced by digital technologies inaugurating a regime of unprecedented traceability. Just as increasingly refined examinations of the Zapruder tape yield ever more finely calibrated timelines of the event in Dallas of November 22, 1963, data plants with yottabyte deepnet processing capabilities are producing ever higher resolutions of our daily deeds and misdeeds. Corporate leaders or serfs, we are all leaking into the future. We have become constant betrayers of ourselves and others because technology has turned us into *Homo vestigia faciens,* Man the Trace-maker, a being defined by inscription surfaces, recording devices, and storage facilities able to capture far more of its signs and traces than it is willing to divulge.

In other words, there is a correlation between traceability and betrayability. The more we can intercept, store, and communicate, the more we can betray; the more we can be traced, monitored, and recorded, the more our digital trails are vacuumed up by insatiable agencies, the more we are being betrayed. Just as the switch from *perduellio* to *maiestas* and the rise of state sovereignty created new possibilities and suspicions of betrayal, every advance in media technology increases the domain of treason. Horn is very clear about this: whether it is a matter of extracting or leaking, of espionage or treason, each epistemic juncture detailed in her study is linked to a particular standard of technology. From the sextants and measuring-chains of Kipling's Great Geographical Game and the synergy of maps and reports in *The Riddle of the Sands* all the way to satellite reconnaissance and the web-based communications around 9/11, media are as crucial a variable in the changing structure of treason as the evolving configurations of sovereignty, enmity, and the secret. Media, too, determine the levels of the secret war. Here we detect the long shadow cast by the late Friedrich Kittler, who is as present in Horn's analysis as he is in several related (and recently translated) studies: Cornelia Vismann's scrutiny of the changing media of the executive branch in *Files: Law and Media Technology,* Bernhard Siegert's study of the discontinuous techno-epistemes of the postal circuit (*Relays*), Philipp von Hilgers's *War Games: A History of War on Paper,* and Markus Krajewski's *Paper Machines: About Cards and Catalogs, 1548–1929.* The Kittler effect is present not only in the emphasis on the foundational importance of media technology, or in the related assumption that perceptible and aesthetic properties are dependent variables of technical feasibility, but also in the focus on *war.* There is not much peace in Horn's book; and while Horn does not share the faint military hardware fetish that is occasionally present in recent German media theory (especially among its male proponents), she does continue employing the concept of war in the intriguing way that Kittler initiated. War is not simply the opposite of peace; it is also the opposite of transparency and publicity. The whole domain of secrecy and *arcana imperii,* the controversial necessity to accept or create a third space between the legal and the illegal, the muddy treacheries of trying to negotiate the shifting boundary between what is above the line and what is below—all this points to a world of subterfuge and confrontation that is always already at war. Montesquieu and Jürgen Habermas yield to Niccolò Machiavelli and Carl Schmitt: clear and public divisions of power invested with the spirit of consensus make way for amoral (not to be confused with immoral) pragmatism and the foundational importance of enmity. Readers of *The Secret War* are entering a world best summarized by the Duke of Wellington, who—as if quoting Sun Tzu, who looms large in Horn's account as the first theoretician of the secret war—famously claimed that war, politics, and life itself are quintessentially the same because they all depend on finding out what "is at the other side of the hill."

But then again, you need media to access the other side of the hill, and once again epistemological problems arise. It is naive to assume that refined tools will automatically bring you closer to the truth. They are just as liable to paint more refined pictures of alternate explanations. To continue the Gibson quotation:

> Regardless of the number and power of the tools used to extract patterns from information, any sense of meaning depends on context, with interpretation coming along in support of one agenda or another. A world of informational transparency will necessarily be one of deliriously multiple viewpoints, shot through with misinformation, disinformation, conspiracy theories and a quotidian degree of madness. We may be able to see what's going on more quickly, but that doesn't mean we'll agree about it more readily. (Gibson 2012, 170)

Which is very much what Horn says. Where everything can be seen, nothing can be discerned; where everything is in sight, nothing is in focus; where all is said, everything can be said otherwise. Increase of information spells an increase of ignorance because the more we know about things, the more we realize that they can be different. The implications are most evident in the final part of Horn's book on 9/11 and the concomitant rise of swarmlike terror networks. While Horn acknowledges that 9/11 spawned countless conspiracy narratives, she tends to agree with William Gibson that "the description of an underlying, literally occulted order is invariably less complex than the surface reality" (Gibson 2012,

119). So many nefarious machinations, so much subtle puppeteering—and it all boils down to a couple of suits or uniforms seated around a table? Horn's point is more subtle: nowadays conspiracy theories are not (to use Luhmannian terms) reductions of the complexities of an event but an increase in the complexity *of the communication about the event.* This sets 9/11 apart from the Kennedy assassination. JFK conspiracies attempt to reveal a signified that determines the event's many signifiers ("The CIA did it!"); by contrast, 9/11 conspiracies multiply and recombine the signifiers to erode and challenge any imposed signified ("What about this? And consider that! Connect it in a different way!"). The former arose before the arrival of a global digital network that facilitates instantaneous dialogic and participatory communication structures, thereby promoting open questions rather than closed truths. It is no longer a matter of revealing what "really" happened but of following links and references and scouring sources indicating alternate explanations. The technological mediation of communication opens up precisely those domains that conspiracy theories thrive on and then try to shut down. And—in line with the basic structure of treason introduced at the outset—this new, open-ended, "headless" way of communicating does its share to turn states and enemies into increasingly dispersed, shadowy, head- or faceless entities. But how is this to be depicted? How can we narrate the multiple explanations jostling underneath all the delirious misinformation, faceless enemies, and constantly shifting treachery?

Narrative Recursions

The subtitle of *The Secret War* is *Treason, Espionage, and Modern Fiction.* It is crucial to pinpoint the relationship between fiction on the one hand and treason and espionage on the other. Yes, *The Secret War* is very much about fictions that depict treason and espionage, but though written by a professor of literature, it is *not* a *literary* study of fictional representations of treason and espionage. The relationship established by Horn between fiction and espionage is a great deal more complex and will no doubt irritate intelligence and literature practitioners alike.

To grasp what is at stake, let us stage a brief grudge match between the business of literature and the art of espionage. Representing literature we have the irrepressible William Somerset Maugham, author of *Ashenden,* a string of stories based on Maugham's experiences in the British Intelligence Department during the First World War. Much like his creator, Ashenden is an author who finds his temporary profession aesthetically unsatisfactory: "The work of an agent in the ID is on the whole extremely monotonous. A lot of it is uncommonly useless. The material it offers for stories is scrappy and pointless: the author has himself to make it coherent, dramatic, and probable" (Maugham 1967, ix).

And even if intelligence work should now and then manifest some dramatic coherence, it is no more than a cheap knockoff. When "R.," Ashenden's recruiter, tries to impress him by telling the story of a French minister robbed of some very important documents after spending the night with a yellow-haired lady of questionable reputation, Ashenden remains unimpressed: "We've been putting that incident on stage for sixty years, we've written it in a thousand novels. Do you mean to say that life has only just caught up with us?" (Maugham 1967, 3). The routines of espionage do not live up to literary standards. They require selection, dramatization, a sense of beginning and end, the ability to "choose from life what is curious, telling, and dramatic"; otherwise they remain "as unsatisfactory as those modern novels that give you a number of unrelated episodes and expect you by piecing them together to construct in your mind a connected narrative." Literature 1, Espionage 0.

In the other corner, representing espionage, we have Frederick P. Hitz, former legislative counsel to the director of central intelligence, deputy chief of operations for Europe, and first statutory inspector general of the Central Intelligence Agency (CIA). Hitz knows the business, as is evident from his ambitiously titled *The Great Game: The Myth and Reality of Espionage* (2004), a scrutiny of spy fiction from *Kim* and *Ashenden* all the way to the latest le Carré from the point of view of a seasoned pro. Hitz is a fair and appreciative reader, but in the final analysis, after comparing fictional accounts of treason and espionage to real-life cases, his verdict—delivered with numerous invocations of *reality* and *real*—is negative. "Real-life spy heroes don't look or act like Winie Verloc, Davies and Carruthers, or Richard Hannay" (Hitz 2004, 78). "Reality is neither as romantic as Kipling suggests in *Kim,* nor as cynical and manipulative as Greene and le Carré paint it" (ibid., 142). Le Carré's *A Perfect Spy* may be "brilliant" (ibid., 36), but the novel's "obsession with the burden of betrayal . . . may emanate from roots more personal than the verisimilitude of his [le Carré's] ordinary observations on the world of espionage" (ibid., 35). The "amoral exploitation" and "cold calculation" in *Tinker, Tailor, Soldier, Spy* and *The Spy Who Came In from the Cold* is in "the real world" more likely the result of "bureaucratic ineptitude" (ibid., 42). In short, "the real world of spy villainy may be more pedestrian" (ibid., 120). Precisely the techniques of dramatization, streamlining, and emplotment advocated by Maugham make literature (the eponymous "myth") fall short of reality: "The truth that makes you free in the real world of espionage is that no fictional account adequately captures the remarkable variety of twists and turns that a genuine human spy goes through in pursuit of his mission of treachery and betrayal" (ibid., 189). Unreal Literature 0, Real Espionage 1.

So far we have a draw. But while each side considers itself superior, both agree that they are clearly separate. There may be a lot of borrowing but there is no mingling. And if there are breaches, genre markers act with the intransigence of East German border guards. A case in point is *A Man Called Intrepid,* the highly questionable 1974 biography of Sir William Stephenson, "which was reclassified as fiction by Macmillan Publishers in the United States following complaints and bad reviews" (N. West 2004, 122). Formidable discursive regimes are charged with securing the boundary between fiction and reality. But just as the modern institutionalization of literature draws attention away from the profoundly *literary* activities of those claiming to deal with real things, the institutionalization of intelligence work has blinded us to the fact that so many of its basic activities—from mapping terrain to interpreting data—are part and parcel of the business of literature.

But now things get interesting—that is, both entertaining and unsettling. Have another look at the last *Ashenden* quotation given earlier. Maugham compares the routines of espionage work to a modern novel; in fact, he likens it to an eventless Chekhov story extended beyond its natural (and bearable) boundaries. The fiction/reality boundary is reentered on the side of fiction. Fiction already contains espionage because the fiction/espionage boundary is made to coincide with the boundary between Maugham's idea of palatable fiction, able "to excite, interest, and absorb the reader," and "unsatisfactory" modern literature that evinces all the drudgery of intelligence work. Horn performs the same operation on the other side of the fiction/intelligence boundary by insisting that intelligence work always already contains the practices, modes, and operations of fiction. In the best of several well-chosen examples she focuses on the 1973 thriller *Three Days of the Condor,* in which Robert Redford plays a CIA operative by the name of Turner holed up in a New York office calling itself the American Literary Historical Society. This is both a cover name and a highly accurate description, for Turner spends his time scouring all kinds of books in search of material for historically important intelligence analyses. He is such a dedicated reader that he has difficulties accepting the fact that some of his less bookish colleagues go around killing people, including members of their own team. But more important than the incessant reading is the subsequent communication of the information gained by means of a particular form of *writing*—or, to be as precise as Horn, the communication of various, occasionally mutually exclusive interpretations of information while both advocating and relativizing one particular interpretation. At rock bottom, intelligence reports are literary, Horn says, since they manifest

> the difficulty of writing a text that can be read in many different ways but that nonetheless will and must result in one particular reading, a text whose meaning is so clear that it cannot be obscured by any changes from above—a text, in other words, that is both one and many. The reader—the political decision maker—is to be offered the full range of possible hypotheses but is then supposed to arrive at one decisive conclusion. In short, [it is] a text that cannot be. It exists only in the head of an author who does not yet know which words he will use, and in the head of a reader who has either missed or already forgotten the many possibilities of reading.

Spies read the world; readers spy on texts. To rephrase this in terms that come more easily to literary theorists: fiction is, on the one hand, a selection of information that by virtue of its selection is invested with significance. Literature—large parts of our education system would collapse if we did not believe this—is a meaningful reduction of the complexity of reality. At the same time any piece of fiction paradoxically and self-consciously presents itself as *one* particular selection against the background of other, nonselected but equally plausible selections. Undermining the simple contrast between intelligence fact and spy fiction, Horn focuses on a basic similarity: good fiction and actionable intelligence (fiction worth reading and intelligence worth pondering) are both structured by selection and contingency. No literary texts manifest this quality better than those of Jorge Luis Borges, which is why Horn centers one of her introductory segments on selected short stories by Borges. The genius of Borges's narratives, however, is not only their ability to deconstruct, defer, and question their narratives by always already including the exclusion that made the story possible in the first place, but also the fact that the best of them do this by centering on historically informed narratives of treason and secrecy. Literary fiction—for Horn, especially the fiction of Borges, DeLillo, and le Carré—is able to capture the slippery status of secrets and the changing structure of treason that political narratives tend to gloss over by claiming to present the truth. Fiction, the old saying goes, is the truth inside the lie (and who would deny that politics, by contrast, is the lie inside the truth?). But this saying still presupposes a clear distinction between truth and lies with the former in the privileged—and ultimately accessible—center. Horn is more cautious: fiction shows that truth comes about by a strategic arrangement of one explicitly presented and alternate implied truths. And the more truth denies the selections it is based on, the more it is a lie.

It is fitting that Horn concludes with a paean to *Our Man in Havana,* Graham Greene's tragicomedy of treason featuring vacuum salesman Jim Wormold, who is hired by the British secret service and proceeds to invent a fictitious network of Cuban sources and agents. Wormold, a minor demiurge of intelligence with money issues, soon loses control of his creations; he initiates and is then sucked into a fact/fiction feedback. He invents characters that turn into files containing actionable intelligence in need of real-life interventions—which in turn necessitates further fabrications by Wormold. Horn speaks of a "recursion of fiction into reality and reality into fiction." It is also a recursion of fiction into history and history into fiction. Greene based his novel in part on the exploits of Joan Pujol Garcia, aka "Garbo," the Catalan double agent who managed to convince the German Abwehr that he was running a spy network in Britain made of more agents and subagents than can be found in a Tom Clancy novel. An alternate source of inspiration for Greene has recently been suggested in the unlikely shape of Heinz Lüning, "Hitler's Man in Havana" (Schoonover 2008), a pathetically inept German spy sent to Cuba who was arrested and executed soon after his arrival. In this case the fabrications were the work not of the spy but of his captors, especially J. Edgar Hoover. Never one to miss out on an opportunity to promote himself and his agency, Hoover concocted tall tales of Lüning the Nazi master spy that were no less fanciful than Wormold's intelligence reports. But the interweaving of reality and fiction goes further back in time, for Pujol's exploits are a real-life recursion of a literary story told by none other than William Somerset Maugham. Ashenden is sent to Basel to meet up with "Gustave," an agent who provides the British with reports from his travels into Germany. Ashenden finds out that Gustave is making up all his reports because he no longer ventures into Germany. His reason for not traveling: there is a war on, and he loves his wife. Given that Ashenden's exploits come close to what Maugham himself experienced, the origin of intelligence fabrication is lost somewhere between fact and fiction.

But the recursions also go forward in time. Greene's Wormold reappears in the shape of Harry Pendel, John le Carré's eponymous tailor of Panama. (Indeed, what are intelligence experts other than hybrids of vacuum salesmen and tailors? They suck up whatever data they come across and stitch it into a fitting garb.) Like Wormold, Harry is an increasingly desperate liar whose fabrications cater to the gullibility of a postimperial intelligence service eager to revive its bygone glory days. Harry is the last, pathetic example for Horn's concluding statement that no matter how much secrets and treason may have changed throughout the many historical contexts of the last century, the lonely figure of the traitor remains a fixture. Like so many of his predecessors, Harry is lost between nations, races, languages, ideologies, and women; but he is also lost between fact and fiction, intelligence and literature. For Harry—and this may serve as an epitaph for Horn's study—there is nothing left but an anguished outcry which reveals that, sometimes, the traitor's love of fiction is a fiction of love: "Everything in the world is true if you invent it hard enough and love the person it's for!" (Le Carré 1996, 77).

University of British Columbia, 2012

Introduction: Treason, Secrets, and Fiction

The political secret has acquired a bad reputation. It was not always regarded as suspect: for centuries, the clandestine arts practiced by far-sighted rulers and skilled generals belonged to an arsenal of techniques designed to support the execution and maintenance of power. Since the arrival of the modern ideal of political transparency, however, any state secret removed from public scrutiny has aroused suspicion. What governments keep secret is likely to be seen as something that could not be legitimized if it were made public. In modern democracies, state secrets are suspected to be state crimes. The entire realm of state secrecy, with its intelligence services, classified information, and rituals of diplomatic discretion, is seen as a "pathology" of politics, or, at best, a necessary evil (Friedrich 1972). And yet modern states have not only built up a massive, highly professional intelligence infrastructure; they also depend on espionage, secret operations, surveillance, and the classification of information, which are indispensable governmental and military tools. Modern power fundamentally hinges on secrets and secrecy. If, as some have argued, treason has become the signature of the political in the twentieth century, it is because its secretive structure has made power "betrayable" (Boveri 1956–60). However, unlike premodern regimes that viewed their *arcana imperii* as a legitimate part of governance, modern governments tend to make a secret of their dependence on secrets, most famously in the "plausible deniability" that, for a long time, was used by the U.S. government to dissociate itself from the activities of its own intelligence services. Today, secrecy is mostly dealt with in the form of the scandal: if political secrets are exposed or betrayed, the leakage will occur as a fundamental disturbance of political order. Most often this will trigger a debate that is not limited to the mere content of the disclosure but will question the legitimacy of political secrecy altogether.

As a result of this bashful treatment of secrets, we have a public obsessively interested in ferreting them out. Every day books and articles appear, from journalistic scoops to painstaking historical reconstructions and insider memoirs, that aim to reveal the "truth" behind the silence of the intelligence community and the "real" events covered up by government communiqués—an approach to political secrecy that is as necessary as it is legitimate. This book, however, will pursue a different path. It aims not at disclosing, criticizing, or justifying state secrecy but at inquiring into the *structure* of the political secret. This requires, first, that we analyze the specific type of knowledge produced by modern secret services. How do they separate knowledge from speculation, theory from paranoia? What constitutes the inner goals and logic of intelligence work and military reconnaissance? What happens when state secrecy—as a result of treason or conspiracist fantasies—begins to spread beyond anybody's control? An inquiry into the structure of modern political secrecy, however, requires, second, an analysis of the discourses and narratives surrounding the secret. Secrets generate conjectures; they trigger narratives designed to make sense of events that are removed from knowledge. When we are unable (or unqualified) to know what "really" happened, the only thing left to do is to construct plausible versions.

This study, therefore, is not concerned with historical documents but with fictions: literature and film. Fiction—this is the basic thesis of this book—is the most lucid way of shedding light onto the structure of the modern political secret. Since fictions do not, like works of journalism and history, claim to offer the *one* historical truth of an event, they are better suited to analyzing how secrecy functions; they can explore *possible* versions of an event but refrain from settling on an "ultimate" solution. Fictions illuminate secrecy's structure because they reconstruct its logic, its subtle and mysterious economy of light and dark, truths and lies, presence and absence. Unlike memoirs or historical accounts, fiction is able to circumvent the legal interdictions that necessarily surround state secrets, whether gag orders and secrecy clauses imposed on insiders or the classification of certain types of information. "Invention" has always been a mask to reveal otherwise "unspeakable" truths. But the main reason for fiction's lucidity lies in its poetic structure: through the form of its narrative, its subtle play of allusion and mysteriousness, implication and explication, the literary narrative can make the secret "readable," decipherable without explicitly solving it, thereby rendering visible the structure of a type of knowledge inextricably entangled with nonknowledge, truth blended with lie.

To provide an example for this intricate structure of fiction revolving around secrecy and betrayal as well as for the difficulties of reading such a narrative, we will first explore one of the most notorious cases of betrayal in occidental culture: the story of Judas. This archetypal case clarifies what a "betrayable" secret is, to what extent betrayal is a moral and political action, and what historical and historiographical consequences it inevitably entails. As is evident in the Gospels, however, the story of Judas also demonstrates how unreadable and mysterious all histories of betrayal necessarily must be. The story of Judas is a narrative that contains its own structural mystery; and unlike Judas, who delivers his master, it retains its own secret, refusing to hand it over to its readers.

The Mystery of Judas

> Also Judas, the traitor, they say, had exact knowledge of these things, and since he alone knew the truth better than the other apostles, he accomplished the mystery of the betrayal. Through him all things in heaven and on earth were dissolved. This fiction they adduce, and call it the Gospel of Judas.
>
> —Saint Irenaeus, *Against Heresies* (about 175–85 C.E.; translation emended)

The story that ushers in the history of Christianity is, at first glance, deceptively simple: a group of men, a charismatic leader, and one of the followers who delivers the leader to his enemies. The leader turns into a martyr, the deliverer into a traitor; a Judas becomes *the Judas*. Whether we are dealing with a group of political conspirators or Jesus and his disciples, the act of betrayal unfailingly marks the point at which secrets are revealed, plans are thwarted, the group is dispersed, and hopes are buried. From here on, history will take a different turn. It is the moment at which the hero loses his life and the traitor his integrity by committing the most despicable act a human is capable of. "The Son of man goeth as it is written of him," notes the Gospel of Matthew, "but woe unto that man by whom the Son of man is betrayed! It had been good for that man if he had not been born" (Matthew 26:24). The betrayal is as inevitable as it is reprehensible, the traitor is necessary but beyond redemption. His very existence is void, he should never have been born—and yet he is the instrument to bring about what has to come about. The act of betrayal is the mystery of a predetermined yet contingent act, an act both foreseen and unforeseeable.

At first glance the story of Judas—as told in the Gospels and retold and reread countless times thereafter—may appear very simple, but on closer inspection it becomes extremely enigmatic. The Gospels do not agree with one another, and none of them is without internal contradictions. The story is dispersed across versions and variants engaged in a dazzling struggle for consistency. Treason is an act that in the final analysis cannot be clearly ascribed to political, psychological, or historical motives, intentions, or power structures; neither can it be endowed with a determined "historical meaning." But precisely this inscrutability calls for constant interpretations and narratives eager to furnish a plausible explanation of what "really" happened. Treason betrays a secret—but above and beyond this "delivery" of secret knowledge the act of treason is itself a secret that persists throughout the many versions. It hints at something elusive yet powerful, the mysterious character of historical tradition.

A comparative reading of the Gospels and of the enigmatic fragments from the Gnostic Judas tradition suggests that, as Hans-Josef Klauck has argued, "The writing of the New Testament must have been preceded by a wholly different Judas tradition and a wholly different reality" (Klauck 1987, 144).[1] Obviously, the Gospels—and with them all later attempts to relate the act of betrayal—are residues, screen memories of something that cannot be told. They indicate that vested interests are at work in the retelling of an event that can no longer be reconstructed; it has fallen into the darkness of a history which is only present in a multitude of *stories* that conceal as much as they reveal. From the very beginning, that is, starting with the story of Judas the question arises how a betrayal and its secret can be represented. Betrayals generate narratives that are forced to deal with ruptures and mysteries, resulting in ambiguous tales that offer one particular version at the price of concealing equally possible alternatives. What needs to be deciphered is precisely this structure of concealment. Narratives of betrayal are positioned in a framework of lies and enmity and therefore require a reader's distrust. They are always already political insofar as they are polemical, that is, agenda-driven versions of a conflict they obscure rather than illuminate.

Approaching the various versions of Christ's Passion thus calls for a view toward a hidden subtext, a secret political agenda that came to shape the authoritative tradition. One of the first thoroughly political and highly skeptical readings of this kind was presented by the Marxist theoretician Karl Kautsky. In his reinterpretation of the foundations of Christianity he offers a radically new reading of Christ's Passion as a muddled, politically motivated concoction of lies. Underneath all the "tangle of concoctions," "strange subterfuges," "contradictions and absurdities" he detects a biased, decidedly political agenda aiming at moving Christianity closer to Rome and away from Judaism (Kautsky 1953, 338–39).[2] In the inconsistencies within and among the Gospels' versions, Kautsky deciphers the narrative attempt to enable Christianity's "peaceful subjugation" to Rome and the covering up of the class struggle within the Jewish people that Jesus was about to bring to a revolt: "The trick was . . . to give the tradition such a twist that the guilt of Christ's Crucifixion should be shifted on to the Jews and Christ himself cleared not merely of any violence but of any feelings of Jewish patriotism or enmity to Rome" (ibid., 339). Not surprisingly, Kautsky sees Jesus as an early socialist fighter. What is interesting, however, is not so much Kautsky's own version, but the way he subjects the biblical text to a highly suspicious reading exposing the gaps, inconsistencies, and overly neat connections—signs of a narrative distortion of the true events. While Kautsky's own reconstruction falls prey to the illusion of knowing what *really* happened, his polemical and politicizing gesture of deciphering brilliantly reveals the mysterious structure of the Judas story. This enigmatic character of the Passion narrative has produced an unending chain of exegeses and deliberations (see Klassen 1999), revolving around the implausibility and mysteriousness of the very act of betrayal. I will briefly sketch three of these mysteries, though not to provide yet another psychological, political, or theological solution, but rather to point out some of the *questions* they raise. As we shall see, the mysteries of Judas contain *in nuce* three basic elements of the political secret: first, the mystery of the subject entangled in secrecy and betrayal; second, the mystery of the political *arcana* themselves; and third, the mystery of the political secret as it relates to the problem of its representation.

The Motive

The first problem: Why did Judas betray his friend and master? What was the motive of his deed? The infamous thirty pieces of silver are mentioned only by Matthew, and their relatively small value rather underscores the lack of motive than explains the deed. For Judas, the keeper of the disciples' purse, thirty silver coins are a meager reward (roughly the equivalent of the price of a slave). Besides, after carrying out the deed he throws the money at his clients' feet. Luke and John, in turn, note that Judas was possessed by the devil. This, however, would imply that his betrayal does not constitute a deliberate, premeditated act for which he can be held accountable. Judas would be no more than a vehicle, the bodily appearance of a principle of evil that acts through him (see Daub 1816–18).

This indeterminacy of motive and ostensible lack of reason have given rise to countless psychological, political, and theological readings. Judas appears as a jealous friend distraught over Jesus's lack of interest and the contempt of the other disciples (Andreyev 1947, 15–106); as a revolutionary eager to force Jesus to fulfill his mission as the leader of a Jewish revolt (De Quincey 1873; Kazantzakis 1960); as a pious Jew who has realized that his master is a self-proclaimed false Messiah; or as the very incarnation of human weakness and malice (see Pfaffenroth 2001). These narratives foreground the betrayer to explain the betrayal; they attribute to him a psychic life and inner depth that the Gospels' texts lack. Modern sociological and psychological attempts to explain the more secular treason in the twentieth century (Boveri 1956–60) follow the same path: the mystery of betrayal is solved by exploring the inner conflicts, origin, and tragedy of the renegade. Psychologizing treason is one—though not the only—possibility of filling with a plausible narrative the gap left by the motive. Peter Paul Rubens's painting *The Last Supper* (figure 1) stages

Figure 1. Peter Paul Rubens, *The Last Supper* (1693), Pinacoteca di Brera, Milan. Under license from the Italian Ministry for Cultural Goods and Activities.

an intricate constellation of glances to depict this view of Judas: while Christ, who is blessing the bread, is turned toward the light falling in from above announcing his divine mission, Judas turns his back on the pious community. He is still sharing the table with the other disciples, but his gesture indicates his ambivalent status as both member and defector. Fully engrossed in thoughts about his coming action, he appears to be looking out of the painting—and meets the eyes of the beholder. With his gaze directed at the viewer rather than at Jesus, Judas appears to be communicating the problem of the traitor's "psychology" to the audience. But the gaze also refers to the problem of observing and depicting the act of treason. Looking into the eyes of Judas, the viewer is caught up in an uncanny ambivalence of complicity with and recognition of the traitor. The depiction itself is "tarnished" by an act of betrayal that cannot be captured by any innocent tale or portrayal.

The alternative to psychologization is demonization, as proposed by Luke and John. This simplifies both motive and iconography: Judas is identified by either a black aura (as opposed to the golden halo of Jesus and the other disciples) or a shadowy devil lurking behind his back. The demonization of Judas and his deed, however, seems to take recourse to a premodern, nonsecular motivation of political actions. If one uses the story of Judas as a model for a modern theory of treason and political secret, one begins to wonder what in secular politics corresponds to the theology of Satan. In the modern age, the secularization of Satan, I would like to suggest, is the enemy: he deceives, seduces, entices us to switch sides. And just like Satan he assumes deceptively harmless shapes. The secularization of Satan, however, indicates the irreducibly theological residue of all political apostasy: it always points to a fall from faith and to a betrayal of a community of believers. The modern version of demonization, then, is that powerful "interested third party" (Rolf Schroers, Carl Schmitt) that emerges as the instigator and profiteer of treason. This may be a state, a principle, an "ideology" (as the Cold War discourse on treason liked to call it), a faith, a lifestyle, a revolutionary movement. There always is a principle that transcends the traitor. The question regarding the motive of treason thus unfolds a tension, an antinomy of individual motivation and political-theological meaning. Restricting the question of motive to the psychology of the traitor, then, means effacing this antinomy, as is the attempt to turn Judas into a principle of evil (as Carl Daub, among others, has done). The first mystery of betrayal consists precisely in the unsolvable ambiguity regarding the question of who commits the act of treason in whose name. Reading narratives of treason and betrayal throughout the twentieth century, this book will offer readings that try to take into account both sides of this ambiguity: the complicated subjectivity of traitors and defectors as well as the historical forces and circumstances that frame their decision.

The Secret

The second problem: What exactly is the object of betrayal? What knowledge is passed on by treason?—which secret is divulged? What is the "content" of political secrets? Acclaimed by the Jewish populace, Jesus enters Jerusalem shortly before Passover; his public disputes as well as his violations of Jewish religious laws provoke the scribes and high priests; and he attacks the Jewish authorities who are using the temple as a place of business. In the tense situation involving a discontented population, collaborating Pharisees, and Roman occupiers, Jesus of Nazareth embodies an irritation that threatens the fragile truce between Jews and Romans as well as that between priests and populace. Jesus emerges as both political revolutionary and religious reformer; his political volatility arises from his lack of respect for the Pharisees and his scriptural superiority over them. His true secret, however, is that nobody knows who he really is. Given the popularity of Jesus, the action of Judas does not consist in the act of identifying a person, something Jesus himself already comments on during his arrest: "Every day I was with you, teaching in the temple courts, and you did not arrest me. But the Scriptures must be fulfilled" (Mark 14:48–49). In his conspiracist reading of the Gospels Karl Kautsky makes the fine comparison that betraying Jesus's identity would be "a good deal like having the Berlin police pay an informer to indicate the person called Bebel" (Kautsky 1953, 313).

As indicated in the Gospels (Matthew 10:4, Mark 3:19), the betrayal amounts to a handover. Someone has to *deliver* the Son of Man. The Greek word used, παραδίδωμι, means "to hand or give over," "relinquish," or "surrender," rather than "betray" (προδίδωμι, as in Luke 6:16).[3] The same term is used to designate God's act of "delivering" his beloved son (Romans 8:32; Romans 4:25) or that of "giving oneself over" (Isaiah 53:12; Ephesians 5:2; Galatians 2:20).[4] What the Pharisees need to know is the opportune moment at which Jesus can be arrested without witnesses. "But they said, Not on the feast day, lest there be an uproar of the people" (Mark 14:2). Thus the knowledge betrayed and passed on by Judas appears at first glance to be a piece of tactical intelligence rather than a grand secret. But this makes his almost obscene gesture—the kiss—and the address "rabbi" (in English, "master") all the more perplexing:

> And while he [Jesus] yet spake, lo, Judas, one of the twelve, came, and with him a great multitude with swords and slaves, from the chief priests and elders of the people. Now he that betrayed him gave them a sign, saying, Whomsoever I shall kiss, that same is he: hold him fast. And forthwith he came to Jesus, and said, Hail, master; and kissed him. And Jesus said unto him, Friend, wherefore art thou come? (Matthew 26:47–50)

To use the respectful address and to pervert the kiss, a gesture of friendship, into a sign of attack is obscenely theatrical—and completely unnecessary. From a tactical point of view Judas's betrayal is carried out with the cool deliberateness of a police operation, yet both the act and its strange gestural embellishment point toward more. The act and gesture of the betrayal fluctuate between two possible interpretations: on the one hand, they represent a purely tactical assistance that enables the arrest of the popular preacher Jesus of Nazareth; on the other, they function as a revelation aimed at the hidden "essence" of the betrayed. Thus, the secret betrayed by treason is always a double: a simple fact and an auratic mystery revealing the "historical" meaning of treason—in this case Jesus's messianic nature.

Taking issue with the unsatisfactory hypothesis that the act of betrayal was merely a tactical expedient, the theologian, physician, and philosopher Albert Schweitzer proposed an alternative. His hypothesis centers on the spiritual existence of Jesus, which he considers the real threat to both the Jewish establishment and the Roman occupiers. The true mystery of Jesus consists in the fact that he is the Son of God and the Messiah, something that Jesus himself repeatedly tells his disciples not to pass on (Matthew 16:20, Matthew 17:9). "In the betrayal," Schweitzer notes, "there were two points, one more general and one more specific: the general fact by which Judas gave Jesus into their power, and specifically the undertaking to let them know of the next opportunity when they could arrest him quietly, without publicity. But the decisive thing was the betrayal of the messianic aspect. Jesus died because two of his disciples had broken his command of silence: Peter when he made known the secret of the Messiahship at Caesarea Philippi; Judas Iscariot by communicating it to the high priest" (Schweitzer 2001, 353). Schweitzer is anticipating an insight supported by the Gospel of Judas, which was published in 2006. In this Gnostic text, probably written around the second century C.E., Judas receives special mention as the "thirteenth disciple" and as the one who was privy to a grand cosmological vision. What sets Judas apart, this text suggests, is that he is the only one to recognize the divine nature of

Christ. Here, Judas says to Jesus: "I know who you are and where you have come from. You are from the immortal realm of Barbelo. And I am not worthy to utter the name of the one who sent you" (Kasser, Meyer, and Wurst 2006, 22).[5]

Schweitzer's reference to the double nature of betrayal—"general and specific"—highlights the second antinomy of treason, which concerns the nature of the communicated secret. The mystery of betrayal is caught in the tension between purely tactical intelligence and eschatological or historical secret—the identity of the savior. Once again the act of betrayal encompasses a contradictory double: on the one hand the divulged secret is tied to military cunning; it is a piece of hidden information, a finite object quickly used up in the fog of war. On the other hand it represents auratic knowledge: the very mystery of faith or sovereignty. It is this second dimension that turns the secret into a historic agent, bringing forth a turning point in history. Treason must be analyzed considering both sides, its technical aspects, the epistemic structure of the knowledge that is being passed on—but also the historico-political dimension that lends historical meaning to the act of treason.

Hero and Traitor

The third problem: What is the relationship between Judas and Jesus, betrayer and betrayed? How do narratives organize this relationship? Who assigns the positions of "good" and "bad," "hero/savior" and "traitor"? Apart from the remarkable scene at the Last Supper, we know very little about Judas, other than that he was responsible for the group's finances. Jesus had announced on several occasions that he would be handed over and killed, a prediction repeated during the Last Supper: "And as they did eat, he said, Verily I say unto you, that one of you shall betray me. And they were exceeding sorrowful, and began every one of them to say unto him, Lord, is it I? And he answered and said, He that dippeth his hand with me in the dish, the same shall betray me . . . Then Judas, which betrayed him, answered and said, Master, is it I? He said unto him, Thou hast said" (Matthew 26:21–25). Both betrayer and betrayed know what is about to take place, but the latter does not prevent it from happening, and the former does not desist. While the Synoptic Gospels leave it at this exchange of glances between Jesus and Judas, John offers an even more puzzling version of events. Once again Jesus announces the betrayal and is asked by John who the culprit is. "Jesus answered, He it is, to whom I shall give a sop, when I have dipped it. And when he had dipped the sop, he gave it to Judas Iscariot, the son of Simon. And after the sop Satan entered him. Then said Jesus unto him, That thou doest, do quickly" (John 13:26–27). This gesture is deeply ambivalent: it fluctuates between exposure ("I know it is you") and assignment ("It is to be you"). It is as if Jesus were appointing Judas to be the betrayer and insisting on his order: "That thou doest, do quickly." The breaking of the bread, the *communio* between Jesus and his disciple, turns into an incisive *excommunicatio:* Judas is part of the disciples' community to the extent that he assumes the function of traitor, apostate, and outcast. The Gospel of Judas goes a step further. Jesus explicitly orders Judas to betray him: "But you will exceed all of them. For you will sacrifice the man that clothes me" (Kasser, Meyer, and Wurst 2006, 43). Between Judas and Jesus, betrayer and betrayed, there is a moment of furtive agreement, if not a form of "consent," that Bertolt Brecht will later address as the ethical quandary of treason (see part 5, "Agents of the World Revolution"). The exchange of glances during the Last Supper and the infamous kiss in the garden of Gethsemane point toward an agreement that blurs the distinction between friendship and enmity. The traitor is both friend and enemy, closest confidant and most dangerous antagonist. Only as a friend can the traitor turn into the most pernicious enemy; only as a friend can he access closely guarded secrets and inflict the serious damage.[6] Yet he also demonstrates a strange, perverted, or paradoxical form of loyalty, for the betrayal implies an intimacy that even at the very end neither Jesus nor Judas is willing to relinquish. Taking seriously this mysterious agreement between Jesus and Judas opens up the vertiginous dialectics of treason: maybe, as argued in countless literary speculations from Friedrich Gottlieb Klopstock, Johann Wolfgang von Goethe, and Christian Friedrich Hebbel to Nikos Kazantzakis and Jorge Luis Borges, the betrayal of Judas is nothing but a final, extraordinary, and sacrificial gesture of loyalty. Judas's treason could be an attempt to force Jesus to fulfill his mission as either Messiah or king of the Jews. "The scripture has to be fulfilled," the Gospels reiterate, and without a doubt Judas (whether deliberately, possessed by Satan, or mandated by Jesus) turns out to be the unfortunate and accursed, yet nonetheless indispensable tool of salvation. Goethe, among others, suggested that Judas was a disciple who saw Jesus more as a Jewish revolutionary than as a spiritual reformer. Kazantzakis, in turn, depicted Judas as the mentor of and driving force behind Jesus. Summoned by Jesus to betray him to the authorities Judas hopes that the arrest will trigger an uprising—a plan that is thwarted by Jesus himself. Not coincidentally, Kazantzakis's historico-theological speculation, which centers on a deeply torn, ambivalent Messiah with Judas as his mentor and friend, gained notoriety in the wake of Martin Scorsese's controversial *The Last Temptation of Christ* (1988). It is Judas who guides and protects the self-doubting Jesus, and it is Judas who ultimately persuades Jesus to reject all worldly temptations and accept his destiny as the Messiah. Other interpretations foreground Judas's attempts to force Jesus to reveal that he is the Son of God. Hebbel noted for a planned Christ drama: "Judas is the most fervent believer" (quoted in Sauerland 1992, 105). Gnosticism offers a similar proposal: Judas—and he alone—understood what Jesus really meant when he announced to his disciples that he would soon appear in a different shape. By bringing about the emergence of Jesus as the Messiah, Judas demonstrated his awareness of Christ's secret essence. In the Gnostic tradition Judas figures as the true agent of salvation, possessing a knowledge that puts him immediately adjacent to Jesus.[7] Jorge Luis Borges gave the final, most radical twist on this millennia-old dialectic by presenting the traitor as the real savior (see part 1, "Borges—A Poetics of Treason").

Hence the third antinomy of betrayal emerges from the tension caused by the irresolvable politics of friendship and enmity: betrayal is an ambivalent gesture, an act of enmity based on friendship, but maybe also a form of friendship in disguise, an act of moral self-mutilation. The breach of loyalty and trust, then, always implies both proximity and distance, affiliation and exclusion. This is precisely why Judas's betrayal fluctuates between assignment ("That thou doest, do quickly") and condemnation ("Woe unto that man by whom the Son of man is betrayed!"). Treason masks itself much like a traitor: it adopts the guise of friendship and loyalty to pervert and exploit them. Yet it may, under the guise of infamy and disloyalty, be an opaque form of faithfulness and loyalty, a cryptic form of obedience (see Horn 2009a).

This third antinomy has both historical and historiographical consequences. Jesus and Judas, hero and traitor, are figures that depend on each other. Every sacrifice, every heroic deed needs its traitor to achieve a narrative contrast between light and darkness. Jesus and Judas, betrayed and betrayer, are a pair: they refer to each other; the hero needs the traitor, a vicarious agent and historical counterfigure, as his negative reflection. The traitor defiles himself to the same extent that the hero acts as a paragon of moral integrity; the former is the shadow that allows us to see heroism in all its light. What unites them is that they both *make* history—for better or worse. They embody the human ability to decide and act, finding themselves at the turning points of history. The hero appears as savior or martyr, as a figure of memory and identity that enables communities, mythologies, and religion to crystallize. His deeds are exemplary;

they can be told, commemorated, and celebrated. The traitor, on the other hand, is the dark side of history, that which cannot appear in canonical narratives—or can appear only as something "infamous," hostile, or demonic. The nauseating details of Judas's death demonstrate the exaggerated abjection he is subject to: he hangs himself, and his body becomes an abject symbol of his crime, the belly bursting open and the entrails gushing out (see Matthew 27:5, Acts 1:18). The devil snatches his departing soul. The obscene existence of the traitor is subject to what Jorge Luis Borges called the "modesty of history": an intrinsic law determining what can and cannot be represented, as a result of which "essential dates may be, for a long time, secret" (Borges 1964, 167). To allow for the possibility of history, then, the story of the betrayal both relates and withholds its "essential dates."

Fiction and Political Secrecy

The story of Judas with its three problems allows us to develop the three basic issues this book intends to pursue. The question of motive leads into the domains of politics and ethics while also pointing toward the psychology and sociology of the traitor. On the one hand we are probing a subject whose actions constitute a violation of affiliation and trustworthiness; on the other hand we are concerned with the framework of allegiances and enmity inside which the act of treason gains meaning and impact. Who is the betrayer and apostate? What are the principles and goals of his covert actions? If the act of treason involves a decision, then what were the initial options, and what position did the traitor come to occupy within the political domain? Was it a matter of changing sides or of attempting to find a "third way"? Is the traitor betraying his community, or are we dealing with a form of power that will inevitably turn each and every person into a traitor? These are the questions at the very core of the discourse on the twentieth century as an "epoch of treason" (see part 2, chapter 1, "The Age of Treason"), questions that—for example, in Cold War America—have led to the common suspicion that conspirators and traitors were lurking around every corner. As a symptom, the discourse on treason indicates a crisis of the political arising from both a crisis of allegiances and a crisis of enmity. In modernity, the multiple forms of loyalty the individual is caught up in mutually exclude one another and make treason all but inevitable. The traitor becomes a paradigmatic figure that reveals as much the irritations of modern society as the blurring of enmities. As a remote-controlled agent or assassin the traitor is the emblem of a society that observes its inner mechanisms—its circulation of knowledge, use of media, and social and communicative interconnectedness—with a maximum degree of ambivalence and suspicion. Friends and enemies are no longer identifiable; they have turned into abstractions in need of constant phantasmagorical determination. The traitor reveals and embodies something *irregular* in the relationship between subject, community, and sovereignty. He incarnates the modern individual's political unreliability, but also the modern subject's faculties of role-play and seduction. The traitor's many appearances—defector, partisan, sleeper, mole, agent, saboteur, renegade, or conspirator—embody clandestine tactics and conduct that are not necessarily linked to irregular political activities but seem to underlie every aspect of social behavior. Role-play, disguise, and betrayal are part of the modern individual's social and erotic survival techniques (see part 4, "Spies, Male and Female"). If spies and traitors have become one of the most pervasive motives and fantasies of twentieth-century culture, it is because they embody a social life that cannot do without secrecy and betrayal.

But traitors are a symptom not only of modern social life but also of a political state of affairs. While the political ideals of modern democracy emphasize transparency and participation, the "betrayability" of modern power reveals its fundamental dependence on a sphere of secrecy: the world of intelligence agencies and military secrets, of secret knowledge, silent control, and manipulation. In a culture of publicity these *arcana imperii* represent a double-edged element of power: they are necessary means of defense, self-protection, and military efficiency, but they also constitute a space exempt from public control and the rule of law. On the one hand, modern state secrets are legitimized as the "trade secrets" of efficient governance and as necessary defensive measures. On the other hand, their mysterious status opens up a realm of hidden violence or secret intrusion into the private sphere (see part 2, chapter 2, "Logics of Political Secrecy"). Here, in this realm of suspended public control and legality, a basic feature of modern power becomes manifest: power is not only a matter of enforcing the rule of law; it also consists of suspending it. From this point of view the modern *arcana* are the sphere of a covert but continuous state of exception, the *irregular* side of power itself.

What exactly did Judas betray? What was the *nature of the secret* he divulged? These questions open up the epistemological dimension of our inquiry. What is the form of the knowledge that is deposited as a secret and passed on by treason? Is it a simple fact, a tactical or technological secret, or a *mysterium*—the secret of Messiahship whose disclosure violates both divine and human injunctions? The tension between tactical information and salvational *mysterium,* as presented in the story of Judas, indicates that the value and impact of a secret lies not in the mere content of information but rather in its epistemological form, that is, the specific economy of knowable and unknowable, manifest and latent. Analyzing political secrets requires a political epistemology, a theory of the specific type of power-knowledge used to guarantee social control, military success, and political foresight. This political epistemology of arcane state knowledge, or, to use the technical term, this "secret intelligence," is at the center of this book. Secret intelligence is a type of knowledge that is primarily geared not toward truth but toward effectiveness in the face of an enemy (see part 2, chapter 3, "Secret Intelligence"). The enemy is the basis and precondition of secret intelligence. Intelligence may consist in collecting correct information about this enemy, but also in engineering deceptions, disseminating disinformation, or providing false clues. It is tactical and strategic knowledge, a weapon in current, future, or imaginary confrontations; it involves exploring strategically or tactically important spaces, reconnoitering the enemy, and uncovering invisible internal enemies. The fact that this knowledge has to be acquired, evaluated, and used in secret, however, has grave consequences for its epistemological structure as well as for the strategic decisions based on this knowledge. Indeed, what do secret services really "know"? How do they derive large-scale prognoses from isolated bits of information? How can they double-check their theories if everything is subject to secrecy? How can they trust their sources (Horn 2011)? Analyzing the epistemological structure of secret intelligence must deal with the dialectics of blindness and insight at the basis of this knowledge, a knowledge that is haunted by the powerful phantasm of "the enemy." The enemy is—to use a formulation introduced by Carl Schmitt—"the figure of our own question" (Schmitt 2007, 85; translation emended). Whether as the mirror image of a hyperrationalist superpower during the Cold War (see part 6, chapter 2, "War Games") or the distorted reflection of a global, highly mediatized network (see part 9, chapter 2, "The Future of Enmity"), we cannot help but project into the phantasm of the enemy the structures and pathologies of our own society. This may either fuel the rationalization of methods and models (see part 6, chapter 2, "War Games") or, by contrast, accelerate an unstoppable dynamics of suspicion and paranoia (see part 7, "State Paranoia"). The question concerning the essence of the secret political knowledge points not only to the logic of its knowledge but also to its inevitable delirium.

The third mystery of the Judas narrative, the unacknowledged complicity between savior and betrayer and the intimation of a historical plan realized by treason, points toward the *poetological* core of secrecy and treason. The contradictions between the Gospels as well as the infinite number of interpretations and retellings reveal both the necessity and the difficulty involved in furnishing an account of *what* happened. The mutual dependence of savior and betrayer produces a puzzle picture or ambigram: whether you see the hero or the villain depends on the narrative perspective. But precisely this ambiguous constellation renders treason, to draw on Jorge Luis Borges, a musical "theme": a stable basic structure, yet so infinitely variable that there is no real original or "true" version of the theme. Betrayal demands never-ending narration. Whatever version is offered points not only toward other versions that have been concealed or silenced but also toward the possibility that the narration itself is nothing but a lie, a cover story made up of half-truths. This scandal, which is always already a scandal of narration and depiction, reveals the close ties between fiction and political secret.

But why resort to literature and films when chronicling the political secrets of the twentieth century? Why not simply reconstruct historical cases, devise a sociology of the traitor, or attempt a political theory of modern state secrets? In the face of the narrative difficulties involved in depicting treason, and faced with the double-edged epistemology of the political secret in the modern age, fiction comes with the advantage of being able to reflect these difficulties in its very structure. Fiction alone can *narrate something* and at the same time *hint at something else to be deciphered* underneath the obvious plot. Even more so, literature is able to make the narrative's unstable basis itself a part of the narrative. While secret intelligence by definition involves the withdrawal of truth and the opacity of positions and affiliation, fiction enables us to see through the thicket of interested versions. Fiction helps us catch a glimpse of the underlying rules that determine what can be seen and known and what remains invisible and unknowable. This is the peculiar lucidity of literature as opposed to historiography or journalism that claims to reveal "the whole truth." Once we enter the domain of enmity and clandestinity, nothing is given as a simple *factum brutum*. We are left with nothing but one version of the truth, implicitly or explicitly referring to other, contradictory versions. Novels, plays, films, autobiographies, military war games, and the instructions given to secret service staff are all "fictions" of this sort. Exploring the field of the political secret, fictions are aware of the fact that any "truth" is at best (and for the time being) nothing more than the most plausible among an infinite number of other possible versions. If there is no "truth" of treason because everything could have taken place differently, the narrative positions of savior and betrayer, hero and villain can be switched—renarrating or rereading the whole story from an opposite angle.

As a result the traditional opposition between "fiction" and "literature," on the one hand, and historical "reality" and "politics," on the other, has to be readjusted. By speaking of things whereof one cannot speak, literature touches on—and even interferes in—the very structure of political secrecy. The fictions in this study are political not because they deal with politics, war, treason, espionage, or conspiracies but because they present active interventions into the order of the political secret. These interferences assume different shapes: for instance, there are fictions that stage future threats and conflicts with the implicit or explicit intention of highlighting potential dangers, rehearsing potential crises, or devising new defensive measures. Despite their appearance as thrillers, these fictions are primarily a matter not of entertainment but of political mobilization. To read Erskine Childers's *Riddle of the Sands* (which aspires to warn Britons of a secret German attack), Rudyard Kipling's *Kim* (which develops a completely new type of colonial agent), or the nuclear satire *Dr. Strangelove* (an intelligent Third World War scenario) as mere tales of adventure is to drastically underestimate their political impact, not to mention their detailed knowledge of the minutiae of espionage techniques, crisis simulation, and agent-handling procedure. Reconstructing the intimate ties between these fictions and the world of secret intelligence requires not only that we uncover the secret political knowledge that informs these texts but also that we reveal their political goal: for example, the warning of a looming danger, the justification of necessary military measures, or the analysis of political conflict.

While some forms of political fiction target potential or future enemies, others attempt to hypothetically reconstruct past, silenced events in the shape of a retrospective narrative. They do not want to solve the riddle as much as approximate it with various versions: how could it have been? Such fictions form an alternative historiography of the political *arcanum*. The story of Judas, as related in the Gospels, is part of it, as is John le Carré's *Tinker, Tailor, Soldier, Spy,* an infinitely subtle and extraordinarily well-researched novel that centers on the greatest Cold War espionage fiasco, the case of Kim Philby, the British MI6 agent who was a Soviet mole. To classify such texts as popular spy novels ignores their role as profound reflections of—and interventions in—the political. It is not a mere American media anecdote that Oliver Stone's movie *JFK* triggered the presumably last official investigation into the assassination of John F. Kennedy. Fictions like these *are* politics, because they are often the *only* way the most secret and dangerous state knowledge can be addressed in public. Fiction, therefore, is frequently one of the most effective disguises for that which political discourse is not allowed to express. It is both part of the secretive structure of modern power and, at the same time, its most insightful critique.

But fiction's incursion into politics goes even further. Fictions are more than encrypted politics transposed into the playful domain of the imagination. Rather, they expose the fictionality of the political itself. When modern states and modern wars depend on the dimension of the secretive, on deception and disguise, they are always already involved in narratives of plausibilization and legitimization. The narratives employed in actual politics are subject to the very economy of light and dark, narratable and non-narratable, that is manifest in the story of Judas. What enters the public sphere, the domain of representation and negotiation, is always already a product of this economy of representation. Politics is a fiction in the sense that its pronouncements and legitimizations, its attempts at presenting and locating itself, are just one *presentable* variant among other less opportune versions of an event. Politics is fiction insofar as its visible side hides as much as it reveals. It may depend on evidences, on clearly identifiable friend/enemy distinctions—but it operates precisely by undermining these evidences. If literature is the narrative medium par excellence for revealing the mechanisms of narrating and concealing, of making readable and rendering unreadable, then it is the ideal medium to reflect the inevitable *fictionality of politics.* Self-reflexive fiction can illuminate the secret of the political—if not its (forever inaccessible) content, then at least its form and function.

Fiction's reflection of the political has its theory and history. My deliberations have as their point of departure a segment on Jorge Luis Borges, who did not focus on any specific historical "case" of treason or secrecy but instead analyzed treason as a ubiquitous historical structure, thereby providing a basic theory of the secret and its narratability (see part 1, "Borges—A Poetics of Treason"). Borges is the most advanced literary theorist of the secret and its underlying friend/enemy constellations. It is precisely for this reason that he develops a concept of fiction that arises from the necessity and the difficulty involved in transforming this precarious secret into a narrative. Borges and his poetological concept of "fiction" (*ficción*) and bifurcation (*bifurcación*) serve not only as a theoretical foundation for my concept of fiction but also as a model for a form of narration that tells one version while keeping other versions of the events decipherable beneath the surface of a seemingly simple plot.

This theoretical outline, which will be demonstrated by way of a close reading of four texts from Borges's *Ficciones,* will be followed by a discourse history of twentieth-century theories of treason and the political secret (part 2, "Treason and Secrecy in the Modern Age"). Its point of departure is the debate about the twentieth century as "The Age of Treason." The notion of "treason" sparked a debate about those going rogue, a theory of political *irregularity* whose most advanced embodiment is the partisan/agent (part 2, chapter 1, "The Age of Treason"). While this debate was primarily concerned with irritations of the political, the theory of the state secret was traditionally focused rather on stability than on risk or disturbance. Antique and early modern doctrines of the *arcana imperii* and the raison d'état make the secret an essential instrument of a politics of the conservation of power. Only with the arrival of the modern ideal of complete public transparency did this start to arouse suspicion (part 2, chapter 2, "Logics of Political Secrecy"). Intelligence agencies today embody a new ominousness of political secrecy, which is why their structures, not to mention their covert operations, have become preferred objects of political fantasies and conspiracy theories. These phantasms manifest themselves in various accounts—from spy novels and political thrillers to investigative journalism, historical reconstructions, and memoirs by members of the secret service—as well as in the specific structures of knowledge produced by intelligence services. Genealogically, secret intelligence derives from military stratagems and techniques of deception, from the arts of reconnaissance and skillful camouflage (part 2, chapter 3, "Secret Intelligence"). However, by institutionalizing this martial knowledge intelligence agencies become caught up in the epistemic aporias and paranoid structures produced by the imperative of total secrecy. The epistemology of secret intelligence sketched in the third part of this introduction leads us back to the question of how the "betrayable" secret knowledge is structured, revealing the inner dynamics that locate the fictions at the very core of knowledge and its political transpositions. Caught in its secretive hall of mirrors, intelligence tends to produce nothing but hypotheses, theories, probabilities, suspicious facts, and, in the worst case (as during the preparation for the second Iraq War), opportunistic lies—that is to say, fictions that can assume reality as secret coups, covert operations, and occasionally even open wars.

The individual analyses following this exposition are historically situated case studies. Each segment will focus on one epoch, one case, or one specific aspect of the political secret in the modern age; and each is concerned with fathoming its theoretical structure as well as its imaginary representations. Each historical scenario will foreground a systematic approach permeating the historical and local examples: spatial reconnaissance, cartography, and geopolitics in the case of the British Empire (part 3, "The Great Game"); the forms of role-playing and disguise involved in gender performances and modern social techniques (part 4, "Spies, Male and Female"); the structures of modern sovereignty and the conduct of clandestine revolutionary politics (part 5, "Agents of the World Revolution"); and the specular and speculative structuring of the enmity between the superpowers of the Cold War (part 6, "Cold War"). The last three sections are devoted to fantasies revolving around the depths and shallows of the political secret in postwar America, from the McCarthy era to 9/11. The ambivalent structure of a state paranoia that turns every citizen into an enemy and the government into an extralegal sphere of violence and manipulation will be the focus of two cases from the McCarthy era: the case of the "atom spies" Ethel and Julius Rosenberg and the movie *The Manchurian Candidate* (part 7, "State Paranoia"). With the assassination of President John F. Kennedy this paranoia gives birth to the notion of an "invisible government," in which arcane powers are bent on eroding and extinguishing sovereignty (part 8, "Invisible Government: JFK"). Finally, the ubiquitous post–9/11 talk about "terror networks" will serve as a point of departure for inquiring into the epistemic and political structures of projected "future enemies" located beyond all ideological and national affiliations (part 9, "After 9/11").

The historical readings and accounts presented here do not claim to provide a continuous history of intelligence agencies and activities. This book aims to present some of the historical cornerstones supporting the grand edifice of the modern *arcana imperii,* not a comprehensive coverage of the entire building. A literary epistemology of state secrets is concerned not with the history of secret operations and their administrative reorganizations but with the internal logic that structured this secret at a given historical moment. And of course this is not another literary history of the spy novel. Genre histories concentrate on allegedly homogeneous groups of texts and trace their generic rules and conventions, but the texts and films that will be discussed here cannot be subsumed under one specific genre label. We are dealing with poems, short stories, and plays, war memoirs and agents' autobiographies, techno-thrillers, war game scenarios, a children's book, novels and films of the most varied genres, and, last but not least, the scattered life traces of a Friesian nudist dancer whose minutely staged vita is as mysterious as a novel. The goal of a detailed analysis of the constellation of enmity, secret, and treason in these highly diverse fictions can only be to expose their eminently political foundation. Fiction appears to be a burning-glass, a medium that is able to reveal in particular clarity the political epistemology of the secret because it doubles the ambivalence and indescribability of the secret state knowledge. Fiction can tell a story—yet at the same time it tells us that, and in what ways, certain things *cannot* be told.

Part 1

Borges—A Poetics of Treason

Fictions

In December 1944 Jorge Luis Borges finished his most important and influential collection of stories. Its title is as unspecific as it is programmatic: *Ficciones*. It contains fictions and metafictions, made-up stories and stories about making up stories, seemingly more straightforward narratives and texts that recursively loop back into themselves. In fact, the volume comprises two collections. The first, *El jardín de senderos que se bifurcan* (*The Garden of Forking Paths*), had already been published in 1941; the second, *Artificios,* appeared in *Sur* in 1944.[1] While the famous texts contained in *Jardín*—such as "Tlön, Uqbar, Orbis Tertius," "Las ruinas circulares" ("The Circular Ruins"), "La biblioteca de Babel" ("The Library of Babel"), and "Pierre Ménard"—offer a kaleidoscope of imaginary realms, dreamworlds, library fantasies, and fictitious authorships, the texts of *Artificios* are "crypto-political" in the sense that they venture into the world of history. Their plots and protagonists are located in historical scenarios and locales, and their heroes become entangled in—and ultimately succumb to—ongoing struggles between political and theological parties. The following remarks are concerned with this crypto-political dimension of Borges's stories. Our particular focus will be on the way the plots are permeated by constellations of enmity that point to what Carl Schmitt determined to be the essence of the political. Moreover, the narratives develop an intricate theory of what it means to speak of the political. Borges's concept of fiction reflects on the possibility and impossibility of speaking of political secrets, or even of the political itself. Indeed, it may only be possible in the medium of fiction.

Not that Borges has much to say about current events. Neither the turmoils of Argentinian politics between 1941 and 1944 nor the rise to power of Juan Domingo Perón (detested by Borges) are explicitly mentioned in these texts. Nonetheless, a number of them reflect on the political by conjuring up distant scenarios such as the Irish uprising, the First World War, or the Passion of Christ. In these texts the political—conceived of as the antagonism of parties and positions—appears as something concealed, a structure of secrecy: something that questions depiction and narration as such. In line with its programmatic title, *Ficciones* offers texts that probe the possibilities of artifice and imagination and delve into the conditions of memory and the combinatorial possibilities of signs. The many inquiries into the political secret condense into one "topic": that of betrayal. For Borges, betrayal is more than a mere motive; it combines a poetological examination of "fiction" with a focus on history as the space of secrets. Betrayal is like a musical "theme" that is reprised at different times and places, obsessively reenacted and transformed throughout Borges's work in the countless showdowns between gauchos, scholars, painters, and even impersonal objects such as daggers ("El encuentro" ["The Encounter"]). For Borges, betrayal is the paradigmatic case of the inextricable nexus of secret and narration, of the necessity and impossibility of narrating the secret.

More than any other modern author Borges transforms betrayal itself into a model, a constituent element of universal history, to probe the conditions of both history itself and the writing of history. His obsession is most clearly expressed in the title "Theme of the Traitor and the Hero" ("Tema del traidor y del héroe"). Traitor and hero are inseparably welded to each other; together they form a basic constellation of treason that reemerges throughout history. His stories condense and unfold questions of secrecy and betrayal, narratability and readability, fiction and historical frame, in the smallest possible space, without, however, offering an explicit poetics of betrayal. Reading these stories means deciphering their implicit theory of the entanglement between secrecy, fiction, and narration, reading them against the grain and with a fair amount of suspicion.

"*I* am Vincent Moon. Now, despise me," says one of Borges's traitors—arguably the most pathetic—to his listener after having told him his own private story of betrayal (Borges 1998, 138–42). The contempt demanded by the traitor is the inevitable gap that opens up between those who participated in an event and those who are confronted with the story. Every tale of betrayal bridges this gap by positioning both narrator and audience on the same (political) side, that of the hero, the savior, the betrayed, not that of the betrayer—just as we saw in the Gospels. The betrayal cannot be told from the perspective of the traitor. Fully aware of this difficulty, the protagonist of "The Shape of the Sword" ("La forma de la espada") resorts to a basic stratagem: he relates the story from the point of view of the betrayed hero who had saved the life of the "hopeless coward" Vincent Moon only to be handed over by the latter to his enemies for "Judas silver." The story, which like so many of Borges's texts is in fact the story of a story (the first-person narrator listens to Moon's story without knowing that his interlocutor is Moon), relates a betrayal while simultaneously relating that the betrayal itself, the muddy constellation of "traitor and hero," cannot be related. Narrating the betrayal requires a narrative displacement such as the one undertaken by Moon, who both reveals and denies himself in a confession that defers the moment of self-disclosure to the very end: "*I* am Vincent Moon." In "Guayaquil," a story contained in the collection *Brodie's Report,* Borges writes that "when one confesses to an act, one ceases to be an actor in it and becomes its witness, becomes a man that observes and narrates it and no longer the man who performed it" (Borges 1998, 390). Moon's tale, then, enacts the switch between the two positions required by every act of betrayal: traitor and hero.

Neither confession nor lie (though a bit of both), but above all a tiny yet decisive shift of perspective: that seems to be the only way to narrate treason. It marks the poetic program alluded to in the title of Borges's collection. The Borgesian notion of "fiction" is central to our investigation because it addresses the difficulties involved in narrating betrayal, that is, in revealing how a secret was revealed. What is at issue is the possibility or impossibility of exposing a forbidden knowledge, and of narrating an act that subverts the conditions of its own narratability. Here, fiction is not just an artifice generated by creative imagination, but a moment of deviation: the precise distance between two mutually related and yet diverging versions of an event, the deviation between two mutually exclusive truths.[2] Moon's "fiction" emphatically refers to a truth precisely by deviating from it, and this deviation is rendered transparent by the story. "The Shape of the Sword" offers both the truth *and* its variant, yet this truth—that Moon was betrayed by the very friend he saved—can be disclosed only in distorted fashion. Borges's fiction marks the distance, the possible space between two (or more) variants or "versions" of an event. These versions, however, are not arbitrarily chosen; they all point toward something essential, a "real" truth behind the lie, the solution to the riddle. Borges's use of the word "fiction" thus evokes the original meaning of the word *fingere,* which means not only "invent, create, shape," but also "feign, lie, deceive." Moon's tale is fiction because it is a "false" version, but this "falseness" remains tied to a truth—in this case, an identity that may even reach beyond the final confession "*I* am Vincent Moon."

The story of and about Vincent Moon is a model of the way we tell tales of secrets and betrayal. If "the Englishman at La Colorada" (Borges 1998, 138), as the protagonist is called before he reveals himself to be Vincent Moon, had remained silent, he would never have been recognized as Moon the Irishman, Moon the traitor. To tell a story, therefore, is to betray oneself. The story's point of departure is a "symptom," a clue in need of explanation: "a vengeful scar, an ashen and almost perfect arc that sliced from the temple on one side of his head to his cheek on the other" (ibid.). This "vengeful" (*rencorosa*) scar has the shape of the scimitar that made it and thus resembles a sickle-shaped moon—thereby pointing to the name of the protagonist. This overdetermined clue is the result of a "marked reference," creating an *effet de secret* (see Haverkamp 1993). It is an ostentatious sign, the trace of a story that has to be lured out and told. In fact the tale appears to have been told once before: when the former owner of La Colorada was reluctant to sell that scarcely profitable estate, "the Englishman plied him with an argument nobody could have foreseen—he told him the secret story of the scar" (Borges 1998, 138). Even though it remains unknown why the owner changed his mind and what exactly Moon told him, however, what is clear is the power of Moon's story. The *effet de secret* is an extremely *effective* piece of fiction: it has a direct impact on audience, content, and narrator. The act of narration alters the reality in which it takes place; it performs yet another betrayal by passing on a piece of knowledge that is as secret and efficacious as the betrayal itself—both decide over life and death, guilt and innocence, victory and defeat, purity and defacement. But the more the truth can only be told by replacing it with "fiction," the more difficult it becomes to listen to or read the tale. Clues like the name "Moon" and the moon-shaped scar are pieces of evidence in need of interpretation, even though it may be impossible to fully resolve them.

Name, scar, and their story, however, are traces not only of an individual crime but also of a historical event: the Irish struggle for independence in 1922. With this larger historical frame of reference the fiction leaves the exclusively literary domain. It is no longer a mere *story* but now also a piece of *history.* Exposing this historical frame of reference moves Borges closer to other texts that refer to political and historical matters, thereby shedding light on hitherto neglected aspects of his work. Critics have time and again described how his texts stage—if not simulate—apocryphal knowledge and open up the infinity of a library universe in which texts refer to nothing but other texts.[3] Borges, so the mainstream appreciation has often concluded, is part of the tradition of a "literature of unreality."[4] But rather than crediting him once again with producing "texts about texts," it may be more precise to describe Borges's tales as *stories about history.* More to the point, they are stories about the conditions that determine the way history is constructed. No matter how arbitrary and diverse the names and locations, no matter how fictitious the accompanying notes, Borges's historical scenarios are always both exact and explicit.[5] At the core of the stories, however, is a crucial tendency toward secrecy marked by what Anselm Haverkamp, modifying Sigmund Freud's "consideration of representability," has called a "consideration of concealability" (Haverkamp 1991, 24). History, Borges notes, is "modest" in the sense that "its essential dates may be, for a long time, secret" (Borges 1964, 167). Nobody illustrated with greater clarity than Borges the idea that history is the labor of the secret.

What distinguishes Borges's narratives from other explorations of the secret, however, is their extreme degree of self-reflexivity. For all their irritating precision, the dates, names, and locations specified in the stories are marked as random: "In 1824, let us say, for convenience's sake," utters the narrator at the outset of "The Theme of the Traitor and Hero," "in Ireland, let us say" (Borges 1998, 143). It could just as well be Poland or 1922 or any other specific time or place. Borges's tales present the reader with possible though indeterminable versions of a historical truth; they are *fictions* precisely in the degree to which they take on history and historiography. They may utilize the generic characteristics of fantastic literature and create unreal worlds out of texts, dreams, memories, delusions, and myths, but the fictional core of *Ficciones* is not the frequently emphasized *contrast* to reality but the presentation of an alternative, *equally "real"* reality. Ironically, it is exactly this celebratory foregrounding of historicism that serves to reveal the contingent and textual character of the historical. Fiction thus becomes a *possible* version of our knowledge of reality, just like a "heuristic fiction," a fiction that serves to explore the logical consequences of a problem or situation.[6] Fictions are hypotheses, explorations of assumptions or sophisms, narrative unfoldings of possible worlds and chronologies. *What if? What's behind this? What really happened?* To decipher tales of betrayal and treason always implies the reconstruction of the underlying historical scenarios, scenarios that determine what is or has been at stake in the very act of treason. Nevertheless, we cannot expect such stories to faithfully depict what really happened. The necessary deviation—in terms of both structure and content—can only be gauged by tentatively referring to a historical substrate that can never be grasped "as such" but that is encrypted in the narrative—crossed out, denied, manipulated.

Betraying, Narrating, Reading

From the *Universal History of Infamy* to the perfidiously innocent Emma Zunz in the short story of that title (Borges 1998, 215–19), Borges remains fascinated by betrayal and treason as particular species of infamy. *Infamia* and *fama* are not only linked to moral judgment (including the contempt solicited by Vincent Moon) but also, above all, to historical transmission. While *fama* or fame refers to the heroic glory from which we weave the tapestry of history, *in-famia* is that which cannot or should not be communicated. For Borges, history is "the history of a few metaphors" (Borges 2000, 351) or themes: heroes and traitors, duels, visions and dreams, recursions in time; it is nothing but the variation of a limited number of types of events. The *infamia* of betrayal, however, immediately raises problems of narration and narratability,[7] which Borges passes on to the reader by highlighting the difficulties of reading and deciphering historical narratives. In setting after setting Borges depicts the historical event as a contingent course of events that later is transformed through the act of narration into a necessary, logical logic of things. To read history is to retrieve the element of contingency from the closure of historical tradition.

Borges refers to this as a "bifurcation" (*bifurcación*) in time that allows for the precise rendering of alternate, equally possible options. He projects possible worlds, possible sequences of events, whose consecutive realizations remain aware of the unrealized concurrent options. In "A Survey of the Works of Herbert Quain" he provides a sketch of these bifurcations:

$$z\begin{cases} y_1\begin{cases} x_1 \\ x_2 \\ x_3 \end{cases} \\ y_2\begin{cases} x_4 \\ x_5 \\ x_6 \end{cases} \\ y_3\begin{cases} x_7 \\ x_8 \\ x_9 \end{cases} \end{cases}$$

(Borges 1998, 109)

Betrayal is the event par excellence, a caesura at which history bifurcates, the moment in which one possible course of events is enacted while many others are discarded. It is the starting point of a narrative that will present this particular course *and no other* as true, necessary, and above all *noncontingent,* thus elevating the chosen story to the status of *history.* But if this particular story-as-history is tied to the implicitly suppressed versions, it can be recognized as something manufactured and artificially created—as fiction. The act of narration inevitably silences something else. To read and unearth the latter is the adventure faced by Borges's readers—and most of his heroes. In "A Survey of the Works of Herbert Quain," which could serve as a reading guide for all of *Ficciones,* Borges laid out the theory of such a reading in the disguise of a fictitious obituary of a fictitious writer, Herbert Quain. Describing four texts by Quain, each of which embodies a certain riddle structure, Borges in effect offers nothing less than a poetics of investigative reading and narrating—a set of instructions for how to read his own texts.[8] The text summarizes *The God of the Labyrinth,* one of Quain's apocryphal works, as follows:

> There is an incomprehensible murder in the early pages of the book, a slow discussion in the middle, and a solution of the crime toward the end. Once the mystery has been cleared up, there is a long retrospective paragraph that contains the following sentence: *Everyone believed that the chessplayers had met accidentally.* That phrase allows one to infer that the solution is in fact in error, and so, uneasy, the reader looks back over the pertinent chapters and discovers *another* solution, which is the correct one. (Borges 1998, 108)

This device attributed to the fictitious Quain enables the reader to be more perceptive than the detective who fails to solve the murder. Text and plot are at odds; the latter is a cover story for a secret contained but not narrated by the story. The clause "everyone believed" is a code indicating that the text has to be reread using the proper key. To follow this hint and find the "correct" solution to unveil the secret of the text rather than that of the plot implies a backward motion aimed at exposing the deceptive narrative order. Following Borges, we start at a given point *z* and determine what other (perhaps hidden) prehistories in the shape of *x* and *y* are possible. Reading, then, amounts to the decision between two mutually exclusive versions, the reconstruction of multiple irreconcilable pasts that nevertheless, coexist.

Borges presents the works of Quain as basic narrative models that refer to a secret either reconstructed in the past or projected into the future.

They are models of how narratives are doubled into a secret and a public meaning. Borges's tales are reflective textual models for all texts that revolve around secrets and disclosures: from the poetics of shame or mendacity in the autobiographies of traitors and bearers of secrets (from T. E. Lawrence to Kim Philby), to the forensic reconstructions of "what really happened" undertaken in spy thrillers (for example, John le Carré), to conspiracist uncoverings (such as the vast literature on the assassination of John F. Kennedy). Borges's models teach us how to read those texts by insisting that we must also decipher *possible* alternatives, all which is left unsaid, when reading the *given* version (nowhere more so than in le Carré's cryptic dialogues). To decipher the secret implies that whatever is narrated may be only a twisted, perverse, or apologetic—but in any case effective—cover-up of an entirely different story. And that is how Borges himself has to be read.

The Dialectic of God: "Three Versions of Judas"

If the betrayal of Judas is the primal scene of treason that spawned countless versions and interpretations, then Borges boldly offers the last, final twist. "Three Versions of Judas" ("Tres versiones de Judas") tackles the act of betrayal as an incomprehensible *mysterium iniquitatis,* a mystery of iniquity in need of a solution, by offering a scandalously blasphemous speculation.[9] Not coincidentally, we are again confronted with the adventures of a reader, in this case those of the Swedish theologian Nils Runeberg. Following the Gnostics, Thomas De Quincey, and "a certain German" (Borges 1998, 165)—Kautsky? Schweitzer?—Runeberg attempts a new interpretation of the betrayal of Jesus. His point of departure is the familiar premise that it would not have required the services of a traitor to identify such a well-known preacher: "He observes (as Robertson had) that to identify a teacher who preached every day in the synagogue and worked miracles in plain sight of thousands of people, there was no need of betrayal by one of the teacher's own people. That is precisely, however, what occurred" (Borges 1998, 164).[10]

But unlike Kautsky, Runeberg does not venture into the political; instead he (like Schweitzer) insists on sharpening the theological interpretation. The iniquity of Judas, Borges's theologian argues, parallels the humiliation of God becoming man. "Judas is somehow a reflection of Jesus" (Borges 1998, 164). According to this first version Judas would be the "secret mirror" of Jesus, the slightly gruesome repetition of God's incarnation. The crux of Runeberg's dialectic meditation is that it gravitates in ever tighter interpretive circles toward the constellation of "hero" and "traitor": once you conceive of heroes and traitors as mutually dependent figures, there is no end to this "dizzying dialectic" (ibid., 167). Years later, in the story titled "The Sect of the Thirty" ("La secta de los treinta"), the very same idea is attributed to a heretic sect: "Of knowing actors [that is, those aware of the deeper significance of the Crucifixion], there were but two: Judas and the Redeemer . . . The Sect venerates the two equally" (ibid., 445). In a second, even more scandalous publication Runeberg goes a step further by claiming the identity of Redeemer and Judas:

> God was made totally man. But man to the point of iniquity, man to the point of reprobation and the Abyss. In order to save us. He could have chosen *any* of the lives that weave the confused web of history: He could have been Alexander or Pythagoras or Rurik or Jesus; he chose an abject existence. He was Judas. (Ibid., 166)

The secret of redemption, then, no longer consists in a mirroring. Now it involves an exchange of positions: Judas sacrifices himself, while Jesus of Nazareth suffers no more than "the agony of an afternoon on the cross" (ibid., 166). To elucidate this version the text refers to Isaiah 53:2–3: "He shall grow up before him as a tender plant, and as a root out of dry ground: he hath no form nor comeliness . . . He is despised and rejected of men; a man of sorrows, and acquainted with grief" (ibid., 166). By rereading the Gospels from this particular passage Runeberg hits upon the "correct solution" among the many logically and theologically plausible explanations—just as God, choosing among so many different human fates, chose to be incarnated as Judas.

However, this contingent and awful decision must remain undisclosed: "God did not want his terrible secret spread throughout the earth" (Borges 1998, 167). God makes a decision in much the same way as the reader (in this particular case, the scriptural reader Runeberg), choosing among alternative versions, chooses a *different* version according to which Judas is the true Messiah. But redemption only comes with the price of misapprehension; the true Redeemer must remain damned and despised, both in death and in tradition. This variant serves to radicalize the complicity between Jesus and Judas hinted at in John 13:26–27. The redemption of mankind is possible only if it remains a secret, for while a religion may involve a god's sacrifice, it can hardly be based on his crime. The betrayal, abjection, and redemption of Judas can fulfill its historical mission only if it remains secret. As a result, the failed theologian Runeberg turns into the third—and worst—version of the Judas the betrayer:

"Runeberg realized that the hour was not yet come. He felt that ancient, divine curses were met in him" (ibid., 167). Nils Runeberg (who strangely enough shares the second half of his surname, his translator Emil Schering, his home country of Sweden, and the year of his death with August Strindberg) is the betrayer of divine secrets. His "Revelations" in the form of two publications, however, remain unread. Like Judas he is left to walk through town in a contrite daze: "Drunk with sleeplessness and his dizzying dialectic, Nils Runeberg wandered the streets of Malmö, crying out for a blessing—that he be allowed to share the Inferno with the redeemer" (ibid., 167). In death his body explodes like that of Judas, as depicted in gory detail by Giovanni Canavesio, although in the end it is, medically speaking, no more than a "ruptured aneurysm" (ibid., 167).

In Borges's structurally cool (though theologically dashing) analysis of the Passion there is no Redeemer without a betrayer—but through his act of betrayal the latter moves into the position of the former. Borges depicts betrayal as a constellation of positions choreographed by the secret: the "Redeemer/hero" position, the "traitor" position, and the "narrator" position. The subjects move from traitor to Redeemer to narrator (who in turn comes to occupy the position of betrayer). The secret doesn't circulate; it assigns positions and has the subjects circulate through time and space. The (provisionally) last turn of the events from 30 C.E. takes place in early twentieth-century Sweden and—if you like—in the Buenos Aires of Jorge Luis Borges, who in telling the story moves into the position hitherto occupied by Runeberg. Borges emphasizes this universal, transhistorical iniquity of treason with an epigraph that establishes a link to another case of betrayal. It is a quotation from *The Seven Pillars of Wisdom,* T. E. Lawrence's account of his part in the Arab uprising against the Ottoman Empire (see part 3, "The Great Game"): "There seemed a certainty in degradation" (T. E. Lawrence 1991, 564). In the passage in question Lawrence dissects his double role as organizer of the Arab insurgency and British agent, a double role that makes him both liberator and traitor. "There seemed a certainty in degradation, a final safety"—the safety offered by degradation reflects the inescapable shame of treason, a shame that in Borges's dialectic constitutes the secret core of Lawrence's heroism. (It should be noted that in 1942, just prior to the appearance of *Ficciones,* Borges's friend Victoria Ocampo published one of the many admiring books on Lawrence.)[11] In Lawrence, hero and traitor melt into one. By contaminating the theological implications of the Passion of Christ with the political treachery of T. E. Lawrence, Borges underlines the universality of the hero/traitor/narrator constellation. Underneath the incisive historical event lies a secret, the secret of treason.

The Silence of History: "The Theme of the Traitor and the Hero"

How can such a deeply ambivalent event be narrated? The poetics of treason is at the heart of "The Theme of the Traitor and the Hero," a story whose title and epigraph underscore the universal status of treason and the return of all historical events in the "Platonic year."[12] The story is no more than the brief sketch of a plot, the narrative of a historian trying to write the life of his great-grandfather, who is an Irish national hero. In this tale, more than in any of his others, Borges emphasizes the arbitrariness, the "made-up" nature of his story (the original refers to it as a *argumento*): "I have conceived this plot—which I will perhaps commit to paper . . . Today, January 3, 1944, I see it in the following way" (Borges 1998, 143). It may be no coincidence that on the following day, January 4, 1944, the *New York Times* reported on the beginning of a trial against thirty conspirators who allegedly had tried to install a fascist regime in the United States.[13] The date may not be so arbitrary after all.

Once again, readers are faced with a doubly nested and canceled narrative—the *untold* narrative about a narrator who, in the end, will *not* relate what he nonetheless will have found out. The narrator and protagonist is the historian Ryan, "the great-grandson of the young, heroic, beautiful, murdered Fergus Kilpatrick" (Borges 1998, 143). On the occasion of its centenary, Ryan wants to retell the story of the Irish conspirator who in 1824, shortly before the successful uprising, was assassinated in a theater. What he unearths is, in short, that Kilpatrick (kill-Patrick!) may have betrayed his own organization and that the conspirators, unwilling to lose their leader under such inglorious circumstances, condemned him to die a martyr's death modeled on Shakespearean drama. The "dizzying dialectic" of treason is at work again: the hero is the traitor is the martyr. Borges borrows this complicity of friend and enemy from G. K. Chesterton, who is mentioned at the outset of the story and whose novel *The Man Who Was Thursday* tells the story of a conspiracy in which the head conspirator is in cahoots with the police (Chesterton 1908).

Once unmasked, the hero and traitor Kilpatrick consents to his theatrical demise because his dismissal from the ranks of the insurgents would jeopardize the imminent uprising. To safeguard the insurgence and preserve the charismatic leader, the person must disappear without harming the position. This is achieved by means of a tragic martyr's death staged for (and against) Kilpatrick by his friend and comrade James Alexander Nolan. Not coincidentally, Nolan chooses Shakespeare's *Julius Caesar* and *Macbeth,* thereby alluding to the wicked and conspiratorial murder of rulers—Caesar and Duncan. The idea is to make Kilpatrick appear as innocent as good king Duncan in *Macbeth.* The *imitatio Christi* of the martyr is clearly spelled out: Kilpatrick, the text intones with scriptural inflection, "entered Dublin, argued, worked, prayed, reprehended, spoke words of pathos" (Borges 1998, 145). These words are provided to him by Nolan (plagiarizing Shakespeare), whose mise-en-scène manages to construct a memorable event that will install Kilpatrick as national martyr and saint. He stages a story to be remembered and retold. To *make* history, Borges claims, is to provide material for a narratable story, that is, to produce *representable* events. As a narrative, history is not simply the retelling, manipulating, or falsifying of prior events; it is itself, in all its theatricality, already manipulation, secret, conspiracy (see Horn 2009a).

At one point Ryan, belated reader of this highly artificial performance, realizes that the Shakespeare quotations inserted by Nolan into his political melodrama are aimed at him: "Ryan suspected that the author interpolated them from Shakespeare so that someone, in the future, would be able to stumble upon the truth" (Borges 1998, 146). If Kilpatrick, like Judas and Lawrence, wavers between hero and traitor, Nolan represents a new figure of no less importance for the functioning of the *arcana imperii:* the scheming intriguer, the gray eminence who pulls the threads and retains powers even though it may involve sacrificing the sovereign. (As we shall see in part 6, chapter 3, "The Human Factor," John le Carré's mole Bill Haydon is a late, dastardly manifestation of this figure.) Nolan guards the secret, and both hides *and* betrays it by means of his politico-historical stage performance. Given the secret's inscrutable ambivalence, Nolan's role in the events, however, is anything but clear: he is not only Kilpatrick's closest friend and confidant but also the one who unveils his treachery, and he may even have wrongly accused him—the narrative leaves it all open. Ultimately Nolan even betrays the great cover-up he himself staged. By inserting the Shakespeare quotations, Nolan reveals the citational and thus artificial nature of the events to a very careful future reader, such as Ryan. While a confused Ryan is at first left to ponder the return of certain events in history,[14] he finally comes to realize that it was all nothing but forgery.

Yet the question arises *how* Ryan solves the puzzle. The critical clue, we may assume, is *Macbeth.* As is well known, Shakespeare's play is not only about the murder of a legitimate king but also about the disgrace and downfall of Duncan's usurper, Macbeth. The allusion to *Macbeth* is every bit as ambivalent as Kilpatrick himself: it both conceals and betrays the latter's double nature. To the intertextually versed Borges reader, Nolan himself is marked as suspicious. His name is no less telling than that of the cowardly traitor Moon, for "Nolan" happens to be the name of the traitor in Liam O'Flaherty's *The Informer*, a novel that Borges, an outspoken admirer of O'Flaherty, was sure to have known. It deals with a group of Irish revolutionaries whose leader is betrayed by Nolan, the eponymous informer. Like Kilpatrick, Nolan is both hero and traitor; he ingeniously saves the revolution yet also betrays the secret to the readers, including Ryan. The latter receives the message, but unlike C. Auguste Dupin in Edgar Allan Poe's "The Purloined Letter," he does not pass it on but keeps it to himself: "He [Ryan] published a book dedicated to the hero's glory" (Borges 1998, 146).

Secrecy is here revealed as a hidden dimension of history, a dimension that makes the reading of history—both as event and as story—an act of intense deciphering. Following the transmission of the secret from Kilpatrick to Nolan and finally to Ryan, Ryan is now in the precarious situation of owning the secret. As Jacques Lacan's reading of "The Purloined Letter" emphasizes, this position holds both power and danger (further see part 2, chapter 2 "Logics of Political Secrecy").[15] Ultimately it is the reader who is placed in the position Ryan eventually refuses to assume. Reading thus means being drawn into a game of secrets, becoming part of the constellation of truth and lie—in other words, becoming part of the fiction itself. Borges's stories reveal that fiction combines an *effet de secret* with an *effet de vérité:* they involve the reader in the fiction and force her to assume a position.

Transmission: "The Garden of Forking Paths"

The story "The Garden of Forking Paths" ("El jardín de senderos que se bifurcan") is one of Borges's most complex texts. It introduces a different type of political secret: the military secret. Unlike the mystery of Judas, military secrets do not linger for centuries in the undergrowth of tradition; they are as powerful as they are short-lived. "The Garden of Forking Paths" is less concerned with the depths of the *arcana imperii* than with secret intelligence (on the distinction between the two, see part 2, chapters 2 and 3, "Logics of Political Secrecy" and "Secret Intelligence"). The story revolves around one of the basic problems of espionage, the secret transmission of messages: in the days leading up to the Battle of the Somme an agent working for the Germans is charged with communicating the location of enemy artillery positions to his superiors in Berlin. Ostensibly mimicking the spy genre of the 1920s, the text leads off with a reference to the Serre-Montauban line at the end of July 1916, as it allegedly appears on page 242 of Basil Liddell Hart's famous *History of the World War* (see Borges 1998, 199).[16] Once again, historiography is at issue, in this case that "missing dimension" (Andrew and Dilks 1984) of official military historiography known as espionage. The story purports to offer additional information that "throws unexpected light" (Borges 1998, 199) on certain apocryphal events of the First World War. What follows is a fragmentary confession, written by a Chinese spy working for the Germans prior to his execution, which contains an alternate version of Liddell Hart's official account.[17]

The Chinese spy in question, a man called Yu Tsun from the former German colony Tsingtao, has found out "the name of the exact location of the new British artillery park on the Ancre" (Borges 1998, 120)—a secret he must quickly pass on to his handler in Berlin. Since his fellow agent, a spy with the familiar name Runeberg, has already been unmasked and shot, Yu Tsun is under extreme pressure to find a way to communicate the information. He decides to kill a man who happens to have the same name as the town in question (Albert) in the hope that a public connection between his own name and that of his prey will alert his German superiors. After perusing the local directories in search of a convenient victim, he travels to the nearby village of Ashcroft, where he kills one Stephen Albert, a sinologist, before being apprehended and handed over to the authorities by his antagonist, Captain Richard Madden. The plot, in short, revolves around a vital piece of information that has to be encoded and transmitted at great risk and at the greatest possible speed. The medium of each transmission is death: Runeberg's death signals the urgency of the situation to Yu Tsun; the death of the sinologist Albert, allegedly a random victim, signals to the Germans the position of the English artillery. Again, Borges depicts the secret as an arrangement of positions: here the doomed bearer and messenger of the secret, there the murderer whose crime enables the transmission in the first place. Captain Madden, pursuer of German spies, kills Runeberg, who knows the secret, thus alerting Yu Tsun, who by killing Albert manages to warn the Germans. The actual communication is enabled by Madden, who by arresting Yu Tsun establishes a publicized connection between the latter and the name Albert. Finally, the condemned Yu Tsun communicates the riddle's (alleged) solution to his judges and readers. The secret assigns positions to the subjects of the story: whoever is in possession of the vital piece of information has to kill or die to pass it on.

Despite the many dedicated pursuits, the tale also raises the question of the protagonists' loyalty: strangely enough, neither the Chinese Yu Tsun nor the Irishman Madden belongs to the warring nation he supports. Dr. Yu Tsun, a former lecturer in English at the German-Chinese *Hochschule* at the one-time German colony at Tsingtao, is now working for the Germans in England, while the Irishman Madden—in the immediate aftermath of the Easter Uprising of 1916—fights for Britain. Both are, by the very nature of their allegiances, traitors, but their loyalty is so steadfast precisely because their superiors don't expect it from them. Indeed, Yu Tsun identifies the fact he is a "yellow man" as a prime motivating factor: "I did it because I sensed that the Leader looked down on the people of my race . . . I wanted to prove to him that a yellow man could save his armies" (Borges 1998, 121). No matter how determined the figures may act, the boundary between friend and enemy is no longer clear—a diagnosis of pivotal importance in the "century of treason." (On the complex and bewildering identities and loyalties in colonial espionage and its protagonists, see part 3, "The Great Game.") Borges plays with this lack of clarity of friend and enemy, the signature of enmity in the modern age, by depicting how contingent even the most courageous efforts are.

But at the core of the tale is a mysterious nested narrative, the aesthetic if not completely ethereal conversation between Yu Tsun and his victim, the sinologist Stephen Albert. It suspends the hurried spy plot in the timelessness of a discussion of Chinese literature, which, significantly, has time as its content. As idle and out of place as it may seem in the midst of the desperate chase for time, the conversation confronts the reader with nothing less than a theory of secrets and fictions at the heart of which Borges locates a theory of time. The main topic of conversation between the Chinese spy and British sinologist is an apocryphal Chinese novel, a manuscript of which has been discovered and analyzed by Albert. Yu Tsun happens to be a descendant of its author, Ts'ui Pen. Its bizarre title, "The Garden of Forking Paths," gives the story its name. Albert is in possession of an incomplete draft and has managed to reveal its secret structure. As he explains to Yu Tsun, it "suggested to me the image of a forking in time, rather than in space . . . In all fictions, each time a man meets diverse alternatives, he chooses one and eliminates the others; in the work of the virtually impossible-to-entangle Ts'ui Pen the character chooses—simultaneously—all of them" (Borges 1998, 125).

According to Albert the novel's unspoken secret can only be glimpsed in its bifurcating structure: "[The novel] is a huge riddle, or parable, whose subject is time" (Borges 1998, 126). Time is the sum total of all possible and conceivable pasts and futures, a virtual reservoir of history that is nothing less than the totality of *all* alternative individual histories. Time, which to Borges was the center of all metaphysical inquiries (Christ

1974, 400), is both the Chinese novel's and the story's deepest secret. But it is also the cipher for Borges's notion of "fiction": the alternative presence of possible worlds composed of all yet-to-be-unfolded future and the many prehistories leading to the same present. Ts'ui Pen's novel is the fiction of fictions because it not only reflects alternative pasts and presents but also manages to realize *all of them*. It is a total and therefore altogether impossible book. Indeed, it is a cryptic model of Borges's own narratives: not coincidentally, "The Garden of Forking Paths" was the title of his first collection that subsequently became part of *Ficciones*. Borges's own tales are gardens of forking paths, labyrinths of fiction that focus on the contingencies and possible decisions of their own narrative threads. Last but not least, the Chinese novel about time is a model of the secret itself: as Albert explains, while time may structure the entire text, the word itself is not mentioned once in the text. It is marked by its absence. The secret constitutes an empty space, an absence that organizes everything around itself.

Yet the tale's metapoetical center is anything but a world of scholarly serenity removed from the harsh wartime reality. At the end of the brief, yet deep conversation Stephen Albert is struck down by a bullet from Yu Tsun's gun. Their serene dialogue, too, is permeated by war, enmity, and treason. Albert illustrates the principle of alternative bifurcation of causal chains by reading an excerpt of the Chinese novel that centers on a battle:

> In the first [version], an army marches off to battle through a mountain wilderness; the horror of the rocks and darkness inspires in them a disdain for life, and they go on to an easy victory. In the second, the same army passes through a palace in which a ball is being held; the battle seems to them a continuation of the *fête*, and they win it easily. (Borges 1998, 125 and following)

What the passage indicates leads right back into the context of the story: victory is a result that can be deduced from highly divergent prehistories. The bifurcations are in a past that has to be unrolled in reverse: how do different pasts arrive at the same present? The secret is distended across binary bifurcations that determine life and death, friendship and enmity. War and enmity are the paradigm of inevitable and yet equally contingent *bifurcaciónes*. Both Albert and Yu Tsun address this fundamental logic of war: "In one of the possible pasts," Albert remarks, "you are my enemy, in another my friend" (ibid., 125). Yu Tsun, in turn, comes up with a double lie when he claims: "The future is with us . . . but I am your friend" (ibid., 127). Neither is the future already "with us," a given thing, nor is he Albert's friend. Enmity in Borges is mostly deadly, but also radically contingent (see Horn 2009a). Hence the binary logic of enmity not only structures the story's military frame and the labyrinthine work of Ts'ui Pen. It also structures the dialogue itself, including the theory of time and its implicit theory of fiction as the network of bifurcations. Bifurcations structure the entire text—there are always pairs of two: two spies (Yu Tsun and Runeberg), two men who are killed in the midst of a labyrinth by an unknown man (Albert and Ts'ui Pen), two connoisseurs of Chinese literature (Albert and Yu Tsun), two deaths that transmit a message (Runeberg's and Albert's). Borges's world is a series of branching binary alternatives, of decisions being made—but in which the other, not-chosen alternative still lurks as the uncanny and secret underside of the given reality and the narrative.

But time is not just a garden of forking paths, of latent possibilities in need of decision—it is also a merciless linear stream pushing forward. In Borges's spy story, it is a matter of speed and acceleration, deadlines and windows of opportunity, such as the forty minutes that the railway timetables (and the time it takes Captain Madden to figure out what is going on) leave Yu Tsun for his conversation with Stephen Albert. This dimension of time as speed constitutes the temporal structure of the military secret (see part 2, chapter 3, "Secret Intelligence"). It is a matter of *up to* a certain point acquiring and passing on knowledge *before* the enemy. The military secret is knowledge with a sell-by date, something you know *before* your enemy does. Yu Tsun is on the run; whatever chance he has depends on his being faster than his pursuers. It is no coincidence that his name recalls that of the Chinese strategist Sun Tzu, who first conceived of time as a decisive military factor. Sun Tzu's *Art of War* was later equipped with an introduction by the very same Basil Liddell Hart whom Borges quotes at the beginning of the story. Sun Tzu famously emphasized that the value of a military secret solely rests in the speed with which it is communicated: "Speed is the essence of war" (Sun Tzu 1963, 134).

The tale's overly elegant plot, however, contains a riddle, an unsolvable contradiction that specifically deals with these two dimensions of time: time as a "garden of forking paths" and as speed. By murdering Albert, Yun Tsu, the story claims, manages to communicate the name of the city that the Germans must target. "Yesterday," he writes, "it was bombed—I read about it in the same newspapers that posed to all of England the enigma of the murder of the eminent sinologist Stephen Albert by a stranger" (Borges 1998, 126 and following). However, this results in a logical quandary: if it is the newspaper's mention of the murder that reveals to the German side which town they have to attack, then bombardment and murder *cannot* be mentioned "in the same newspapers," given that the murder is the causal and temporal precondition for the attack.[18] There must have been another, *earlier* transmission. Could it have been by Runeberg, Yu Tsun's fellow agent who was killed by Madden? At the beginning of the story it is mentioned that the first two pages of Yu Tsun's confession are missing. Maybe they contained the solution.

In this unsolved mystery of communication the model of a flowing, accelerating, or delayed time intersects with the temporal model of the bifurcation and the branching of various solutions and events. Based on this model it is possible that two alternative routes of transmission lead to the same result (just as the Chinese novel shows). If there was indeed a different, earlier transmission, then Yu Tsun would not have "most abhorrently triumphed" (Borges 1998, 127) but rather committed a completely unnecessary murder. Underneath the text—which is, after all, the confession of an agent sentenced to death, and thus not a particularly trustworthy source—tiny fissures of implausibility reveal traces of a completely different drama that contradicts all previous accounts. This possibility, however, is hinted at rather than redeemed. The meshwork of the secret war unraveled by Borges is so obscure that even when you believe that you have "won" you can never be certain was "really" happened. Although betrayed, passed on, exploited, or revealed, the secret remains ineffable.

Borges turns secret and betrayal into a *structure* underlying history as a universal "theme." This is why Borges's theory of betrayal is so central for the obsession of modernity with treason as *the* political decision. Betrayal—more precisely, the doubling of secret and betrayal—attains the status of an erratic and incisive moment, the very paradigm of an event. By depicting a structure that allows for constant arbitrary rearrangement of different stakes, scenarios, and protagonists, Borges paints a picture of betrayal as a typical, indeed omnipresent symptom for the state of the political. But Borges not only uncovers the dialectic entanglement of hero and traitor, of betrayal and allegiance that marks the political in the twentieth century; he also develops a poetics of secrecy and treason as that which can only be deciphered underneath the "official" stories and histories, always failing to uncover the "ultimate truth."

Part 2

Treason and Secrecy in the Modern Age

1 The Age of Treason

In view of the countless historical and literary settings featuring heroes and traitors, the latter appears to be a universal figure. In the twentieth century, however, the traitor has emerged as nothing less than the signature of an epoch, an unmistakable indication that the political is afflicted by two crises: a crisis of loyalty eroding the individual's allegiance to a national community, and a crisis of enmity. Time and again the twentieth century has been labeled the Age of Treason, an epoch of blurred loyalties and conflicting allegiances. The belief in abstract ideologies has come to replace the affiliation with nations or ethnic communities; in turn, throughout the tumultuous and bloody century states have repeatedly deprived citizens of their rights and branded them as traitors and domestic enemies. Margret Boveri's *Treason in the Twentieth Century* (Boveri 1956–60; Boveri 1963), an epoch-making analysis that already at midcentury was attempting to describe modern politics as a whole in terms of treason, offers a phenomenology of what Carl Joachim Friedrich later called the "pathology of politics" (Friedrich 1972). Looking back on two world wars and forward to an increasingly icy Cold War, treason emerges as the signature of a century that like no other is marked by total and shifting enmities.

Treason in the Twentieth Century appeared in four volumes as part of *Rowohlts deutsche Enzyklopädie* (*Rowohlt's German Encylopedia*), a series whose universal scope corresponded to Boveri's monumental title. Boveri, however, demonstrated little interest in systematic theorizing, she was aiming for a total overview of a whole range of different symptoms that reveal a crisis of the political: propaganda, resistance, the proliferation of intelligence agencies, collaboration, ideology, and last but not least "the epidemic of treason" in 1950s America (see part 7, "State Paranoia"). Boveri's "treason" functions as a concept encompassing very heterogeneous forms of political ambiguity: the ambiguity of affiliation and the opacity of enmity, the intrinsic paranoia of state power, and the global reach of conflicts. Essentially, Boveri is interested in figures *between the fronts:* apostates, dissidents, defectors, partisans, collaborators. In foregrounding the various shapes of political apostasy, each nation is processing its own trauma: Germany, the Third Reich; Britain, the politics of appeasement and Nazi sympathizers and, later, the slew of Cambridge spies; France, the collaboration; and the United States, the state paranoia of McCarthyism. On the one hand, the concept of treason allows Boveri to conjure up all that appears to have been dissolved by it—a sense of home, old bonds of loyalty, and forms of belonging that have dissolved in modernity. On the other hand, the epidemic use of treason as a stigmatizing label indicates a political state of emergency that goes beyond any individual act of betrayal. For Boveri, treason is a prime symptom of a pathology of modern politics. But that means we must also ask what the discourse of treason itself betrays (Boveri 1956–60, 4:311).

Figures of Apostasy

The traitor is the human manifestation of a political landscape marked by obscurity, abstraction, and lack of transparency, a crisis of both community and enmity. This situation evokes a whole range of political figures whose common denominator is—in the words of Carl Schmitt—their "irregularity" (Schmitt 2007). Among them are Jünger's "forest dweller," Boveri's "traitor," the "partisans" of Schmitt and Schroers, and their siblings in the shape of agents, agitators, saboteurs, and spies (Boveri 1963; Jünger 1960; Schroers 1961b). It is not by accident that an array of texts revolving around the figure of the traitor and apostate appeared after World War II and in the coldest phase of the Cold War—from Boveri's highly influential book and Rebecca West's postwar essays collected in *The Meaning of Treason* (West 1947) to André Thérive's *Essai sur les trahisons* (Thérive 1951) and Hans Magnus Enzensberger's "Towards a Theory of Treason" (Enzensberger 1982). While postwar societies had tackled the question of loyalty in terms of collaboration and resistance (both of which are forms of "treason"), the Cold War turns affiliation itself into an impossibility. We are, as it were, always already on the wrong side; we are always caught in the structure of "East vs. West," which renders an individual choice of allegiance almost impossible. Personal forms of loyalty (to friends, colleagues, family, and so on) enter into dramatic, if not tragic, conflict with political allegiance. It is practically inevitable, Enzensberger argued, that we turn into traitors—or that we are at least denounced as such. The texts on treason and apostasy published in the 1950s and 1960s must be seen as a political anthropology of dissidence, attempts to reconceptualize enmity in times when the figure of "the enemy" becomes increasingly unrecognizable. The discourse on treason revolves around three basic political relations or tensions: first, the bonds between sovereign and citizens; second, the distinction between friend and enemy; and third, the tension between a democratic ideal of transparency and the need for certain types of secrecy in politics. The individual's answer to this political intransparency is what Carl Schmitt has called "political irregularity" (Schmitt 2007). The "irregular" individual exits a political structure marked by clear-cut front lines between friends and enemies.[1] Treason, apostasy, going rogue, are the epitome of irregular conduct, a breaking of rules intent on opening up a space for different forms of allegiance and alternate political choices. The traitor or apostate is both the victim of and the solution to a political crisis that consists in the tragic impossibility of allegiance. The traitor is the one who leaves his or her nation, ideology, religion, or scientific community behind. This is why the traitor becomes not only the hero of theoretical discourse, the "Gestalt" (figure) of the individual's tactics in the face of crisis, but also the hero of political fiction. While political theory dwells on a situation that renders treason inevitable, political fiction elucidates the tasks and tactics of irregular conduct and the psychology of the traitor as well as the betrayed. Fiction must thus be seen as a different form of political anthropology, sketching the inner world of the dramas and tragedies of apostasy.

Sleepers: Jünger's "Retreat into the Forest"

With his infallible sense for timely topics and stylistic mastery in formulating matters as vaguely as possible, Ernst Jünger opens the discussion with his 1951 essay "The Retreat into the Forest" (Jünger 1960).[2] Jünger's basic proposal, later honed by Boveri and Schmitt, is to link a political figure he calls the "forest dweller" (*Waldgänger*) with a spatial concept referred to as "the forest." The forest dweller—and the same will apply to partisans and spies—is a figure tied to a specific space in which he takes shape, moves, and acts. Jünger starts with an example that highlights one of the basic dilemmas of any politics of publicity: given a manipulated vote that produces a 98 percent agreement, how can one express dissent? In face of such an overwhelming majority, the dissenting voice merely serves to confirm the alleged tolerance of the dominant position while simultaneously revealing the presence of an "enemy on the inside." On the level of the plebiscite—a mechanism that ostensibly embodies freedom of expression—there is nothing to be done. Jünger's theory of resistance—or, in his diction, the "retreat into the forest"—concerns the "freedom of the individual" (Jünger 1960, 307), that is, his ability to withdraw from the game of power no matter how total and inclusive it may be. For Jünger this is the gist of irregular political behavior: stepping out of the official electoral games while also abstaining from any open revolt. As a surreptitious dissident the forest dweller is isolated, homeless, and "targeted for annihilation" (ibid., 317), yet within the forest he enjoys miraculous protection. The forest, a clandestine underground domain, is a sphere of freedom that offers a way out of the ongoing constraints imposed by the state. The forest is "home and harbor" (ibid., 325), where the solitary individual finds "a third way" (ibid., 337) that consists neither in "running with the pack nor in taking up arms" (ibid., 336). For Jünger, this act of apostasy is the very prototype of a political decision, in the original sense of the term "decision": a cut.[3] It implies abandoning a structured state order that always already allocates to each individual a certain freedom of action and expects loyalty in return. The "retreat into the forest," then, is a move away from the established breakdown into friends and enemies and their regularized conflict: it is the act of determining one's own enemy.

The forest, therefore, is not a preexisting space. Created by the maverick individual, it is a familiar environment that suits his actions: hideout, masked location, known terrain, impenetrable maquis, partisan underground. Jünger's "forest" creates a political topography marked by a split between a public domain and a secret sphere into which renegades may flee—and from which they may launch an attack. Jünger writes, somewhat enigmatically: "It could also be said that the individual sleeps in this wood." But what is this wood he sleeps in? And what kind of sleep? "The wood is secretive,"[4] Jünger writes, it is both hidden and familiar, the element in which the individual may find his way. The wood wherein he "sleeps" is a zone of politics that contains the possibility of dissidence, revolt, sabotage, or civil war, a zone of proto-enmity that has yet to determine the true enemy. The sleep the forest dweller may enjoy in the forest does not only imply a form of innocence and ethical integrity; it also suggests that he is waiting to awake and take action, much like the "song" that is "asleep in everything."[5] It is a state of latent possibilities that have not yet become manifest by crystallizing into a stable form. The forest dweller is a "sleeper."

Jünger's forest is a first, somewhat nebulously phrased attempt to sketch a space of politics that in the course of the twentieth century has assumed fundamental importance. It is a subterranean zone of latency. Jünger's use of nature metaphors like forest and sleep, however, reveals his intention to endow this space and its emblematic figure both with a certain heroic glamour and a degree of naturalness. "Forest" and "sleep" are, after all, innocent and harmless. Jünger's wood is far from being a dangerous thicket of clandestine tactics that demand dirty work and impossible ethical decisions—such as are presented in all brutality in Brecht's *The Measures Taken* (Brecht 1977; see part 5, "Agents of the World Revolution"). Margret Boveri or Rolf Schroers would, unlike Jünger, focus precisely on these dirty and tragic aspects. By contrast, Jünger's theory of apostasy and political irregularity emphasizes the potential to withdraw from given constellations of friendship and enmity without dirtying one's hands. Jünger's forest dweller is the epitome of the politically solitary and autonomous individual—which is precisely the image of himself that Jünger liked to project throughout the Third Reich and the postwar years. Jünger's self-stylization implicit in the concept is more than obvious: a highly popular author with his memoirs of World War I in the Weimar Republic, Jünger had been part of the so-called conservative revolution, an intellectual movement that prepared the rise of the Nazi Party to power. His war memoirs belonged among Hitler's favorite books. After 1945, however, Jünger, like many other Germans, claimed to have been part of the "inner emigration," a tacit attitude of disapproval avoiding any open confrontation with the Nazi Party. His vague and allegorical style made it possible for him to continue to publish throughout the National Socialist years, but it also allowed for a reading of his texts as documents of veiled resistance and disapproval. The forest dweller is Jünger's unabashed self-image, safely enshrouded in misty nature metaphors.

Crisis of Loyalty: Boveri

Jünger's contemporaries and friends, such as Boveri, Schmitt, and Schroers, are more explicit. When Jünger's sleeper awakes he becomes a traitor, partisan, assassin, or saboteur. The "landscape of treason" surveyed by Boveri depicts the renegades, refuseniks, and enemy collabora-

Figure 2. The influential German intellectual Margret Boveri (1900–1975), daughter of German-American parents, graduated with a doctorate in history in 1932. She served as foreign correspondent for the *Frankfurter Zeitung* from 1939 to 1943, then returned to Germany. After 1945 she became one of the most influential conservative authors for the *Frankfurter Allgemeine Zeitung* and *Merkur.* Boveri was a firm opponent of the policy of Western integration and an equally staunch supporter of German reunification. Her circle of friends included such highly diverse personalities as the East German author Uwe Johnson (who edited her autobiography), Ernst Jünger, Gottfried Benn, Theodor Heuss, and Wilhelm Conrad Röntgen. Photograph by Loni Liebermann, 1970.

tors out in the open. Her extensive study turned her into one of the leading postwar German intellectuals and enshrined treason as the signature phenomenon of the twentieth century (figure 2). Her encyclopedia of contemporary treason encompasses figures as diverse as Claus von Stauffenberg and Carl Friedrich Gördeler, T. E. Lawrence and Richard Sorge, Klaus Fuchs and J. Robert Oppenheimer, William Joyce and Ezra Pound, Vidkun Quisling and Henri Pétain, Arthur Koestler and Ernst Reuter, Otto John and Rudolf Rössler.[6] For her, "treason" is an umbrella term that covers collaboration, propaganda, intelligence work, the betrayal of secret scientific information, and apostasy in general. Her detailed compilations deal with those "pathologies of politics" that Carl J. Friedrich later grouped around secrecy and treason and analyzed in terms of their functionality for the historical evolution of liberal societies (Friedrich 1972). Unlike Friedrich, however, Boveri is far from delivering a functionalist account of her object; her goal—supported by psychological and sociological case studies—is to arrive at a diagnosis of the political transformations whose endemic symptom is treason.

Boveri attributes the ubiquity of treason to a crisis of loyalty. The replacement of monarchical by popular sovereignty, Boveri's profoundly conservative argument goes, has weakened the ties that bind people to power. "Originally, treason and loyalty were affairs which depended on a relationship to a certain person"—a protector, the head of the family, a chieftain, or a king; in turn, the promise of loyalty obliged the leader to "protect, help, nurture, guide and instruct" his followers (Boveri 1963, 17).[7] Oaths of allegiance were pledged to the sovereign lord; as late as 1914, the German pledge was to Emperor Wilhelm II, not the German nation. Only after the war was the sovereign replaced by the constitution. The "depersonalization" of sovereignty entailed a secularization of power that dissolved the religious and personal ties between sovereign and subjects. "It was the transition from a feeling of belonging that, regardless of whatever regime happened to be in power, had its roots in the land, its soil, traditions, language, and familiar surroundings, to a revolutionary patriotism that depended on the belief in the *volonté générale*. The latter, however, was more a matter of the head than the heart, and it was prone to identify the nation with a political slogan" (Boveri 1963, 21 and following; translation emended).

This "depersonalization" assumes its most frightening shape in Communism, regarded by Boveri as an internationalist ideology that specializes in disregarding borders and boundaries. For Boveri, the decline of a divinely ordained and yet personal sovereignty is a basic motive of the modern conceptualization of treason. Treason is a stigma of political modernism.

In other words, treason reveals the price for the rationalization and secularization of power—a story of decline, incidentally, that is not only told by conservatives. In his review of *Treason in the Twentieth Century*, the young Jürgen Habermas sharply rebuked Boveri for the conservative romanticism with which she promoted the allure of the Fatherland: "The fictitious and historically untenable notion of 'patriotic' loyalty forces the author to view—and condemn—any transfer of such loyalty as its dissolution" (Habermas 1956, 11). For Boveri, the irruption of rationalism into the political (as embodied in the modern concepts of publicity, transparency, equality before the law, participation, and representation) gives rise to treason as the dark side of a politics ostensibly committed to the public sphere: it is both a symptom of such politics and its affliction. "Social levelling and technological simplification," the "Holy Trinity of capitalism, bourgeoisie and natural science," are fertile ground for the hidden countercurrents that give birth to treason, even though treason may unite such heterogeneous figures as "romantics, reactionaries and non-Marxist socialists" (Boveri 1963, 348–53). Nevertheless, Boveri concedes to the traitor a certain tragic justification. She sees him as a "displaced person," emanating from the large number of emigrants and expatriates in the wake of the Second World War. In a similar fashion, Rebecca West in *The Meaning of Treason* views treason as the tragedy of severed home ties: "They had forsaken their familiar medium; they had trusted themselves to the mercies of those who had no reason to care for them . . . they needed a nation which was also a hearth. It was sad to see them, chilled to the bones of their souls" (West 1947, 306 and following). The coldness Boveri's and West's traitors venture into is the coldness of crisis-ridden modern societies. Treason is the act of crossing a border and defecting to an enemy who, in the case of Communism, negates the very principle of national loyalty. In turn, any form of internationalism or loyalty to something other than a territorial home constitutes a potential act of treason. Cosmopolitan figures who are suspected of having no fatherland, like Mata Hari (see part 4, "Spies, Male and Female"); secret agents such as T. E. Lawrence (see part 3, chapter 3, "The Partisan, the Traitor"); and Jews like Ethel and Julius Rosenberg (see part 7, "State Paranoia") will pay the price.

In her autobiographical conclusion Boveri, who was the daughter of a German-American couple, portrays herself as someone whose own life had been scarred by dislocations, double cultural identities, and conversions (Boveri 1956–60, 4:326 and following).[8] The personal reference reveals the core of her approach: treason can be elucidated only by reconstructing individual cases—an approach Boveri shares with novelists like Graham

Greene or John le Carré. Her "novelistic" approach becomes clearest in her analysis of the case of J. Robert Oppenheimer. In many ways a character from a Graham Greene novel, Oppenheimer is the embodiment of an identity dispersed across incompatible affiliations: Jew and antifascist, leftish American democrat, friend of Haakon Chevalier (who lost his university position due to Oppenheimer's incriminating testimony), member of the scientific community, former lover of a Communist, member of the armed forces, father of the atomic bomb. Boveri writes:

> Almost all of [Oppenheimer's] actions and convictions were by one party or another construed as treason or transgression. Antifascism, support of Spanish-aid committees, and friendship with communists all amount to a betrayal of Americanism . . . The development of the bomb equals genocide. The refusal to name Chevalier: putting national security at risk. The naming of Chevalier: betraying a friend. Lack of support for the hydrogen bomb: another security risk. Later support of the hydrogen bomb: abetting genocide. (Boveri 1956–60, 4:276)

Boveri is hinting at the inevitability of treason in modern society. It is less Oppenheimer's personality than the contradictory social and political inclusions or exclusions, the incompatible affiliations and enmities, that turn individuals into renegades and defectors. The individual must choose something—and thus becomes guilty of excluding something else. Modernity opposes localized or rooted loyalty with the inevitable diffusion of social and political affiliations. One is never in one's place, because this place does not exist.

State Treason: Enzensberger

Precisely this inevitability of betrayal is the point of departure for Hans Magnus Enzensberger's 1964 essay "Toward a Theory of Treason" (Enzensberger 1982). Enzensberger is an attentive student of Boveri's and yet, as a leftist, a stern political opponent of her conservatism. He shares her view of treason as a symptom of political crisis, but he effectively turns it on its head. While Boveri's focus is on the deviance of subjects, Enzensberger's theme is the betrayal of subjects by their sovereign. Like Boveri, Enzensberger emphasizes the nonsecular, magical qualities of the ties that bind subjects and power. Referring to Freud's *Totem and Taboo,* he unfolds the "double meaning" of the "ruler taboo": "The ruler taboo not only protects the ruler from the ruled, but also the ruled from the ruler" (Enzensberger 1982, 82). The magical aura surrounding the ruler ensures that any violation of the latter by his or her subjects constitutes both a sacrilege and a political offense. At the same time, however, it binds the ruler: the taboo keeps him or her from assaulting his or her subjects. For Enzensberger, the erosion of the magical portions of power leads to a dissolution of these reciprocal attachments: "The subjects of treason now are the people, its object the ruler. A reversal of this relationship has become almost legally unthinkable" (ibid., 83). Unilateral loyalty exclusively burdens the citizens with potential treason; the ruler is now by definition incapable of any act of treason because she is under no obligations of loyalty. This development becomes apparent in the first law concerning high treason, the English Treason Act of 1351. Divine right and laws against high treason, Enzensberger objects to Boveri, were not the golden age of contained treason but the first step toward a corruption of power that would soon unleash a flood of accusations of treason. The moment treason and traitor are criminalized, the charge of treason turns into a convenient means of maintaining power. As a result we are faced with an "oilspotlike spreading of the definition of treason" (ibid., 84). Anyone can be declared, prosecuted, and condemned as a traitor. The vicissitudes of twentieth-century history with the rapid succession of short-lived regimes, Enzensberger concludes, make it almost inevitable that at one point each and every one will be marked as a traitor, domestic enemy, or security risk.

The proliferation of the accusation fuels a paranoid fear of treason. Rulers see themselves surrounded and subverted by traitors. "By the logic of paranoia no one is innocent; there are only those who haven't yet been convicted of treason" (Enzensberger 1982, 85). Whoever happens to be "in touch" with an alleged traitor turns into one. It is only a short step from laws against high treason to a state paranoia that constructs and incessantly hounds its enemies. Hidden within Enzensberger's text, written in 1964, is the arguably most dramatic case of state paranoia, the trial against Julius and Ethel Rosenberg, who had been accused of being "nuclear spies" in the United States in 1951 and were executed in 1953. The state paranoia that marked both this trial and the public reaction to it are the implicit core of Enzensberger's legal theory and criticism of the concept of treason. By linking the accusation of treason to the increasing paranoia of state power in the 1950s and 1960s, Enzensberger arrives at a theory of treason diametrically opposed to Boveri's. For Enzensberger, treason is less a symptom of the political irregularity of the individual than of power itself. Power is violating the very rules it is supposed to watch over and defend. The epigraph of the essay, from Franz Kafka's "On the Question of the Law," illustrates Enzensberger's argument:

> Our laws are not widely known. They are the secret of the small group of nobles that rules us . . . It is tradition that the laws exist and are entrusted to the nobility as a secret, but it is no more and cannot be more than an ancient tradition which has become credible through its very age, for the character of these laws also require that their content be kept secret. (Quoted in Enzensberger 1982, 79)

Kafka's secret laws—guarded and wielded by a nobility that is "above the law"—point toward a paradox of sovereign power scrutinized by Giorgio Agamben. Based on Carl Schmitt's thesis that the structure of modern sovereignty reveals itself in the state of exception,[9] Agamben focuses on the constitutive relationship between legal order and exception. The rule of law is guaranteed by an authority that is above the law and that has the power to suspend any and each law whenever it appears threatened. The true execution of sovereign power, Agamben argues, is the act of suspension, the exception from the regularity of the law. In Kafka's small text the unknown—and hence impossible-to-follow—laws coincide with the arbitrariness of sovereign power. The secret laws—and this is the crux of Enzensberger's argument—are not rules but "irregularities," a form of governmental arbitrariness that may use the stigma of treason to get its hands on any subject. Like Agamben, Enzensberger is focusing on an element of totalitarian power within societies that appear to be based on the rule of law. In the laws against treason, legal order and arbitrariness, law and extralegal exception, Enzensberger argues, coincide. With this in mind, the allegedly disloyal citizen, branded a traitor, is the *Homo sacer,* the "bare life" that according to Agamben corresponds to the structure of modern power. "Bare life" is the life that has fallen from the legal order; it involves the marking of an individual by a sovereignty that no longer *includes* it within the legal domain but instead *excludes* it from the space of law and order. "Bare life" may be killed without any legal procedure—and without legal consequences for the killer. Rather than being tried and sentenced before a court, the victim is declared an outlaw (*Vogelfrei*). "Bare life," Agamben writes, "is the life of *Homo sacer* (sacred man), who *may be killed and yet not sacrificed*" (Agamben 1998, 8; emphasis in the original). By virtue of the fact that his life may be taken with impunity, the outlaw enters a zone in which he is neither protected nor punished but rather "abandoned" by the law. This zone is the extralegal domain of those who have come into contact with a secret dimension of the political, either because they voluntarily ventured underground or because they have become the target of clandestine state activities. Agamben's zone of a permanent state of exception is the world of the modern *arcana imperii:* a world in which the suspension of public control coincides with a suspension of law (see part 2, chapter 2, "Logics of Political Secrecy"). Agamben listed a few candidates for the *Homo sacer* as a symptom of modern sovereignty. With Enzensberger in mind we can add the "traitor" and his variants, the renegade or the "domestic enemy."

Theories of the Partisan: Schroers, Schmitt

By concentrating on the relationship between subjects and sovereign, both Boveri and Enzensberger miss out on a dimension of the political that is equally indispensable for understanding treason: the structure of enmity. In two texts of unequal fame, Rolf Schroers's forgotten *The Partisan* (1961b) and Carl Schmitt's notorious *Theory of the Partisan* (2007), enmity figures as the basis for tackling the question of political irregularity. Both texts continue to pursue the question of apostasy that Jünger and Boveri dealt with, but from a different angle. Schroers and Schmitt refer to the apostate as a "partisan." They are less interested in the irregularity of the state and its subjects than in that of enmity. Within the structure of enmity, that is, within the division into friend and enemy—which according to Schmitt is the elementary gesture of politics—the traitor represents a maximum of irregularity by blurring distinguishable front lines.

Schroers's partisan is the heroic, activist variant of Jünger's forest dweller: emerging from the latent existence of the sleeper, the isolated individual turns against a technologized state and its powerful administrative and disciplinary mechanisms. The partisan is the antagonist of the "machinist," the technologically versed pillar of modern power (Schroers 1961a). He embodies pure resistance and autonomy—and his dignity, Schroers adds, ultimately rests in his fighting for a lost cause. Changing sides or clandestine operations are manifestations of an irregular struggle, though highly dubious ones. As an "agent" the partisan becomes himself part of the techno-political structure he rises up against (Schroers 1961b, 117–19). As the most radical variant of the partisan, traitors and agents embody this ambivalence in particular clarity: as lone warriors they represent individual apostasy, yet as technicians and experts they are part of the technologized, "formed" world. In doing so, however, the agent thwarts Schroers's ambition to present the partisan as a figure of heroic resistance against the triumph of technology. In the final analysis even Schroers has to concede that agents and traitors are part of this technologized world they are fighting against.

Spies, agents, traitors, and saboteurs also make their appearance in Schmitt's *Theory of the Partisan,* which is obviously inspired by Schroers, Boveri, and Jünger but takes their argument much further into a general theory of warfare and enmity (see Horn 2004). For Schmitt, the agent represents an extreme variant of the partisan as the epitome of irregular warfare. The partisan deserves recognition as the "autochthonous defender of the homeland" (Schmitt 2007, 30). But Schmitt's essay makes a sharp distinction between, as it were, good and bad partisans; the former are "telluric" defenders of their home turf, whereas the latter are motorized, technologically equipped "globally aggressive revolutionary activists" (ibid., 30). The agent-partisan is an advanced form of technologized warfare that turns humans into mere instruments:

> In the situations of the Cold War, he [the partisan] becomes a technician of the invisible struggle, a saboteur, and a spy . . . Such a motorized partisan loses his telluric character and becomes only the transportable and exchangeable tool of a powerful central agency of world politics, which deploys him in overt or covert ear, and deactivates him as the situation demands. (Ibid., 22)

Once he evolves into an agent, the partisan's dignity—his autonomy as well as his defensive posture—turns into a purely instrumental, highly dangerous functionality.

In the figure of the agent the irregularity of the partisan, including his civilian cover and the preference for ambush operations in familiar terrain, is twisted into a furtive, globally operating secret fighter, who in Schmitt's words "is simply used as cannon fodder, and is deceived about why he undertook the struggle and about the roots of its telluric character and of his partisan irregularity" (Schmitt 2007, 74; translation emended). To use Cold War jargon, he ultimately turns into a pawn, a minor sacrifice in a game of grand-scale politics (see the section titled "Pawn Sacrifice" in part 6, chapter 3, "The Human Factor"). As a clandestine agent of a state-sponsored or revolutionary power, the partisan forfeits the innocence of Jünger's forest dweller, though he acquires the formidable tactical efficiency of the irregular combatant. "The dead ride fast, and if they become motorized, they move even faster" (ibid., 76). The figure of the agent-partisan is linked to a completely new movement in space: a dislocation, a tactical use of space, a becoming-invisible—T. E. Lawrence, aka

"Lawrence of Arabia," will be one of the most brilliant strategists and theorists of these tactics (see part 3, chapter 3, "The Partisan, the Traitor"). The traitor not only switches sides; in the shape of the agent he also destabilizes space and dissolves the principles of territorial sovereignty.

But the question that haunts Schmitt's essay is: who motorizes "the dead"? Who facilitates the dynamics of dislocation that turns the *guerrillero* defending his homeland into a globally operating agent? Schmitt calls this instance the "interested third party" (Schmitt 2007, 75).[10] It is the player that provides the decentered partisans with logistical, ideological, and technical support. This "party" represents the *novum* introduced by Schroers and Schmitt. The interested third party is a sovereign power with a vested, though hidden, interest in the conflict fought by the partisans. It pursues this interest not publicly but rather by means of technical support and official recognition of the partisan cause. From the partisans' point of view the interested third party is an enemy of their enemy and hence their friend, or so it appears. The interested third party does not operate openly in the conflict, preferring to remain, as it were, in the wings of the war theater. It is an enemy that acts undercover and by proxy. In a way, the "interested third party" corresponds to the demon that according to Luke and John took hold of Judas: a hidden power that instigates and supports the act of apostasy and invests it with its true historical significance.

If the partisan already obscures the clear-cut enmity between two warring parties, the traitor, as an undercover agent operating in isolation, adds to the confusion. The distinction between friend and enemy is blurred by the possibility of enemies within one's own ranks. If the motorized partisan disguised as civilian brings about a significant expansion of the combat zone, treason and espionage entail an even more radical dislocation. Traitors, spies, moles, saboteurs, agitators—they are all appearances of the enemy within; they allow the outside "interested third party" to become an inner "*invisible* third party." They dislocate enmity and disperse it, as it were, across the smallest capillaries of society and potentially into all governmental institutions, thereby extending the enemy's reach into the innermost sanctums of power. Given this dispersion, the traitor is no longer, as Boveri would have it, a mere symptom or result but rather an agent of the age of global ideologies that have replaced and undermined regional or patriotic loyalty.

With his emphasis on the interested third party Schmitt effectively destroys the pathos of radical autonomy that from Jünger to Schroers creates the fascination of political apostasy. Schmitt locates the partisan in the realities of a Cold War that no longer allows mavericks to go it alone.

In the Cold War you may change sides, but there is no place "between the fronts." Treason loses its individualist glamour; there is no "third way," no matter how fervently some traitors may have claimed not to belong to any side. Whenever there is an interested third party, the world inevitably is split up into two sides. Even though Schmitt's text, published in Berlin in 1963 in the midst of the Cold War and the aftermath of the Cuban Missile Crisis, is clearly aiming at the partisan as a figure able to break up the deadlock of the Cold War, it ultimately leads back to the dead end of inescapable binary decisions. For Schmitt, there is no innocent and autonomous apostasy, no retreat into the forest.

Theories that present treason as the very signature of modern politics tend to view it as a breakdown of community and friendship. What the anthropological approach from Boveri to Schmitt and Enzensberger misses, however, is the epistemological condition of treason: the secret. The fact that transmitting secrets and operating in secrecy are capable of fundamentally disturbing the political process reveals the degree to which the latter depends on secrets and secrecy. It is necessary, therefore, that we analyze the role of the secret in modern politics as well as the shapes it may assume: the secrets of maintaining power, the *arcana imperii,* or the stratagems and hidden knowledge of the enemy, *secret intelligence.*

2 Logics of Political Secrecy

> Real power begins where secrecy begins.
> —Hannah Arendt, *The Burden of Our Time* (1951)

What makes modern power "betrayable" is the fact that it fundamentally hinges on a vast range of secrets and secrecy. However, unlike premodern regimes that regarded secrecy as a legitimate and necessary instrument of power, modern governments tend to make a secret of their dependence on secrets. Today, secrecy is mostly dealt with in the form of the scandal: if political secrets are exposed or betrayed, the leakage will occur as a fundamental disturbance of political order, often calling into question the legitimacy of political secrecy altogether. However, the simple opposition of transparency and secrecy, as well as the latter's identification with political crime or corruption, falls short of a more complex and substantial understanding of the structure and the workings of political secrecy (see Birchall 2011). Such an understanding must start with a view of the complex "logics" of political secrecy, that is, the historical and epistemological structure of these logics, which are best illustrated by the different Latin terms for "secret": *mysterium, arcanum,* and *secretum.* These logics not only organize different relations between the known and the unknown, between things that can be discussed and those that are not open to debate; they are also helpful in analyzing the transformations of the structure of political secrecy in modernity. Historically one must distinguish between different cultures of secrecy: the medieval "mysteries of the state," the early modern doctrines of *arcana imperii,* and the modern "secret of the state." What becomes clearer from such a genealogical perspective is not only the different logics of secrecy that these models imply but also the profound ambivalences regarding the political status and the usage of secrecy in modern democracies. As a result of modern democracy's ideal of transparency and the moralization of politics, secrecy has become precarious and problematic, something seen as both necessary and noxious, constantly in need of legitimization yet never really legitimate.

Attempts to repress secrecy, however, do not make political secrets disappear. Secret operations are not only an integral part of democratic policy, domestic or foreign; political secrets are also an obsession of the public sphere, an object of permanent suspicion and speculation as well as a source of frequent outrage and scandal. Today, we can see a deadlock between two opposing attitudes: a political pragmatism that accepts or even promotes secrecy as a necessary evil, and an obsessive public curiosity and indignation in regard to it. However, these antagonistic views of political secrecy are two sides of one and the same coin: a specifically modern logic of secrecy that combines an unavowability of the secret with its permanent *mise en discours.* Political secrecy today is a "public secret" (Taussig 1999, 50–51), one that functions much like sexuality in Foucault's description of the "repressive hypothesis": "What is peculiar to modern societies is not that they consigned sex to a shadow existence, but that they dedicated themselves to speaking of it ad infinitum as the secret" (Foucault 1980, 35). That's the political secret today: a thing spoken of ad infinitum.

A brief genealogy of the conceptualizations of political secrecy can illuminate the logic as well as the blind spots of a modern culture of political secrecy.

Skeletons in the Closet of Power

The first coining of the term "secret of the state" (*arcana domus,* literally "the secrets of the emperor's house"), as well as a phenomenology of its mechanisms and uses, can be found in Tacitus's *Annals:*

> The new reign's first crime was the assassination of Agrippa Postumus. He was killed by a staff-officer—who found it a hard task, though he was a persevering murderer and the victim taken by surprise unarmed. Tiberius said nothing about the matter in the senate . . . But when the staff-officer reported in military fashion that he had carried out his orders, Tiberius answered that he had given no orders and that what had been done would have to be accounted for in the senate. This came to the notice of Gaius Sallustius Crispus, who was privy to the secret [*secretum*], for it was he who had

> sent instructions to the colonel, and he was afraid that the responsibility might be shifted to himself—in which case either telling the truth or lying would be equally risky. So he warned Livia [the adoptive mother of Tiberius] that palace secrets [*arcana domus*], the advice of friends [*consilia amicorum*], and services performed by the army [*ministeria militum*] were best undivulged [*vulgare*]; and Tiberius must not weaken the throne by referring everything to the senate. The whole point of autocracy, Crispus observed, is that the accounts will not come right unless the ruler is their only auditor. (Tacitus 1996, 34, translation emended.)

Tacitus's terse account of events relating to the accession of Augustus's successor Tiberius provides a paradigmatic case study of state secrecy: the removal of politically inopportune family members, the subsequent denial of the orders that led to their removal, and finally the advice of a clever and cautious confidant to avoid any public debate. The dynastic secrets (*arcana domus*) Tacitus has in mind are a matter of both family and government; they are as private as they are political. Sallustius's counsel demarcates the space of the ancient *arcana:* it contains crimes such as the murder of the politically intolerable Agrippa, confidential advice by friends (*consilia amicorum*), and discreet services of the military (*ministeria militum*). As a means of securing the stability and legitimacy of the principate of Tiberius, Agrippa's removal is part of the attempt to replace Augustus's personal *auctoritas* with institutional authority, yet this would be called into question if it became known that the order to assassinate Agrippa had been issued by Tiberius rather than the late Augustus. The slain grandson is, quite literally, a skeleton in the closet of power. The strict secrecy recommended by Sallustius fundamentally differs from Tiberius's awkward attempt to publicly shift the blame to someone else. *Vulgare* (to make common) is the opposite of *arcanum;* it implies the obligation to legitimize questionable actions, something Sallustius knows can be achieved neither by lying nor by telling the truth.

The state secret, then, concerns something that precedes the decision between truth and falsehood or justice and injustice: namely, the decision between silence and speaking. It is "something manifest that nonetheless is not open to negotiation" (Haverkamp 2004, 106). The prerogative of power is to withhold certain issues from debate, avoid justifications, and instead take care of business behind closed doors. However, political secrets are not necessarily synonymous with political crimes—they do not even have to be something unknown; it is enough that they are *left unsaid.* Another episode in the *Annals* illustrates this. Gallus, a member of the senate, had suggested that magistrates and praetors be nominated well in advance of their tenure, a motion that was designed to make senate politics more predictable but that would also severely constrain the emperor. "This proposal obviously had profound implications attacking the whole unspoken premises of autocracy [*arcana imperii*]" (Tacitus 1996, 94). In this particular case, the secret identified and targeted by Gallus is imperial power as exercised in short-term appointments. Here, the *arcana imperii* are the functional principle of power and must remain off-limits at all times. They are the unspoken basis for the preservation of power—a basis strictly removed from debate. Indeed, the essence and principle of power consists in preventing such debates (as Tiberius did when he swept Gallus's motion off the table with a clever though thoroughly hypocritical rejoinder).

Starting with Tacitus, then, the notion of the state secret is marked by a profound ambiguity: on the one hand, it intimates a political crime that drives a sharp wedge between the legitimacy and the preservation of power. On the other hand, the state secret appears to be nothing more than a sign of prudence—a neutral, precautionary measure beyond good and evil. What the two meanings have in common is an awareness that the stability and preservation of power requires a withholding of knowledge and a refusal to communicate. Power is that which is neither subject to debate nor forced to justify itself. This does not in itself constitute a crime—it does not necessarily involve any intent to act in a morally or legally dubious way—yet it does contain the possibility of criminal acts. Being withdrawn or exempt from public control and debate, political secrecy opens up a discretionary space for actions that do not have to be accounted for, that will not have to stand the trial of legitimization, that will not have to be justified—since, ideally, they will never be known or discussed.

Mysterium, Arcanum, Secretum

This withdrawal from knowledge, communication, and debate, however, can be enacted in different ways. There is not just one "logic of the secret" (Marin 1998); there are several logics or models of secrecy that are best illustrated by the various Latin words for "secret": *mysterium, arcanum, secretum. Mysterium* emphasizes a dimension of the unknowable, the religious or cultic secret, the inscrutability of God, nature, or the human soul. The mystery in question is fathomless and auratic. As Ernst Kantorowicz pointed out, the medieval *mysteries of state* are very different from the *arcana imperii.* While the latter are thoroughly secular political techniques associated with antique or absolutist dynasties, the *mysteries of state* are a theological concept, tied to the late medieval construction of the sanctity of the sovereign as a supernatural, immortal *corpus mysticum* (Kantorowicz 1965). By contrast, *arcanum* and *secretum* deal with entirely mundane issues. *Arcanum* (from *arca,* meaning "chest," "coffin," or "treasury") is that which is locked away and hidden in a container: it is not available because it has been removed by lid or lock from visibility and use. As the noncommunicable and nondebatable basis of state power, the *arcana* are essentially linked to a technique of silence and concealment which, as Niklas Luhmann points out, is first and foremost a form of political time management. Silence—the limitation or deferral of communication—facilitates a head start for any kind of political (or, for that matter, military) action; it is also a way of gaining time for decisions or of keeping options open. The ruler who keeps his plans under wraps cannot be forestalled and beaten to the punch. Thus secrecy guarantees viable possibilities, not least the possibility of communication itself: "Whoever is silent may still speak. But those who have spoken about something can no longer be silent about it . . . Speaking procures connectivity, silence enables reflection" (Luhmann 1997, 105). The kept secret preserves the status quo. This fundamental asymmetry of speaking and silence is the basis for the conservative power of secrets and secrecy, yet it is a force directed toward the future in that it keeps open future possibilities. The *arcanum* is an essential tool of security, protecting sensitive forms of information from abuse—today most prominently in the form of classification. Its effectiveness arises from the stabilization of the given and the planning of the future; it secures the here and now of the state, its *status*.

Unlike *arcanum,* which emphasizes withdrawal from communication by locking something away under a lid of silence, *secretum* defines secrecy in terms of social inclusion or exclusion. *Secernere,* from which *secretum* is derived, means "to exclude, to segregate, to secrete"; its antonym is *confundere*—"to mix, to confuse, to become indiscernible in a mass or crowd." Paradoxically, the verb *cernere* also refers to clarity: "to survey, part, distinguish, recognize." *Secretum* is marked by an invisible though nonetheless highly effective referential structure: it is pointing to itself as something that has to be sought out, found out. The *secretum* is not, like the *arcanum,* a given yet hidden piece of information, but rather a relation: a relation between the known and the unknown, between those who suspect and those who are "supposed to know." Derrida called this the "secrecy effect" (*effet de secret*) (Derrida 1994, 245). This effect is the awareness (or belief or suspicion) that a secret exists, which, especially in the context of power relations, can have a greater impact than a real secret: "the secret . . . consists in knowing how to make one suppose knowledge and believe in the secret" (ibid., 246). Everything, Derrida claims, depends on the supposition that there is a secret, not on its actual existence or its content.

Secrecy, then, is about the workings of this secrecy effect, for which Edgar Allan Poe's famous short story "The Purloined Letter" may serve as an allegory. A compromising letter to the French queen has been stolen, under the queen's eyes, by the Minister D—, which puts him in a position to blackmail the queen with the threat of revealing the letter to the king. Desperately the queen tries to retrieve the letter, first with the help of the police, later and more efficiently with the help of Poe's mastermind detective, Dupin. The letter is the physical form of a political secret—a secret whose power arises from the mere threat that it may be revealed. But throughout the story the letter remains sealed; its content remains unknown and is never of any importance to the story. What counts is the potential for abuse by Minister D—. The secret thus indicates a certain "aggregate state" of knowledge, a form of looming latency or potentiality that is more powerful than its actual content. The potential for future disclosure is what constitutes the power that its holder has over others. As Poe's story illustrates, the secret and its inherent "power effect" are based on a social constellation made up of three basic positions: first, person A, who knows the secret; second, person B, with whom A shares it; and third, person C, who is kept in the dark about the secret and is thus excluded from the knowledge shared by A and B (see also Marin 1998). The *secretum* is inextricably linked to communication; a secret locked into a single mind that is not at least potentially "shareable" is not a secret (it is rather, one might say, a *mysterium*). In this sense, secrecy structures social or political relations of exclusion and inclusion by separating those who know from those who do not (but who at one point may know, or who doubt or suppose that there is a secret). Poe's story displays this structure as a choreography of positions between knowledge and ignorance, power and powerlessness. The characters in the story move through these positions: the queen and Minister D— (in positions A and B) share a secret (the knowledge of the ominous letter), and D—'s power relies on the fact that the king, occupying position C, is excluded from this knowledge. Later in the story, the tables have been turned: Dupin has stolen the letter from D— and returned it to the queen without D—'s knowledge, so D— now finds himself in the uncomfortable position C, that of the one excluded from knowledge. The secret thus functions as an organizing principle of social relations: states of knowledge, positions of power, bonds of allegiance, or intentions of betrayal.

Lacan's ingenious reading of Poe's "Purloined Letter" highlights the structural inevitability of this constellation and its consequences for the persons subjected to this logic of the secret. Lacan identifies the secret with the signifier, which compellingly organizes the subjects' desires and positions:

> You think you act when I stir you at the mercy of the bonds through which I knot your desires. Thus do they grow in force and multiply in objects, bringing you back to the fragmentation of your shattered childhood. So be it: such will be your feast until the return of the stone guest I shall be for you since you call me forth. (Lacan 2006, 29)

Within the entanglement of desires and intentions the secret is that which returns, either to restore order or to draw everything into its abyss, just like the "stone guest," the murdered *commendatore* in *Don Juan.* The secret structures and haunts the symbolic order as well as the political. It is both defensive and stabilizing, yet it also marks—with increasing insistence—the moment of crime that reveals the illegitimacy and vulnerability of power. On the one hand, the state secret acts as a constituent element of power; on the other hand, it fuels its excess, marking or, more precisely, secreting the state's vulnerable spot, the turn to violence, corruption, and chaos.

The Suppression of the *Arcana* in the Modern Age

Historically, the different logics of secrecy indicated by the terms *mysterium, arcanum,* and *secretum* refer to the political contexts from which they originated. While the *mysteries of state* belong to the transcendent and religious foundation of the medieval state, *arcanum* and *secretum* belong to a modern, secularized form of politics. In the footsteps of Tacitus and Machiavelli, political theorists of the sixteenth and seventeenth centuries developed a rich corpus of rules and guidelines for a rational and efficient political conduct that grants a prominent role to the political secret, following the logic of the *arcanum* as a stabilizing, defensive form of secrecy. In the early modern era the principal political goal is to secure and expand the power of the sovereign. Political doctrines often run under the heading *arcana imperii* (see Stolleis 1980). These *arcana,* however, are less a body of dark secrets than a prudent code of conduct for princes who are neither particularly godless nor amoral. Authors like Botero, Bodin, Ammirato, and Clapmarius treat the *arcana imperii* simply as governmental techniques, or, to quote Botero's classical definition, as "notitia mediorum & rationum, quibus fundatur, firmatur & augentur status" (notes on the means and rules through which the state is founded, strengthened and augmented) (Botero 1997, 87). Since discretion and secrecy are viewed as the most important conditions for sustaining and expanding power, the authors recommend a variety of social techniques designed to hide a person's thoughts and intentions, such as deception and dissimulation, cunning, waiting, silence, and self-control. Here, state secrecy is a form of managing information that restricts politically relevant knowledge to the smallest possible group. It implies, in Helmut Lethen's words, a form of "cool conduct" that privileges discretion, dissimulation, and opacity over communication, authenticity, and morals (Lethen 2002). The basic idea of the *arcana* doctrine is not altogether unreasonable: decisions should be left to small groups, and the most efficient way to pursue one's goals is in secret. The split between personal morality and public good is viewed as a necessary differentiation for the sake of political stability. In light of the confessional wars of the sixteenth and seventeenth centuries it makes sense to keep personal faith and conscience out of politics. Bracketing morality, then, is a means of pacifying society. Only in the twentieth century will this separation of politics and morality be recast as an inherently contradictory and tragic conflict (Meinecke 1957). However, the *arcana* approach to secrecy as a necessary and rational political instrument has not disappeared altogether. Carl Schmitt, in particular, can be seen as a modern heir to the *arcana* tradition.

But the onset of political modernity, the establishment of popular sovereignty and democracy, starts with the "purging" of the *arcana* from politics—and, simultaneously, the establishment of an entirely new culture of secrecy (Koselleck 1988, 53). The bourgeois criticism of absolutist sovereignty involves more than the demand that politics be opened to participation and publicity. According to Koselleck, the birth of modern political man in the eighteenth century takes place within the confines of secret societies, that is, under the protective cover of a bourgeois culture of secrecy that is directly opposed to the clandestine operations of the state, the *arcana imperii.* Questions of conscience and morality that the absolutist state had relegated to the private sphere reappear in enlightened secret lodges such as the Freemasons and Illuminati as benchmarks of political conduct. "It was in the lodges and through them that the bourgeoisie acquired a social form of its own. In imitating both, its mystery won a place beside the ecclesiastical mysteries and the arcane politics of States" (ibid., 72). The lodges' secretiveness provided a protected space in which an enlightened critique of the state could be unfolded, a critique that would eventually come to focus on the state secret. The new space of the political that the citizen's emancipation brings about essentially relies on its claim for transparency, while at the same time applying moral standards from the private sphere to the political world. The public aspires to be the arbiter of public matters, since it is the ultimate instance of sovereignty and legitimacy.

With this new distribution of secrecy and publicity, however, political secrecy does not vanish altogether. Instead, modernity replaces the *arcana imperii* with the logic of *secretum,* establishing a much more complicated relation to secrecy and its political uses. On the one hand, modernity discovers secrecy as an essential basis of society, a common good worth protecting. It sees privacy as a protective space that contains the secrets of individuals, souls, families, groups, and associations. While in Tacitus the *arcana domus,* the secrets of the emperor's family, are clearly both private and matters of the state, modernity sharply separates politics from private issues. Georg Simmel has argued that the secret is constitutive both of modern societies and of the concurrent emergence of individuality (Simmel 2009, chap. 5). His sociology of the secret refers to that particular reserve of nondisclosure that enables the intimacy and private nature of individual communication, and that constitutes social groups by drawing boundaries between the initiated and the excluded. Secrecy, Simmel (1906) argues, is the basis of bourgeois society, a private domain that is no longer burdened with too much knowledge of the other. Although secrecy, in the form of privacy, has now become constitutive of society, secrecy in "public matters" is no longer acceptable. The modern moralization of politics and the secretiveness of the private sphere turn the political into the other of the private; nonetheless, the standards of the latter are applied when judging the former. As a result, political secrecy arouses both profound suspicion and intense curiosity, and this is precisely what makes the logic of *secretum*—rather than that of *arcanum*—the specifically modern logic of the secret: while *arcanum* is the secret "locked away" and silenced, the secret as *secretum* is a form of social relation, that is, more an effect than a muted form of real information. The secrecy effect of the modern state secret consists in its permanent and intense relation to a sphere of publicity. Everybody either doubts or knows that "there is something"; the secret is what has to be sought out, "read between the lines"—as the Latin word *intellegere* suggests. This curiosity revolving around the political secret comes with a considerable degree of moralization: in a political culture that favors publicity and transparency, anything that refuses to be subjected to public scrutiny and debate is a priori unlawful and immoral; as a result, the secret becomes the antonym of law and social contract. "The social contract," Alain Dewerpe summarizes,

> abolishes any possibility of secrecy in the execution of power, any lack of transparency in the intentions of the sovereign, any excess in carrying out government business, and any legal threshold region that would allow for the employment of clandestine means. All power will be dominated by the principle of publicity. Liberal thought . . . censures the space of the secret. (Dewerpe 1994, 78)

Secrecy and the Law

However, the early modern tradition of thought on the *arcana imperii* involves a more complex understanding than the modern rejection of the secret from a sphere of legality and morality. It is important to recognize that the assumption that whatever is not public is a priori reprehensible blurs an (albeit complicated) boundary that has been an integral part of classic theories of state secrecy: the boundary between government's rational rules and its vices. Here the early modern doctrines are highly instructive: following in the footsteps of Tacitus, Arnold Clapmarius, one of the German authors of the *arcana* doctrines, sharply separates the *arcana dominationis*, the "secure and secret privileges of maintaining power," from the *flagitia dominationis*, the misdeeds and infamies of power (Clapmarius 1602). Clapmarius's differentiation aims at purging the *arcana* of the moral ambivalence that marked Tacitus's phenomenology of the political secret: they are clandestine means for achieving laudable goals, while the *flagitia* are the elements of mere corruption. Yet because they remain mere means and do not amount to rules or norms, Clapmarius introduces a terminological differentiation designed to separate *arcana* from laws: "I furthermore distinguish the secrets of ruling from the laws of power" (Clapmarius 2009, lxiii; see Stolleis 1980, 17–19). This hints at the complicated legal status of secrets: *arcana* are not necessarily crimes requiring cover-up; rather, they are measures and decisions outside the purview of the law. They are even outside the law of exception, the *iura dominationis*, as opposed to the *ius commune*. Even though they are not crimes, the secrets of the state cannot be bound by any kind of law.

This is how, without lapsing into a simplistic logic of good ends justifying bad means, the classical theory of the *arcana imperii* draws a careful line between the realm of the law and the realm of secrecy. Secrecy has its own rules and limits, rules of caution, rational foresight, and strategic shrewdness that often preclude violence—but for reasons of efficiency, not ethics. As a modern heir to the *arcana imperii* tradition, Carl Schmitt in his 1921 study on dictatorship outlines a theory of *arcana* adapted to the modern bureaucratic state. Schmitt interprets Clapmarius's theory of *arcana* as a reflection of the operating principles of power beyond legal norms. The *arcana* are rules of efficient governance that enable the law to operate or that are used to reestablish the rule of law in times of turmoil and crisis (Schmitt 1995, 14–16). He emphasizes the extramoral neutrality and functionality of those rules. Always critical of the modern moralization of politics, Schmitt is concerned with removing the ominous and suspicious reputation that secrets have acquired in the modern age. "The concept of arcanum, when it means state secret, is not more or less mystical than the modern concept of the secret 'know how' of a business [*Betriebs- und Geschäftsgeheimnis*]" (ibid., 13). There is no doubt of Schmitt's intention here: to compare state secrets (*Staatsgeheimnisse*) to simple trade or business secrets (*Betriebsgeheimnisse*) is a way of "sanitizing" political secrecy to eliminate its noxious aftertaste. A trade secret, after all, is a purely defensive secret; located on the border between what may not be told and what is not worth talking about, it serves to protect a business against potential competitors. Schmitt's sanitization of political secrecy into pure functionality, into what one could call the political "tricks of the trade," puts the emphasis on secrecy's defensive aspect, on its stabilizing and security-related functions. Secrecy, he argues, is a functional principle at the core of the governmental apparatus, an apparatus that cannot operate if it is constantly subject to debate. Beyond the modern moralization of politics, beyond the legal order and the structures of political representation, the state apparatus and its modern raison d'état are, for Schmitt, a domain of mere "technique":

> Historically, the modern state emerged from a politically neutral technique [*Sachtechnik*]. With it begins the doctrine of the raison d'état as its theoretical reflex, that is: a sociopolitical maxim which is above the dualism of legality and illegality and which is derived only from the necessity to maintain and extend political power. The military and bureaucratically trained officialdom, the "executive," are the core of this state which is essentially executive. From a technical point of view the executive does not care in whose service it operates. (Schmitt 1995, 12)

For Schmitt, this apparatus is politically "neutral," presumed to function regardless of what particular political representation or laws and forms of government happen to be in place. It is mere infrastructure, a functional basis comprising administration, supply, and the circulation of humans, goods, and information—and is also, of course, what provides the security for all of this, what ensures the absence of coups, acts of sabotage, or terrorism (see Friedrich 1957; Horn 2003b). What makes Schmitt crucial for an understanding of the status of secrecy in modern states is precisely his *neutralization,* the idea that secrecy must not be moralized as such but is an essential and functional element of politics. Secrecy for Schmitt is part of this basis, neither part of the law nor subject to it. It is an element of the paradoxical operation of suspending the law to preserve it. In this act of "putting the law into practice" (*Rechtsverwirklichung*), Schmitt sees the essential function of dictatorship as a temporary state of exception (Schmitt 1995, xviii, xx). Its justification thus can only lie, as Schmitt has it, in "ignoring the law but only in order to allow it to become effective [*verwirklichen*]" (ibid., xviii). Following this logic, we might say that the state secret is the exception of the political in the modern age, the moment in which the transparent legal order, the commitment to representation and legality, willingly suspends itself in the name of the functioning of the state apparatus, thus creating space for something beyond the reach of its principles. This sphere, however, is to be conceived not, like the classic "state of exception," as a temporary suspension of the entire legal order but as a permanent possibility inherent in the state itself.

Schmitt's neutralization of the state secret certainly helps to free a theory of political secrecy from the hysteria of an ideal of total transparency and of the fallacies of the secrecy effect. It offers a conceptualization of secrecy that makes the secret acceptable as a functional *souterrain* of politics, as it were—as a stabilizing basis, albeit removed from sight. His paradoxical formula—"ignoring the law but only in order to allow it to become effective"—certainly has its appeal when it comes to the defensive and security-related functions of secrecy, such as data classification, diplomatic discretion, or security measures. Whether we are dealing with know-how related to the state's infrastructure, with the protection of certain technologies, or with the opacity of administrative procedures, the state secret remains defensive in nature. To draw on a recent example: as of 2002, as a protection against potential terrorist attacks, the U.S. government classified as secret all technical information regarding U.S. electric power stations, nuclear power plants, chemical factories, and other sensitive infrastructure. Secrecy here protects what one could call the "material basis" of the state. This material basis normally comes into sight only when it is the target of disruption or sabotage—and preventing such disturbances is precisely what the functional secret is designed to do.

Such a functionalist view of secrecy in the tradition of the *arcana* theory also offers criteria for an assessment and critique of the forms and uses of state secrecy from a nonmoralizing viewpoint. Instead of questioning the very use of secrecy, a functionalist approach to secrecy must ask precisely how its usage helps pursue the proclaimed goal of stabilization and security of the state of law. It must ask, for instance, whether the practice of classification is actually an efficient means of protecting sensitive data or infrastructure—or whether it is, rather, obstructing the accessibility of information important for technology or research. Or, to give a more controversial example: from a functionalist point of view one can legitimately question the effectiveness of secretly financing and supporting guerrilla groups (such as the contras, the mujahideen, or the Arab fighters led by Lawrence of Arabia) in foreign countries by considering long-term consequences. In most cases, the investment either doesn't pay off (contras) or backfires in the long run (from the Arab revolt in 1916 and its geopolitical consequences for the Middle East to the mujahideen, who eventually turned into Al-Qaeda). So, even if one does not want to address the moral issues of this type of intrusion into a foreign country's conflict, from a functional perspective financing guerrillas is dysfunctional. The functionalist view forecloses moral or legal concerns; forms and practices of secrecy must first and foremost stand an efficiency test. Of course, functionalist conclusions might chime with moral and legal ones, but the harmony is no more than coincidental.

Even if it has the advantage of a certain pragmatism, the functionalist approach nevertheless misses a core point of political secrecy: its profound and irrepressible ambivalence. There is the world of aggressive secret operations, coups d'état, assassination plots, interventions into the domestic affairs of other states, secret police actions against potential terrorists, abductions, torture, and, last but not least, intrusive forms of surveillance, interception, and other ways of invading citizens' privacy. Though the secret services of Western democracies are nowadays regulated (at least to a certain extent) by statutory laws such as, for example, the U.S. Intelligence Authorization Act of 1991, contained by internal rules and codes of conduct, and supervised by parliamentary committees, secrecy opens up a universe of unfettered violence. For whatever happens in the impenetrable world of covert operations is, first and foremost, veiled under the shroud of noncommunication, nondocumentation, and nonreporting, and thus essentially withdrawn from the reach of law enforcement as long as nobody reveals it. This is what secrecy is all about: the logic of *arcanum* keeps compromising information locked away not only from public scrutiny but also from government scrutiny. No form of parliamentary control, as it has been established since the 1970s in the United States and Europe, can overcome this essential dilemma: control is possible only to the extent that the controlled institution cooperates, not only by operating by the book but also by documenting and reporting each and every one of its own misdemeanors. From Director of Central Intelligence William J. Casey's famous dictum "The business of Congress is to stay the fuck out of my business!" to George Tenet's stonewalling vis-à-vis the Joint Committee in 2002, this hasn't always been the case (L. Johnson 2007, 176, 182). And control is possible only to the extent that the controlling organ really wants to know: "Congress is informed to the degree that Congress wants to be informed," as former Director of Central Intelligence William E. Colby put it (ibid., 181). Critical research on intelligence control has often complained about the "flaccidity" of parliamentary committees (ibid.). The intelligence world's refusal to debate and justify its activities is oddly paired with the parliamentary control system's inability or unwillingness to ask the right questions.

This fundamental dilemma of control and law enforcement within the sphere of secrecy sheds light on the paradoxical relation between state secrecy and law in modernity. The relationship between the secret and the law tends to correspond to that between the state of exception and the rule of law, that is, between suspending and securing the law in emergency situations. Dewerpe interprets the old axiom *Necessitas legem non habet* as an expulsion of necessities from the legal sphere (Dewerpe 1994, 84). The state secret opens up an "extralegal space" in which state power, no longer under any control, asserts itself in its purest fashion. It is, in fact, a space of war where the rules of civil life are replaced by those of engagement. The secret torture camps of the CIA and the avenging assassinations carried out by Mossad or the Russian FSB (Federal Security Service) are only the most glaring recent examples of legal deregulation enabled by political secrets. Here, secrets of the state are no longer part of a cunning power game but the occasion for the state to transgress its own legal regulations. The modern secrets of the state thus amount to an ongoing state of exception, a permanent (self-)suspension of the rule of law that introduces the possibility of pure, "extralegal" violence.

Radicalizing Carl Schmitt's idea of state power "ignoring the law . . . in order to allow it to become effective," Giorgio Agamben has argued that it is precisely this permanent exception and suspension that enables law and order in the first place (Agamben 1998, 18). From this perspective, the state secret can be seen as a permanent exception that constitutes the rule—that is, the state of lawfulness and publicity. Agamben writes, "The exception does not subtract itself from the rule; rather, the rule, suspending itself, gives rise to the exception and, maintaining itself in relation to the exception, first constitutes itself as a rule. The particular 'force' of the law consists in this capacity of law to maintain itself in relation to an exteriority" (ibid., 18).

The state of law, Agamben contends, constitutes itself by opening up another space that precludes questions of legitimacy. Secrecy is one element, perhaps crucial, of this "exteriority." Agamben highlights the ideological "fiction" that this space maintains a regulated relationship to the rule of law. For him, law and lawlessness mutually enable each other, while remaining, as he insists, substantially incompatible (see Agamben 2005). Less radical than Agamben's, however, Schmitt's formula—"ignoring the law but only in order to allow it to become effective"—may offer a model for this necessary "relation" that must bind every use of extralegal means to the goal of stabilizing and securing the sphere of law. All of the attempts to control and contain the violent and lawless momentum in the employ of secrecy—laws, formal and informal codes of conduct, parliamentary control—must be seen as attempts to maintain this relation, sometimes more successfully and sometimes less. Nevertheless, the uncontainable momentum in secrecy, its profound and irredeemable ambivalence, remains.

Transparency and the Secrecy Effect

This deep legal and functional paradox of the *arcanum* is far from being addressed in today's public sphere, no matter how obsessed it may be with the subject of political secrecy, from the CIA and army scandals in the context of the Iraq War and the "war against terror" (torture, extraordinary renditions, the shooting of civilians, and their respective cover-ups), to the disparaging remarks in confidential diplomatic cables (revealed in the context of WikiLeaks's "Cablegate" in 2010), to the ongoing surveillance of communication, travel patterns, and cash flows in the fight against terrorism. A political culture that stresses transparency and moralizes the political cannot accept the constitutive role of the secret; it will, at best, treat it as a regrettable necessity. This is the secrecy effect today: the employment of clandestine means and practices may be officially admitted, but their details are, as much as possible, hidden deep within the administrative infrastructure and the pervasive reticence of the intelligence agencies. Secrecy remains both unacceptable and unavowable, promoted only by a blunt pragmatism or an alarmism that applies the rules of war to civil society. What neither position sees is the essential paradox of secrecy.

But the secrecy effect adheres to the rule that the suppressed always returns. Instead of being part of the sphere of political rationality, the secret today is relegated to the domain of slipups and indiscretions. It can come to light only in the form of scandal, fiction, or a pervasive sense of being betrayed and manipulated. The rise and popularity of conspiracy theories, especially in the wake of traumatic political events calling for explanations, such as the assassination of John F. Kennedy or the attacks of 9/11, can be understood as a symptom of the secrecy effect (see part 7, "State Paranoia," and part 8, "Invisible Government: JFK"). Conspiracy theories offer answers to the unanswerable questions that permeate a political culture breeding scandals and revealing secrets on an almost daily basis without ever reaching a point of clarity or "ultimate truth." The secrecy effect opens up a space of speculation, conflicting versions, distrust, and paranoia: suddenly there are secrets everywhere; every political decision points to hidden vested interests; every ordinary or extraordinary event is controlled by clandestine networks. Paradoxically, this conspiratorial view, or, in Richard Hofstadter's words, this "paranoid style" (Hofstadter 1965) in politics, not only represents the outcome of a repression and rejection of secrecy but also reveals, as its reverse side, a naive call for total transparency.

Nobody in recent times has expressed this interdependence between a paranoid political worldview and the emphatic claim for total transparency more succinctly than Julian Assange, the head of and driving force behind the Internet platform WikiLeaks, which, among other materials, leaked military footage from an American airstrike in Iraq ("Collateral Murder") and 92,000 classified U.S. diplomatic cables in 2010. Assange's professed ideal is one of total transparency, the absence of any *arcana imperii,* including the embarrassing chitchat of diplomats. From this perspective, the state's secrets can never be anything but its crimes; having secrets is already proof of criminal and immoral political activities. In a (mildly confused) online article titled "Conspiracy as Governance," published in 2006, he equates any kind of government with conspiracy marked by "collaborative secrecy" (Assange 2006, 2). His suggestion for undermining and destroying these conspiratorial structures is to disrupt the secret networks of "authoritarian governments" by destroying or disturbing their modes of communication. Which is exactly what leaking does: it disrupts communication channels by intercepting secret information and leaking it to a global audience. Leaking is a way of disrupting what is believed to be a ubiquitous and immense body of (criminal) secrecy present in virtually all governments today. This attitude reduces the intrinsic ambivalence of secrecy to one lurid picture of crime, corruption, and repression. Such a view of the *arcana imperii* falls prey to the modern secrecy effect and its dialectical intertwining of secrecy and the public sphere: on the one hand, it is marked by an almost paranoid belief in the ubiquity of secret political machinations and crimes; on the other, it believes that the only remedy is a political culture of total transparency. The latter, however, is a result of the former; this idea of transparency is, as Jodi Dean has argued, nothing but the reverse side of secrecy: "Secrecy generates the very sense of a public it presupposes. The secret designates that which is desired to be known, that which hasn't yet been disclosed. In so doing, it presupposes a subject that desires, discovers, and knows, a subject from whom nothing should be withheld" (Dean 2002, 10).

The logic of the secret that organizes the modern *secretum* tends to draw everything into the vortex of its secrecy effect—the secret as much as the public, political crimes as much as the rules of prudent discretion, an all-embracing suspicion as much as a gullible belief in the power of revelation. What we should wish for is a better understanding not only of the functionality of secrecy but also of the highly precarious tension between the *arcanum* and the state of law. In other words, we should replace the hysteria that accompanies the logic of *secretum* by the functional perspective that the *arcana imperii* tradition has to offer, without falling into a pragmatism whereby the ends justify whatever means. All in all, it would be beneficial (and more functional) to adopt a more candid policy of (and attitude toward) secrecy, openly avowing that certain things are not open to debate and public insight, but also acknowledging secrecy's irredeemable ambivalence and the fundamental dilemma inherent in it.

Secrecy and Fiction

Today fiction may be the only way to speak, as it were, "openly" about the precise structure and nature of political secrecy without falling into the trap of the secrecy effect. The mass media in particular appear to be dedicated to revealing political secrets, yet by constantly trying to destroy them, they *create* secrets. In the words of Alain Dewerpe, it is a "secret de Polichinelle" (Dewerpe 1994, 89), a secret that everyone knows and is interested in and claims to have been privy to. The political secret is as popular as it is precarious: intelligence activities are incessantly discussed and researched; they fuel political phantasms that detect all kinds of insane adventures, crimes, and disasters lurking beneath the tedium of parliamentary debates. Not coincidentally, the highly secretive decades from the 1950s to the 1980s, when intelligence agencies had no addresses (let alone home pages) and the U.S. cryptology agency NSA was dubbed "No Such Agency," were the golden age of political thrillers and spy movies as well as of conspiracy theories and great scandals. The modern state secret is not, unlike the ancient *arcana imperii,* silenced and tucked away; it is a constant source of speculation, dramatization, and fictionalization. So-called investigative journalism, the no less investigative spy thrillers and movies, autobiographical accounts penned by traitors and former agents, and the historiographic reconstructions of secret service affairs and conspiracies are all part of a discourse enthralled by the political secret, a discourse that itself is nothing but a secrecy effect. Every gesture of revelation, speculation, variation, or reconstruction is under the spell of this effect: the act of revelation may not be more than the act of covering up something else, something more important; the "tell-all" memoir may be nothing but the biased narrative of the author's own private truth; the neutral historical reconstruction may be nothing but an abyss of uninteresting details and dead facts. Within a culture of the secrecy effect, the difference between "reality" and "fiction" is hard to maintain. Instead, we deal with fictions that produce an *effet de réalité*—and we can analyze the workings of this reality effect. The much-lauded "realism" of spy thrillers, frequently identified as the hallmark of the genre, has nothing to do with any closeness to a "reality" under the shroud of secrecy; rather, it arises from a narrative strategy in the course of which the *effet de secret* turns into an *effet de réalité:* it is the narrative unfolding of the complex distribution of light and shadow, the knowable and the unknowable within a given political situation. The reality effect of political fiction lies in the way it renders transparent the workings of the secrecy effect, being a relation between those who are "supposed to know" and those excluded from knowledge. Fiction casts a light on the mechanisms of the secrecy effect, whether as a phantasmal entanglement between enemies (see part 6, chapter 3, "The Human Factor"), a colonial dream of local knowledge (see part 3, "The Great Game"), a code of conduct for clandestine work (see part 5, "Agents of the World Revolution"), or the irruption of the political into intimate relationships (see part 4, "Spies, Male and Female"). If characters like James Bond do not seem realistic, it is not because "in reality" there are no handguns disguised as fountain pens but because Fleming's novels have no political stake and harbor no secrets.

If modernity is engaged in suppressing the state secret, then fictions dealing with the latter are, no doubt, a symptom of this suppression. The disclaimer at the beginning of many films and novels informing the audience that the events depicted are fictitious is nothing more than a transparent ploy designed to create a reality effect. Jorge Semprún prefaces his novel about an agent who calls himself Ramón Mercader, which happened to be the name of Leon Trotsky's assassin, with this disclaimer: "The events described here are entirely fictitious, any connection with reality would not be merely accidental but scandalous" (Semprún 1973, iv). The disclaimer alludes to and then immediately cancels any historical reference. This straightforward erasure, however, opens up a space in which everything may be said, in which secrets are divulged, tactics explored, conspiracies revealed. In the sense of Borges's *ficción,* fictions amount to variations and versions; they present themselves as *one possible version* of an event that can never be narrated "as such." It is an integral part of *fiction* to point toward this basic deferral—the double gesture that both reveals and conceals—inherent in all treatments of the secret. This is why fiction is the reflexive space—and true medium—of modern secrecy.

Nevertheless, fiction may elaborate and condemn the trade secrets of power, but it will not seriously question their form and existence. On the contrary, it might often be complicit with the logics of political secrecy. Literature may convey instructions for clandestine work, as in the case of Brecht's intricate poem "Cover Your Tracks!" (see part 5, "Agents of the World Revolution") or Kipling's guide to creating an efficient colonial secret service (see part 3, chapter 2, "Local Knowledge"). In turn, novels such as Childers's *The Riddle of the Sands* may be nothing but a fervent call to establish a naval intelligence service (see part 3, chapter 1, "Strategic Space"). Fictions can be useful instruments in understanding the logics of political secrecy, but they themselves can also be tools for deception and subterfuge. They can spread versions of a given event that are designed to distract from certain causes and connections; think, for instance, of the autobiographical accounts by ex-agents and traitors (an exemplary case is Kim Philby's memoirs; see the section on *My Silent War* in part 6, chapter 3, "The Human Factor"). As Louis Marin points out, both the rhetoric of disclosure and the confession of a secret may serve to obscure rather than clarify a given case. A spectacular revelation may be part of a concealment and thus part of the secret itself, or, in the intelligence jargon, it may be "chicken feed"—useless or misleading information "fed" to the enemy or the public sphere. The reflective moment of fiction consists in the fact that *we are given a story in need of deciphering,* that is, we are always dealing with *one* version of events, a version possibly covering up a different, more plausible, more compromising version. Fiction highlights and renders intelligible and communicable the essential ambiguity of the political as it appears in the structure of the modern state secret: its dependence on secrecy and suppression as well as its coupling of legality and violence, transparency and deception.

3 Secret Intelligence

> Force, and Fraud, are in warre the two Cardinal vertues.
> —Thomas Hobbes, *Leviathan* (1651)

The institution that embodies both the ominousness and the efficiency of the secret in the modern age is the intelligence agency. Operating in a twilight sphere removed from public debate and control, it is the preferred focal point of the many fictions that depict the modern secrets of power. Intelligence agencies, however, are not only instruments for secret political interventions: they are also first and foremost *epistemic institutions,* administrations involved in generating and processing a specific type of knowledge known as "secret intelligence." What kind of knowledge may become its object? How is it structured? What rules underlie its production, circulation, and impact? Obviously, intelligence is a form of knowledge that refers to some potential or actual conflict; it is inevitably linked to some visible or invisible threat. The secrets handled by intelligence agencies are, as it were, the aggressive, martial side of the *arcana imperii.* We are no longer dealing with the protocols of discretion and prudent silence; instead we are dealing with the military arts of secretly transmitting information and reconnoitering the enemy in an acute situation of armed conflict. Intelligence is thus a knowledge suffused by the danger and cunning of its origin: war. Despite all the administrative rationalization and technological objectification it has been subjected to, intelligence ultimately remains suspect, prone to violence, and risky both to those who produce it and to those who strive to make it an object of institutionalized knowledge. The epistemology of secret intelligence is the epistemology of enmity.

Nonetheless, definitions of "intelligence" tend to assume a surprisingly academic veneer that centers on the tripartite epistemic operations of capturing, collecting, and evaluation. "Intelligence is a kind of knowledge; the type of organization which produces the knowledge; the activity pursued by the intelligence organization," writes the founding father of postwar intelligence, Sherman Kent (Kent 1965, xxiii). Referring to Karl Popper, Paul Feyerabend, and Imre Lakatos, theoreticians have addressed the specific problems of gathering and processing intelligence knowledge in terms of new theories of science (Ben-Israel 1989). The questions they raise seem to stem directly from a philosophy seminar: Is there something akin to a "paradigm change" in the world of intelligence gathering? Do practitioners progress from individual data to theories and prognoses, or do theoretical presuppositions determine the collection and evaluation of data? Given this unabashedly scientific approach, intelligence has for a long time been presented as a subspecies of the empirical social sciences, a prototype of "applied" science, equipped with clearly defined questions, quantifiable data, and falsifiable theories. Yet there is a small but crucial difference: the object of the social sciences is society, whereas that of intelligence is "the enemy." The scientific terms in the self-descriptions of modern intelligence agencies serve to create the impression that this enemy is no less predictable and rule-bound than nature in the natural sciences (ibid., 693). The basic assumption was that the "enemy" can be reproduced as an accumulation of data (troop strength, gross national product, deployment plans, images, and transcripts of intercepted communications), which in combination with a reliable evaluation of political circumstances allows for the description of actionable scenarios. Ideally, computer simulations of global conflicts were supposed to result in prognoses able to inform and assist political decision makers. Game theory in particular, which during the Cold War emerged as the preferred method for modeling future wars and conflicts, presented politics as nothing less than mathematics with other means (see part 6, chapter 2, "War Games").

Yet this quasi-scientific approach to intelligence arose at a fairly late stage in the history of a knowledge that above all is characterized by its affinity to power and conflict. The basic premise of intelligence activities is not that an enemy is quantifiable, observable, or predictable, but simply that he is *the enemy* (see Horn 2003a). As Michael Herman notes, "Intelligence is about 'them,' not 'us'" (Herman 1996, 34). Whoever becomes an object of intelligence is by definition an enemy: conspirators, revolutionaries, the notorious "Reds under the beds" of the Cold War, traitors, moles, agitators, or terrorists that hide in the undergrowth of our own society. The targets may also comprise "enemy territory," our adversaries' troops, plans, and administrative structures and institutions, their internal conflicts, and above all *their* intelligence agencies. Whatever stumbles into the crosshairs of intelligence is dangerous and has to be identified, controlled, and, if need be, destroyed—even citizens of one's own country. If intelligence agencies tend to violate citizens' rights, it is because intelligence introduces a logic of war and enmity into the civilian sphere. Through the lens of this type of knowledge, citizens become—at least hypothetically—enemies. The secret of war follows a logic of suspicion and constitutive distrust while availing itself of all the means of deception and camouflage. Thus intelligence moves the secret from inside government to outside, either into the realm of interstate wars and conflicts or toward those who, though still inside society, are perceived to be on its outside: the domestic enemy, the traitor, the terrorist.

War and Deception: Sun Tzu

It therefore comes as no surprise that the first theory of intelligence is part of a treatise on war. Sun Tzu's *Art of War* (*Sūnzǐ Bīngfǎ*) is not only one of the oldest and most brilliant handbooks on tactics but also an ingeniously elaborated doctrine of military deception and intelligence. The treatise presumably originated during the warring states period, between 400 and 320 B.C.E., and was translated into French in 1772 by the Jesuit priest Joseph Amiot. Even though historians have speculated that it was the secret of Napoleon's military success, it did not truly gain prominence in Europe until the twentieth century. Without a doubt it served as an inspiration for the partisan tactics and revolutionary war techniques of Mao Zedong.[11] These days military handbooks apply *The Art of War* to the history of European warfare and compare it to the seminal writings of Carl von Clausewitz and Antoine-Henri Jomini (for example, McNeilly 2001). And of course there is hardly a CIA publication that does not feature a Sun Tzu quotation.[12] Paul Virilio, whose writings on psychological warfare, space, and speed are greatly indebted to Sun Tzu, uses a saying from the *Bīngfǎ* as a heading for one of his programmatic essays (Virilio 1989, 5–10). Nonetheless, the truly pathbreaking aspect of Sun Tzu's thought is not the psychology involved in deceiving the enemy, which has now become a staple in popular guides for managers and brokers; it is his theory of a kind of warfare that makes the most economical use of humans, weapons, and material.

The short treatise, which Sima Qian compiled in the shape of short, thematically arranged axioms (with historical examples added by subsequent commentators), offers a basic theory of warfare whose ideal goal is the submission of the enemy without the use of arms. It is a theory of *pure war,* a war that consumes as little human material, weaponry, and money as possible.[13] Sun Tzu's theory of war is in fact an economy of war, one whose most important resource is secrecy and cunning. It aims for the greatest possible strategic effect with the smallest possible use of means: "To subdue the enemy without fighting is the acme of skill" (Sun Tzu 1963, 77). Sun Tzu is advocating a virtually immaterial war, devoid of battles—a war of mind and intelligence. Victory is based on rational planning and tactical superiority alone rather than on greater material and technological force; it hinges on the commander's decisiveness and acumen rather than his chivalry. The immaterialization of war into a war of intelligence(s), however, is tantamount to the suspension of any sense of fairness and respect for the enemy. It is an unleashed war no longer contained by rules, a thoroughly rationalized test of strength whose guiding principle is the rigorous economy of means.[14] Sun Tzu's concept of war is radically opposed to an occidental, modern concept of war: following Clausewitz, modern strategy conceives of war not only as a different form of foreign policy and thus as a continuation of the goals of the state; it is also above all "a duel on a larger scale," an "act of force to compel our enemy to do our will" (Clausewitz 1976, 75). However, once we think of war as a struggle between two states undertaken for political gain, its goal is the defeat of the state rather than that of the hostile army. This Clausewitzian model emerges fully in total war, which aims for the complete destruction of an enemy state. The notion of a frontal competition of strength based on Western traditions of the duel implies symmetrical enemies, the struggle ultimately being a Hegelian "struggle for recognition." This equality of combatants is the basis for a moralization of the struggle and its means—that is, it implies the ostracism of ruses and other perfidious or cruel means. The employment of ruses and other means of deception belongs to the art of asymmetrical war. Indeed, the efficacy of military secrecy lies precisely in sabotaging symmetrical conditions: where two armies are opposing each other in the open, there is no need for further knowledge of the enemy; the result will boil down to greater numbers, superior technology, better tactics. A full reconnaissance of the enemy in combination with subtle deceptions, however, may enable the weaker party to win. Military secrets and deceptions, therefore, belong to the domain of asymmetrical warfare, a type of combat that tends to include "amoral" means.

Sun Tzu's basic axiom is "All warfare is based on deception" (Sun Tzu 1963, 66). Deception is to be accomplished by way of ruses and traps, ambush and confusion. He advises, for example, that mysterious objects be smuggled into the enemy's camp so that opponents will lose time examining them, and that one should conceal one's own strengths and weaknesses. "Therefore, when possible, feign incapacity: when active, inactivity. When near, make it appear that you are far away; when far away, that you are near. Offer the enemy a bait to lure him; feign disorder, and strike him" (ibid.). He also gives advice in what today would be called psychological warfare, for instance, to leave escape routes for surrounded troops to enable them to break off an engagement and not fight until the bitter end. Sun Tzu's techniques are the opposite of the Western understanding of war as an open trial of strength. The secret war is not fought for recognition; it is, quite to the contrary, a victory of misrecognition and misperception. Sun Tzu's military means—ambushes, ruses, surprise attacks, secrecy, camouflage, diversions, and disinformation—are as pragmatic as they are perfidious: "As unfathomable as the clouds, move like a thunderbolt" (ibid., 106). Distracting the enemy and keeping one's own moves unpredictable are one side of a double strategy composed of deception and intelligence: "Know the enemy and know yourself" (ibid., 84). Sun Tzu stresses the importance of reading traces and interpreting hints: the commander and his spies must learn to deduce the fatigue of enemy soldiers from their curses, the speed of approaching troops from the shape and height of the rising dust clouds, the enemy soldiers' nervousness from the clamor they make at night (ibid., 116–23).

This combination of actively deceiving the enemy while simultaneously spying on him and gaining knowledge of his plans constitutes Sun Tzu's decisive insight: "If I am able to determine the enemy's dispositions while at the same time I conceal my own, then I can concentrate and he must divide" (Sun Tzu 1963, 98). One's own knowledge of the enemy must be complemented by the enemy's ignorance. Intelligence, in other words, is always already counterintelligence, that is, the deflection and systematic confusion of enemy intelligence. The essence of intelligence is precisely this mixture of truth and lie, recognition and deception, information and disinformation. It cannot be reduced to understanding and preventing enemy plans; it is always also a matter of deception, disinformation, distraction, agitation, and deterrence.[15]

Such fundamental duplicity is in dire need of specialized operators, which is why Sun Tzu's astonishing text develops an essential theory of espionage and its applications. Spies are the instruments for obtaining the commander's most precious possession: foreknowledge of the future. With casual dryness, Sun Tzu contrasts the employment of spies to the invocation of gods and spirits: "What is called 'foreknowledge' cannot be elicited from spirits, nor from gods, nor by analogy with past events, nor from calculations. It must be obtained from men who know the enemy situation" (Sun Tzu 1963, 145). Spies know more about the future. Their multifaceted activities and functions prompt Sun Tzu to develop an intricate typology of secret agents centered on the double doctrine of intelligence gathering *and* deception; hence spies are introduced not only as scouts but also as active disseminators of disinformation. Sun Tzu distinguishes (1) native agents (traitors from within the enemy's country); (2) inside agents (enemy officials who have been turned against their country); (3) double agents (caught and employed enemy spies who can provide information); (4) doomed agents (expendable deliverers of fabricated information designed to confuse the enemy); and (5) living agents (those who infiltrate enemy towns and camps and return with information). Spies, then, do not necessarily have to be your own people; they do not have to survive; they do not even have to be upright and dependable. Loyalty is irrelevant; what counts is the specific function the spy has to fulfill.

Despite their questionable allegiance spies are to be a commander's closest confidants and highly valued advisers, worthy of the most generous rewards (Sun Tzu 1963, 147). Spies are responsible for a subtle politics of information that will supply the basis for all tactical decisions: "Upon them the army relies to make its move" (ibid., 149). While the moralizing tendencies of European warfare viewed espionage and treason as necessary evils and denounced the spy as unheroic and infamous—as someone, Frederick II declared, who was "needed but not esteemed"—Sun Tzu appreciates the instrumental role of spies when it comes to securing unbloody victories:

> One who confronts his enemy for many years in order to struggle for victory in a decisive battle yet who, because he begrudges rank, honors and a few hundred pieces of gold, remains ignorant of the enemy's situation, is completely devoid of humanity. Such a man is no general; no support to his sovereign; no master of victory. (Ibid., 144)

Spies are the most important instruments for an economy of war that strives to minimize the loss of humans and material. The secret war, the war of cunning and ruses, of deceptions and dissimulations, is a war of minor means, a war of daggers instead of swords.

Next to the duplicity of information and disinformation located at the core of the knowledge of the enemy Sun Tzu highlights another aspect of the war secret, which Borges—possibly alluding to the great Chinese sage—presented in his story "The Garden of Forking Paths": the military secret is subject to a dynamics of acceleration. It is about striking *before* the enemy knows it. Troops must attack the enemy with the speed of a striking hawk that "breaks the body of its prey" (Sun Tzu 1963, 92). "Speed is the essence of war" (ibid., 134), Sun Tzu observes. The military secret, the information on which the outcome of a battle depends, has an extremely limited half-life; it is a type of knowledge measured not by the simple, homogeneous passage of time but by its acceleration. It is a matter of knowing something *faster* than the enemy, of knowing it up to a certain point in time—after which it will be useless. The military secret is not structured by the difference between *knowing/not knowing* but by *knowing something sooner/later.* It is not concerned with stabilizing matters; its goal is to lie in wait for an opportune moment to change things. It is threatened less by disclosure than by obsolescence, something that is not lost on the hero in Borges's "Garden of Forking Paths," who is running against time. The military secret is always part of a race, a race between spies and, as Virilio notes, communication technologies: "If the secrets of war are always written in the air, only high-speed transmission allows their importance to be usefully deciphered" (Virilio 1989, 75).

Origins: Police and Military

Intelligence shaped by the cunning of war is a structural part of the "war machine," which Gilles Deleuze and Félix Guattari have opposed to the hierarchical stratification of the "state apparatus" (Deleuze and Guattari 1987, 351–423). War, the authors insist, is the principle of acceleration, secrecy, violence, and cunning, while the state sees itself as fixity, location, representation, and law. Hence the war machine is external to the state, though it may be incorporated by the latter in the shape of military and police forces and, we may add, intelligence agencies. The war machine, however, embodies "furor"; it brings "celerity against gravity, secrecy against the public, a power [*puissance*] against sovereignty, a machine against the apparatus" (ibid., 352). With its metamorphoses and deceptions, traversals, and accelerations, its unlimited mobilization of means and aggressive force, it embodies the martial dynamic. State apparatus and war machine follow different rules. Secrecy and treason, disinformation and breaches of contract, propaganda, and conspiracy are the elements of a war machine that cannot be made to smoothly serve the interests of the sovereign state without risking its subversion and malfunction. As noted, this is precisely why the secrets of the state are an unsolvable paradox at the core of the state. The "exteriority" of the war machine to the state apparatus turns intelligence agencies into highly hazardous state institutions.

Nonetheless, the modern age has sought to integrate the dynamics of the war machine into the hierarchical state apparatus in the shape of police and military. Together with the famous C^3 triptych—communication, command, and control—obtaining strategically advantageous information on the enemy is "the fourth dimension of war" (Howard 1976, 127). But the military is only one of the two origins of intelligence; the other is the police. This double origin is still visible in the separation between domestic and foreign intelligence. However, for a long time the tasks and functions of those organizations hailed as the precursors of modern intelligence agencies remained unclear; they ranged from protecting the sovereign and snooping at foreign courts to masterminding secret communications and keeping tabs on the postal system. In its early incarnation intelligence arises from the private initiative of courtiers, who by discreetly dispatching agents and secret diplomats sought to satisfy royal curiosity. Think, for instance, of Sir Francis Walsingham, who largely by drawing on his own funds created a deciphering office at the court of Elizabeth I, or Cardinal Richelieu, who benefited from the services of the Capuchin friar Père Joseph (François Leclerc du Tremblay), one of the most skilled and versatile secret diplomats of the day. Among the more infamous precursors of modern domestic intelligence services are the "Black chambers" intercepting and deciphering mail communication, and various nineteenth-century secret police organizations such as Joseph Fouché's *commissaires spéciaux* or the Czarist *Okhrana,* whose fear of agitators and anarchists prompted them to place informers and agents provocateurs on literally every street corner. Nonetheless, the major and highly professionalized intelligence agencies of today only came about during and after the First World War. Only then did European states, especially Germany, France, and Britain, start to merge isolated spying units that hitherto were part of the army or the navy into professional divisions, whose sphere of activities rapidly expanded from reconnoitering theaters of war and enemy installations to capturing all possible information on the enemy: from the mood on the home front, to supply and provisions, to enemy battle plans, the exact location of units, or the interception and deciphering of enemy communications.

But even though the fear of omnipresent enemy spies decisively shapes the phantasms of the First World War, these pristine intelligence agencies had a fairly limited impact on the course of the war. Their professional extension and restructuring took place between the wars. Though founded in 1909, MI5 and MI6 did not come into their own until the 1920s, when they started posting agents in all British embassies, began to support counterrevolutionary anti-Bolshevik actions, and created within MI6 a department that specialized in counterespionage. In Germany, military intelligence services were dissolved together with the army after the First World War; subsequently a new, specialized Reichswehr unit under Friedrich Gempp was established, but it remained organized along military lines and devoted itself to weapons or regions. While—in one of the more notorious cases of German personnel continuity between National Socialism and postwar Western Germany—Reinhard Gehlen, head of Fremde Heere Ost (Foreign Armies East, the German intelligence evaluation section for the Eastern front), turned into the founder and long-serving director of the foreign secret service Bundesnachrichtendienst (Federal Intelligence Service), its domestic counterpart, the Bundesamt für Verfassungsschutz (Federal Office for the Protection of the Constitution), is a postwar creation. In France, the foreign intelligence service DGSE (Direction Générale de la Sécurité Extérieure) emerged from the Deuxième Bureau, originally a section of the general staff responsible for topographic reconnaissance that increasingly took over intelligence activities.

The United States is, relatively speaking, a latecomer to the game. The OSS (Office of Strategic Services), headed by William J. Donovan, was not officially established until 1942. From the very beginning, however, it devoted itself to a task that its successor organization, the CIA, still pursues today: collecting not only military but also more general information related to questions of security and foreign policy. Following the war, historian Sherman Kent would write the first theory of this "holistic" intelligence approach (see the section titled "Intelligence" in part 6, "Cold War"). But despite all the long-term continuities that conventional histories of intelligence like to construct, one thing is striking: professional intelligence agencies that amass, process, and apply a totality of politically and strategically relevant knowledge are not only inventions of the twentieth century—they are also the brainchild of modern democracies.

The qualitative jump that separates the work of modern intelligence agencies from their precursors is first and foremost an epistemological rupture. Modern intelligence exhibits a will to *total* knowledge: "It is an apparatus that must be coextensive with the entire social body and not only by the extreme limits that it embraces, but by the minuteness of the details it is concerned with. Police power must bear 'over everything': it is . . . the dust of events, actions, behaviors, opinions—everything 'that happens'" (Foucault 1977, 213).

The desire for a *totality* of knowledge that characterizes modern intelligence agencies transforms the knowledge of a *factual* enemy, which had been the focus of Sun Tzu's deliberations, into a science of *potential* enemies (see Horn 2003a). Anyone can turn into an enemy the moment they arouse the interest of the secret agencies. Knowledge of the enemy takes on an imaginary dimension: "Who could potentially be an enemy?" "What could the enemy possibly plan?" This suggests that "the enemy" is nothing but an artifact, a projection extrapolated out of the bits and pieces of gathered knowledge. In pursuit of military and strategic insights, knowledge of the enemy expands from preparing a battle to preparing or preventing a war; it focuses less on enemies' specific circumstances than on their overall *capabilities*. Military effectiveness, economic stability, international alliances, and geopolitical interests are now all subject to intense scrutiny. As a result, the focus of intelligence work is both infinitely large and infinitely small: the political clout of fringe groups, the structure of private networks, the behavior of the press and, frequently, the secret vices and ambitions of foreign governmental officials all move into the crosshairs of intelligence work.

"Domestic intelligence," in turn, targets all the possible sources and signs of inner subversion; it scrutinizes the entire population in search of the hidden secret "enemies of society." Intelligence guarantees what has come to be known as "national security"—a security that has to be strengthened against forces from within and without and that derives its legitimacy from a rhetoric of prevention and defense. And it is the latter rhetoric that seeks to draw a dividing line between "inside" and "outside," citizens and external enemies. That is why, in modern democracies, we always have (at least) *two* intelligence agencies, foreign and domestic, that see it as their task to separate politically deviant citizens from foreign infiltrators.

The Frenzy of Analysis

Intelligence agencies do not only ferret out secrets, they also produce secret knowledge themselves. The exclusivity of the latter, however, constitutes an epistemological burden: while scientific research can publish results that are corrected or confirmed in subsequent discussions, intelligence remains "blind" to correction. Its data, hypotheses, and theories arise, circulate, and disappear in secluded intelligence networks marked their own unique concerns, evaluation protocols, and internal power struggles (see Horn 2011). It is no surprise, therefore, that especially during the Cold War intelligence had a tendency of "mirror-imaging," as a result of which the enemy turned into an imaginary construct that was nothing more than a mirror image of one's own shape, interests, and plans. "The enemy is the figure of our own question" (Schmitt 2007, 85; translation emended), Carl Schmitt famously decreed, pinpointing the ongoing epistemological travails of identifying and giving a shape to the ever-elusive enemy targeted by intelligence (see part 9, chapter 2, "The Future of Enmity"). John le Carré's Cold War spy novels in particular set out to explore the phantasmal "cold" space of the enemy from which nobody returns (see part 6, chapter 3, "The Human Factor"). Not coincidentally, one of his novels is called *The Looking-Glass War:* behind the epistemological mirror of the enemy's shape lies an unfathomable world whose secrets, in case of doubt, happen to be precisely what one is looking for. The very concept of secrecy implies that those in possession of intelligence are fundamentally alone, locked up in the mirror-cabinet of their findings (or conjectures); and the highly selective circulation of information makes it hard to question these findings (see the section titled "Classified Knowledge: Nuclear Secrets" in part 7, "State Paranoia"). Unlike academic research results, intelligence has no "second-order observer" who, driven by methodological doubts, chance, or academic idiosyncrasy, will focus on the blind spots inherent in an approach and the results it has produced. As a form of knowledge deprived of methods of self-correction, intelligence is so concerned with its own reality status that it is constantly forced to doubt and reevaluate itself. While Sun Tzu's treatise radiates the optimism of the infallibly cunning commander, the doubling of reconnaissance and deception in modern intelligence agencies results in an abysmal logic of suspicion. For the epistemology of the secret, the enemy is as vexing a demon as René Descartes's *genius malignus,* "an evil genius, supremely powerful and clever, who has directed his entire effort at deceiving me" (Descartes 2006, 12). The omnipotent demon of deception is the essence of modern enmity: "In the case of enmity, the probability, indeed, the certainty, of being deceived is a priori a given" (Sloterdijk 1987, 331).

But it is not only the enemy that deserves distrust but also one's own practices of obtaining and processing information. Who can guarantee that an ambitious field agent hasn't been taken in by an overly boastful or moneygrubbing source? Who can tell whether or not he is being fed disinformation? (Further see Horn 2011.) As we shall see in part 7, "State Paranoia," after years of unchecked paranoia in which any hypothesis or nugget of information appeared credible as long as it appeared to confirm the ruling anti-Communist mind-set, Western intelligence agencies in the 1970s introduced a strict division of labor designed to separate the procurement of data from its evaluation. This was more than a merely functional split; it amounted to a fundamental differentiation of epistemological agendas. While those involved in procuring information (that is, agents and their handlers) tend to give credence to the data obtained, those charged with evaluating the incoming data are encouraged to remain suspicious and question its reliability. While field agents are interested in *what a source knows,* the analysts back home are more concerned with *who this source is.* Where did the information originate? What are the motives for passing it on? What networks are involved? To ensure a modicum of self-reflexivity, intelligence agencies deliberately produce an internal antagonism at the very core of their administration that is designed to structurally replace the lacking outside perspective.

However, the internal tension between the collection and evaluation of data does not change the fact that there is something profoundly "unreal" about the knowledge produced by intelligence. Intelligence practitioners may not like it, but their activities come dangerously close to literature. Indeed, there is more to the affinity between intelligence knowledge, political secrecy, and modern fiction than just the popular fascination with espionage. Maybe it is less a matter of literature portraying secret services than of the latter resembling novelists. Both hatch plots and invent worlds that dissolve into alternative possibilities or get bogged down in dialectic assumptions and counterassumptions. Fiction appears to be itself an integral part of the epistemology of secrecy and enmity that no rational or methodical cleansing can fully eradicate. This is especially obvious in the case of the "textual work" required to turn the mass of collected data into coherent assessments. Secret services produce texts that process hypotheses into arguments able to provide guidance to political decision makers. It is a daunting task: a heady mix of hypotheses and counterhypotheses, available and missing data, experiences derived from past operations and unverifiable predictions of future events have to be distilled into a sufficiently unequivocal proposal capable of informing a clear decision. This synthesis of alternative hypotheses, partial arguments, and side aspects is a matter of reading and writing, a practice succinctly summarized by John Whitman, a former drafter for the National Intelligence Authority (NIA):

> The author will give a scrupulously complete list of arguments why the enemy might do what we want him to do. Then he will give an exhaustive set of reasons why the enemy might do just the opposite . . . It gets the policy maker to think about all the factors, the unpleasant as well as the pleasant ones. And it insures that he cannot dismiss the conclusion which follows on the ground that

> the intelligence people forgot something important . . . A competent drafter will marshal his facts and his ideas and construct an argument which leads to a single or a few major conclusions. If he does not, there is no use writing the estimate. If he does, and if he constructs well, then his betters may tug and pull his paragraphs, alter his adjectives and qualify his estimate passages, but his message still comes through. (Whitman quoted in Laqueur 1985, 35)

It's all about the "construction." Whitman is in effect describing the difficulty of writing a text that can be read in many different ways but that nonetheless will and must result in one particular reading, a text whose meaning is so clear that it cannot be obscured by any changes from above—a text, in other words, that is both one and many. The reader—the political decision maker—is to be offered the full range of possible hypotheses but is then supposed to arrive at one decisive conclusion. In short, Whitman is describing a text that cannot be. It exists only in the head of an author who does not yet know which words he will use, and in the head of a reader who has either missed or already forgotten the many possibilities of reading. It may well be that the political makers and shakers poring over intelligence reports are prone to such negligent reading habits. But Whitman's ideal text will always exhibit a gap between the "pleasant" and "unpleasant" factors as well as between the plurality of factors and the simple-mindedness of conclusions. It is through this gap, however, that fiction makes its entry; it is the point at which alternate possibilities, alternate readings, challenge and invalidate one another as plausible and contingent options. The gap is the moment of undecidability (in the textual as well as in the political sense) that arises from the blindness of the secret. The difficulties involved in writing down and "reading" a secret stem from the epistemological difficulties of outlining a form of knowledge that is as elusive as it is hypothetical.

Part 3

The Great Game

When everyone is dead the Great Game is finished. Not before.

—Rudyard Kipling, *Kim* (1901)

A short text by Jorge Luis Borges tells the story of two kings and two labyrinths. A Babylonian king builds a labyrinth so complex that nobody who enters it ever manages to find a way out. "In time there came to the court a king of the Arabs, and the king of Babylonia (to mock the simplicity of his guest) bade him enter the labyrinth, where the king of the Arabs wandered, humiliated and confused, until the coming of the evening, when he implored God's aid and found the door" (Borges 1998, 263). After promising his host that he will show him his own labyrinth, the king of the Arabs attacks the city, vanquishes the empire, and takes the Babylonian king captive. On a swift-footed camel he brings him to the middle of the desert and leaves him there to die.

Two labyrinths, two kings: the "simple" Arab nomad is pitted against the shrewd Babylonian builder of hybrid cities and towers; the simpleton faces off against the ruler of the complex and confusing. The two labyrinths are the respective domains of two very different sovereigns, and their antithetic structure forms the basis of their power. The bronze labyrinth is a hyperstructured space whose stairs, doors, and walls determine what can be traversed and what remains inaccessible. It is a space that both channels and prohibits movement. By contrast, the Arab labyrinth is nothing but an open expanse—an empty, "smooth"[1] space; an ocean, inexhaustible in its endless openness—yet neither divine aid nor Babylonian cleverness will help the captive king escape. Borges's two labyrinths symbolize space as a scene of power and a dangerous terrain. As a labyrinth, space itself becomes problematic, an object of a knowledge in need of orientation; it requires the ability to turn space into an ally rather than see it as an obstruction. The labyrinth, in short, represents space as a secret.

Spatial Reconnaissance: Labyrinth, Wall, Pixel

As an object of knowledge and a scene of battle, space is the military secret par excellence. Military reconnaissance begins with scouts and spies exploring the terrain and becomes increasingly professionalized following the introduction of media technologies that render space transparent and disposable—from topographical maps to aerial photography and satellite imaging. As the principal media for vital military knowledge, detailed maps were long kept secret; they were covertly produced or stolen, while faulty or incomplete versions were leaked to the enemy (Dewerpe 1994, 235). Sketches of strategically important terrain and fortifications were classified as military secrets. But the reconnaissance of military space involves more than exploring its topography; it also aims at revealing the enemy's positions, plans, and overall condition. Not coincidentally, Sun Tzu's theory of strategically important knowledge is to a large extent a theory of spatial reconnaissance in which exploration of the terrain is a prerequisite for obtaining knowledge about the enemy. How can the particular features of the terrain be exploited, and what dangers may be lurking there? What are the enemy's plans, weapons, and resources? The Arabian Desert and the Babylonian cityscape are locations that call for wholly different forms of warfare. Spatial reconnaissance thus constitutes a *tactical and strategic space,* a constellation of geographic features, humans, weapons, and means of transportation to which the chosen tactical procedures have to adapt. Scouts and spies gather information that will enable them to develop a tactic that will take advantage of the particular spatial features. The tactical space, however, is "formatted" and framed by *geopolitical space:* the form of major zones of conflict between nations or alliances, or an imperial space that links the colonies to the motherland, or a space that defines where the hegemonic center and the peripheries of a political structure are located. Geopolitical space is defined by the potential for conflicts that it contains: Which sphere of influence is the enemy targeting? What are the inroads and barriers of our terrain? How can the periphery be controlled from the center? It is the overall geopolitical situation, then, which structures the space that needs to be explored—and which therefore also determines what kind of knowledge must be obtained.

For the modern age we can roughly distinguish three such geopolitical formats that have shaped the basic structure of the "dangerous space" of vital interest to intelligence activities. We could name them after the basic component that limits spatial reconnaissance: *labyrinth, wall, pixel.*

The *labyrinth* is a mysterious space that cannot be easily surveyed. It poses considerable problems to the mapmakers; meticulous reconnaissance is necessary to render it transparent and reveal its dangers. But the labyrinth also has the structure of a terra incognita, for even if it can be entered, it remains a dangerous space precisely to the extent to which it is not understood. It can, however, be exploited politically and militarily if you adapt to its local—that is to say, linguistic, cultural, and geographical—features. The following sections on scouts, spies, and partisans of the British Empire will focus on this labyrinthine space.

As opposed to the labyrinth, the *wall* surrounds an inaccessible space. It is difficult and dangerous to enter and almost impossible to leave, and there are real and imaginary threats within its boundaries. It is no coincidence that the wall became the emblem of the Cold War's insurmountable global division. Spatial reconnaissance in the age of the wall no longer relies on the adventurism of scouts and cartographers; instead, secret agents must enter a potentially deadly zone of "coldness" from which there may be no escape. The many spies that venture across this heavily fortified border (we will revisit them in part 6, chapter 3, "The Human Factor") are one possibility of reconnoitering this hazardous space, and flyovers that penetrate deeply into Soviet space (made famous by the Gary Powers U2 incident) are the other. A lot of what is hidden in the space on the other side of the wall can be glimpsed from the air: military arsenals and installations, or the number and location of missile launching pads. This is very different from the "local knowledge"—the familiarity with social and cultural customs and codes—that was of such importance to the agents of the British Empire. As a type of knowledge gained from flyovers or dangerous missions into forbidden territory, the spatial reconnaissance of the Cold War depends on highly specialized arts of evaluation and interpretation (aerial images have to be carefully "read"), yet it is also susceptible to phantasmal projections (see the section titled "Behind the Border: *The Looking-Glass War*" in part 6, chapter 3, "The Human Factor").

Finally, *pixel.* If the wall creates inaccessible and invisible geopolitical zones that require risky exploration, the new post–Cold War lack of transparency is, simultaneously, also one of (almost) complete transparency of space. The desire of Cold War intelligence to "look into" enemy space and the growing distrust of human sources (aka HUMINT) fueled the rapid development of satellite imaging. Satellite-based IMINT (imagery intelligence) appears to offer a solution to the phantasms produced by inscrutable agents and paranoid intelligence administrations while rendering unnecessary manned surveillance flights; it provides objective and comprehensive surveillance from space. Exposed to the gaze of the satellite cameras, reconnoitered space is smoothed out; it becomes homogeneous and (ideally) completely transparent. New means of camouflage defense against aerial reconnaissance are countered with infrared technologies and electronic image processing that can distinguish over two hundred shades of gray. Satellite reconnaissance renders space almost completely controllable: nobody and nothing can move without being observed and pinpointed. Nonetheless, even this infinitely controllable space has two limits: resolution and transmission time. Resolution is the representation of spatial units as image units; for example, in a one-meter resolution every meter is represented by one pixel. Whatever is smaller is not represented, hence the *pixel,* the smallest unit of resolution, defines the limit of all spatial reconnaissance. According to my present research commercial satellite imagery by the GeoEye satellite generation is able to achieve forty-one-centimeter resolution; publicly available images, however, are restricted to fifty-centimeter resolution. Military intelligence satellites may even reach ten-centimeter resolution. Flyovers are riskier and more expensive, but they yield even greater detail (figures 3, 4, 5, and 6). Today, satellite imagery may allow the distinction of different car models but not the reading of a license plate or the identification of a person. The other limit is the passage of time that separates the moment at which the photo was taken from its evaluation. Images have to be transmitted, scrutinized, and interpreted, and they can never be anything but a snapshot of a given moment. In times of crises, however, only fully up-to-date images are of any use. Transmission and processing times must therefore be minimized.[2] Just as resolution limits the visualization of space, transmission time limits the use value of information. Within hours, highly sensitive imagery can transform into nothing but historical material.

A literary history of spatial reconnaissance is always a history of the geopolitical conflicts that mark a given space and epoch—whether the rule of the British Empire (with the problems arising from its vulnerable insular position within Europe and its colonial policies in Asia and Africa), the Cold War confrontation between East and West, or the desire of the United States or China to monitor virtually every corner of the planet. The British Empire, however, is a specifically productive case in point, especially regarding the "Great Game," the simmering conflict that for over a century pitted Russia against the British Empire. It produced its share of brilliant writing from Kipling to T. E. Lawrence, and it allows

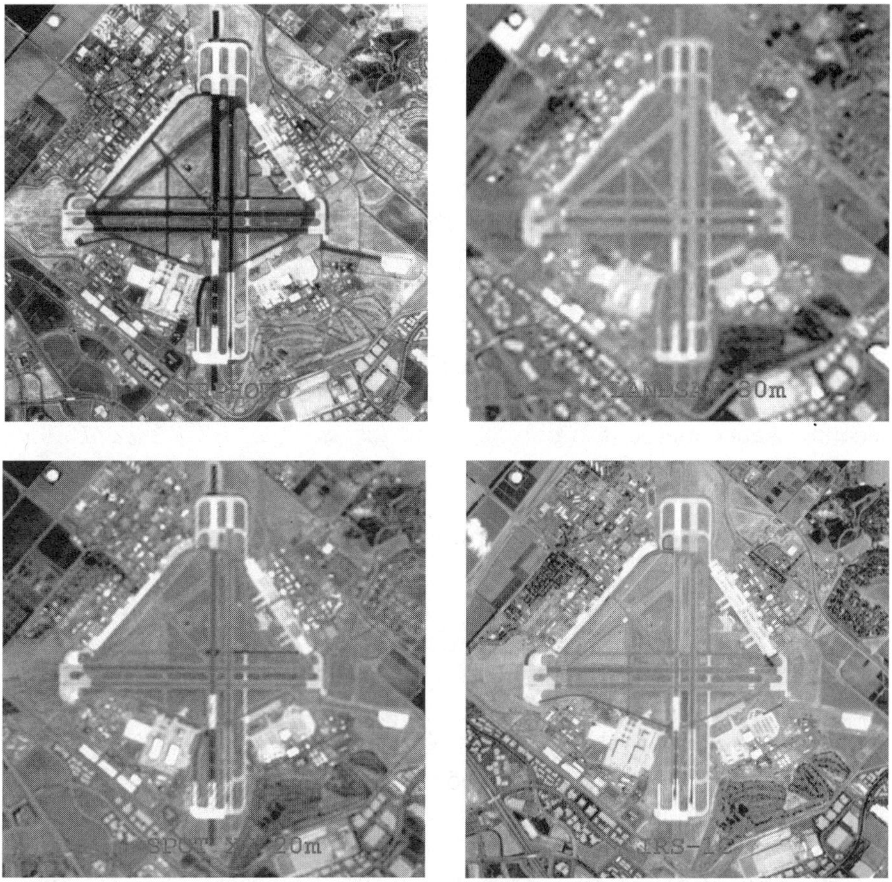

Figures 3, 4, 5, and 6. Four pictures of an airport show the varying quality of images provided by aerial photography and different types of satellites. Figure 3 (*upper left*) is an aerial photograph on a scale of 1:600,000. Figure 4 (*upper right*) is an image from Landsat 7 with a resolution of thirty meters. Figure 5 (*lower left*) is from a SPOT satellite with a resolution of twenty meters. Figure 6 (*lower right*) is an image from an IRS–1C satellite with a resolution of five meters. (www.landinfo.com)

us to trace the gradual emergence of modern agents and their specific cultural, technical, and psychological skills. The metaphor of the "Great Game," however, not only refers to the specific Anglo-Russian conflict in and about Central Asia; it also is the guiding metaphor for espionage as a whole at the beginning of the twentieth century: a mixture of child's play and theatrics, sports and adventure, a seemingly lighthearted form of war. The decidedly tragic dimensions of this game will become apparent in the case of T. E. Lawrence.

The texts under discussion here were written in the twilight of the British Empire: Erskine Childers's *The Riddle of the Sands,* Rudyard Kipling's *Kim,* and T. E. Lawrence's *The Seven Pillars of Wisdom.* They create colonial and European scenarios of the secret war—the efficient defense of the British island against German invaders or Britain's conflict with other colonial powers. In addition, they foreground the role of fiction in these conflicts: the texts by Childers, Kipling, and Lawrence not only depict intelligence work but also offer compelling evidence that the "writing of novels is a continuation of espionage by other means" (Kittler 1993, 42). Going beyond mere entertainment, the texts are concerned with constructing "dangerous spaces" in need of control; they are explorations of alien, inscrutable territories. In them, literature and military reconnaissance merge into one.

Knowledge of the Empire

The British Empire was a power structure rooted in the administration and control of an immense and extremely heterogeneous space. As Thomas Richards has argued, it took a specific regime of knowledge to guarantee its spatial coherence, an "imperial archive" designed to collect, store, and classify information from all parts of the world. "They surveyed and they mapped. They took censuses, produced statistics . . . In fact they often could do little other than collect and collate information, for any exact civil control, of the kind possible in England, was out of the question. The empire was too far away" (Richards 1993, 8). Pursuing the ideal of a unified and complete representation of the world, the imperial thirst for knowledge arose from its specific spatial structure: an empire spanning the globe with Britain as its undisputed political, economic, and military center that nonetheless had to nurture and facilitate a certain amount of "local" self-organization to maintain control over such a vast domain. Local features in colonial territories had to be harmonized with imperial centralization—that is, remote control and self-control had to be coordinated. The Victorian colonial will to knowledge is a will to power grounded in control over space.[3] Geography and hydrography, institutionalized in the Royal Geographical Society (founded in 1830), are the basis for the administration and military control of the colonial territory. As such they are not simply areas of knowledge among others but the royal disciplines of colonialism. "State nomads," that is, world travelers, explorers, cartographers, and the empire's more or less amateurish secret agents, are the actual heroes of this kind of spatial power:

"Nineteenth-century geography was the continuation of politics by other means" (ibid., 17).

Nonetheless, the empire's exploration of space is far from a peaceful land survey. The knowledge of space under discussion here is nothing but the preparation or preemption of war. Gazing at deserts, mountains, cities, roads, canals, and even the sea serves to reveal the tactical and strategic opportunities space has to offer. This gaze discerns the tactical opportunities of a landscape, the logistics of transportation routes, and the geopolitics of a terrain; it therefore requires adepts and experts. Kipling's Kim is taught the basics of surveying at the Catholic School in Lucknow. Prompted by an almost fatal encounter with an enemy agent, the amateur yachtsmen of Childers's *Riddle of the Sands* start exploring the sandbanks and tideways of the North Sea. And T. E. Lawrence, archaeologist, British agent, and tactician of partisan war, learns from his Arab comrades how to tactically exploit the endless, inhospitable expanse of the desert that will entrap his enemies just as it had Borges's unfortunate Babylonian king.

Apart from the skills of observing, investigating, recording, and exploiting space for military purposes, secret spatial reconnaissance calls for an art of deception not required of civilian geographers. In the words of French general Jules-Louis Lewal, "It is a matter of getting there, collecting information, disguising oneself, acting quickly, and returning even more quickly" (Lewal 1876, 364). Since it involves gathering information in hostile terrain without tipping off the enemy, scouts and spies have to specialize in inconspicuous movements, and they need to disguise themselves as idle tourists, traveling salesmen, or, as in Kim's case, disciples of a mendicant. The necessity to adapt and disguise oneself and merge with "the people" gives rise to a special type of cultural mimicry, a hybrid, polyglot, and protean subjectivity (see Horn 2008a). Its fictional but nonetheless politically most influential model is certainly Kipling's Kim, while T. E. Lawrence appeared to his contemporaries as its most heroic and exotic embodiment. In the case of these imperial agents, fictional or real, the idea of *going native* is less a real process than a *program* related to political and military exigencies. Ideally, the colonial spy should be able to turn into a native: that is, not only should he be able to speak all the necessary languages and dialects with no discernible accent, he should also (like Kim) be able to imitate all segments of the population and be fully familiar with curses, prayers, holy texts, and the medical properties of local drugs. The agent is a cultural chameleon. One of the most powerful fantasies of the late empire is the agent-traveler who has mastered the skills of cultural mimicry so perfectly that he is able to fool his enemies—and baffle his readers. He dominates the regions and locales he reconnoiters precisely because he manages to be at home in all of them.

As a result of this cultural adaptation, however, the imperial spy is caught in the fundamental tension of colonial space: while the motherland is the goal and origin of his mission, that mission takes place in the imperial periphery, where the interests of competing colonial powers and the native populations clash in the "Great Game." Scouts and spies operate in marginal spaces on the edge of frontiers where friends and enemies confront each other yet are hard to discern. It is this marginal position that turns space into a dangerous secret. This liminal zone, however, need not be the North Indian Himalayas or the desert of the Hejaz. It can just as well be located only a few hundred miles from Britain: for instance, in the shallow waters of Germany's Frisian coast.

1 Strategic Space

Erskine Childers: *The Riddle of the Sands*

The Riddle of the Sands, frequently hailed as one of the first spy novels, was published in May 1903. The original subtitle, *A Record of Secret Service Recently Achieved,* was followed by the publisher's announcement *Edited by Erskine Childers.* Posing as the editor of an authentic secret intelligence report, Childers claims that his two heroes, the yachtsmen Charles Carruthers and Arthur Davies, presented him with their diaries and nautical charts so that he could turn the material into a novel with wide audience appeal (figure 7). Childers the author retreats, yet he emphasizes his affinity with his sea-bound protagonists by presenting himself as a sailor and naming his own boat after the novel's *Dulcibella,* which was originally the name of Childers's own sister (see Piper 2003). In his preface Childers reveals the tangible political reasons for Carruthers's request. The alleged report, chronicling the adventures of an autumnal sailing trip in the German North Sea, contains information about an imminent threat to Britain. Cruising off the East Frisian Islands, the yachtsmen had stumbled upon secret preparations for a German invasion of England. They risked their lives to spy on German agents until they had fully grasped their plans: the invasion, which would come as a complete surprise to Britain, was to be launched from the shallow tidal waters of the Wadden Sea. The preface further relates that immediately upon their return Carruthers and Davies communicated their discovery to the proper authorities, yet they were forced to realize that their infor-

Figure 7. Robert Erskine Childers (1870–1922), *center,* around 1902. Of Anglo-Irish descent, Childers fought on the English side in the Second Boer War and World War I and wrote several military publications. In the wake of the bloody suppression of the Easter Rising in 1916 he became a radical Irish nationalist. He opposed the Irish Free State established in 1922 and was executed during the Irish Civil War. From Jim Ring, 1996, *Erskine Childers* (London: John Murray).

mation, gathered under such perilous circumstances, had no discernible impact. By presenting their findings to a common readership, they are forcing the government to take precautionary measures, while signaling to the Germans that their plans have been foiled. In other words, literature directly intervenes in matters of national security. Billing itself as a "record of secret service," the novel comments on the status—or nonexistence—of a fully functioning British naval intelligence apparatus at the beginning of the last century. The novel claims that it is up to private citizens to risk their lives in the service of their country and publicize their findings—but of course matters ought to be handled by professional agents whose reports should without delay translate into military action. In the unorganized early days of the intelligence business, literature is not espionage by other means but its only possible form.

Known as the Intelligence Branch, the late nineteenth-century British secret service had in 1873 emerged from the War Office's Topographical and Statistical Department. In line with Britain's imperial ambitions it was especially concerned with securing the northwestern border of India, the main target of the Great Game described in *Kim*. By contrast, defending the island against a European aggressor appeared to be a remote issue, although it was increasingly spurring literary fantasies. It was not until 1910, after several successful German invasions had been played out in best-selling fiction, that James Edmonds, head of MO5, the organization that later evolved into MI5, started to build up professional sections for espionage and counterespionage (see Andrew 2009, 10–21). "The British Secret Service," David Trotter writes, "like the British spy novel invested in . . . the same phantasy" (Trotter 1991, 31): invasion. Peacetime reconnaissance around 1900 was chiefly the task of geographers and hydrographers; the navy, even slower than the Intelligence Branch, had only a tiny office for "naval intelligence" staffed with one officer and three clerks (Andrew 1985, 10–12). In any event, covert reconnaissance remained such an underpaid and poorly equipped venture that agents were frequently forced to cover their own expenses. Spy novelists like William Le Queux took to writing marketable shockers to indulge their patriotic passion for spying. "The ID's [Intelligence Division's] system," Christopher Andrew concludes, "remained amateurish. Secret intelligence arrived . . . 'heaven knows how,' rather than from any organized network" (ibid., 23).

No wonder, then, that two amateurs, the sailing enthusiasts Davies and Carruthers, take it upon themselves to assume the duties of a secret service chastised as amateurish. While the orphaned Kim, working for the Survey of India, receives a solid education in surveying and sketching, Childers's heroes have to rely on their own skills. More precisely, like all amateur spies they willy-nilly receive on-the-job training. The somewhat cranky Davies, often understood as the author's slightly idealized self-portrait, is an excellent and intrepid sailor—he can read maps and charts and orientate himself at sea, and he has a passion for naval strategy—but on land he feels like a fish out of water. Carruthers, on the other hand, undertakes a couple of highly informative forays on dry land; he even manages to eavesdrop on vital German meetings (Childers 1978, 235–44) and observe a nightly maneuver (ibid., 300–318) that helps solve the eponymous riddle. While Carruthers's diaries are the basis of the novel, Davies contributes the necessary maps and nautical charts that serve to improve the "prehistoric rottenness of the English charts" (ibid., 96). The two are a felicitous combination of complementary skills: experts for land and sea, text and graphics—the ideal spying team.

Reconnaissance: Map and Report

This complementary competence in matters of media and terrain is more than a fancy idea on Childers's part. It reflects the constitutive elements of any reconnaissance operation: the combination of mapping and reporting. The former may be a detailed topographical rendition or a crude

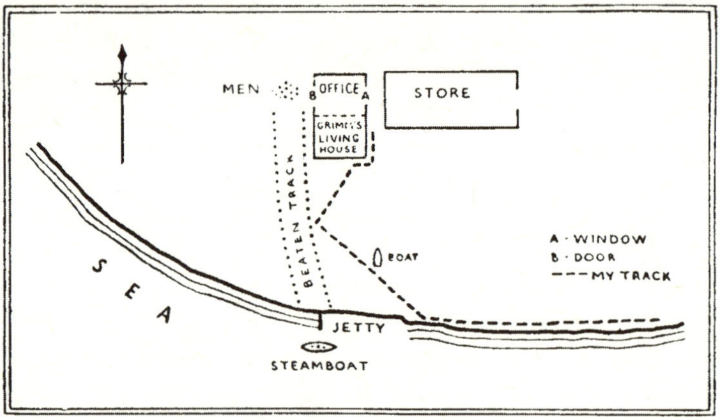

Figure 8. A sketch of German buildings made by one of the heroes, Charles Carruthers, in *The Riddle of the Sands.*

sketch (figure 8) such as the one Carruthers makes of the house of the German planning staff (Childers 1978, 237)—what counts is that

> 1. A sketch and report should convey no faulty information, inaccurate intelligence being worse than none at all. 2. Objects should be considered solely with reference to their military value, and those which, even if otherwise remarkable, are unimportant from this point of view should be omitted, unless their presence assists in the recognition of the area or road sketched. (Parker 1898, 9 and following)

The double criteria of accuracy and relevance have to be applied to the poetics of the novel itself. By brushing aside the overly detailed descriptions of the *Dulcibella* and the coastline as superfluous embellishments of a mediocre novel, critics have overlooked their military relevance in the nefarious plan that the two sailors gradually uncover—a plan that entirely depends on technical and hydrological details. To dismiss *The Riddle of the Sands* as mere entertainment[4] and the maps and the scenic depictions as narrative deficiencies completely misses the point of Childers's text. "Its structure breaks down," Leroy Panek remarks in his history of the British spy novel; "its dependence on maps betrays considerable narrative weakness, and surely even sailors find that all of the messing about in the *Dulcibella* is a bit much" (Panek 1981, 32). On the contrary, the link between maps and story—Childers had in fact planned to include more maps, including a sketch of the fortifications around Esen—is not an aesthetic shortcoming but fulfills the novel's task to render all the tactically relevant details of space as clearly as possible. The novel, in short, is reconnaissance in the technical sense: a combination of sketch and report. As E. D. Parker writes in *Outline of Reconnaissance,* it is the function of the report to add to the map what the latter cannot convey: it reveals details that are too small, all that is hidden, and, finally, anything that moves and changes in the observed terrain (Parker 1898, 9).[5] Reconnaissance is not exclusively a matter of maps, for maps cannot replace a visual inspection of the situation in the field, and its tactical-strategic dimension can be rendered only by a text (see Baden-Powell 1899). "The best spatial reconnaissance," a French textbook notes, "remains unintelligible if it presumes to replace the map. One complements the other" (Cambrelin 1874, 17). The text adds a temporal dimension to the map, supplying what is hidden, what cannot be seen or graphically represented. Of Davies it is said that he can smell the shape of the waves, as it were. But that is precisely what is at stake in Childers's novel: his text provides a type of information that maps can represent only in part—the military secret as the secret of space. Not surprisingly, a contemporary critic remarked that "the book can only be read by the aid of large maps, railway guides and special information about things nautical" (quoted after Piper 2003, 75).

The novel's most astonishing chart was a minor sensation because it offered a more detailed rendition of the terrain in question than anything else that could be purchased in Britain at the time (figure 9). It illustrates one of the most thrilling scenes, related in chapters 7 and 8. Here, Davies encounters the strange yachtsman Dollmann, an English traitor who works for the Germans. Dollmann lures Davies, who is sailing on his own, into dangerous shallow waters in the hope that the inconvenient sailor will capsize and drown. During this almost lethal incident close to the mouth of the Elbe, Davies first catches sight of the eponymous riddle: he comes to realize the strange structure of the North Sea coast as well as the strategic importance of the surrounding space. Between the charted and well-marked navigable channels are flat sandbanks traversed by small channels and tideways, hidden under the surface of the water. Carruthers, who later returns with Davies to these treacherous waters, describes them as a "labyrinth of detached banks which obstruct the

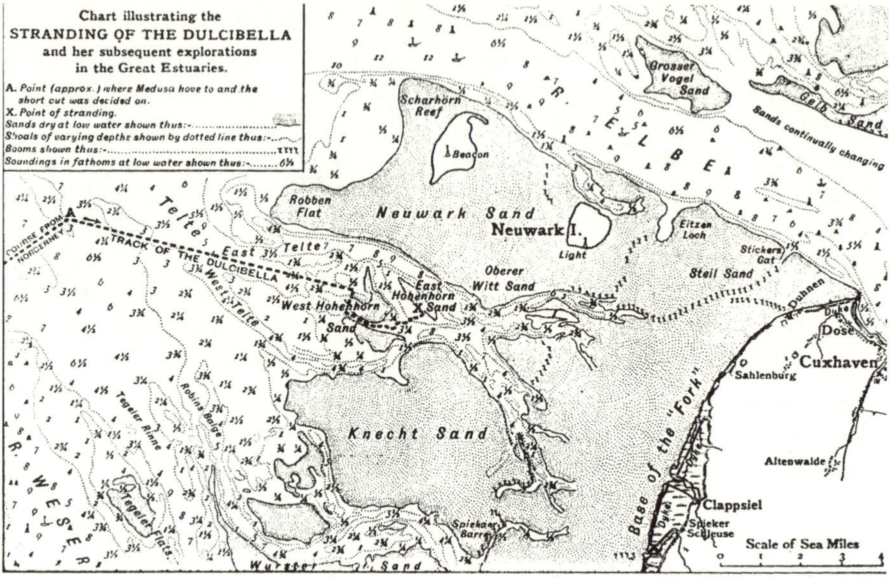

Figure 9. A nautical chart of the Wadden Sea off Cuxhaven, Germany, with the route of the *Dulcibella* (from *The Riddle of the Sands*). Childers uses maps, sketches, and nautical charts to add verisimilitude to his novel.

funnel-shaped cavity between the upper and middle prongs" (Childers 1978, 135). The problem of this space is that even though it may appear to be a plane, uniform surface, its navigability dramatically changes with the tides. It is, in fact, a "hidden maze":

> This I knew [the fact that he is in the labyrinth] from the chart. My unaided eye saw nothing but the open sea, growing dark green as the depths increased; a dour, threatening sea, showing its white fangs. The waves grew longer and steeper, for the channels, though still tortuous, now begin to be broad and deep . . . Partly by sight and mostly by touch we crept around the outermost alley of the hidden maze. (Ibid., 135)

Childers inserts a nautical chart complete with the depth markings of the channels and tideways as well as the route of the *Dulcibella* during her first, almost deadly encounter with Dollmann. That particular incident would be all but incomprehensible without the map; by the same token, the text reveals the relevance of the chart with its maze of sandbanks and varying depths. The text teaches us how to read the naval space: under the seemingly plane surface of the water lurks an ever-changing dangerous labyrinth that can be navigated only with the help of precise nautical charts. In turn, Carruthers's remarks on the color of the water and the shape of the waves indicate how this labyrinth may be deduced from certain signs on the water's surface. Chart and text are thus mutually indispensable, complementary media providing information about the ephemeral labyrinthine seascape that can be revealed only by astute observation and meticulous hydrography. *The Riddle of the Sands* is eager to provide both because, as author and protagonist keep emphasizing, the British charts of the North Sea are imprecise and useless in comparison to the German ones (see Drummond 1985, 182). Consequently, the chapter's goal is ultimately not to thrill but to give a lesson in hydrography.

Tactical Space

A second necessary step in spatial reconnaissance is to decipher the terrain's tactical and strategic relevance. Why is detailed knowledge of the German North Sea coast of such vital importance to Britain? Davies introduces his fellow sailor—and the reader—to the "strategic channel theory" that ties the geopolitical circumstances of Germany and Britain to the complex structure of the North Sea coast, resulting in a unique invasion scenario. Germany, Davies expounds, has no colonies to speak of, yet it is building a mighty fleet to remedy matters:

> Think of Germany as a new sea-power . . . The next thing is, what is her coast-line? It's a very queer one, split clean in two by Denmark . . . Far the most important bit of coast-line . . . looks on the North Sea . . . Now it must strike you at once that it's ridiculously short compared with the huge country behind it . . . In the event of war it seems to me that every inch of it would be important, sand and all . . . It strikes me that in a war a lot might depend on these, both in defense and attack. (Childers 1978, 101, 103)

Davies's reasoning, according to which the covert German coastal activities are preparations of a coming war, explicitly draws on the bible of geopolitical naval theory, Alfred Thayer Mahan's *Influence of Sea Power upon History 1660–1783,* first published in 1890. Conceiving of the sea as both highway and theater of war, Mahan emphasized the vital importance of access to the sea and the relationship of land to sea. In other words, the sea is much like land, a surface suited for the communication of goods and people, "a great highway; or better, perhaps, a wide common, over which men will pass in all directions, but on which some well-worn paths show that controlling reasons have led them to choose certain lines of travel rather than others" (Mahan 1918, 25). Davies's reading of the importance of the Wadden Sea is in effect a small-scale application of Mahan's idea that the sea is a system of lanes and passages. The basis of the German plan, which the protagonists finally come to understand as an offensive rather than defensive scenario, consists in using their knowledge of the Wadden Sea channels for a covert launch of troop transporters rather than having to rely on (easily controllable) German harbors. Under the cover of night an armada of shallow-draft boats will cross over from Germany to Britain and invade the island. The entire secret—and with it the surprise effect the Germans are banking on—hinges on their exclusive knowledge of the navigability of the Wadden Sea. The latter is an ever-changing labyrinth of channels with the tides opening and blocking passages, and shoals and watersheds producing constantly changing currents—and to top it off, the Germans are secretly adding dykes and canals to the labyrinth. Only precise knowledge of land and sea will enable one to safely traverse this dangerous space. As a result, knowledge of the terrain amounts to a tactical weapon.

Davies's explanation starts with a bird's-eye view of the entire region of the North and Baltic Sea and then draws small-scale conclusions: "Every inch of it would be important" (Childers 1978, 103). A large-scale geopolitical perspective raises questions that can only be fully answered by scrutinizing all the details of a specific location. The sweep of Davies's argument closely follows the thrust of political-military intelligence: a global view of the power distributions, spatial configurations, inroads, borders, and coastlines—and a local, on-the-spot assessment of tactical possibilities. Davies's move from grand view to regional and local detail links heterogeneous perceptual fields: geopolitics on the one hand, "local knowledge" on the other.[6] It is not only a matter of geography on differing scales but also a matter of complementary ways of apprehending and exploring space. Scouts focus on details, on whatever is unique, hidden, or subject to change. Unlike regular troops, they do not try to traverse space as quickly as possible; they move slowly and inconspicuously and seek to avoid the enemy (Henderson 1915, 11). The slow exploration dissolves the apparent homogeneity of cartographic depictions and instead registers space as a mutable, opaque, and dangerous zone. Ultimately, amateur spies like Davies and Carruthers turn out to be a great deal more versatile and intellectual than the professional agents who came to replace them: they combine political insight with technical know-how, geopolitics with surveying skills, the global perspective with local knowledge. They are as talented at sailing, eavesdropping, and (if need be) handling guns as they are at deliberating future European colonial politics and its impact on the empire.

The truly remarkable quality of Childers's epochal novel has little to do with the practicality of its invasion scenario, of which Prince Louis of Battenberg, director of naval intelligence, remarked: "As a *novel* it is excellent, as a *warplan* it is rubbish" (Battenberg quoted in Drummond 1985, 153). Together with George Tomkyns Chesney's *The Battle of Dorking* (1871) and William Le Queux's *The Invasion of 1910* (1906), Childers's novel inaugurated a new genre of invasion literature and fueled political fantasies that had immediate military consequences.[7] A few years after its publication *The Riddle of the Sands* was, as it were, replayed by two adventurous British officers. In August 1910 Lieutenant V. R. Brandon and Captain B. F. Trench were arrested in East Frisia for trying to spy on coastal fortifications. In their trial they stated that they had read Childers's novel—in Brandon's case, "three times."[8] What is unique about *The Riddle of the Sands* is an observation and transformation of space that places it alongside the strategic conceptions of space on display in Kipling's *Kim* and Lawrence's theory of partisan war. As Kipling does with India, Childers projects the German coast as a tactical space—and he also sketches the outlines of the figure that will explore and itemize these terrains to decipher or prevent coming wars: the modern agent.

2 Local Knowledge

Rudyard Kipling's *Kim*

Published two years before *The Riddle of the Sands,* Rudyard Kipling's *Kim* shares with Childers's novel the fantasy of an adventurous space that needs to be explored and surveyed. Kipling's India is, no doubt, far less dangerous and a great deal more colorful, burlesque, and "orientalist" than the uncanny German Wadden Sea. Despite this difference, both novels are concerned with the basic problem confronting the underdeveloped state of imperial intelligence. India is far away, an alien country at the margins of the empire, and the need to secure this periphery is at the core of Kipling's novel. More precisely, *Kim* is concerned with the simmering geopolitical conflict that for over a century pitted the British Empire against Czarist Russia in a struggle over supremacy in Central Asia: the so-called Great Game. While the East India Company had in the nineteenth century relinquished the administration of India to the British government, Russia had from 1813 on expanded its sphere of Central Asian influence ever closer to the northern borders of the Raj. By 1900 the boundaries of the Russian and British spheres were only twenty miles apart. Vigorously pursued by both powers, the mapping and exploration of largely unknown territories in Central Asia, especially in the region of present-day Afghanistan, was less a matter of geographical interest than part of major geopolitical conflict.[9] Kipling's novel uses this conflict as a backdrop for Kim's coming-of-age story. Yet the novel is not simply a bildungsroman but, more to the point, the portrayal of the formation of a new type of agent. Despite his young age, Kim is already what Davies and Carruthers still have to become in the course of their novel: a youthful but professional scout with a sense of mission and adventure, an expert for spaces and the secret wars that inhabit them.

Kim tells the story of a transition to adulthood in the midst of the Great Game, a tale of apprenticeship, adventures, and travels across the Indian subcontinent. Kim—Kimball O'Hara, orphaned child of impoverished Irish parents employed in the colonial service—meets an aged Tibetan lama who is on a quest to find a holy river. Kim becomes the lama's pupil and disciple (*chela*) and accompanies him on his spiritual journey through India while running occasional errands for his friend, the horse dealer Mahbub Ali—who is in fact working as an agent for the British. Kim is eventually sent to an English school in Lucknow by Colonel Creighton, where he receives training as a geographer. Thanks to Kim's adroitness and linguistic skills Creighton entrusts him with secret delivery and spying missions, which he carries out during his holidays under the loose supervision of Mahbub Ali and other agents posing as traveling salesmen or Bengali anthropologists. Following further training under the gem dealer Lurghan Sahib, Kim—still acting as the *chela* of the traveling mendicant—pulls off his greatest feat: in the foothills of the Himalayas he manages to steal from two Russian spies dispatches containing instructions for rebellious princes in the northern regions of the Raj. After receiving a sound thrashing at the hands of some villagers, the Russians are forced to return home empty-handed. By blurring the boundaries between child's play, apprenticeship, and highly dangerous secret mission, Kim becomes the empire's first professionally trained agent.

Right at the outset, the novel's famous opening lines cut straight to the heart of colonial matters: "He sat, in defiance of municipal orders, astride the gun Zam-Zammah . . . Who hold Zam-Zammah . . . hold the Punjab . . . There was some justification for Kim . . . since the English held the Punjab and Kim was English" (Kipling 1987, 49). But how "English" is Kim really? He is introduced as the son of a destitute Irish father, "a poor white of the very poorest," raised by a native foster mother; his Hindi and Punjabi are better than his English, and he is "burned black as any native" (ibid., 49). By presenting a cannon as the emblem of colonial power and then adding a map of northwestern India to get the plot under way, the novel wastes no time in conjuring up the basic constellation of the Great Game: the stakes are nothing less than British control over an India whose northern border is increasingly threatened by local rulers who prefer to collaborate with the encroaching Russians. The truly remarkable aspect of the opening image, however, is that a *child* astride Zam-Zammah has come to embody British domination. The colonial agenda of the novel is obvious, yet the text will be less concerned with military power than with more subtle forms of control.

As Thomas Richards notes, Kipling's novel depicts in singular clarity a transformation of imperialism from the reliance on ethnocide, enslavement, or unfettered exploitation, that is, from the direct use of violence, to the skilled management of information—and of intelligence, for that matter (Richards 1993, 23). However, colonial intelligence as the accumulation of knowledge pertaining to the control of colonial territory is always encumbered by problems of communication and interpretation. Hence there is an urgent need for multilingual agents familiar with the many cultural codes, laws, and taboos of an extremely heterogeneous society such as India. In other words, the political and military reconnaissance of colonial space involves more than scouting and spying missions to explore the terrain and eavesdrop on the enemy; it also requires cultural fluency and social acumen. In short, it depends on "local knowledge."[10] As the British had been forced to learn during the Indian uprising of 1857, they could not secure their rule if they disregarded local codes and customs. The uprising, known as the Indian Rebellion or Mutiny of 1857, was an armed insurrection of Bengali and Indian soldiers triggered by reports of cultural insensitivity: rumors began to circulate that the cartridges of the newly introduced Enfield Rifled Musket had been greased with either lard or tallow, which was unacceptable to Muslim or Hindu soldiers, respectively. Throughout 1857 the revolt spread across central and northern India and ultimately put an end to the rule of the East India Company; from now on India was to be administered by the British government.

The agents in possession of the indispensable cultural knowledge, whose vital importance became apparent during the Rebellion of 1857, had to be supremely assimilated individuals capable of moving around the Raj without attracting any attention. Kipling's novel introduces a veritable typology of such agents: Colonel Creighton—the multilingual colonial officer with years of experience in India who recruits Kim for the Great Game; Babu Hurree Chunder Mookerjee—the ambitious, British-trained Bengali, a brilliant and burlesque ethnographer who has set his sights on advancing up the ladder of the colonial administration; Mahbub Ali—an Afghan merchant loyal to the English; and of course Kim himself—an orphan descended from poor "whites" and reared by a "half-caste" Indian foster mother.

Education and Equipment

If you read Kipling's novel not as the fancy description of a sentimentally idealized colonial India but as a training manual for British imperial agents, Kim's educational journey becomes highly revealing. It leads through various stages of apprenticeship: Kim is a *chela,* a spiritual disciple and worldly servant of the itinerant lama, whom he accompanies and assists on his quest; an occasional apprentice to the horse dealer–cum–spy Mahbub Ali; and finally a reluctant pupil at Saint Xavier, the British Indian school for prospective colonial civil servants in Lucknow, where at the instigation of Colonel Creighton he receives a triple education in Catholic piety, British culture, and the techniques of surveying and mapping (see Wilds Craft 1998). It is typically ironic for Kipling to present a Catholic institution as the best English education center in the Raj and a learned Bengali, the Babu Hurree Chunder Mookerjee, as the one who introduces Kim to the Western European high school canon, comprising Wordsworth, Shakespeare, Burke and Hare, Latin and French. It appears that more than others these somewhat un-English servants of the empire have to put their loyalty on a sound cultural basis. The most important prerequisite for Kim's future work as an agent, however, is a technical skill, "the art and science of mensuration" (Kipling 1987, 211). "A boy who had passed his examination in these branches," the Babu promises him, "could, by merely marching over a country with a compass and a level and a straight eye, carry away a picture of that country which might be sold for large sums in coined silver" (ibid.). Even though Kim receives a solid education as a "chain-man" that qualifies him for employment in the lower ranks of the Survey of India, the central engineering agency in charge of mapping and surveying, there is more to it than merely geographical training. The Survey of India is a cover for Kim's and the Babu's secret service activities. In practical terms, to "carry away" the picture of a landscape refers less to geological mensuration than to surveillance and reconnoitering by doing away with "adventurous aids" and complex instruments and instead relying on careful observations. Kim is taught to use his own step as a measure of length and to employ such simple and inconspicuous tools that nobody will recognize him as a geographer (or even as English). From the very beginning Kim is trained to be a secret scout rather than a harmless surveyor. As the military treatises keep emphasizing, the most important tool for scouts is the power of observation, which Kim acquires under the systematic guidance of another mysterious player in the Great Game, the spy trainer Lurgan Sahib, who poses as a gem dealer. The "jewel game," a kind of memory training that also uses photos of natives and weapons, increases the ability to absorb and retain a wealth of details. Known as "Kim's Game," it is still used today to train the powers of observation and short-term memory. Later on, Kim practices his skills observing Lurgan Sahib's—mostly disguised—customers. What is at the core of Lurgan's education program is to observe, to take in even the smallest detail. Yet it also involves *not* seeing anything that is merely suggested. Part of Kim's training is a hypnotic experiment conducted by Lurgan, in which he tries to convince Kim that a broken jar on the floor has reassembled itself. Kim successfully resists Lurgan's attempt to hypnotize him by switching to English and reciting multiplication tables.

Kim's powers of observation are not simply claimed by the narrator; they are performed by the text itself. Kipling's famous depictions of Indian folklore, from the market of Lahore to the hustle and bustle on the Grand Trunk Road that runs from Peshawar over Delhi to Calcutta, are a literary reflex of the colonial agent's observation skills. The painstakingly precise ways in which the narrator quotes folk sayings (the novel originally contained passages in Hindi), describes the clothes and physiognomy of each and every social type, and depicts local customs, all of which have frequently been dismissed as orientalizing embellishments, is indebted to the attention to detail that is also required of good spies. The novel's scopic qualities, then, are less an effect of imperial panopticism than the perspective of an agent scrutinizing each and every surrounding detail.[11] The narrator "reads" the figures according to their behavior and social background, always in search of peculiarities and discrepancies. Which is precisely what Kim excels at: he unmasks a spy disguised as a fakir. The colorfulness and attention to detail that characterize Kipling's portrayals are a form of social reading directly linked to the novel's intelligence agenda. Both narrator and protagonist are able to observe and narrate in great detail, making the novel a "continuation of espionage by other means."

Part of this visual regime is the art of disguise, including all the appropriate dialects, curses, prayers, and gestures. Kim is a natural: during his first break from school he runs to a prostitute to have his head shaved and his body rubbed in black lotion to remove his formal English haircut and darken his lightened skin. In fact, Kim's greatest skill is that of cultural mimicry—a skill he is, as it were, naturally predisposed to, given his hybrid, Indian European upbringing. While Kim's training centers on observing and mapping techniques, his aptitude arises from his cultural versatility. He can be anything: Indian street urchin and British scion, crafty messenger and pitiful servant of a mendicant. But above all, Kim is a child—and it is his mixture of childishness, malleability, inconspicuousness, and playfulness that in Kipling's eyes constitutes the ideal basis for the creation of the colonial agent. As Edward Said remarked, Kim's aptitude for perfect mimicry, his ability to wholly blend into the colonized culture, embodies a central "wish fantasy" of this "reformed" colonialism—not only to fully understand the dominated Indian culture but also to be able to slip it on and thus acquire a new identity: "[It] is the wish-phantasy of someone who would like to think that everything is possible, that one can go anywhere and be anything . . . Was there ever a native fooled by the blue or green-eyed Kims and Lawrences who passed among the inferior races as agent adventurers?" (Said, in Kipling 1987, 44). For Kipling, at least, this seems possible.

Kim's activities for the British Indian secret service, which operates under the guise of the ethnographic section of the Survey of India, lead off with a simple errand for the horse dealer Mahbub. He has to transfer a message concerning the conspiracy of "five confederated kings" and a "Northern Power"—easily identifiable as Russia—to Colonel Creighton (Kipling 1987, 69). Kim proves himself to be a natural at clandestine activities. Not only does he immediately grasp the conspiratorial nature of his mission; he also avails himself of the pious lama as a cover and secretly observes the impact of the message transmitted. Kim is an agent who wants to know what is going on. The three secret service employees Kim will collaborate with fulfill three different functions: Colonel Creighton is in charge of the agents. He is the one who recruits Kim, sends him to school for further training, and watches over him. He is, in Richards's words, a "cybernetic character" (Richards 1993, 30) who masterminds and controls Kim's many seemingly random encounters on the road. Creighton is the switch point of an intelligence apparatus whose efficiency arises primarily from the fact that it is decentralized, mobile, and skilled at improvisation. Mahbub Ali, a British agent "registered in one of the locked books of the Indian Survey Department as C25 1B" (Kipling 1987, 69), pursues his own missions but also acts toward Kim as a kind of agent handler avant la lettre. Finally, the fat Babu Hurree Chunder Mookerjee is a shrewd colleague and a brilliant teacher of practical matters. At the end he bids Kim farewell in a caricatured mix of Bengali and English that reiterates the basic rule of deception and disguise: "Good-bye, my dear fallow [*sic*], and when next you are under thee emotions please do not use the Mohammedan terms with the Tibetan dress" (ibid., 330).

Despite the many successes achieved by Creighton's agents, the Survey's network seems strangely disorganized: agents appear only to vanish again, and encounters, no matter how dramatic they turn out to be, seem to be completely random and thus call for extensive improvisation, as in the case of the injured fellow agent on the train to Delhi, whom Kim is forced to dress up to avoid detection by the police (Kipling 1987, 247 and following). Everybody is constantly on the move and flitting about—Kim accompanying the lama, Mahbub buying and selling horses, the Babu posing as a Survey ethnographer, and so on. Nobody has a fixed address, but somehow they always manage to know where to find one another in the immense space of northern India when the need arises. This lack of a clear destination, which is most obvious in the case of the lama's aimless quest for a sacred river, appears to be the essence of intelligence work. Babu Hurree Chunder Mookerjee invariably manages to locate Kim, no matter where he is. During their operation directed against the Russo-French agents in the middle of the Himalayas, both Kim and the Babu are always able to predict what the other is about to do; as a result they are eventually reunited at their point of departure, and Kim hands over the enemy papers to his mentor. "There was no means of communication with the boy, but he could be trusted" is the basic principle according to which agents organize their joint efforts (ibid., 299). As opposed to World War and Cold War intelligence, unquestioned loyalty here is not yet a moral category but simply a matter of organizational dependability. There is no question about Kim's loyalty. His reliability as an agent rests on his ability to understand critical situations and come up with improvised solutions. As the model of a—yet to be created—colonial secret service, Colonel Creighton's network is a miracle of ongoing improvisation, fortunate circumstances, and impeccable timing. Measured against the bureaucratic organization of modern intelligence services, his small brigade appears hopelessly chaotic, yet proves to be miraculously efficient.

During the historical period in which the novel takes place (around 1870, between the First and Second Anglo-Afghan Wars) there was no centralized intelligence service in the Raj, only a loose assortment of departments attached to the police or the foreign office responsible for suppressing the violent Thuggee cult, fighting the radical Wahhabi, and other policing activities. Prior to 1904, when Viceroy Lord Curzon (perhaps under the influence of Kipling) began the training of secret agents in the service of the Raj, it was in particular the Thagi and Dakoity Department that in its struggle against organized crime engaged in gathering secret information, employing snitches, and evaluating intelligence reports. Following the Rebellion of 1857 it became ever more important to identify and suppress rebellious movements in time.[12] One of the great fears was that an Indian insurrection or a ruler on the margins of the empire would form an alliance with Russia (Popplewell 1995, 17).

This, precisely, is the conspiracy code-named "the pedigree of the white stallion" in the first message Kim has to convey:

> It concerned all manner of out-of-the-way mountain principalities, explorers of nationalities other than English [that is, Russian agents disguised as explorers and geographers], and the gun-trade—was, in brief, a small portion of that vast mass of "information received" on which the Indian Government acts. But, recently, five confederated Kings, who had no business to confederate, had been informed by a kindly Northern Power that there was a leakage of news from their territories into British India. (Kipling 1987, 69)

Such information was collected either by officers of the Indian army, by the political department of the Indian colonial government, or by more or less solitary travelers, explorers, and adventurers. Much like in the British mother country, intelligence work in the Raj was primarily a matter of individual initiative. Resourceful explorers and adventurers were the real players of the Great Game—and frequently its victims. Exploring the northwestern Indian frontier as well as the Indian portions of the Himalayas and Tibet (which at this point had barely been mapped at all) was a joint venture involving geographical exploration, military reconnaissance, and occasional secret diplomatic missions to local rulers that were under pressure from both sides. However, the extent of the Russian threat remained as unclear as the plans and conduct of the Central Asian sovereigns. It was not unusual for European travelers to be arrested and executed as colonial emissaries.

It therefore makes a lot of sense for Kipling to assign Colonel Creighton to the Survey of India. His function corresponds to the double duty of surveying and scouting that characterized the office toward the end of the nineteenth century.[13] Given the tense political situation, however, it was extremely hazardous for European surveyors to venture into the unknown mountainous regions. An officer of the Survey, Lieutenant Colonel Thomas George Montgomerie (1830–1878) hit upon the idea to train native Indians from the Punjabi region as geographers and send them across the northwestern border into Tibet (see Hopkirk 1997, 120–32; Hopkirk 1990, 330–32). It is reasonable to assume that Kipling was familiar with Montgomerie's reports that appeared in the *Journal of the Royal Geographical Society* between 1866 and 1875. Kim receives the same training and is given the same mission as the native pundits. Sent by Montgomerie on arduous and dangerous explorations to Tibet, Nepal, East Turkestan, and Yarkand, "Their scant instrumental equipment consisted of no more than two large sextants, two box sextants, prismatic and pocket compasses, thermometers for observing temperature of air and boiling water, pocket chronometer, and common watch, with apparatus, the latter reduced as much as possible" (Montgomerie and Pundit 1868, 132).

In Montgomerie's publications the pundits are frequently referred to by their code number ("Native Explorer Nr. 9") or simply called Pundit (but occasionally listed as coauthors), though a few did gain a prominence under their own name.[14] Kim's desire to have a code name—"the dignity of a letter and a number"—as well as "a price upon his head!" (Kipling 1987, 209) is the desire to become a pundit. To avoid detection as geographers and Western agents, the pundits dressed as priests. In addition, Montgomerie notes, they were provided with a box of medications to ingratiate themselves with the local population.[15] Hurree Chunder Mookerjee equips Kim with a similar box when he sends him off on his mission. The instruments of Montgomerie's emissaries were specially designed to be as small as possible, and the staff of the native *moonshee* was equipped with a compass. "Every endeavor was made to prevent the instruments from being conspicuous," Montgomerie notes in his first report (Montgomerie 1866, 158). Likewise, in *Kim* religious artifacts like rosaries and the small container for betel nuts are converted into surveying tools: "As it was occasionally inexpedient to carry about measuring-chains [because they would have revealed their bearer to be a scout] a boy would do well to know the precise length of his own foot-pace . . . To keep count of thousands of paces, Hurree Chunders's experience had shown him nothing more valuable than a rosary of eighty-one or a hundred-and-eight beads" (Kipling 1987, 211).

Surveying the wild northern frontier of India around 1900 and reconnoitering it as a spy are one and the same.[16] What is remarkable is that Kipling chooses the same disguise for his protagonist that Montgomerie chose for his pundits: religious garb. Kim's best cover is the lama whose *chela* he pretends to be; he enables Kim to successfully pose as a traveling disciple—because he, the lama, believes it himself. Throughout the novel the dignified old monk takes Kim's restlessness as an indication that he is looking for the river of healing, which he eventually does find.

Kipling explicitly (and polemically) contrasts Montgomerie's pundits and his protagonist to a different type of agent embodied by their Russian and French counterparts, whom Kim encounters in the Himalayas. By comparing Kim and the Babu to these thoroughly European agents, the novel stages a colonial clash between two very different types of secret service employees. On the one hand we have the European chauvinist agent-surveyors; they ascend the mountains equipped with heavy theodolites and a strong dose of imperial snootiness and proceed to tear up the lama's precious drawing, until they are finally beaten up and chased away by irate villagers. On the other hand we have the multilingual, highly adaptable British Indian agents, who carry out spatial reconnaissance by means of cultural mimicry. The Franco-Russians view space as mere terrain, and their surveys rely on expensive instruments that Kim eventually casts into a deep ravine. Space has no more than purely material properties; they understand neither the language nor the mentality and social rules of the region they happen to be in. Nonetheless, they have a ready-made theory of "India" that they see embodied in the Babu: "'He represents little India in transition—the *monstrous hybridism* of East and West,' the Russian replied. 'It is *we* who can deal with Orientals. He has lost his own country and has not acquired any other' " (Kipling 1987, 288; emphasis added). Those who believe in clear-cut cultural affinities and "nationalities" cannot but view Hurree Chunder Mookerjee's cultural mobility as monstrous, yet it becomes increasingly obvious that the Russians are incapable of dealing with Orientals. Kim and Hurree are indeed Eastern-Western hybrids, but this is precisely what Kipling's vision of the imperial agent (and, more generally, of the colonial subject) is aiming at. They are not only mapmakers, ethnographers (like the Babu), and messengers; they are also *both native and colonial.* They embody "local knowledge" as mimicry of whatever local culture they happen to encounter. As the very essence of this "locality" the novel presents religion and religious piety, embodied by the lama. It comes as no surprise, therefore, that even Lurgan Sahib—teacher of agents, dealer of gems, and merchant of information—is prone to discuss "metaphysics in English and Bengali . . . He was always interested in religion" (Kipling 1987, 206). To the degree that Kim cares for and adores the lama, to the degree that despite and beyond all irony and guile he really is his master's *chela,* he is also moving within a hybrid region *between* Indian and colonial, spiritual and material spaces. While this interim space, especially in the case of the cartoonish (yet intellectually brilliant) Babu, serves to exacerbate the monstrous nature of hybridity, precisely this hybridity serves as an example for adept, versatile agents. The Kims, the Hurree Chunder Mookerjees, and the Lurgans are the models of the new, auspicious servants of the empire.[17]

The Great Game: Boy Scouts and Geopolitics

Whatever Kim may be, he will only be within the confines of the Great Game. As he comes to realize, whatever happens, whatever he himself has done and will do, is part of the game:

> Well is the Game called great! . . . Now I shall go far and far into the North playing the Great Game. Truly, it runs like a shuttle throughout all Hind. And my share and my joy . . . I owe to the lama here. Also to Mahbub Ali—also to Creighton Sahib, but chiefly to the Holy One. He is right—a great and wonderful world—and I am Kim—Kim—Kim—alone—one person—in the middle of it all. (Kipling 1987, 273)

Kipling's novel was instrumental in popularizing the metaphor of the Great Game for the Anglo-Russian conflict, after which it turned into a metaphor for espionage itself; and even though the First World War banished the ludic element from the secret war, the war games of the Cold War resurrected the metaphor. Playing games as a form of inauthentic behavior allows for the acting out of enmities that no longer permit real war (see part 6, "Cold War"). A history of espionage must therefore also be a history of this metaphor and its ironic—not to mention frequently euphemistic—content. And it is this euphemistic quality, rather than its frequently discussed orientalism, that marks the ideological content of Kipling's novel.

Around 1900 the game of espionage is associated with levity, childishness, lack of professionalism, adventurousness, and the art of improvisation; yet at the same time it is framed by large-scale geopolitical issues such as those raised by Childers's jolly yachtsmen. Obviously, the Great Game involves more than open-air adventures. The term itself was coined by one of its most famous victims: Captain Arthur Conolly, who introduced it in his *Journey to the North of India* (1834) and who later lost his life in one of his missions.[18] The game metaphor comes with two major references that serve to close the gap between espionage and civilian life: sports and geopolitics. In both cases the metaphor enables a distancing from actual events that is typical for the self-understanding of the colonial subject. One form of distancing is to adopt a bird's-eye view of political conflicts, an approach that marks Halford J. Mackinder's take on geopolitics. Mackinder located his "pivot area"—the geopolitically most central region—right in the middle of the Eurasian continent, that is, in the principal playground of the Great Game (Mackinder 1904).[19] The totalizing and homogenizing geopolitical gaze is focused on large-scale territories: "Geopolitics is a new way of seeing international politics as a unified worldwide scene" (Ó Tuathail, Dalby, and Routledge 1998, 16). What turns geopolitics into a "game," then, is not the lack of seriousness with which it is pursued but the abstract modeling of space. The "greatness" of the Great Game consists of this global dimension that is no longer concerned with valleys and villages but with populations and cultures.

The geopolitical gaze disregards localized threats to specific borders in favor of generic "margins" and "heartlands," as Kipling's contemporary Mackinder has it. In this perspective, India's unstable northern frontier is nothing but a particularly sensitive region at the turbulent periphery of the giant empire. From the perspective of the Kims, Creightons, Montgomeries, and pundits roaming and exploring the area, on the other hand, northern India is a labyrinthine, adventurous, dangerous space with its own complex local logic. Thus the Great Game implies two very different, indeed mutually incompatible concepts of space: the global view of geopolitics and the local perspective of the spy.[20] For T. E. Lawrence, this tension between large-scale colonial politics and local claims to sovereignty will result in a political and personal tragedy.

By contrast, Kim embodies the other ludic dimension of the Great Game. As Feroza Jussawalla puts it, he "is simply in it for the adventure and fun" (Jussawalla 1998, 118). To him, the secret war is a kind of athletic competition, and the mortal danger it entails is a thrilling risk. Scouting manuals of the day tend to describe scouts as both courageous and cautious, given that a dead or injured scout is of no use to anybody (Henderson 1915). But while real scouts seek to avoid contact with the enemy at all costs, Kipling's protagonists move about with the instinctive sureness of sleepwalkers. Any danger is quickly overcome by means of an improvised ruse (which normally tends to come with a comical effect, for example, when the Babu fools the Russian agents or Kim engineers the arrest of the fakirs who are planning to kill Mahbub). In *Kim* the games of scouts and spies contain neither tragedy nor risk. All possible threats and risks are defused by playful irony; the enemy is an object of ridicule rather than of fear or hatred. This is how a child can become the hero of the intelligence game.

Around the turn of the last century, intelligence is modeled as a child's game. Kipling's friend Lord Baden-Powell, himself on spying missions in Germany, praises the game of hide-and-seek as an excellent preparation for intelligence work. Before the shock of the First World War, espionage is a form of higher amusement, a gentlemanly game of wit and subterfuge. Baden-Powell describes it vividly in his little book *My Adventures as a Spy*. The lovable dilettantism of the spy trade is evident in its fuzzy results: in his booklet Baden-Powell proudly presents sketches of leaves and butterflies containing the hidden outlines of a fortress (figure 10). He subsequently emerged as the most outspoken proponent of a pedagogy merging war, espionage, civic education, and the idea of fairness in sports: the Boy Scout idea. During the Second Boer War, while trapped in Mafeking for seven months, he compared the siege to a cricket match and let

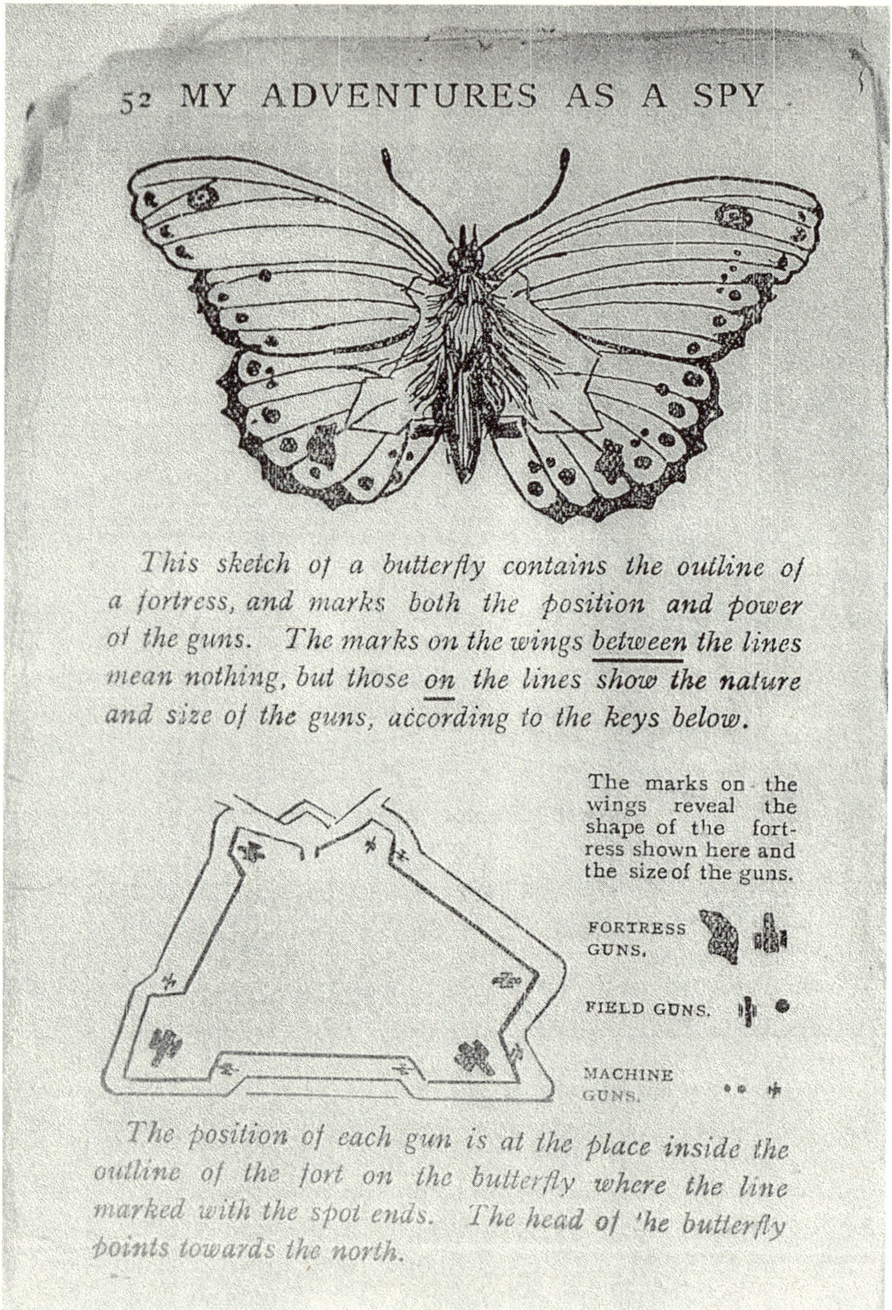

52 MY ADVENTURES AS A SPY

This sketch of a butterfly contains the outline of a fortress, and marks both the position and power of the guns. The marks on the wings between the lines mean nothing, but those on the lines show the nature and size of the guns, according to the keys below.

The marks on the wings reveal the shape of the fortress shown here and the size of the guns.

FORTRESS GUNS.

FIELD GUNS.

MACHINE GUNS.

The position of each gun is at the place inside the outline of the fort on the butterfly where the line marked with the spot ends. The head of the butterfly points towards the north.

Figure 10. A spy sketch by Robert Baden-Powell (1857–1941), founder of the Boy Scouts, cartographer in India, and secret agent who spied on German fortifications. The butterfly, a ruse to fool his captors in case of an arrest, conceals a sketch of a fortress (Baden-Powell, 1915).

his enemies know that he was having "a very enjoyable game" (quoted in Ferguson 2002, 274). Inspired by Kipling's heroes Kim and Mowgli, Baden-Powell envisions the Boy Scout as an athletic and adventurous civil servant. He demands physical fitness, team spirit, independence, fairness, a sense of duty, and unquestioned submission to the rules of the game (and war, he declares, is a game). The goal of this apparent civilizing of war is to fashion characters in the mold of the gentleman spy: "A good spy—no matter which country he serves—is *of necessity* a brave and valuable fellow" (Baden-Powell 1915, 28; emphasis in the original). Rather than facing the realities of war, the harshness of colonialism, and the evil ploys of espionage, this public school games ethic recasts them as adventurous field trips in exotic countries.[21]

Obviously, this vision of espionage doesn't encompass the fundamentally tragic or "dirty" dimensions of deceit, treason, and abandoned loyalties. Only the First World War would excise all notions of nobility from the spy trade. Hannah Arendt interpreted this ideological self-fashioning of the imperial subject as the realization of a pubertal fantasy. Despite all administrative efficiency and war-related violence, the colonial subjects remain trapped in their self-image as "dragon slayers who went enthusiastically into far and curious lands to strange and naive peoples to slay the numerous dragons that had plagued them for centuries" (Arendt 2004, 272). Imperialism, Arendt claims, rested on the shoulders of civil servants who pictured themselves as Kim or Colonel Creighton; the two "key figures in this system are the bureaucrat on the one side and the secret agent on the other" (ibid., 280). The seductive purposelessness of Kim's never-ending Great Game, the love of playing it for its own sake, Arendt points out, was part and parcel of an ideological illusion. The enchanting figure of Kim degenerates into "the vulgar duplicity of a spy," and the enchanted players of the Great Game "are duly cheated when a few decades later they met the players of the game of totalitarianism" (ibid., 282). But while it lasted, this illusion, whose most powerful literary voice was Kipling's, tempted two generations of Britons to serve the empire by joining a game that never was. Among Kipling's readers, the best and most tragic was T. E. Lawrence.

3 The Partisan, the Traitor

Lawrence in Arabia

With one of the most successful agents of the late empire, Thomas Edward Lawrence—better known as "Lawrence of Arabia"—there is a marked change of terrain and tone (figure 11). He does not move around the labyrinthine spaces of Childers's Wadden Sea or Kipling's colorful India; his theater of operations is the desert, Borges's *other* labyrinth. It is neither overcrowded nor mysterious but an empty, barren space, and Lawrence's task is not to explore but to tactically and strategically exploit it. In this terrain the Great Game of spaces and frontiers acquires the bitter taste of colonial realpolitik, and the adventure ends in the acrimony of inevitable betrayal. But what is so fascinating about Lawrence is not only his work as an agent of the British Empire but also, above all, the fact that he subsequently described it in a highly perplexing literary text: his war memoirs, *The Seven Pillars of Wisdom.* The media persona—the celebrated, professionally marketed "Lawrence of Arabia"—is of less interest than Lawrence as the author of one of the most ambivalent and complex texts to emerge from the secret war.

Lawrence first arrived in the Middle East in 1909. He returned in 1911 to participate in the excavations at Carchemish and then, at the behest of the British military, to prepare a detailed map of the Sinai—the latter in preparation for a possible campaign against the Ottoman Empire. At the outbreak of the First World War his cartographic skills ensured his employment at the Geographical Section of the General Staff in Lon-

Figure 11. T. E. Lawrence (1888–1935) in Arab dress (1919). Photograph by Harry Chase, Imperial War Museum QT 2217.

don; his knowledge of the Middle East, in turn, prompted his transfer to Cairo Military Intelligence and later to the Arab Bureau. Here, Lawrence emerged as a dedicated supporter of plans to fan the growing Arab insurrection against the Ottomans. In 1916, he was sent as military adviser and liaison officer to rebellious Arab tribes; in due course he turned into an unofficial military planner and leader of the insurrection. For two years he had a commanding role in the successful Arab partisan war in the Hejaz—two years of extreme exertions, permanent marches, dogged negotiations with tribal leaders and colonial officers, and occasional skirmishes with Ottoman troops. He was instrumentally involved in the capture of Wejh, Aqaba, and Damascus. His return to Europe in 1918 was marred by his disillusionment over the peace negotiations at Versailles, in which he unsuccessfully tried to promote Arab interests. In 1919 he started work on his almost seven-hundred-page account of the Arab campaign, *The Seven Pillars of Wisdom*.[22]

At first glance the account appears to have a clear political agenda. Countering the way the Versailles negotiations had denied to the Arabs the territories they had conquered, the account recalls the independence and glory of the Arab movement "that everyone may see how natural the success was and how inevitable, how little dependent on direction or brain, how much less on the outside assistance of the few British. *It was an Arab war waged and led by Arabs for an Arab aim in Arabia*" (T. E. Lawrence 1991, 23; emphasis added). But Lawrence's book, printed at his own expense and initially only available to friends and subscribers, hardly qualifies as a political pamphlet, given how its complex ambiguities undermine the prerequisite heroism.[23] E. M. Forster succinctly described *Seven Pillars* as "granular," "a succession of items which . . . have some sort of intervals between them" (A. W. Lawrence 1962, 58, 61). Despite its overly precise renditions of minor conflicts within the Arab camp, endless camel rides, accidents, diseases, and squabbles with various Bedouin tribes, all of which bear the mark of the notebooks Lawrence kept during the campaign, *Seven Pillars* does not furnish a complete account, not only because it limits itself to a sequence of unconnected scenes but also because it keeps pointing out its own gaps, which contain something unspeakable that was elided although it should have been put into words: "Our life is not summed up in what I have written (*there are things not to be repeated in cold blood for very shame*); but what I have written was in and of our life" (T. E. Lawrence 1991, 31; emphasis added). This mixture of shame and exhibitionism characterizes the text as a whole. Not all can and should be said, but rather than merely concealing matters, the concealment itself is emphasized with painstaking accuracy. Lawrence's wartime memoirs are marked by a structure of the *secretum*—an inscribed secret that contains both the admission and the concealment of treason.

Geopolitics and Partisan War

In October 1916, when Lawrence joined the insurgent Arabs led by the grand sharif of Mecca, Hussein ibn Ali el-Aun, and his sons, the

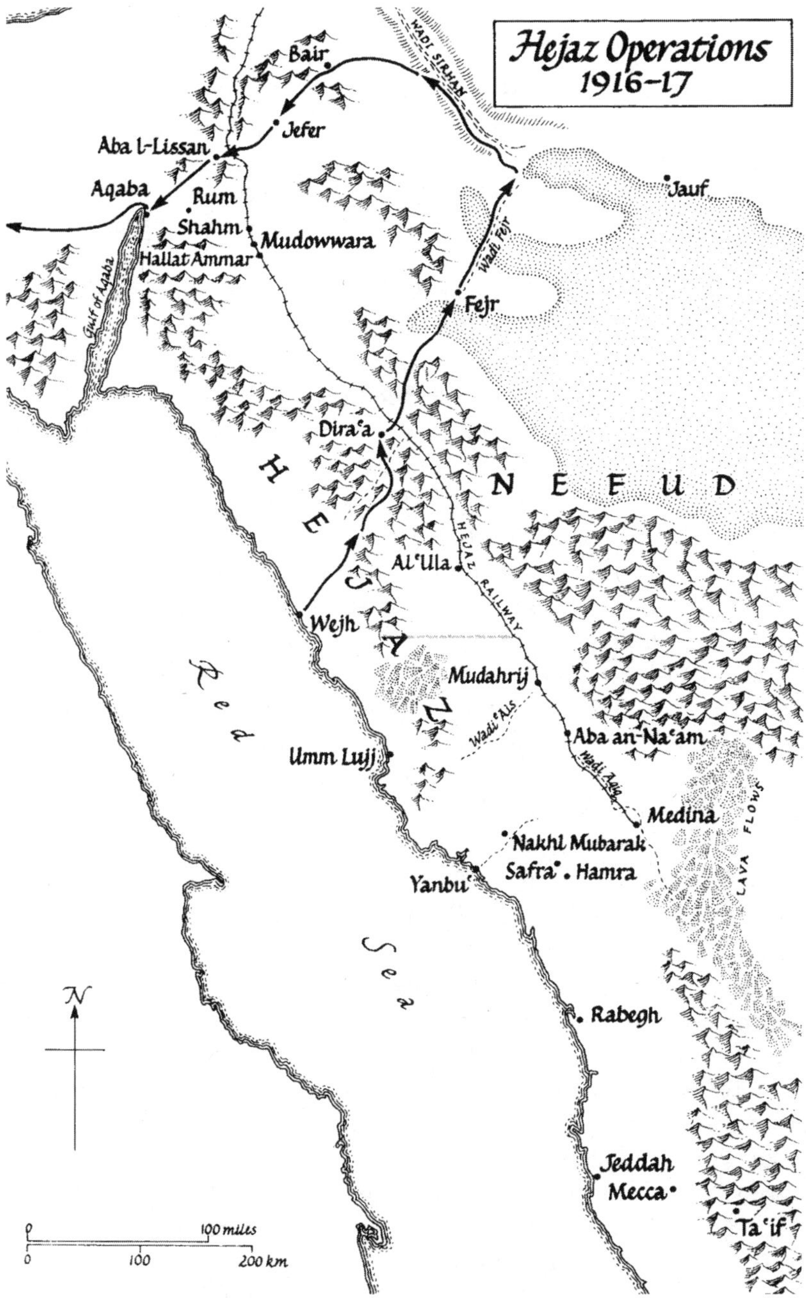

Figure 12. Map of the Hejaz operations undertaken by Feisal's troops from Wejh to Aqaba, an Ottoman port on the Red Sea. Lawrence proposed that the Arabs start from Wejh and cross the desert to attack Aqaba from the land side, not the heavily fortified sea side. The Arabs surprised the Ottomans and captured the port. Copyright © The National Archives, London.

Turks had already been driven from Mecca, Jidda, and Rabegh. *The Seven Pillars of Wisdom* records that he undertook the journey on his own initiative while on leave from the Arab Bureau; in reality Lawrence was on a secret intelligence mission to obtain reliable information concerning the goals of the uprising as well as topographical data of military importance (the photos, complete with precise geographical notations, are on display in the Imperial War Museum in London). The second part of his mission was to act as a liaison officer and to influence the Arab tactics against the Turks in accordance with British interests.[24] Lawrence's first piece of advice sets the stage for the entire strategy: he persuades the Arabs led by Emir Feisal to abstain from taking Medina, has British arms delivered to Rabegh, and instructs the insurgents to capture Wejh instead. As a result the isolated Turkish garrison is forced to rely on the Hejaz railroad to maintain contact with Turkish-held territories. Lawrence is now in a position to develop his famous partisan tactics that shunned direct confrontations and instead relied on sabotage and scouting skills. He blows up the Hejaz railroad tracks and restricts himself to minor raids. After a march covering six hundred kilometers, the Arabs succeed in storming Aqaba from the rear—an achievement that ranks as Lawrence's most celebrated stroke of genius. The map illustrating his route offers a glimpse of the extensive, space-consuming tactics designed to avoid sieges and battles in favor of prolonged marches and sudden attacks (figure 12). Rapid raids and immediate retreats enable Feisal's troops to capture Tafileh, surround Dera'a, and finally defeat the retreating Ottoman Fourth Army in the horrendous massacre outside Damascus. *The Seven Pillars of Wisdom* concludes with the entry into Damascus—as did Lawrence's mission in the Middle East.

Yet from the very outset Lawrence's military genius and the courage of the Arab revolt play out against the background of a decision that undermined Arab aspirations for political independence: the Sykes-Picot Agreement. Already in 1916, prior to the insurrection and the subsequent British intervention, the British diplomat Mark Sykes and his French counterpart François Georges-Picot had in anticipation of a successful uprising defined the British and French spheres of influence in the Middle East. In other words, the Arab independence Lawrence fought for had been betrayed from the very beginning. Following the liberation of the Hejaz and the occupation of Damascus, Mesopotamia (today's Iraq) and Jordan were to be subject to British rule; France was allocated Syria, Lebanon, and southwestern Turkey; and Palestine was to be an Allied Condominium.[25] The Sykes-Picot Agreement was basically a map—blue for France and red for the British Empire—showing how in anticipation of its downfall the Ot-

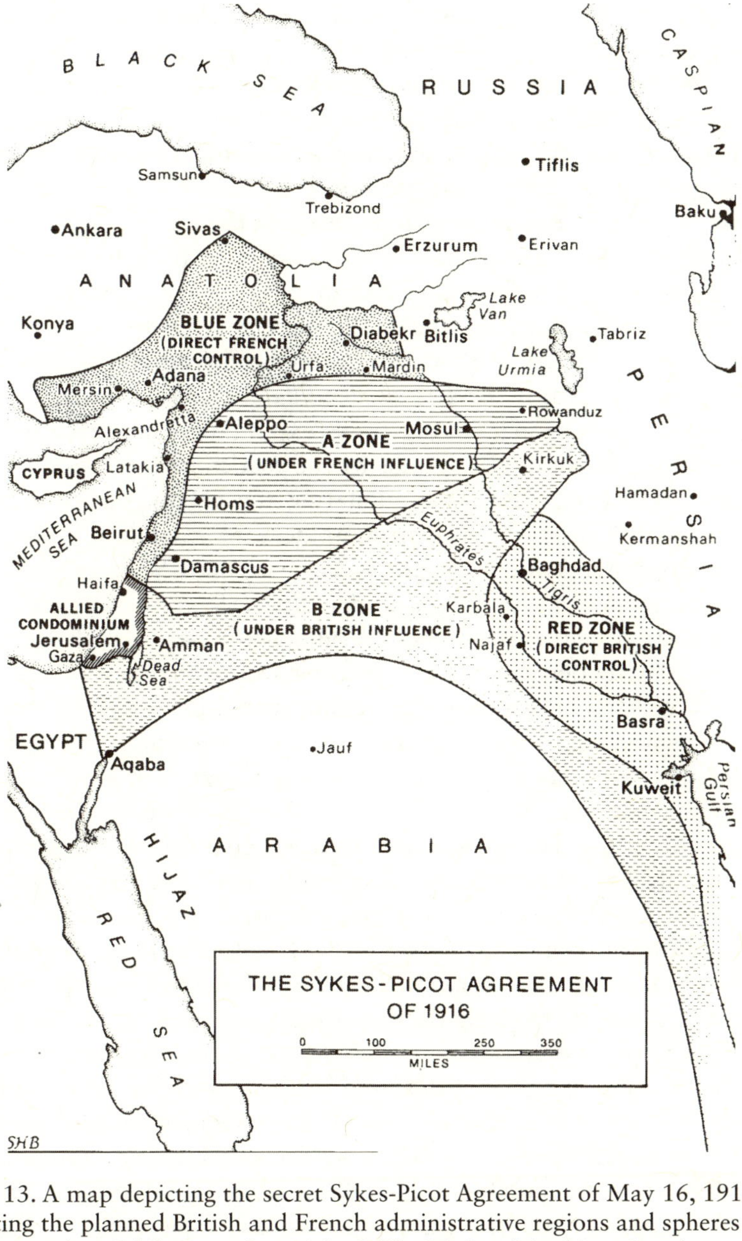

Figure 13. A map depicting the secret Sykes-Picot Agreement of May 16, 1916, indicating the planned British and French administrative regions and spheres of influence in the Middle East. Copyright © The National Archives, London.

toman Empire had already been divvied up by the colonial powers.[26] The map symbolizes the willingness of the Great Game to override local knowledge and local interests in favor of geopolitical abstractions (figure 13). Sykes-Picot is Lawrence's political and moral burden: he is aware of the agreement even before he joins the Arabs; and while he may enthusiastically support the uprising and contribute to its success, he is conscious of the fact that he is betraying the Arab cause. The colonial tension between geopolitics and local knowledge, imperial rule and local self-government that Lawrence is caught up in foreshadows the conflict of loyalties that will shape the political in the twentieth century: treason.

Leaving aside the geopolitical tension that characterizes imperial politics, Lawrence's military approach to space is truly remarkable. He is the twentieth century's first theoretician of irregular warfare. His partisan war is a war of scouts and intelligence that centers on the reconnaissance and exploitation of space. The tactics he develops in the Hejaz are—to quote the subtitle of *The Seven Pillars of Wisdom*—a "triumph" of the local over the global, an ingenious exploitation of both terrain and Arab mentality. In marked contrast to the tactics of the Western Front, the Arabs are focused not on annihilating the enemy but on conquering space itself: "Their aim was geographical, to extrude the Turk from all Arabic-speaking lands in Asia" (T. E. Lawrence 1991, 191). This becomes apparent in Lawrence's counterdraft to the Sykes-Picot Agreement, a remarkable map featuring spheres of influence with blurred boundaries rather than clearly demarcated occupied territories (figure 14). This is the basis for the war of liberation Carl Schmitt will call "telluric" (Schmitt 2007, 20): a war fueled by the emotional ties to a home territory that has to be cleansed of occupiers. It is a pure war of space in which, as Lawrence emphasizes, casualties are not necessary as long as the occupiers are expelled: "The Arabs fought for freedom, and that was a pleasure to be tasted only by a man alive. Posterity was a chilly thing to work for" (T. E. Lawrence 1991, 191). As in the case of Sun Tzu, this calls for a highly economical use of military force.[27] Employing tactics of sabotage and small, unnerving raids, Lawrence focused on the destruction of material by systematically destroying the Hejaz railroad. Since his side lacked the capacity to mount a defense, there must not be anything worth defending: no positions, no weapons, no food supplies. The most important quality of the Arab troops was spatial dispersion. Their permanent movement forced the Turks to expand their defensive lines across the entire occupied territory of "perhaps one hundred and forty thousand square miles. And how would the Turks defend all that? No doubt by a trench line . . . but suppose we were (as we might be) an influence, an idea, a thing intangible,

Figure 14. A map of the Middle East presented to the British Cabinet in 1918 shows Lawrence's marking of the regions and spheres of influences as envisaged by the Arabs. Note the sparing use of boundary lines. The British administrative zone (under Abdullah's rule), the Arab region under the British influence, and the independent Arab territory under Feisal are marked by different color shadings and lack clearly drawn boundaries. The map also indicates an Armenian territory, a Palestine under international administration, and a Lebanon administered by France. The dotted line bears the inscription: "No foreign power other than Great Britain to be allowed any voice in the government of the country south of this line." Copyright © The National Archives, London.

invulnerable, without front or back, drifting about like a gas?" (ibid., 192). Lawrence deploys the expanse of space itself against the Turks; its emptiness—as opposed to force or material—is the true weapon of the Arabs. Such mobility turns the desert into a "smooth space" (Deleuze and Guattari 1987), an empty surface whose only measure of size is speed.

However, highly mobile tactics, knowledge of the terrain, and averting direct confrontations are not, as Liddell Hart argues, an early form of the "indirect approach" but rather an application of scouting principles to the entire force (see Liddell Hart 1937, chap. 9). Successfully spying on enemy troops precludes direct enemy contact. Patrols and reconnaissance parties, Henderson writes, "seek to obtain their information without being observed, and are not intended to fight but to elude the enemy" (Henderson 1915, 11). Lawrence, in effect, merges scout and warrior, or secret agent and commander:

> The corollary of such a rule was perfect "intelligence," so that we could plan in certainty. The chief agent must be the general's head; and his understanding must be faultless, leaving no room for chance. Morale, if built on knowledge, was broken by ignorance. When we knew all about the enemy we should be comfortable. We must take more pains in the service of news than any regular staff. (T. E. Lawrence 1991, 194)

Lawrence combines spatial reconnaissance, obstruction of enemy communication and supply lines, and ambush tactics into a guerrilla war in which space is an ally and intelligence the most valuable resource. His Arab partisan war merges tactics and intelligence into a type of war that is as fleeting as a breath of air.

Politics of the Agent

In light of Lawrence's commanding role in the uprising, the question arises: Why were the Arabs willing to accept him as a leader in the first place, rather than avoiding him as an agent in the pay of their dubious British allies? If Edward Said is right to rhetorically ask whether there ever was "a native fooled by the blue or green-eyed Kims and Lawrences who passed among the inferior races as agent adventurers" (Said, in Kipling 1987, 44), we may add that it is even more astonishing that the Arabs came to *respect* him as a key adviser. The fictitious Kim was able to draw on his natural knack for languages to pass as a native, but the real-life Lawrence was forced to resort to a different form of cultural adaptation. While Kim was born and bred in India, Lawrence came to Arabia as an adult, hence there was nothing natural in the ostentatious "Arabness" with which he tried to adapt to the Hashemites. His adaptation is both highly reflexive and deeply phantasmal, for whereas Kim can easily assume all conceivable cultural roles because he always already "is" what he plays, Lawrence is fully aware that he is a complete outsider: "I was sent to these Arabs as a stranger, unable to think their thoughts or subscribe their beliefs . . . I could at least conceal my own, and pass among them without evident friction, neither a discord nor a critic but an unnoticed influence" (T. E. Lawrence 1991, 20).

For Lawrence cultural mimicry is less the adoption of a new cultural identity than a form of self-erasure, a cleansing of one's own identity. What separates him from the classic orientalist desire is his awareness that the Arabs whose language he speaks, whose clothes he wears, and whose war he advances are nothing but his own phantasm. As he admits to himself and to his readers, his treacherous balancing act between the Arabs and his British superiors is undertaken in pursuit of a *fantasy* of "Arabness" culminating in the cultural and political unity and independence of all Arab tribes. He describes himself as a political dreamer—or, more precisely, as a political actor bent on translating a phantasm into reality:

> All men dream: but not equally. Those who dream by night in the dusty recesses of their minds wake in the day to find that it was vanity: but the dreamers of the day are dangerous men, for they may act their dream with open eyes, to make it possible. This I did. I meant to make a new nation, to restore a lost influence, to give twenty millions of Semites the foundations on which to build an inspired dream-palace of their national thoughts. (T. E. Lawrence 1991, 24 and following)

War and politics are revealed as dreams put into action. History, Lawrence implies, amounts to acting out phantasms; in the final analysis it consists of transforming dreams and fictions into reality—in this particular case, the dream of a cultural and political unity that the Arabs lack but are now being inspired to achieve.

But Lawrence knows better than anyone else that "the Arabs" do not exist. "A first difficulty of the Arab movement," he notes laconically, "was to say who the Arabs were" (T. E. Lawrence 1991, 33). They are little more than quarreling tribes that are suddenly expected to set aside their differences and dedicate themselves to a common goal, "a manufactured people" as "unstable as water" (ibid., 42). The only thing that unites them is their language and, Lawrence adds, a proclivity for abstractions that fuels both their appreciation of the desert and their nonpictorial religion. "Children of the idea" (ibid.), he calls them, ascetics, idealists without an ideal. Lawrence's strategy initially consists of a frictionless, almost unnoticed exertion of influence. He does not make decisions—he lets them be made, but in accordance with his interests. His most important move involves the choice of leader. When he joins the Hashemites, they are still being led by the old Sharif Hussein, emir of Mecca. Unwilling to accept Hussein's leadership, Lawrence sets out in search of a younger and above all more charismatic figure. His chosen alternate is Hussein's third son, Feisal. It is he rather than one of his elder brothers who will become the leader of the great uprising that will carry him all the way to Damascus and then on to the peace talks in Versailles. Feisal's military skills, however, appear to have been of less importance to Lawrence than his beauty and prophetlike charisma: "I felt at first glance that this was the man who would bring the Arab revolt to full glory. Feisal looked very tall and pillar-like" (ibid., 91). Lawrence wastes no time in pitching his strategy to Feisal; already during their first encounter he suggests that instead of falling back to Yenbo or laying siege to Medina, Feisal should march on Aqaba with a view toward taking Damascus and asserting his claim to power in Syria. This momentous piece of advice foreshadows Lawrence's role as Feisal's adviser, mouthpiece, and right hand, but also as the one who will constantly remind him of the original mission. Lawrence leads the uprising—but in the shadow of the man he counsels and influences.

Lawrence must have intuitively grasped that he can exert his "power" as an agent only by remaining hidden behind the image of the official leader. Especially in light of his deliberate self-erasure, the case of Lawrence demonstrates that the effectiveness of agents depends on the degree to which they act as a medium rather than as a leader. Lawrence is the channel that links the Arabs to the British, Feisal to General Edmund Allenby; he is an intertribal communicator and, ultimately, the translator and voice for the Arab independence that European politicians choose to ignore. But Lawrence is a medium, hence he does not speak (for) himself, he does not act in his own name, and he does not pursue his own interests. The principle guiding this policy of self-erasure is described in the *Arab Bulletin* of 1917: "Your ideal position is when you are present and not noticed . . . Wave a Sherif in front of you like a banner and hide your own mind and person."[28] Feisal is brandished by Lawrence so that he may hide himself and his intentions. Indeed, Lawrence's conduct brings to mind that old staple of secret European diplomacy, the privy councillor, the scheming éminence grise whose great influence is due to the fact that he shuns the limelight. This does not mean, however, that he is plotting to subvert or overthrow his master. On the contrary, Lawrence believes in Feisal and remains loyal to him, even during the disastrous negotiations in Paris after the end of World War I. In the mold of the secret councillor he sees himself as a "servant" who serves his master best by correcting, interpreting, and occasionally manipulating his instructions. Feisal is the figurehead—that is, he is the outward appearance, a representative of the power exerted by Lawrence.

The basic prerequisite for a successful Arab campaign as well as for their political autonomy is their national unity *as Arabs*. However, what it means to be an Arab is precisely what Lawrence intends to demonstrate to the Arabs by imitating them. The goal of his cultural mimicry is not to trick the Arabs into believing that he is one of them but "to imitate them so well that they spuriously imitate him back again" (T. E. Lawrence 1991, 31). It is, in Kaja Silverman's words, a strategy of "double mimesis," a cultural masquerade that apes the other to present to him as in a mirror what he *could be*.[29] The objective, Lawrence warns, is not disguise, which (as in Kim's many metamorphoses and costume changes) is nothing but the attempt to assume a false identity by dressing up as someone else. Though he may have disdained British uniforms in favor of Arab garments—as in the photo from 1919 (figure 11)—Lawrence emphasizes that he was not out to hide his Englishness. The Arab dress, which has become emblematic for his public persona, is not an attempt to look like an Arab but a signal that he is on their side. The arguably most famous photo of Lawrence, then, is not a deception but an enactment addressed mainly to Britain and the British press. Deception is only used against an enemy—as in the traumatic event in Dera'a when Lawrence was arrested, tortured, and raped by Turks who took him for a fair Circassian and failed to realize whom they had caught:[30]

> Disguise [Lawrence notes his *Twenty-Seven Articles*] is not advisable . . . At the same time if you can wear Arab kit when with the tribes you will acquire their trust and intimacy to a degree impossible in uniform . . . You will be like an actor in a foreign theatre . . . Complete success, which is when the Arabs forget your strangeness . . . is perhaps only attainable in character . . . If you wear Arab things wear the best . . . Dress like a Sherif, if they agree to it. (Quoted in Liddell Hart 1937, 111–12)

Lawrence stresses the theatrical aspects of mimicry by invoking the double meaning of theater as stage and battleground. The theatricality of the agent is grounded in method acting: it is an internalized acting-out of an Arab identity that first needs to be emotionally experienced or constructed. But what is presented by the actor is not just any form of Arab identity but its most noble, elevated rank: "Dress like a Sherif." Lawrence doesn't want to get by as an inconspicuous spy; he wants to play—discreetly, yet efficiently—a leading role. However, this role—

represented by the garments Feisal hands to him—clearly requires the consent of the imitated: "Dress like a Sherif, *if they agree to it.*" In other words, Lawrence's Arab dress is not a form of disguise but an instrument of mutual recognition.

Nonetheless, Lawrence's "double mimesis" is neither a program of postcolonial self-reflection nor, as Said would have it, a performance of the orientalist wish-fantasy. It is instead a paradoxical and highly idiosyncratic attempt to both comply with *and* subvert his colonial mission to deploy the Arabs against the Turks but then to withhold the promised independence. From the outset Lawrence is caught between conflicting loyalties: the British want him to organize the uprising of the Hejaz tribes against the Ottoman Empire by holding out the prospect of political independence, yet in light of the Sykes-Picot Agreement the latter appears to be no more than a British lie employed to rally the Arab tribes. Tormented by shame and fueled by daydreams of an "Arabia" that does not yet exist, Lawrence turns the inconsistency—or, rather, mendacity—of his mission into an ambiguous political strategy. Increasingly Lawrence tends to pursue Arab interests rather than those of his British superiors, yet he maintains contact with the latter and implements most of their directives. Caught in the predicament of conflicting agendas, he feels that he has come to betray both sides.

Lawrence—the "successful trickster" (T. E. Lawrence 1991, 26), the agent who crosses borders and in part turns against his own country—is a fundamentally lonely figure: "I had dropped one form and not taken on the other . . . with a resulting feeling of intense loneliness in life" (ibid., 32). In the end the very self-effacement, which he had both dreaded and desired and which allowed him to consort with the Arabs, leaves him the hollow, burned-out receptacle of a glorious reputation he himself considers shameful. Since his power had consisted of his invisibility and mirrorlike qualities, it comes as no surprise that he would experience his postwar fame and visibility as an almost unbearable lack of power—which it no doubt was. As hero and public figure (largely created and promoted by the writer and journalist Lowell Thomas) Lawrence can do little more than participate in futile negotiations, translate, and work as Winston Churchill's special Middle Eastern adviser. As mentioned, his vision of an Arab empire is contained in a map that, significantly, features shaded colors and open boundaries rather than clearly demarcated territories—a counterdraft, as it were, to the geopolitical games of Sykes-Picot. His wartime account *The Seven Pillars of Wisdom* bears all the traces of the ambiguities of Lawrence's contradictory role. He is, as Borges might have put it, a further variation on the theme of hero and traitor.

The Poetics of Shame

If the agent does not speak in his own name but always in that of foreign powers, then what is the position assumed by the narrator of *The Seven Pillars of Wisdom*? Where does Lawrence stand? What gesture underlies the publication and the structure of this text? The principal mark of this strange, highly dispersive narrative is its constant reflection on the possibility, and impossibility, of speaking. Novels like *Kim* and *The Riddle of the Sands* offer designs and programs for a politics of secrecy; they are determined to mobilize a certain type of civil servant whose work guarantees the survival of colonial rule. But while the Great Game had to rely on this programmatic fiction to wage the secret war, Lawrence's book seeks to deconstruct this function: it is a piece of fiction that—in line with Borges's understanding of fiction—is fully aware of the contingent and constructed nature of the version it is narrating. The text itself stages the secrecy, deception, and dissimulation it keeps alluding to. Lawrence announces in his preface that he is going to tell neither the "true story" of the Arab uprising nor even the one the Arabs themselves would tell, but merely his own version, "a personal narrative pieced out of memory" (T. E. Lawrence 1991, xi). But right from the outset this version is already tinted, distorted, and fractured by the ambiguous position Lawrence assumes. It is the position of the hero-traitor: he is telling the story of an event he participated in, yet the manner in which he participated is—to use one of Lawrence's favorite words—"unspeakable."

Given that Arab interests had already been undermined by the Sykes-Picot Agreement, each decision, each goal achieved, amounts to a betrayal of either Arab or British interests. In fact, Lawrence informs Feisal of the secret agreement; the capture of Aqaba and Lawrence's insistence that Feisal enter Damascus prior to Allenby's arrival are attempts to strengthen the Arab position for future negotiations. With the release in 1968 of the files and cables exchanged between Lawrence and his superiors in the Foreign Office, it has become possible to offer a more informed assessment of the historical facts underlying *The Seven Pillars of Wisdom*. Many of Lawrence's alleged intuitions or inspirations turn out to be military orders he was given—or, at the very least, as fortunate convergences of British and Arab interests.[31] The key difference between the documents and the *Seven Pillars* version of things thus lies in the transformation of remote control into self-control. Lawrence's memoir turns decisions that in historical fact were subject to large-scale geopolitical imperatives into decisions made by the Arabs for their own benefit. In other words, Lawrence ascribes to the Arabs an independence from British manipulation they in fact never enjoyed.

In the same vein Lawrence endows his own position with more decision-making ability than he probably ever had. Nevertheless, he openly depicts his actions as a betrayal of both sides: "Here were the Arabs believing me, Allenby and Clayton trusting me, my bodyguard dying for me: and I began to wonder if all established reputations were founded, like mine, on fraud" (T. E. Lawrence 1991, 562). *Seven Pillars* is a document of betrayal, an embarrassing, painful, and idiosyncratic expression of shame—yet it is an unconcealed shame that ostentatiously puts itself on display, reminiscent of Vincent Moon's tale in Borges's "The Shape of the Sword." Moon's final words, "Now, despise me" (Borges 1998, 142), could be an epitaph for Lawrence's narrative. He seems to beg his readers to turn their admiration of his public figure into contempt. However, as Gilles Deleuze notes, Lawrence's ongoing display of shame keeps mutating into pride, into an exhibitionism compelled to revolve around the "unspeakable": "Never before has shame been sung like this, in so proud and haughty a manner" (Deleuze 1997, 120). One of the most symptomatic statements occurs toward the end: "There was a craving to be famous; and a horror of being known to like being known" (T. E. Lawrence 1991, 563). He claims to fear nothing more than his own thirst for glory, yet he also stresses that it was the true motivation behind his words and actions. Another symptom is the reference to the obvious secret underlying both his text and his passion for Arabia: his homosexuality. Hints are generously spread across the text: the dedication to the mysterious "S.A.," the remark in one of the concluding chapters that in the final analysis his motives were exclusively personal, and the puzzling introductory chapter that intimates the topic of gay love in cold nocturnal deserts only to stress a few paragraphs later the abnegation of all physical desire and the purity of Arab ascesis. "Lawrence of Arabia," the great hero glamorized by Lowell Thomas, does not shirk from admitting that he was driven by vanity and did not always believe in the cause, but at the same time he insists with great pathos that he sacrificed himself for a cause that wasn't his own (ibid., 551). Lawrence wavers between confession and concealment, triumph and failure, pride and shame—but in such a way that confessions appear as concealment, triumphs as failures, pride as shame. It is no coincidence that Borges's "Three Versions of Judas" cites Lawrence, in its motto, as a crown witness for the dialectic intoxication of the hero-traitor that leads him to discover punishment and degradation as the only certain thing: "There seemed a certainty in degradation" (ibid., 564).

However, this certainty in degradation, sought for by Lawrence in real life, is not available to the text. It is not centered on a subject in control of speech and memory: instead it disintegrates into "intensive singularities" that keep the narrative from any "semiotic or narrative explanation or logic" (Aldama 2000, 66).[32] The net of mutually incompatible versions neatly unfolded in Borges's poetics of treason is here, as it were, condensed into a poetics of shame that fuses utterance and concealment, signification and its erasure. The hero-traitor who in "unspeakable" ways makes history is caught between the loneliness of his radically solitary decisions and a servitude that according to Hannah Arendt makes him the victim of "secret forces of history and necessity," of which he is "but a function" (Arendt 2004, 266). This is why the text is so "granular," as E. M. Forster remarked—why it offers neither a narrative continuity nor a coherent identity of an autobiographical subject (see also Kaplan 1995). The text fails to align personal narrative with history, because that which historically and politically turns Lawrence into a hero is that which on a personal level makes him a traitor. Unlike Kipling, Lawrence cannot playfully resolve the tension between the two irreconcilable sides of the Great Game, that is, the grand geopolitical structure on the one hand and local and personal ties on the other. A genius when it comes to tactically exploiting space, Lawrence will fail in the face of the geopolitics of colonialism.

Lawrence, who most likely grew up with books like *Kim* and *The Riddle of the Sands,* is a Kim who has reached adulthood. Leaving behind colonial boyhood dreams of "dragon-slayers" (Arendt) and adventurous gentlemen-spies (Baden-Powell), Lawrence is the first agent of the secret war to realize what kind of sacrifice this war demands: namely, the surrender of one's autonomy when choosing sides. He is the first agent to get entangled in the snares of treason that will come to characterize the twentieth century. In addition, he is the first agent who refuses ludic metaphors when describing the political ambiguities of the Great Game and instead re-creates it as complex, highly self-reflexive textual structure. Nonetheless, the Great Game continues to rely on affirmative fictional depictions like *Kim,* not only because texts such as those by Kipling and Childers are directly involved in modeling and creating the first modern intelligence agencies, but also because they popularize the sporty and playful interpretation of the secret war that will determine the self-understanding of civil servants and secret agents until long after the disappearance of the British Empire. According to John le Carré, even the great traitor Kim Philby is, at bottom, a disappointed imperial gentleman-spy (see the section titled "The Betrayed: *Tinker, Tailor, Soldier, Spy*" in part 6, chapter 3, "The Human Factor").

The spirit of the Great Game is one of spatial reconnaissance aimed at scrutinizing and making tactical use of spaces. Its protagonists are modeled on scouts, traveling diplomats, archaeologists, and ethnologists who explore, describe, and map foreign countries. The genealogy leaves no doubt that the professed interest comes with military and political agendas. The representation of foreign areas and cultures (whether in the shape of maps, novels, or autobiographies) inevitably reveals the gaze of geopolitics and the possibility of colonial intervention. But unlike the dangerous, hostile Cold War spaces cordoned off by the *wall* and the seemingly all-knowing, all-seeing, omnipresent controlling gaze of today's IMINT, the Great Game's space is accessible and has to be deciphered *on site*. However, given how comprehensive satellite coverage effectively does away with all unexplored zones that marked the Great Game, it may seem that the old concept of local reconnaissance has become obsolete. For a long time the notion of local knowledge, so important to colonial intelligence, was considered a thing of the past, a part of old-school spy folklore. In the wake of 9/11 things have changed. Already in the late 1990s there were growing complaints that U.S. intelligence services had withdrawn from many of the world's more inhospitable regions, ranging from Peshawar to Kinshasa. As late as July/August of 2001 an online article by Reuel Marc Gerecht quoted one of the CIA's Middle Eastern experts:

> The CIA probably doesn't have a single truly qualified Arabic-speaking officer of Middle Eastern background who can play a believable Muslim fundamentalist who would volunteer to spend years of his life with shitty food and no women in the mountains of Afghanistan. For Christ's sake, most case officers live in the suburbs of Virginia. We don't do that kind of thing. (Gerecht 2001)

Nowadays universities and intelligence agencies are back at work recruiting and training local agents equipped with the necessary linguistic and cultural skills, the Kims of today. In a political conflict that pits Islamic terrorists against Europe and the United States, the local knowledge and cultural dexterity of the Great Game type of agent is once again an indispensable element of global intelligence (see part 9, chapter 2, "The Future of Enmity"). This reemergence of HUMINT as the core of intelligence work, in combination with the awareness that you have to know and understand your enemy, heralds a fundamental change that goes beyond the domain of secret intelligence. It calls for agents who may be more "old school" than they appear to be. Those sporty, occasionally tragic, yet self-reliant local experts recruited as agents by the British Empire are, today, of more than merely historical interest. They might be models for the intelligence operatives of the twenty-first century.

Part 4

Spies, Male and Female: The First World War and the War of the Sexes

Love and War: The Female Spy

There is no place for politics in the intercourse of the sexes. The *rapport sexuel* may involve personal hatred as much as love, but no enmity. According to Carl Schmitt the *hostilitas* that defines the political has to do with the antagonism between "fighting *collectivities* of people" (Schmitt 1996, 29; emphasis added) rather than with any personal animosity. As a strictly private affair involving two people, the sexual depends on the absence of the political. All the worse, then, when the intimacy of the sexual encounter is marred by the suspicion that more than two may be involved. The intrusion of politics into intimacy raises the specter of a third party, that side or group which the two partners belong to—and which they do not cease to belong to even in the intimacy of the sexual union. When the logic of enmity forces itself upon the relationship between the sexes, the sexual becomes political, just as the political and the martial become sexual. It was, not coincidentally, the First World War, the "great seminal catastrophe of the century" (Kennan 1979, 3) and first "total war," which irreparably damaged the privacy of the *rapport sexuel,* thereby generating one of the most pervading phantasms of the secret war: the female spy. She embodies the phantasm that the most private and intimate encounter could itself turn into a secret arena of politics and become part of the *arcana imperii.* With the euphoric and hysterical outbreak of the war in August 1914, the front (including all the ubiquitous machinations of the enemy) appeared to invade civilian life. Long before Britain, France,

Germany, and Austria established professional intelligence agencies, and with no evidence of foreign agents spying on the nations at war, the belligerent populations became obsessed with the idea that anybody could be an enemy spy. As Erich Mühsam noted in his diary in August 1914:

> The excitement of these days has given rise to veritable mass hysteria. Spies are suspected everywhere. People amass in groups, manhandle the unfortunate victims, and deliver them to the police . . . Again, in the afternoon hundreds dragged a girl to a policeman because somebody had accused her of being a man in disguise. (Mühsam 1994, 102)

No doubt this "espionitis" or collective fear of disguised enemies was a symptom of the frenetic identification of civilians with military events; the front, as it were, invaded the entire society (see Altenhöner 2001; Kloth 2004) and triggered a collective paranoia that did not end with the war. It fueled large-scale illustrated books on spying in the aftermath of World War I. This ubiquitous conspiracist scenario is beautifully illustrated by the page decorations in Paul von Lettow-Vorbeck's voluminous book *Weltkriegsspionage* (*World War Espionage*): conjuring up the image of a world ensnared in the secret tentacles of espionage, the page numbers are surrounded and caught by cobwebs distended between blossoms and thorns, appearance and being, friend and enemy (figure 15). The most remarkable feature of this war hysteria, however, is the degree to which this fear is sexualized. In Mühsam's example, the fear of spies turns into an uncertainty regarding the sex of a randomly picked woman: the simple fact that she is female appears to be a deception. Suddenly, the camouflaged soldier appears behind the alleged civilian; the armed warrior rears his head behind the seductive girl. Women, formerly the very

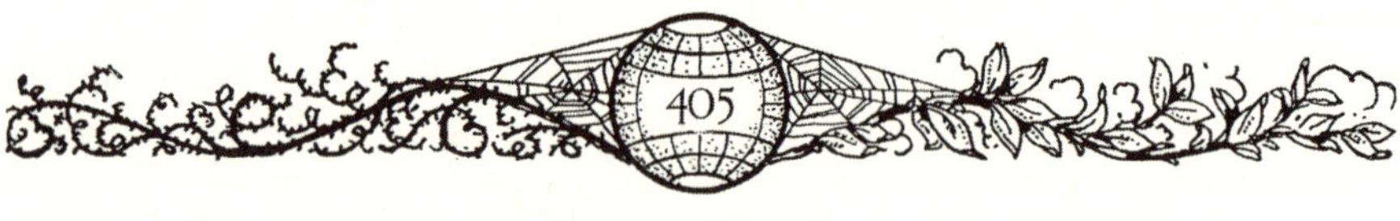

Figure 15. This ornament appears as a running decoration on the pages of Paul von Lettow-Vorbeck's anthology *Die Weltkriegsspionage* (1931). The design of a globe in spiderwebs suggests a world entangled in espionage. Omnipresent spying was a central phantasm of the First World War. The idea was popularized in luxurious coffee table books such as Friedrich Felger and Walter Jost's *Was wir vom Weltkrieg nicht wissen* (*What We Do Not Know About the War,* 1936), first published in 1929, and Lettow-Vorbeck's *Weltkriegsspionage.*

epitome of the private, are now drawn into the martial logic of friend and enemy. They become figures of disguise and deception precisely *as women,* that is, as seemingly apolitical agents of highly political missions. Women become the embodiment of the *secret* side of war and politics.

The figure of the female spy and agent—glamorous and pathetic, seductive and seduced, oscillating between grande dame and prostitute—is a product of the First World War. She is, however, not the brainchild of the classical authors of espionage fiction like John Buchan, whose gentleman-hero, the polyglot and cosmopolitan Richard Hannay, continues to render homage to the old ideal of the imperial agent. In fact, the male world war agents, from Edward Phillips Oppenheim's General Besserley to William Somerset Maugham's Ashenden, hardly go beyond the prewar model established by Childers's sailing sportsman Carruthers or Kipling's childishly playful and explicitly asexual Kim.[1] The female spy, by contrast, is invented by women, not in the realm of fiction but in real life—women like Margaretha Geertruida Zelle, the legendary Mata Hari; the prostitute and aviator Marthe Richer; and the indefatigable Elsbeth Schragmüller, who built up a network of agents for the German General Staff. And she is invented by men who convert the theatrically staged or carefully concealed activities of these women into adventurous, demonic, and highly eroticized narratives—narratives that cost these women their reputation and sometimes even their lives. The figure of the female spy is indebted to fanciful or patriotic life performances that are modeled by literary narratives. Mata Hari, who with extraordinary intuition and clarity of purpose designs her own career and identity to be just such a fiction, is the prime model of an existence that is and wants to be nothing other than appearance, show, and performance—a self-conscious and self-reflexive fiction that in times of war falls prey to the fatal logic of authenticity.

Mata Hari is one model of the female spy—that which involves glamour, seduction, and a comedy of the sexes. The other model is derived from the invisible functionary, the secretary and silent organizer who in times of war replaces the absent men. She is, no doubt, a great deal more effective, but as an expert or specialist, a nondescript switch point, she never transcends the institution she works for. Starting with these complementary models—the great seductress and the little secretary—we can write the subsequent history of all the notorious female spies, though it will on several occasions amount to a mixture of the two. Such a history would range from the femmes fatales of the 1920s (see Horn 2008b) to the Bond Girls of the 1960s and beyond. It would encompass the notorious "loving female agents" who do everything "for love" as well as the coldhearted wife in Len Deighton's trilogy *Game—Set—Match* (1983–85), who betrays both her agent-husband (appropriately named Samson) and MI6. The double phantasm of the woman as seducer/seductress *and* functionary reaches its sad and rarely glamorous nadir with the West German secretaries in Bonn who were ensnared by so-called East German Romeo agents and talked into betraying secrets. It is the most sordid aspect of GDR espionage recalled, not without pride, by the East German spymaster Markus Wolf in his memoirs (Wolf 1997, 123–50). A more complex female figure emerges in Luc Besson's 1990 movie *Nikita,* whose eponymous heroine needs to learn more about makeup than about guns. As a beguiling scene involving the agent (Anne Parillaud) and her instructor (Jeanne Moreau) makes abundantly clear, to become an agent and to become a woman is one and the same thing. The convergence of seduction, femininity, and acting, which was first apparent in the case of Mata Hari, the godmother of the female spy, becomes thoroughly self-reflexive in John le Carré's *The Little Drummer Girl* (1983). Mossad recruits a British actress called Charlie, who as the lover of a PLO terrorist may be able to infiltrate the inner circles of the organization to lay a trap for his brother. Her Israeli handler tempts her with the alluring prospect of acting in the "theatre of the real" rather than on stage. At this point in the secret war nothing—neither Charlie's love of sexual adventure nor her most intimate feelings—can escape the logic of treason.

In due course the two fundamental types of female spies inspired by World War I fictions, the femme fatale and the competent functionary, are blurred. The seductress becomes a technician, warrior, and expert; the clerk, in turn, tends to get embroiled in affairs that make it increasingly difficult to determine who is seducing whom. Moreover, as in the case of the German Romeo agents, men take over the genuinely "feminine" role of seducers. In any case, the female spy represents a fundamental disturbance of the relationship between the sexes, if not of social intercourse itself: Not only does she highlight the theatrical element in the "comedy of the sexes" (Lacan), she also foregrounds the theatricality of erotics and reveals the blind spots in the *rapport sexuel* by merging the secret of this *rapport* with the secret of the political. It is an uncanny mixture, for once the political secret finds its way into the innermost domain of intimate relationships, it changes its own nature as well as that of the conflict it is associated with. Politics and sexuality merge. Once again, the First World War is the seminal scene of this mysterious amalgam that makes it impossible to determine whether desires are exploited and guided by politics, or whether politics is shaped by phobias, phantasms, and sexual desires.

Was die Liebe bei ihr kostet
Zeichnung von K. Sohr

Figure 16. "What Her Love Costs," from Magnus Hirschfeld's *Sexual History of the World War* (1930), shows a woman stealing documents from her lover and slipping them to an accomplice. Translator's note: This illustration was not reproduced in the 1941 English translation.

Klaus Theweleit has provided a compelling account of the sexualization of enmity and politics permeating the war fictions and images of the 1920s (see Theweleit 1987, 2:271–345 and passim). Women—divided into "rifle-women" (Theweleit 1987, 1:70) and syphilitic prostitutes on the one hand, and "brides" devoid of will, name, and life on the other—are the real enemy. They are deindividualized, bestial, and occasionally armed with a phallus or a venereal disease. But worst of all, as "whores dressed up as nurses" (ibid., 1:93) they are not what they seem to be. In this amorphous mass of castrating forces men have to prove the invincibility of their "body armour" as much as their stalwart immunity to seduction. However, the phantasm of the disguised, infectious, and dismembering female opponent is not only, as Theweleit would have it, the defense mounted by a fascist male subject. It also indicates the degree to which the relationship of the sexes has been caught up in war. "Women and diseases as weapons of war" would be an apt summary of this sexualization of politics (see Brack 1931). The female spy is the most dangerous weapon, for femininity is the optimal camouflage in the new dimension of war—a clandestine war that is not waged at the front but marked by the intrusion of an "interested third party," a parasite that feeds off the erotic dyad (see Serres 2007, 79). Where two meet away from the front line, a third is lying in wait (further see Horn 2008b). This "third" haunts the popular tales and illustrations of clueless soldiers enjoying a fatal lovers' tryst; he waits behind the curtain and snatches secret documents from the pocket of a victim lost in the voluptuous embrace of a willing spy, as the illustration from Magnus Hirschfeld's *Sexual History of the World War* indicates (figure 16). While the woman is acting *in front of* the curtain, the man lurks *behind,* coordinating an army of seductive agents or syphilitic whores, transferring the front line into the most intimate and private encounters.

Being or Having a Secret: The Comedy of the Sexes

How are men and women best deployed as spies? According to popular conceptions the female spy always works with and within the medium of sexuality—ranging from passive "sexual dependence" to frigidity and active cunning. This focus on sexuality distinguishes female from male spies; moreover, it implies a histrionic component that marks the basic difference between the sexes in the world of espionage. A text in Lettow-Vorbeck's collection spells it out in all clarity:

> What the male spy can only accomplish by means of cleverness and criminal instinct, the female spy will achieve in a far more direct—and far less restrained—manner. Men use their intellect, women their body; the male spy operates *behind* the scenes, the female spy *in front of* them. Men rely on their powers of intellect, women put their trust in chance and erotic power. (Mühr 1931, 405; emphasis added)

Women "use" their bodies, they rely on "erotic power" and act "*in front of* the scenes." In other words, women indulge in sexual theatrics and stage an erotic performance that awakens desires and captures attention, thereby distracting the attention from the real object of desire—the military secret. Many contemporary illustrations depict dramatically reclining women embracing intoxicated carriers of military secrets while concealed male helpers (or the women themselves) surreptitiously remove—in midact, as it were—a document from an unsuspecting pocket or pour sleeping powder into a glass. While male spies retreat into unobserved shadows, women perform their erotic treachery in the spotlight. He is invisible; she is all show. What makes the phantasm of the female spy so persistent is that she knowingly enacts the "comedic" element at the core of the relationship between the sexes. According to Jacques Lacan, this comedy consists in the asymmetrical desires of the sexes: men want what women are, and women want what men *have*. "These relations [between the sexes] revolve around a being and a having which, since they refer to a signifier, the phallus, have contradictory effects: they give the subject reality in this signifier, on the one hand, but render unreal the relations to be signified, on the other" (Lacan 2006, 582). By staging herself as an alluring erotic secret, the female spy is targeting a secret; as a result the impassioned man may momentarily forget that if he *has* this secret, he can also lose it. Her phallic self-presentation, that is, as something one *has* to have, is not geared toward *being the phallus,* as Lacan would have it, but toward *snatching it.* In this game of having and being, the secret or signifier that everything revolves around assigns a position to each player, as Lacan elaborated in his reading of Poe's "Purloined Letter" (Lacan 2006, 6–48). The game, however, is disturbed by the parasite, the third party that introduces a dramatic asymmetry of knowledge. He issues orders and binds the desire of the women to manipulate her into manipulating her victim; she, in turn, converts the desire for the secret into her erotic theatrics that trap the clueless prey. In the comedy of the sexes the female spy *has* and *is* the secret; the man *has* and *is* nothing.

1 The Female Spy as Hysteric

The image of the female spy as seductress and stealer of secrets is a product of the First World War that emerges (albeit in fantastic and relatively unpractical fashion) in tandem with the gradual institutionalization of intelligence gathering. Secrecy not only becomes an integral part of warfare but also invades the most intimate social junctures. The most prominent suspects are, of all candidates possible, nurses, since they work directly behind the front lines and are particularly apt to gain the wounded soldiers' confidence. While they embody a piece of home in the middle of the carnage, they are suspected of being the enemy's most cunningly disguised gateway. This contradictory mixture of "pure feminine" and "all too male" deceitfulness turns the spying nurse into a demonic figure that requires draconian countermeasures. Think, for instance, of Edith Cavell, the English nurse in occupied Belgium who organized the escape of Allied soldiers and whose execution by the Germans the poet Gottfried Benn starkly justified by pointing out that she had "acted like a man" (Benn 1981, 200). But what makes the figure of the spying nurse all the more uncanny is the fact that she appears as the strange "double" of a particularly dazzling feminine figure, the hysteric. As Freud had noted long before the war, women who take care of bedridden men tend to succumb to hysteria with surprising frequency. "Nursing sick people," Freud noted in a lecture titled "The Psychical Mechanism of Hysterical Phenomena," often "plays a part in the aetiology of hysteria" (Freud 1982, 6:17).

Hysterics are marked by a secret that fascinated nineteenth-century psychiatry and that psychoanalysis later attempted to decode. This secret—which unites hysterics and female spies—relates to women's sexual desire, which is so unutterable that it can find expression only in the deferred language of symptoms. The hysteric, just like the spy, embodies this secret in the most literal sense of the word: she gesticulates, rages, plays, imitates; in short, she playacts—which is also precisely what the female spy does. In the words of Pierre Janet, hysteria is a *maladie par représentation,* a malady as and by representation. The female spy, too, is first of all an actress. The hysteric resorts to foreign languages (as did the most famous "case," Anna O., who for a while only spoke English); the spy hides her nationality by means of polyglossia. She speaks the language of the enemy; as Mata Hari put it, she is *une femme internationale.* And ultimately, both hysteric and spy are characterized by the fact that their "true desire" is unclear, present and yet concealed, encoded in their games and symptoms.

Nothing, therefore, is more fatal than a hysteric at the front. A typical sample of the World War I discourse blending a crude theory of hysteria and femininity with the fear of the female spy-nurse is army captain Wulf Bley's essay "Espionage and Abnormal Predisposition" (Bley 1931). Bley recounts the case of the eighteen-year-old Countess Denise de M., a wealthy and glowingly patriotic convent student who passionately dedicates herself to her work as a frontline nurse for the Germans. Bley emphasizes her erotic attractiveness to the young soldiers, whom she cares for with a certain "voluptuousness of pity" (ibid., 378). However, not long after she commences her duties in the field hospital, she develops symptoms of hysteria: Countess Denise suffers from "nervous toothaches" that force her to seek the service of an American dentist residing in Paris. The beautiful hysteric, of whom it is said that she appears "the more radiating the more she sacrificed herself," enjoys "one-on-one flirtations with artillery officers" (ibid., 379) during which she displays a surprising interest in the military situation in certain sectors of the front. With the help of an ordnance map hanging in her room she extracts detailed information on positions, equipment, trench locations, and supply routes. Of course her interest is anything but innocent, and of course it was her hysteria that turned her into a spy and traitor. Hypnotized by the American dentist (who, of course, was more than a dentist), her toothache is converted into a far more dangerous symptom: espionage. The countess herself does not realize what she is doing—which is why she passes several security controls. Under hypnotic orders she delivers the frontline secrets to her dentist in regular dispatches.

What ties her to the dentist is, of course, more than his ability to cure her toothache. It is what psychoanalysis describes as transference, that delirious attachment which bound Anna O. to Josef Breuer, though Captain Bley prefers to call it "love dependency" (Bley 1931, 381). In times of war this unconscious and unspeakable feminine dependency, which in the case of Anna O. led to a hysterical pregnancy, turns into female espionage. The parallelism established in Bley's story between espionage and hysteria makes spying a conversion symptom of female sexuality. "Love dependency" is the one great risk involved in the wartime deployment of women whose hysteria can no longer find a comparatively harmless discharge in the shape of transference (as Anna O.'s did). In the "love dependency" of the female spy the unconscious force of feminine desire turns into a grave political threat: women can be manipulated by ominous third parties able to inject themselves into their desire; as a result women may abandon their fathers, brothers, and husbands, that is, their *father*land.

Not surprisingly, popular tales and theories like to emphasize the "tragedy" of the female spy. Caught up in her acting frenzy, she either succumbs to the object of her seduction, falls in love, and sacrifices herself and her mission or remains completely cold and, as Mühr puts it, "raises the scale of her emotions to the highest possible peak, but in the knowledge that she will get the job done" (Mühr 1931, 406). The results are ruined officers, doomed agents, and morphine-addicted diplomats. The sexual scandal represented by the cold, treacherous spy is the very same thing that irritated generations of doctors dealing with hysterics: it is, in the words of Georges Didi-Huberman, "that a woman can make her body lie" (Didi-Huberman 2004, 88). The spy simulates and performs a love she does not feel—or she feels a love that will doom her. Obviously the latter variant is a great deal less alarming. The greatest professional hazard for female spies is that an affair may suddenly turn into something serious. Not surprisingly, love—the most basic slipup in any business transaction—keeps recurring in almost all female espionage cases: as in Aleksey Tolstoy's story "Lovely Lady," it is always the beginning of the end of the beautiful spy as well as the proof of her utter ineptitude (Tolstoy 1949).

Mata Hari: The Invention of the Female Spy

Blurry identity, grand theater, glamorous eroticism, all capped off by a tragic demise—the key phantasmal moments of the female spy were set up and acted out by a real-life person: Mata Hari. The dancer and belle epoque demimondaine, tried and executed as an enemy agent in France in 1917, is the mythical prototype of the grand female spy, even though she probably never conducted espionage in an effective way. Even long before she was accused of spying, her case can be analyzed as the very paradigm of the merger of acting, self-mystification, and sexual theatrics fundamental for the image of the female spy. At the same time, however, the charges against her amount to a war-driven reinterpretation of everything the prewar courtesan had stood for: glamour, seduction, cosmopolitanism, hysteria, self-invention.

Her story began under bad circumstances, though they were preferable to those under which it ended. The outset of one of the most astonishing careers of the early twentieth century involves a failed marriage to a much older colonial officer, four years spent on Java and Sumatra in the Dutch Indies studying the local dances, and a narcissistic young woman who, after having eloped from her alcoholic and violent husband, was drawn to Paris. In 1903 the twenty-seven-year-old Friesian Margaretha Geertruida MacLeod, née Zelle, arrived in the French capital with nothing to her name but a swarthy complexion and a pleasant figure. Drawing on her memories of Indonesian dances, she compiled a short program that she first performed in private residences. The collector and connoisseur of the Orient Émile Guimet invited her to perform in his museum, and it was this first performance in the Museum for Oriental Arts on March 13, 1905, that established her fame. The library was covered in carpets and decorated with oriental statues, the pillars wrapped in flower garlands, the light muted. Guimet and his curator Léon de Milloué opened the soiree with a short introduction on Vedic dances. Then the main attraction appeared: a tall, black-haired, and extremely limber dancer dressed in a costume that left little to the imagination. During her last dance, an invocation of Shiva, she started undressing herself. One by one she sacrificed her many-colored veils to the god until finally she removed the baby sling wrapped around her hips to momentarily stand naked (that is, dressed only in flimsy tights) in front of the audience (figure 17). Following this performance she was the toast of Paris. The high society of the belle epoque clamored for private performances, stage managers offered incredible fees, and viewers came in droves.

What is remarkable about the beginning of Mata Hari's public career is that it would not have come about without Guimet's assistance. As a connoisseur of oriental arts he must have seen straight through her amateurish improvisation, but rather than expose her as the dilettante she was, he provided her with jewelry and costumes from his collection and even proposed a new name: Mata Hari, Indonesian for "sun," or, literally "eye of the day." In addition to the fitting accoutrements Guimet also furnished the appropriate discourse. His introductory lecture aimed to transform the Friesian's seminude contortions into a sacred Asian ritual. Mata Hari's appearance at the Musée Guimet was made up of props and vague memories indiscriminately blending Java and India, Shiva and

Figure 17. Mata Hari (Margaretha Geertruida Zelle, 1876–1917) performs the dance of the veils at the Musée Guimet (1905). Copyright © Mata Hari Centrum/ Fries Museum, Leeuwarden, Netherlands.

Buddha into one orientalist phantasmagoria. She was "the museum-bred mannequin of exotic dance" (Brandstetter 1995, 87), a library fantasy pieced together from visual quotations and clichés.

Her dance was anything but artistic; it was unabashedly erotic. The smooth motions, the nudity, the orgasmic climax of the Shiva dance—everything about Mata Hari's dance was unvarnished, orientally embellished sexuality. But Mata Hari herself eloquently denied this erotic dimension. Dance, she informed the eager journalists, is a form of prayer that originally was not intended for profane viewing. To see her was to witness a performance that meant something very different from what it showed. "A master of ceremonies explains the dances that otherwise would remain incomprehensible; but once you understand them," she commented impassively, "then the performance will make you forget the woman" (quoted in Kraus 1906, 42). The notorious killjoy Karl Kraus had a heyday with this wrongheaded denial: "In order to forget the woman within the women . . . women these days become postal clerks or at the very least Buddhist dancers, and if that is not enough Mr Gregory will have to stand next to her and lecture" (Kraus 1906, 42). From the very beginning Mata Hari situated her art in an inauthentic space open to interpretation; she addressed her viewers by prompting them how they were to see things. With this shift a structural affinity arose between Mata Hari and the performances of hysterics: the permanent demand to "decode," to interpret something different from what you see (see Schneider 1994). Slavoj Žižek calls the hysteric symptom a "coded message" (Žižek 1992b, 424). Mata Hari's art, too, was such a code, and there will always be readers more or less willing to decipher it.

Mata Hari did not wait until she was a spy to conceal her background. Long before the war started she had already indulged in the art of permanent self-invention, offering a fantastic, constantly changing history of her origins:

> I was born in Southern India, on the Malabar Coast, in the holy city of Jaffupatam, into a family of Brahmins. My father Suprachetty was called Assivardam, which means the Blessing of God, because of his merciful spirit. My mother, the first bayadere in the temple of Randa Swany, died at the age of fourteen giving birth to me. After the priests had cremated her they adopted me and called me Mata Hari, the Eye of the Dawn. As soon as I took my first steps they confined me to the large underground chamber of the pagoda of Shiva to initiate me into the rites of the holy dance. (Quoted in Kupferman 1992, 24)

Mata Hari did not appear to be overly concerned with the credibility of her accounts; she told each new journalist a new story. Sometimes she was the daughter of a colonial officer and a Javanese and married to a Scottish nobleman, sometimes "the granddaughter of a native regent" (quoted in Lüders 1997, 82). The fact that her biographies, much like her dances, were pure fiction, creating a permanent divide between what you saw and what it was supposed to mean, was obvious to anyone, including Mata Hari herself. Her fascination lay in the tension between shame and shamelessness, between what she tried to be and what she probably was—a tension symbolized by her most important prop, the veil. Already as an artist Mata Hari was a self-commenting illusion, a fiction that presented itself *as fiction.* Of course this ambiguity could easily be turned against her. Very early on embarrassed men and sharp-tongued women accused her of being a fraud. Karl Kraus castigated the "devotion in the face of imposture" (Kraus 1906, 39). Colette commented on her clothes and added: "She an Oriental? Don't be silly!" (Colette 1957, 130). But the indignant declaration that she was nothing but an orientalizing impostor merely repeated what she had been openly doing herself since the beginning of her career. Neither ridiculing her upstart appearance nor exposing her Friesian origins fazed her; it was only when the war arrived and fixed identities became a proof of national trustworthiness that she would be ensnared by her own fiction.

The overriding suspicion, confirmed by her present-day biographers, is that her dancing was a screen behind which she pursued a very different trade: a luxurious form of prostitution. Her dancing, Franz Blei pointed out, was nothing "but an artsy facade . . . for her life as a courtesan" (Blei 1927, 271). Despite her incredible fees Mata Hari mainly lived off generous allowances from rich lovers. They presented her with houses, fur coats, and racehorses, and one of them left her a small fortune at the end of their affair. These are two structural features that, long before the war, anticipate Mata Hari's "career" in espionage: the fictionalization of her biography and her unaccounted income. Where did all the money come from that she spent with such ludicrous extravagance? Once again we are faced with the specter of a third party, a source of wealth that demands risky service in return. The courtesan is always "too expensive" *and* "too cheap," an incarnation of financial excess. This endows her with a mysterious, if not suspicious, trait.

The Courtesan at War

For ten years Mata Hari successfully cultivates her inscrutable identity and immense erotic market value, but with the dramatic change of time and circumstances her mystery becomes her undoing. With the advent of the war the mystery of her extravagant income seems to find a very simple solution: her money must come from a very profitable business, the trading of state secrets. If courtesans and prostitutes have always been associated with espionage, this is not just because of their sexual fickleness but because of the incommensurable economy involved in prostitution. In times of war this economic-sexual mystery of the courtesan turns into the political mystery of treason. What is being exchanged and what interests are being pursued? Under normal circumstances sex is the solution to the "secret" of the courtesan, but in wartime sex suddenly appears to be just a cover. Now one pervading suspicion casts its shadow over the courtesan's business: the money that seems to be coming from beaux and lovers is in fact coming from the enemy. Suddenly the courtesan's extravagant income can be explained by a totally different business: treason. From this angle it becomes clear why a man would spend large sums of money on a woman who in return does not even grant him her exclusive favors but sleeps with a large number of other men—mostly officers. In times of war the courtesan, who hitherto may have bankrupted her lover or, in the words of Mata Hari's judge, "wrecked hearts and devoured fortunes" (Bouchardon 1953, 306), turns into a traitor that may wreck a whole nation.

After years of dazzling success the First World War surprised Mata Hari in Berlin. She moved to Holland, performed in Den Haag and Arnheim, and was caught between boredom and the need to locate new sources of income. At a reception in Den Haag she made the acquaintance of Karl Kramer, the German consul in Amsterdam. For twenty thousand francs he enlisted her to sound out the mood among the Parisian high society and maybe flirt with a couple of officers; he had her equipped with secret ink, a code for transmitting messages, and her last and fatal pseudonym, the code name H 21. In late 1915 she set out on her mission. The German occupation of Belgium forced her to travel by way of England and Spain to Paris, where she arrived in May 1916. It was probably during her second trip that the Dutch and British secret services started keeping tabs on her. The intelligence reports that later provided evidence against her noted numerous contacts with more or less high-ranking military personnel, politicians, and civil servants. Mata Hari appears to have believed that she could best attend to her secret mission by spending suppers and nights with Belgian, Montenegrin, British, French, and Russian officers (Lüders 1997, 34 and following). Thanks to Jean Hallaure, one of her lovers, she established contact with the Deuxième Bureau's chief of counterespionage, Georges Ladoux, who already had her under surveillance. He pretended to hire her for the French secret service (Schirmann 1994, 49 and following). From this moment on Mata Hari was serving two masters, evidently unaware of the dangers involved in this tightrope walk. The crux of the double agent is to maintain the trust of the one side for which he or she "really" works; this side has to remain informed of all hiring attempts by enemy agencies. Mata Hari, who would rather deal with the French than serve the Germans, failed to tell Ladoux that she had been enlisted by the other side—though he already suspected as much.[2] For his part, Ladoux employed Mata Hari not because he expected any special results from her but because it was a better means of controlling her. While during her dancing career her main allure consisted of her fabulous inscrutability, this inscrutability now attracts the suspicion of the burgeoning intelligence agencies.

Mata Hari herself viewed her "spy" activities as the continuation of her artistic and courtesanal career with different means—and different sponsors. She was almost forty and remained the center of a wide network of friends and admirers, but as a dancer she was past her prime and no longer en vogue. She now put everything she had to offer at the service of her new livelihood: in the belief that her intimate friendships with senior officers on both sides of the front would enable her to obtain important military secrets, she bragged about contacts and affairs she probably never had (such as with the German crown prince and the Berlin chief of police). Just as she once had invented her exotic oriental identity, she now reinvented herself as a dazzling spy.

However, even in the realm of espionage she maintained her financial profligacy. She proposed an extraordinary, albeit completely unfeasible coup to Ladoux, for which she demanded one million francs. The proposal in question contained all the leitmotifs of her life: sex and financial excess, glamour and dilettantism. With the help of an admirer in Brussels she planned to infiltrate the German General Staff to steal the German military deployment plans. "I shall proceed to Brussels in dazzling gowns and establish contact with the General Staff" (quoted in Schirmann 1994, 62). Ladoux agreed to the proposal without the slightest expectation of success. Mata Hari traveled to Spain, where she once again met her German contacts, but by now the German secret service was as aware of her amateurish double game as their Allied counterparts were. She told her German contact, Major Arnold von Kalle, that she merely "pretended" to have been hired by the French. Using a code the French had long since broken, Kalle sent a telegram to Germany informing his superiors that agent H 21 had delivered "very exhaustive" reports and was "pretending" to collaborate with the French.[3] These telegrams contained such detailed information about H 21 that it was difficult not to interpret them as a trap knowingly laid by the Germans. In the subsequent trial of Mata Hari the captured missives would serve as the chief exhibit, all the more so as there was little other incriminating evidence.

On her return to Paris in January 1917 she was put under permanent surveillance, her account monitored, and her mail intercepted. She was arrested on February 13; her trial took place in July. In the interim, Pierre Bouchardon, the investigating judge, busily looked for incriminating evidence against the amateur spy, which due to her inefficiency turned out to be a difficult task. Witnesses for the defense were banned from the court; just a few of Mata Hari's old benefactors were allowed to testify that they never talked about anything of military importance. She was interrogated for months, only twice in the presence of her lawyer. Her request to have Ladoux cited as a witness was denied. Ultimately the trial was made possible only by Kalle's strange telegrams. Shipman's recent biography, based on new French material, claims that Mata Hari never really was a double agent but saw herself as loyal to the French, who, well into the fourth year of war, desperately needed a success—and a scapegoat (Shipman 2007). Her trial took place on July 24 and 25, 1917, lasted one and a half days, and ended, as planned, with a death sentence. The president rejected her petition for mercy. The sentence was carried out on October 15, 1917, at a quarter past six in the morning.

Those are the raw facts insofar as they can be reconstructed from a wealth of contradictory material. But what exactly was Mata Hari convicted for? Apart from those charges that in hindsight are either wrong or insufficient for a death sentence, the files of Judge Bouchardon as well as his subsequent memoirs reveal a pattern linked to that particular ambiguity which constituted the allure of the dancer. Bouchardon became her last—and lethal—interpreter. He "read" Mata Hari's prewar life and wartime activities to find a hidden meaning—and this meaning was treason. Following established criminological procedure he searched for the underlying connection that tied events together, turning seemingly insignificant details into clues. His point of departure was precisely what the wagging tongues of the belle epoque had been drawn to: her promiscuity, wanderlust, and extravagance. He attempted to establish that she had been living as a prostitute for years, that due to her extravagant lifestyle she was in constant need of money, and that she therefore had already started to work as a German spy before the war. Cosmopolitanism, multilingualism, promiscuity—in the eyes of the investigating judge all three pointed toward espionage. Bouchardon's reading of her life amounts to a forced change of register: where *sexuality* was, there *politics* shall be. When asked why she in times of war slept with so many officers, and sometimes even for free, she declared: "I love officers, I have loved them all my life. It is my greatest pleasure to sleep with them; I don't think of money. Besides, I like to compare the physique and temperament of men from different countries" (Bouchardon 1953, 320). Mata Hari may have pursued sexual interests, but Bouchardon's comments point in a different direction: "It is not difficult to imagine that a woman like H 21 could use this string of affairs to obtain and assemble information passed on to her in confidence. Her partners were caught off guard. In encounters like these, the man, no matter how skilled, is always the loser" (ibid.). He cannot imagine that her beds and suppers served any purpose other than the exchange of important military secrets. While Bouchardon attempts to deduce her importance and efficiency from the amount of money she received from the Germans, Mata Hari declares impassively: "You do not propose such missions to a woman of my position without offering generous compensation" (quoted in Schirmann 1994, 146). "A woman of my position"—for Mata Hari that means "a woman of my social and erotic standing." For Bouchardon it means "a well-trained master spy." Whereas Mata Hari sees spying as a playful continuation of her serious work as a courtesan, Bouchardon understands the latter to be nothing more than the playful introduction to the deadly seriousness of espionage. In Mata Hari, prostitution and espionage, the world's oldest and second oldest professions, come together.

Bouchardon is following a logic of war that does away with all ambiguities. War renders the alluring mysteries that populated the glamorous salons of the belle epoque deeply suspicious. Bouchardon is intent on installing a semiotic regime of definite meaning that treats appearances as deceptions or clues. War needs and generates certainty, either/or decisions, the dichotomy of enmity. The "ideas of 1914" have spelled it out: the war, as Friedrich Gundolf notes in a letter to Stefan George, has arrived to annihilate a "world of appearance, chatter and luxury" (George and Gundolf 1962, 257) in favor of "spiritual decision" (see Simmel 1917, who is a particularly succinct example of the euphoria at the beginning of 1914). It exorcizes the masquerades and irritating cosmopolitanism of the belle epoque and demands clear, unambiguous identities. An economy of waste yields to an economy of secured values; the exotic games of otherness and make-believe give way to the commitment to national affiliation.

Mata Hari falls victim to this iron logic. She is exposed and uncovered by all too serious men ranging from Karl Kraus to Judge Bouchardon, who tear off the mask of the beautiful oriental and demimondaine to reveal the hustler and traitor underneath. They also burrow through her clothes and legendary beauty to lay bare the aging body of the forty-year-old. Bouchardon comments on the femme fatale's gray streaks and bulging lips; the prison doctor Léon Bizard publishes about her ugly dark nipples (Bizard 1925, 309). Copies of her last photo circulate in the press, showing an exhausted, deeply distraught woman (figure 18). This political and physical *mise à nu* of the great nude dancer is an attempt to complete her demystification. The rhetoric of authenticity, which interprets her flamboyant demeanor and monetary demands as proof of her enormous efficiency as a spy, inserts a "something" where in fact there is nothing. Mata Hari is endowed with a substance, an essential core; though she

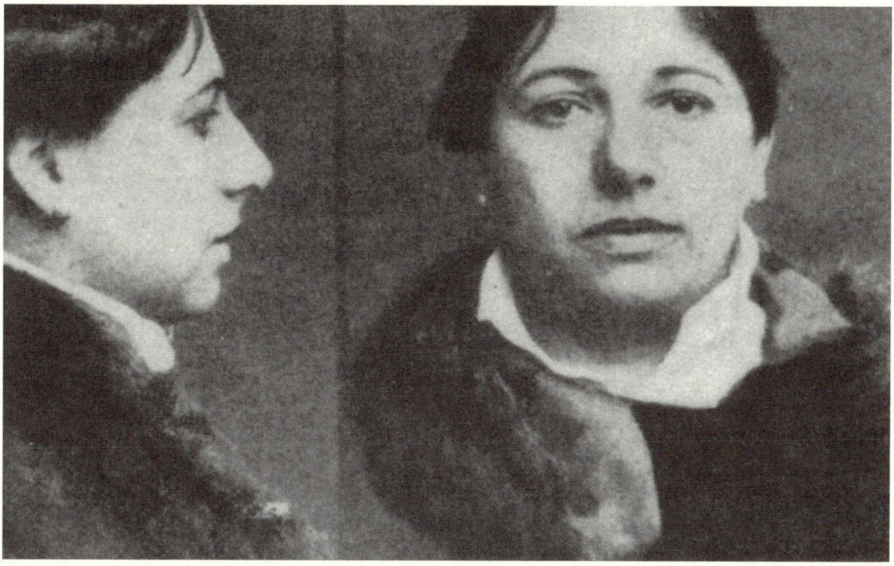

Figure 18. Mata Hari at her arrest in 1917, in a police photograph from the Saint-Lazare prison. The photo is circulated in the French press with gloating comments on the ravaged beauty of the once-legendary dancer. Copyright © Mata Hari Centrum/Fries Museum, Leeuwarden, Netherlands.

probably remained an enigma to herself, her riddle appears to have been solved by her accusers: *she was an enemy; we have uncovered her.* And last but not least there is the generic lapse of the "loving spy," which to this day haunts the biographies of Margaretha Zelle. It is said that during her final year she truly fell in love for the first time—passionately and without any financial considerations. The object of her affections was Vadim de Massloff, a young Russian officer born in the same year as her deceased son. As a love-struck spy she entered the military zone to see her injured beloved; as a lover devoid of her senses she approached Ladoux to obtain a permit. In the end, her "true love" appears as a deadly emotional faux pas, confirming the fallibility of the female spy.

Let us assume that the French were fully convinced of having executed a professional spy responsible for the exposure of a Belgian agent and the sinking of several submarines off the Spanish coast. If that is the case, then in all likelihood they were duped by the Germans, who—as the incriminating telegrams seem to indicate—deliberately sent Mata Hari to her doom.[4] Years later Major von Roepell, her German contact, confirmed the French appraisal: "The two or three letters I received from her via a cover address in Düsseldorf contained, as far as I recall, matters of little importance written in chemical ink. It is conceivable, however, that more important information was intercepted and not communicated to me. She certainly did work as a German spy, and I am of the opinion that—regrettably—the French executed her with good reason" (quoted in Gempp 1939–43, 19; see also Lüders 1997, 109–11). Or did Mata Hari fool both sides? Was she able to convince both parties that she was a spy? "One of the cleverest women I have ever met," Roepell remarks of her. In any case, with her death she confirmed this impression. All witnesses agree that she died "like a soldier." In her final hours Mata Hari may have come to understand that this was to be her greatest performance. Masterfully she played the role of the convicted spy; she went to her death bravely, not without joking about the ungodly early morning hour. One last time she granted her judges what they had wanted to see: a cold-blooded agent. But as she had so frequently and without avail emphasized during her trial, it was "nothing but a show."

2 In Her Place: The Female Secretary

Beyond all the great female spies (who rarely lived up to their reputation), and beyond all the distortions of war and gender relationships they produced and provoked, there were women who really did perform intelligence services. They were so efficient precisely because they remained invisible; they did not indulge in stagelike performances or rely on the power of their erotic aura. In the words of the French aviator and double spy Marthe Richer, of whom Georges Ladoux (of all people) wrote a biography, they "serve":

> To be a spy during wartime does not mean, as sensational novelists picture the role, plunging into romantic adventures to which an additional zest is given by the spice of danger. It does not mean merely playing the part of fatal women, of turning people's heads and of worming out secrets which one can sell for enormous sums of money. Being a spy in wartimes means real hard, risky service. (Richer 1935, ix)

Richer, an excellent pilot before the war, was denied entry into the air force. The only agency willing to employ a woman such as herself was the Service Secret. Intelligence work appeared to be the only way women could enter war. As Richer writes, this service requires complete subjugation to the demands and assignments of an intelligence agency—even when it comes with the constant distrust of one's superiors. No games, no confidential exchange with ominous third parties, no ambiguities à la Mata Hari: these women work hard to prove that they are and remain on the right side (further see Wheelright 1992). They see themselves as aids, messengers, organizers who—if worst comes to worst—will be executed as spies rather than as soldiers.

Edith Cavell, a spinsterish nurse not likely to slip into the role of fatal seductress, was such an organizer. "In the course of a couple of months," the German poet Gottfried Benn writes in his account of the trial against her and her helpers, "her organization had amassed and equipped around three hundred enemy soldiers and Belgians fit for military service and moved them across the Belgian-Dutch border" (Benn 1981, 199). Cavell, then, stands accused not of espionage proper but of participating in the secret war waged behind the front line. Benn makes her part of a perfectly functioning "secret intelligence network of unfathomable precision: within minutes, each step forward or backward on the German front was known to everybody, each and every military occurrence behind the front was immediately communicated to the Allies" (ibid., 197). The remarkable efficiency of the underground communication networks in the occupied territory—Benn appears to consider the hostility of the Belgians toward their German occupiers as a kind of unfair competition on the part of the Allies—is due to the fact that women occupy the key junctures: they cannot be fully prosecuted under martial law. "Women had acted, women had conceived of the plans, women were shipped to Aachen, given work, and turned into heroes and showered with rewards when the war ended. While men remained harmless creatures confined to kitchen duty, women were aglow with an inner fire; they were the great organizers" (ibid., 198). Benn's sarcasm allows for two different readings: are women sent forward because they cannot be punished as drastically as men, or are they in charge of things? But regardless of whether they are real puppeteers, women are placeholders and stand-ins; they replace men. The position of the placeholder confers a value on women—they are now as valuable as, and hence interchangeable with, men. The most unmistakable but also controversial evidence of this equivalence is the fact that women, too, now enjoy the dubious right to be sentenced to death, which is how the Germans justified Cavell's execution. Those who fight like men may and will die like them.

Given the only recently founded German intelligence service's lack of manpower at the outset of the war, female placeholders were indispensable for the creation of secret networks. Section IIIb of the German General Staff, responsible for military intelligence, started setting up "intelligence posts" charged with gathering intelligence both at the front and in hostile or occupied territories. As a rule these posts were staffed by one intelligence officer and his aide; for reasons of camouflage the officer was "his own superior, filing clerk, dispatcher, and scribe" (Gempp 1939–43, 40). The only person close to him, Friedrich Gempp's account notes, was his wife. She had a place in the organization:

> With full knowledge and consent of the leadership, the intelligence officer's wife became his confidante. During his frequent absences she had to take calls and organize meetings with informants and agents; in short, she had to take charge of business in order to avoid frictions and difficulties . . . Nobody else could be made privy to all the secrets . . . Fieldwork aside, most of the activities of the intelligence officer took place in his own apartment . . . Until his arrival his wife managed and transmitted messages to IIIb using her own signature—no doubt a curiosity in the history of the army! (Gempp 1939–43, 41)

In the intelligence service of the First World War, women could take over the position of their spouses or male colleagues. But to assume a man's place meant to be in position when he was not around. Whenever the husband ventured out on risky field assignments, his wife took over the regular intelligence tasks: she instructed agents, transmitted messages, maintained communication, encoded, and decoded. These silent female helpers were the first female actors in the early stage of the intelligence business—not as the demonic antagonists of men but as their better doubles. As Friedrich Kittler points out, by smoothly blending into the symbolic order of the Fatherland as secretaries, helpful spirits, and "typewriters," these women gained astonishing power over "antechambers, access conditions and discourse production" (Kittler 1986, 308). This was the pale but noticeably more effective counterfigure to the Great Female Spy, the hysterical actress and seductress. As clerks and secretaries these placeholders may have disappeared in the great apparatus, but in fact they regulated access, communication, and secrecy. They did not directly engage the enemy; they remained within the agency to perform the tasks essential for any good bureaucracy: recording, evaluating, and storing data; securing access; and organizing joint ventures. Combat and decision, commands and conspiracies were not for them; their lot was administration. The First World War recruited women as clerks, not as pilots. In 1918 the *Zeitschrift für weibliche Handelsgehilfen* (*Journal for Female Clerks*) reported that "the offices of all manufacturers central to the war effort have been occupied with female workers; they have conquered even the orderly rooms of the army administration" (quoted in Kittler 1999, 196). And as clerks employed in secret services they unfolded a potential that dwarfed anything a Mata Hari could ever have extracted from her lovers.

The Medium: Dr. Elsbeth Schragmüller

The prototype is Elsbeth Schragmüller. Not coincidentally, only three very fuzzy photos of her remain (the best is reproduced here in figure 19). In contrast to the relentlessly public and frequently photographed Mata Hari, Elsbeth Schragmüller's allure resided in her obscurity. She completed a doctorate in political economy at the University of Freiburg in 1913 (Schragmüller 1914); shortly after the outbreak of the war she traveled to the front; intercepted General Field Marshal von der Goltz, military governor of Belgium, in the corridor of a Brussels hotel; and asked to be assigned. She was attached to the war intelligence center in Brussels and charged with evaluating confiscated letters. Her reports and summaries were so "extraordinarily professional" and demonstrated such a keen "strategic understanding" that they caught the eye of her commanding officer, who was keen on getting to know this "Lieutenant Schragmüller" (Hieber 2005, 100). On the strength of her talent and zeal she was transferred to the mobile Section IIIb of the General Staff and then put in charge of the war intelligence center (Kriegsnachrichtenstelle) in Antwerp. It was not the allure of conspiracy that prompted Schragmüller to journey to Brussels; in fact, she later admitted that she had no idea what "intelligence works" entailed (Schragmüller 1936, 130). Her duties in Antwerp include securing communication channels and instructing agents as well as checking, summarizing, and transmitting their reports. On her own initiative Schragmüller built a net of French agents recruited from deserters who illegally fled to Switzerland and were then charged with sounding out soldiers on leave from the front. Unlike most civilian agents, these informers, who were provided with money and credible documents, had the considerable advantage of being thoroughly familiar with military matters. Schragmüller's method was simple, cheap, and reliable because she did not have to put her trust in professional agents, some of whom purchased their information from private news agencies (Piekalkiewicz 1988, 299–305). At the end of the war, she settled down in Freiburg and later Munich and published a *Student's Guide to Political Economy,* commissioned and introduced by Karl Diehl, head of the Department of Economics at the University of Freiburg (for detailed biographical information see Hieber 2005). In 1929, she published a short report on her intelligence work in one of the sensationalist volumes on

Figure 19. Dr. Elsbeth Schragmüller (1887–1940) in Berlin in the 1920s. After obtaining a Ph.D. in political economy, she volunteered for office duty in the German army in 1914. She was assigned to German headquarters in Brussels and charged with evaluation of intercepted letters from Belgian soldiers. After training at the Kriegsnachrichtenstelle West (War Intelligence Section West), she transferred to an intelligence-gathering post in Lille, Belgium. In early 1915 she was given the responsibility of the Kriegsnachrichtenstelle in Antwerp until the end of the war. In this function, she briefly crossed paths with Mata Hari. After the war, Schragmüller returned to work in academia at the University of Freiburg in Breisgau, later moved to Munich, and died there at age 52 of bone tuberculosis. From Janusz Piekalkiewicz, 1988, *Weltgeschichte der Spionage* (Munich: Südwestverlag).

World War I espionage, Friedrich Felger and Walter Jost's *Was wir vom Weltkrieg nicht wissen* (*What We Do Not Know About the War*), and later she made a few public appearances lecturing on her wartime experiences (Hieber 2005, 106). By all accounts Elsbeth Schragmüller was a highly reliable woman who discharged her duties with unfailing competence and punctuality as long as her health permitted. She died in Munich in 1940.

The French called her Mademoiselle Docteur and concocted an exhilarating myth that transformed the resolutely low-key political economist into a mixture of cocaine addict and gun-toting dominatrix. In his memoirs, Bouchardon, the judge who sent Mata Hari to her death, raves about Mademoiselle Docteur's tantalizing calves and luxurious gold jewelry (Bouchardon 1953, 296 and following). According to his wife, Georges Ladoux—who following the Mata Hari affair was himself arrested for treason—was killed by poisoned photos sent to him by Mademoiselle Docteur (Ladoux 1937, preface). Public discourse cannot depict female spies as mere replacements and secretaries; it is necessary to mobilize lurid and demonic caricatures. The irritation caused by a woman holding a doctorate working in the intelligence service can be fended off only by means of an exaggerated stylization that turns the academic degree into a perverse prop—just like Mata Hari's veils and robes. The bloody traces of Mademoiselle Docteur can be found everywhere in the shrill accounts of female espionage in World War I, though it is not always clear whether the authors are referring to Schragmüller or to a certain Annemarie Lesser, an allegedly foolhardy, highly intelligent, and unscrupulous female spy in German services, who ended up as a deranged cocaine addict in a Swiss psychiatric clinic (Berndorff 1927). Where Elsbeth Schragmüller was, there Mata Hari must be: better a deceptive facade than the gray cunning of bureaucracy.[5]

Schragmüller herself described the advantage of employing female intelligence officers without any reference to erotics and deceit:

> Structurally, the intelligence service presupposes certain psychological components that can be neither learned nor acquired in the pursuit of a given profession. Just as talent makes the true artist, intelligence work requires certain psychological aptitudes. Among them are, first, the ability to empathize, to enter into the psyche of those charged with carrying out secret operations; second, a knowledge of human nature and leadership skills, including the instinctive intuition about how people can be coaxed to perform at their best; and finally, fantasy, by which we mean the ability to imagine

> and "feel" the external circumstances and possible situations that may arise during an operation. Women possess these psychological skills to the same degree as men. It may well be that women, given their more strongly developed emotional constitution, are better equipped in this respect than men, which explains the role they play in the intelligence service. (Schragmüller 1936, 132 and following)

Sympathy, empathy, and situational instinct—women, according to Dr. Schragmüller, are superior to men at turning themselves into a medium able to register what the other is not yet able to do or say, and they are better at using this knowledge to their tactical advantage. Women master the art of communication, of "handling people," precisely because they do not aspire to become subjects of speech but instead quietly attune themselves to the actions and communications of others. They are the operators at the junctures of communication; they listen to what others think. Indeed, intelligence agencies could not ask for better employees.

Part 5

Agents of the World Revolution

Doubling the Political

But who is the Party?
Does it sit in a house with telephones?
Are its thoughts secret, its decisions unknown?
—Bertolt Brecht, *The Measures Taken* (1937)

In the hot August of 1920 the Second World Congress of the Third Communist International in Moscow passed a resolution that sheds light on the form and essence of the political in the twentieth century. In paragraphs 9 and 12 of its *Theses on the Fundamental Tasks of the Communist International,* all of the national Communist parties belonging to the Comintern are instructed to create secret networks dedicated to agitation, education, and fighting informers:

> In all organizations, unions and associations without exception, and first and foremost in proletarian organizations, but also in those of nonproletarian toiling and exploited masses . . . groups or cells of Communists should be formed—preferably open groups, but underground groups as well, the latter being essential whenever there is reason to expect their suppression, or the arrest or banishment of their members on the part of the Bourgeoisie; these cells, which are to be in close touch with one another and with the Party center, should, by pooling their experience, carrying on work

> of agitation, propaganda and organization, adapting themselves to absolutely every sphere of public life and to every variety and category of the toiling masses, systematically educate themselves, the Party, the class, and the masses by means of such diversified work. (Lenin 1966, 191–92)

The resolution, presented by Chairman Lenin, reveals a politics determined to strive for its most important goals—forming a party and mobilizing the "masses"—in secret. It aims to explore the political climate, collect information, establish contacts, and sow dissent, but all this is to be achieved by means of "skimming off" and "subversion." Next to party soldiers agitating in public there is to be a net of covert and invisible forces fully adapted to the "toiling masses," whose strength arises from the fact that they cannot be politically identified.

The Comintern resolution introduces a basic structure of twentieth-century revolutionary Communist politics. Revolutionary action implies a fundamentally ambiguous mode of operation with an official or "legal" side on the one hand and an arcane or "illegal" one on the other. What is new is that the illegal status is no longer, as in the bygone days of underground Communist movements, the result of a public ban. On the contrary, Communist parties now are part of the parliamentary system. The order to build up so-called secret "apparatuses," however, does not only apply to countries in which underground activity remains the only viable option; it also pertains to countries where there is no longer any need for clandestine operations:

> In all countries, even in those that are freest, most "legal," and most "peaceful" in the sense that the class struggle is least acute there, it is now absolutely indispensable for every Communist Party member to systematically combine legal and illegal work, legal and illegal organizations . . . Illegal work is most necessary in the army, the navy and the police. (Lenin 1966, 195)

The fact that the tactics of infiltration and subversion, spying and sabotage are directed against government institutions charged with upholding law and order, such as the army and the police force, already indicates that conspiratorial politics represent a countermeasure against state instruments. "Illegal," then, does not mean that Communist gatherings and activities are prohibited by law but that they are *concealed* and do not reveal themselves for what they are. The resolutions of the Comintern congress are the basis for a fundamental doubling of all future revolutionary politics. *Visible* politics such as propaganda, parliamentary, and journalistic work will be complemented, supported, and occasionally thwarted by the other, *hidden* side of political action.

This new, double-tiered structure of revolutionary Communist politics matches and mirrors the modern *arcana imperii* that arose at the beginning of the twentieth century. While in the wake of the First World War the nations of Europe set up professional intelligence agencies, reorganized the nineteenth-century system of snitches and informers, and thus demonstrated, according to Carl Schmitt, a new appreciation of *arcana* as the operating principles of power, politics also strove to be increasingly participatory, democratic, and hence necessarily transparent. The secrets of power, however, turn out to be as vital as they are precarious. No matter how much the idea of the Communist world revolution may conceive of itself as a counterproject and an overcoming of capitalist forms of governmental sovereignty, it clearly shares modernity's notion of the political *arcanum*. Power and its revolutionary overthrow equally depend on the clandestine and the conspiratorial, and in both cases this dependence involves not only an operating mode but also a threat to its own legitimacy. The conflicting, opaque, and violence-prone sphere of secrecy constantly demands reflection and justification—especially when the revolutionary project aspires to confront the injustices of capitalism with a different form of order and justice. This not only gives rise to the question of what constitutes the structure, goals, techniques, and tactics of the revolutionary project. Ultimately it also raises questions regarding the common denominator of governmental and revolutionary sovereignty.

To prepare a revolution implies not *having* an enemy but *determining* an enemy to be such in the first place. The enemy envisaged by Communism is both global and undetermined: the "ruling class," capitalism, the bourgeoisie. The "class enemy" of the revolution is a global enemy beyond all national antagonisms, universal and omnipresent. As Carl Schmitt has shown apropos of Lenin's reading of Clausewitz, relocating enmity from the fronts of the First World War to the civil war of the October Revolution changes it in many respects. The "contained" (*gehegte*) enmity of the eighteenth and nineteenth centuries makes way for an "absolute" enmity of global dimensions. The class enemy is a ubiquitous enemy, one whose forces have to be unmasked at each and every point. Enmity thus turns into an epistemological problem—the enemy must be recognized and marked. "Cognizance of the enemy was the secret of Lenin's enormous effectiveness" (Schmitt 2007, 52). Yet rather than solving the problem of knowing one's enemy, the term "class enemy" raises the question in the first place: "Who is it *in concreto*?" (ibid.; translation emended). Indeed, who is a class enemy? Does the term encompass the petty bourgeoisie, the farmers, the kulaks, the intellectuals, the *Lumpenproletariat*? What coalitions make tactical sense, what internal divisions have to be fueled? To what degree is it permissible to strike deals with the enemy? Lenin invests a lot of time and effort trying to determine who is a friend and who is an enemy, who is an acceptable ally and who is a dangerous dissenter. Hardly any other piece of political writing enacts Schmitt's definition of the political as the distinction between friend and enemy so faithfully as Lenin's "Left-Wing Communism—an Infantile Disorder," his tactical deliberations on how the Bolshevik revolutionaries are to distance themselves from Mensheviks, social democrats, social rebels, anarchists, rightist and leftist dissenters, and so on (Lenin 1966, 17–104). Just as it is necessary to recognize and understand the concealed effects of capitalism's mechanisms of exploitation, the revolution demands permanent efforts to determine the concealed enemy. This dynamic of permanent exposure also applies to the party itself, the self-appointed subject of the revolution, which as a result will in the course of its history become entangled in a never-ending process of schisms and purges of "enemies" and "dissenters."

At the same time the revolutionary struggle conceives of itself as the very progress of world history. Nothing, not even the smallest, most confined activity, ever fully terminates in the here and now; it is instead part of a historical teleology culminating in nothing less than the end of history itself—in universal justice and the end of all exploitation of man by man. Communism, Karl Löwith concluded, is a secularized and politicized history of salvation (Löwith 1949, 33–51).[1] And now, thanks to the victory of Bolshevism in Russia, the realization of the Communist project was within reach. The Bolsheviks of the 1920s saw themselves as the historic avant-garde and the 1917–18 revolution as an exemplary pattern for the rest of the world: "The messianic interpretation of Marxism by Lenin and other party leaders gave rise to the expectation that 'world Bolshevism' was bound to arrive sooner or later" (Watlin 1993, 19). The Communist Party of the Soviet Union represented and coordinated all revolutionary movements. The basic idea of the Third International was the notion of a global revolution based on the model of the October Revolution. The party "apparatuses" took on the task of laying the grounds for armed insurrections: they would covertly explore the political situation and manage the clandestine mobilization of the revolutionary forces when the moment had come.

The awareness of the world-historical dimension of the revolution raises the question of timing: at what point is a country "ready" for an uprising? Once the revolution is no longer conceived as part of a more or less automatic historical process but as a moment in time that—as the events of 1917 appeared to confirm—needs to be brought about, recognized, and grasped, the success of the venture depends on recognizing the right moment. It needs to be prepared with great care, and it becomes vitally important to identify the points and junctures that have to be occupied to secure a takeover of power. According to Curzio Malaparte, this art of secret operations was Trotsky's stroke of genius that enabled the Bolsheviks to seize power in November 1917 (Malaparte 1932, 13–55).[2] This is precisely what the party's secret and illegal side is meant to do. It secretly mobilizes the population, observes collective mood changes, and takes care of weapons and logistics. In other words, the secret side of the party embodies its capability to act. The revolution is born in hiding.

The Apparatus

The German Communist Party (KPD) was one of the Comintern's most powerful organizations outside Russia. Since 1920 it had been busy building up several departments dedicated to conspiratorial work, the most important of which was the "M Division." From 1925 until his escape from Nazi Germany it was headed by Hans Kippenberger (figure 20). In addition to military intelligence agencies the KPD established organizations designed to harbor and hide Soviet agents, such as the Russian trade mission, the Western European Secretariat of the Comintern, and the Soviet Embassy in Berlin. This "archipelago of embassies" (Schlögel 1998, 111–35) was the base camp and the point of entry for agents and couriers of the Russian secret service and the OMS (Otdel Mezhdonarodnoi Sviazi), the Comintern's own intelligence agency.[3] Only one year later, the Comintern decided on a program for the "liaison between legal and illegal work" designed to specify the functions of the various sections, such as preparing for armed insurrection,[4] installing precautionary measures against the "infiltration of the party by untrustworthy and unreliable elements," dealing with "snitches and provocateurs," and creating secret communication networks (Kaufmann et al. 1993, 89). Other tasks included military reconnaissance, weapons acquisition, and logistics, subversion of both police and armed forces, establishing links to the ministries of justice and the interior, and acquiring political intelligence. Industrial espionage for the Soviet Union and the creation of assault teams ("T-Apparatus") and units specializing in agitation/"subversion" ("Z-Apparatus") were added later (see Wollenberg 1952).[5]

Figure 20. Hans Kippenberger (1898–1937) headed the intelligence service of the Communist Party of Germany (Kommunistische Partei Deutschlands, or KPD). From 1925 to 1928 Kippenberger was in charge of the Central Committee's intelligence division, then head of the military division until 1935. He had served as a volunteer during the First World War and joined the Independent Social Democratic Party in 1919. During the Hamburg uprising he was the military leader in Barmbek. In 1924 he was among the first to be trained at the M-School, an espionage college in Moscow. He was a member of the Central Committee of the KPD and a Reichstag deputy. Like many other "chekists," Kippenberger was killed during Stalin's Great Purge. From Bernd Kaufmann et al., 1993, *Der Nachrichtendienst der KPD 1919–1937* (Berlin: Dietz).

The secret "apparatuses" that the Communist parties were to establish in accordance with Comintern resolutions had four basic functions: disguise, intelligence, agitation, and networking. Next to disguise (forged identities, covert organizations, indirect discourse), intelligence (exploring the revolutionary potential in their own ranks, scouting the enemy), and networking (developing the remote control exerted by the Comintern center in Moscow), it was agitation in particular that marked the specific style of the Communist agent. Agitation is a technique of political influence based on dissemblance and insinuation, a form of shaping public opinion while avoiding self-revelation, a way of "opening the eyes of others" without having to be explicit about it. The playwright Bertolt Brecht not only made the rhetorical structure of this particular kind of illegal work the subject of his poetry; he also turned it into a theory of political theater (see the following sections).

The net of Communist agitation, however, was extremely centralized. All the threads converged in the headquarters of the executive committee of the Comintern, the legendary Hotel Lux on Lubyanka Square in Moscow. This "Bolshevikization" of the Communist parties combined the creation of secret party organizations with a rigorous centralism dominated by the Soviet Union. The Comintern saw itself as a kind of "world party" responsible for coordinating the actions of the member parties in an overall revolutionary plan. It was this ubiquitous, globally operating, yet excessively centralized structure that turned the Comintern into a political phantasm—a phantasm that adopted the changing names of the Soviet secret police: Cheka, GPU, NKWD, and so on. The party did indeed, as Brecht's *Measures Taken* puts it, "sit in a house with telephones." The telephone became the symbol for a politics that championed remote control exercised by a central command: the GPU renegade Grigori Agabekov later told the story that there was no high-ranking chekist who did not have at least three phones on his desk (Agabekov 1933, 122).

Next to Moscow, Berlin became the most important node in this network,[6] and here we encounter a new type of political operator: the chekist.[7] "Two generations of pre-1917 revolutionists had developed underground techniques to an unprecedented degree. 'Conspiracy,' which in its Russian meaning refers to the totality of rules of clandestine behavior, was habit and hobby to the revolutionists" (Dallin 1955, 1). Unlike the spies of World War I and the Great Game, the agents of the world revolution were neither patriotically inclined nor simply adventurous. Instead, they were full of their historic mission, and their self-image was as modest as it was ambitious: to be, in Brecht's words, "empty pages on which the revolution may write its instructions" (Brecht 1977, 12). They saw themselves as instruments of a historical process that they helped to advance bit by bit. Frequently these advocates of proletarian dictatorship had a bourgeois background and a solid middle-class education. Dr. Richard Sorge, probably the most important agent of his generation, who as a spy stationed in Tokyo managed to communicate to Stalin the date of the planned German attack on the Soviet Union, was, at least in Germany, rarely mentioned without his doctorate. The chekists of the 1920s and early '30s were cosmopolitan intellectuals, skilled in the arts of communication and survival, who pursued their conspiratorial activities in the spirit of revolutionary eschatology.

Crucial for the survival of these "scouts" was a type of autonomy that enables necessary tactical ties on the basis of a complete absence of social bonds. To quote from a letter by Richard Sorge: "In no way, not even internally, do I need another person to be able to live; I mean to really live, not simply vegetate. I have no attachments any more. I am so completely rootless that the road is really where I feel at home" (quoted in Whymant 1996, 22). What sounds like romantic vagabondage is, in fact, the psychological precondition for political activities that require both total self-effacement and active social networking: establishing contacts, communicating information, entering into alliances, changing identities and locations. Socially and psychologically, the chekist is a man without qualities: unattached yet sociable; cold yet fired by the ethos of the revolution; occasionally (like Sorge) a rake, lush, and erotomaniac, yet of iron discipline when it comes to serving the cause. "He plays on the keyboard of historical constellations," Karl Schlögel writes; "he plays parts. But of course he is disciplined even if the part required of him is that of a dandy or bon vivant" (Schlögel 1998, 243).

The demonic, contradictory qualities of the chekist and his network soon turned him into a popular phantasm, resulting in a literary genre that specializes in exposing the workings of the Cheka (and later of the GPU) fueled by an increasing number of renegade Comintern operatives. The rogue GPU agent Grigori Agabekov[8] was one of the first to provide an inside glimpse of the organizational structure and training procedures of the Cheka; in his book *Ch K za rabotoitĭ* (*The Cheka at Work*), which was immediately translated into German, he recounts his recruitment as well as many of the dirty tricks and intrigues he was involved in. Agabekov's account reveals that the autonomy of the agent is a result of the deliberate destruction of all personal ties. Treason, the eradication of all mutual trust, is the initiation ritual into an organization that does not tolerate any ties beyond the offices of the Lubyanka. Agabekov is forced to deliver his girlfriend, a "white guard," to his employers. This breach of trust is emblematic for both the heroic and the demonic image of the chekist: traitors with little regard for private ties, they hand over lovers, friends, parents, and siblings—yet not for any base motive but rather (as apologetic accounts would have it) as the supreme sacrifice in the service of a cause that transcends all private concerns.[9]

Agabekov's betrayal and his subsequent assassination at the hands of the Narodnyy Komissariat Vnutrennikh Del (People's Commissariat for Internal Affairs, or NKVD) prefigured the fate of many chekists. Most of them, including Kippenberger, fell victim to Stalin's purges in the 1930s and 1950s; many others were branded as traitors and killed abroad. In the words of Genrikh Grigor'evich Yagoda, a leading figure in the GPU and later head of the NKVD from 1934 to 1936: "A chekist is either shot by the enemy or by the GPU" (Schlögel 1998, 238). Indeed, Comintern agents were far more likely to be killed by their own people than by enemy agencies. The most prominent case was Walter Krivitsky, an agent who abandoned the GPU in 1937 and published his sensational account *In Stalin's Secret Service* in 1939, only to fall victim to an assassination disguised as suicide in 1941 in New York. Karl Schlögel has explained that the restructuring of the Soviet secret service and the subsequent replacement of the cosmopolitan-intellectual chekist by the new, provincial bureaucrat occurred as part of the Soviet Union's move away from the old revolutionary project:

> The chekists of the first generation were indispensable for the regime as long as its existence was tied to the advance of the world revolution. Their "Communist competence" was irreplaceable. But once the focus of the revolution had shifted to renewing the Russian state apparatus—a task that required civil servants, employees, and superpower chauvinists rather than revolutionaries, agents, and internationalists, respectively—their days were numbered.[10]

As the fixation on the coming world revolution was replaced by Stalin's more pragmatic focus on maintaining power, the glamour and demonic nature of the Cheka and the GPU, which permeate even the writings of victims like Agabekov and Krivitsky, yielded to the uniformity and coarse brutality of the NKVD and KGB. But even if outpaced by history and liquidated by its protagonists, the concept of a world revolution prepared and brought about in secret remains a unique, specifically modern form of the *arcana imperii.* It is worth taking a closer look at its tactics and techniques, not only to scrutinize the revolutionary means in greater detail but also to assess the degree to which these clandestine and conspiratorial means both promoted and endangered the project.

Bertolt Brecht—more precisely, the Brecht of the late 1920s—has provided an analysis of illegal revolutionary politics that is surprisingly well-informed about the techniques and conduct of agitation and covert operations. In several texts, Brecht explores the forms and the implications of illegal operations in the service of the revolution. Especially his controversial play *The Measures Taken* offers, arguably, the most clear-sighted analysis of a revolutionary politics that for the sake of the overall goal "takes measures" which threaten to jeopardize that very goal. In other words, Brecht is attempting to solve the revolutionary paradox arising from the use of means that are as necessary as they are nonjustifiable; he depicts the violence inherent in clandestine activities as a reflex of another, no less hidden form of violence—that of capitalist exploitation. But above all (and more than any of his competitors and successors tackling the same issues),[11] Brecht succeeds in highlighting the rhetorical and theatrical nature of clandestine work by depicting agitation as a conspiratorial performance and rhetorical technique, as the art of acting without an audience. No other modern author has so closely linked aesthetic to political performance by offering both an ethics and a poetics of the clandestine.

1 “Bertolt Brecht, Minstrel of the GPU”

“Cover Your Tracks!”: The Conduct of Illegal Work

In 1926 Brecht wrote a poem titled “Cover Your Tracks!”—also translated as “Erase Your Traces!”—that reads like a condensed primer for conspirators and spies in enemy territory. Brecht was at this point keeping company with members of the KPD and dissident Marxists like Karl Korsch and Fritz Sternheim. He read “Marxist literature,” including Henri Guilbeaux’s biography of Lenin and René Fülöp-Miller’s *The Mind and Face of Bolshevism* (Hecht 1997, 221, 236). And he was—at least certainly during the early 1930s—acquainted with the aforementioned Hans Kippenberger, who had been head of the KPD’s “M Division” since 1925. “Cover Your Tracks!,” which first appeared in 1930 as the leadoff text in Brecht’s *Reader for Those Who Live in Cities,* has so far primarily been read as a document of the urban coldness that permeates the literature of *Neue Sachlichkeit* or new objectivity (Lethen 2002, 133–42). Brecht’s friend Walter Benjamin was the only one to note the affinity between the text and clandestine Communist work: “He who fights for the exploited class is an emigrant in his country. For Brecht . . . the last five years of his political work in the Weimar Republic amounted to crypto-emigration . . . ‘Cover your tracks!’—a rule for those who are illegal” (Benjamin 2003b, 232–33; translation emended). Indeed, the code of conduct—which the text merely quotes rather than elaborates (“This is what they taught me”)—is that of underground work. The text formulates guidelines for avoiding identification and arrest in the big cities, the privileged playground of secret service operations.

The poem, set in the tone of an instruction to an illegal agent about to start his mission, begins with a scene of separation, the moment of initiation into that particular solitude that characterizes the agents of the world revolution. From now on everything they do they must be done alone: work, agitate, die:

> Part from your friends at the station
> Enter the city in the morning with your coat buttoned up
> Look for a room. And when your friend knocks:
> Do not, oh do not, open the door.
> But
> Cover your tracks. (Brecht 1976, 131)

According to David J. Dallin, one of the most important rules of *konspiratcija* is "that agents must not visit one another in their homes or make telephone calls from home" (Dallin 1955, 9). The first piece of advice, therefore, is to sever all ties to the "comrades" and protect the network by ensuring that no one member can be connected to another. Brecht leaves no doubt that the isolation of the agent is less an expression of emotional autonomy (as Richard Sorge would have it) than a precautionary measure for the protection of fellow agents and the network itself:

> If you meet your parents in Hamburg or elsewhere
> Pass them like strangers, turn the corner, don't recognize them
> Pull the hat they gave you over your face, and
> Do not, oh do not, show your face
> But
> Cover your tracks.

Nothing jeopardizes a conspiratorial existence more than an encounter with past acquaintances. For an illegal agent or agitator there is no greater conceivable calamity than to run into his parents, whether in Hamburg or elsewhere. From the point of view of conspiratorial politics, this is less a modern matter of distancing oneself from the father generation, as Helmut Lethen has argued in his influential study *Cool Conduct,* than one of maintaining a threatened fake identity. Private ties, friends, and family relations are formidable risks; even worse, they burden the political warrior with conflicts of loyalty, which is why the betrayal of parents or siblings, lovers or friends belongs as much to the chekist's moral physiognomy as the hat pulled low over the agent's eyes does to his or her physical appearance. The lack of emotional bonds, which Lethen reads as an indication of the "new objectivism" (*Neue Sachlichkeit*) and "cool conduct" of the postwar era, can therefore be politically decoded as a necessary attribute of illegal work:

> Eat the meat that's there. Don't stint yourself.
> Go into any house when it rains and sit on any chair that's in it.
> But don't sit long! And don't forget your hat.
> I tell you:
> Cover your tracks.
> Whatever you say, don't say it twice
> If you find your ideas in anyone else, disown them.
> The man who hasn't signed anything, who has left no picture
> Who was not there, who said nothing:
> How can they catch him?
> Cover your tracks.

No parents, no pictures, no signature, and no clear affiliation. Be someone "who was not there"—otherwise your photo or description will find its way into the police records, your fake signature will be exposed, and you will be identified as someone who was where officially you were not supposed to be. "Erase the traces of your identity" is the rule of conduct; "dissemble your fake ID." "Never say things twice. Never be caught with an opinion or conviction." For Communists imbued with a passion for theory and an ardent belief in the revolution, this rule must have been as difficult as it was necessary. It does not preach revolutionary idealism but instead advises the kind of tactical alliances with the enemy that presuppose rigorous self-denial ("Go into any house when it rains . . . But don't sit long!"). The cause must be strenuously denied in order not to be betrayed. Those involved in illegal work are therefore neither preachers nor confessors, but at best "saboteurs" or infiltrators; they do not proclaim the world revolution but sow doubt, point out grievances, disseminate bad news. The most important thing is not to be "nailed down," not to disclose that all this muted critical discourse stems from one source and points toward one goal. Once the infiltrator's political allegiance has been unmasked, his effectiveness is nil; he must, therefore, always communicate in such a way that others believe they came up with the ideas on their own. This type of insinuation is discussed in the Weimar Republic as the technique of "erosion" (*Zersetzung*) or "subversion," employed both by right- and left-wing agitators.[12] The *content* of what is being said is not important. What counts is its *effect:* destabilizing the esprit de corps in the police or the Reichswehr, for instance, or sowing doubts and class-consciousness among workers, and so on. The ideological source of this discourse, however, must never be revealed. "Subversion" is a rhetorical operation that requires a tactical distancing from one's utterances. The speaker must "erase" himself in favor of a discursive effect. The poem makes abundantly clear that illegal work requires one to abandon all forms of heroism. Therefore, even memories of the agents must be erased:

> See when you come to think of dying
> That no gravestone stands and betrays where you lie
> With a clear inscription to denounce you
> And the year of your death to give you away.
> Once again:
> Cover your tracks,
> (That is what they taught me.)

In its last line the instructive tone of the poem performs the very act of distancing itself from what it preaches: "That is what they taught me" separates the speaker from the instruction. The instruction is itself a quotation, an instance of reported speech, issued by the poem and then immediately repealed. Nevertheless, this strange kind of instruction can be historically localized: the year the poem was written also saw the foundation of the Lenin School in Moscow, designed "to instruct Western European and American Communists in the technique of Bolshevism" (Krivitsky 1985, 56). The syllabus included military crash courses as well as "the fabrication and use of all sorts of explosive devices, industrial sabotage . . . terrorist actions, diversionary tactics and intelligence work" (Wollenberg 1952, 14). Brecht's text *quotes* and repeats the instructions to a future agent. "That is what they taught me" marks the moment when the speaker chooses not to reveal himself but instead pretends to disavow what he just said, thus eradicating himself as a subject of speech. Both the poem's theme and its structure partake in the technique and tactics of conspiracy.

And yet there is a point at which the text, in defiance of its own program, suddenly reveals a detail that can "nail it down," a location: "in Hamburg or elsewhere." A piece of information, even though immediately retracted ("or elsewhere"). Why Hamburg? Hamburg was the scene of the futile attempt to stage an armed insurrection that was supposed to trigger a "German October," the planning and preparation for which was closely linked to the buildup of the German Communist Party's clandestine organizations (Kaufmann et al. 1993, 57–93). In August 1923 the executive committee of the Comintern had determined that Germany was ready for an insurrection modeled on the October Revolution. Military advisers had been dispatched; the civil war was to start in Saxony and Thuringia and spread from there. Reluctantly, the German Communist Party agreed, believing that "the masses could no longer be contained" (ibid., 87)—a blatant misreading of the political climate in Germany. At the very last moment plans to start the uprising were countermanded. Hamburg alone went ahead: street fighting erupted in the district of Barmbeck, resulting in many casualties. For German Communists the party leadership's cop-out was a traumatic experience, but that is precisely what turned the desperate Hamburg riots into a lost, mythical "revolutionary moment." Its military leader, however, was none other than Brecht's acquaintance Hans Kippenberger, who later became the head of the entire military apparatus of the KPD. With this in mind, "in Hamburg or elsewhere" can be read as a cryptic allusion not only to an important area of operations for militant KPD activities but also to Kippenberger himself, who resided in Hamburg at the time and who more than anyone embodied the clandestine side of Communist work in Germany.

Brecht was clever enough to keep his allusions—if the term indeed qualifies—sufficiently vague ("or elsewhere") and hide his poem in a collection titled *Reader for Those Who Live in Cities.* Here we can detect a political gesture that avoids noisy confessions in favor of indirect and (in the rhetorical sense) "ironical" statements. The strange gestures of self-effacement in the poem—allusions only insiders can decipher, the technique of "subversion," and a self-distancing from the instruction the poem gives—these are all elements of a rhetorical irony, a *dissimulatio* that negates what is and a *simulatio* that professes what is not (Lethen 1992, 95). The politics of revolution is, in the rhetorical sense of the word, "ironic." Propaganda and secret networking, covert subversion and public education of the masses, are the two sides of a fundamentally "inauthentic" politics that constantly strives toward the world revolution, its great, "authentic" goal, while simultaneously engaging in maneuvers and alliances and imposing a culture of concealment and deception. "We must . . . agree to make any sacrifice, and even—if need be—to resort to various stratagems, artifices and illegal methods, to evasions and subterfuges" (Lenin 1966, 55). Brecht, however, is not committing himself by justifying or prescribing these "illegal methods"; instead he articulates the techniques and tactics of conspiratorial activities with all the coolness and distance that appertain to them.[13] In other words, Brecht doesn't simply share or condone these ambiguous politics; he *demonstrates* them. The ambiguous, allusive structure of his texts mirrors the structure of the political caught between propaganda and secret agitation, ideological preaching, and covert "subversion." In his undoubtedly most controversial piece of writing, the *Lehrstück* or "learning play" *The Measures Taken* from 1930, clandestine politics will reemerge as a specifically theatrical undertaking. *The Measures Taken* is the most radical analysis of the ambiguity of revolutionary politics, an analysis beyond both affirmation and defamation, a theory not only of tactics but also of the ethics of secret revolutionary politics.

Effacement: Brecht's *Measures Taken*

Unlike the semi-camouflaged poem "Cover Your Tracks!," *The Measures Taken* aims to explicitly stage illegal political agitation.[14] It is the play that prompted an angry Ruth Fischer to bestow upon Brecht the label "Minstrel of the GPU."[15] A note to the audience written on the occasion of the premiere on December 13, 1930, briefly summarizes the plot and message:

> Four communist agitators are facing a party inquiry, represented by the mass chorus. They have been conducting communist propaganda in China, and in the course of this they had to shoot their youngest comrade. In order to convince the court of the need for their decision, they show how the Young Comrade behaved in a number of different political situations. They show him as a revolutionary in his feelings but inadequately disciplined and too reluctant to listen to reason, so that in the end he becomes a real threat to the movement. (Brecht 1997, 232)

Brecht once again seems anxious to elide rather than foreground the conspiratorial content of the text. The playbill ensures that the critique of the premiere revolves around issues of "emotion" and "reason," "discipline" and "humanity."[16] What the text does not mention, although it represents the core of the plot, is the simple fact that the agitators are operating *illegally* in hostile territory. It is their task to prepare, by means of propaganda and cautious subversion, an armed insurrection by Chinese workers in Mukden. The disguised agitators cross the border to bring the "classics" of the revolution and the "ABC of Communism" to China. They are supposed to open the workers' eyes to the exploitation they suffer as coolies, factory workers, and soldiers and prepare them for the coming insurrection. In the course of this subversive mission, however, they "had to shoot their youngest comrade" because he commits several tactical blunders, but also, and more important, because he wants to force a premature uprising—which means that he fails to understand the fundamental issue of diagnosing the right "revolutionary moment." He reveals their identity and thereby endangers the agitators as well as the rebellious workers. The "discipline" referred to in the note is nothing but the tactics of clandestine operations. These tactical aspects, or, rather, the exemplary mistakes made by the Young Comrade, must have been of considerable importance to Brecht. In the four subsequent revisions of the play between 1931 and 1936 he never tempered the apodictic tone of the political songs, but he introduces numerous details that flesh out the tactical problems in ever greater detail. Clearly, the *Lehrstück* or learning play *The Measures Taken* is in large part a school for agitators.

It is therefore not just a theatrical gesture that the events in China begin with an "effacement" of political and national identity symbolized by donning masks: "Then be no longer yourselves: you no longer Karl Schmidt from Berlin; you no longer Anna Kjersk from Kazan; and you no longer Peter Sawitsch from Moscow. You are all without name or mother, empty pages on which the revolution may write its instructions" (Brecht 1977, 12; translation emended). The use of masks is the theatrical symbol for a role-play necessary *outside* the theater, in the "real," that is, the political world. The importance of this effacement in the context of intelligence activities is obvious: it is the cover-up of identities and allegiances, a switch of passport identities that turns Russians and Germans into Chinese, "born of Chinese mothers, yellow-skinned, who in sleep and delirium speak only Chinese" (ibid., 13). It is a disguise in enemy territory, an act of mimicry to fully adapt to the area of operations. To act undetected is the prime command for all subsequent actions—and in each and every case it is violated by the Young Comrade. Every scene shows a different form of lapse in his behavior: When he is sent out to incite the barge haulers to demand better working conditions, he abandons political instructions in favor of ineffective assistance ("The Stone"). When he is supposed to provide workers with "forbidden literature" during a strike, he instead gets caught up in a scuffle with the police, as a result of which the group is on the run for a week ("Justice"). Next he fails to forge a tactically important alliance with a rice merchant, who is to provide the arms for the uprising, because he disapproves of the latter's snappy song in praise of capitalist surplus value ("What Is Man?"). The Young Comrade fails to master the strategy of "self-effacement" and "subversion"; instead he aspires to the heroism of a public confession of faith and immediate, individual help. This may be honorable, but according to the logic of *The Measures Taken* it is a mistake. Secret subversion is not about heroic gestures. The chorus comments on the blunders of the Young Comrade in its song "In Praise of Illegal Work":

> It is good to seize the word
> As a weapon in class warfare.
> To call the masses to battle
> With loud and resounding voices . . .
> Our petty daily work is difficult but useful.
> Tenacity and secrecy are the links
> That bind the Party network . . .
> To speak, but
> To conceal the speaker.
> To conquer, but
> To conceal the conqueror.
> To die, but
> To conceal death.
> Who would not do great things for glory, but who
> Would do them for silence? (Brecht 1977, 123 and following; translation emended)

This gesture of self-denial contains the deeper meaning of the play's initial effacement. The song "In Praise of Illegal Work"—which bears a striking resemblance to "Cover Your Tracks!"—confronts the pathos of grand speeches and noble deeds with the obscurity of the conspiratorial. Those who die unrecognized and unknown for the cause reap neither gratitude nor fame; those who sacrifice themselves sacrifice everything, including all the glamour of sacrifice; they work in the dark and will enjoy neither praise nor commemoration nor victory. The agitator is no hero; he silently turns himself into the instrument of a historical process. The agents of the world revolution vanish completely, physically and symbolically, leaving no legacy—not even their deeds. The conspiratorial existence is the smallest, meekest, dirtiest existence.

"Effacement" is thus both a political and a rhetorical term, one that links the denial of national and political identity to a rhetorical strategy of inauthentic speech: "to speak, but to conceal the speaker." In doing so it touches upon the strange theory and practice of that particular type of drama Brecht referred to as *Lehrstück,* "learning play." The basic feature of the *Lehrstück* is the distancing of speakers from their speech: the text, Brecht notes in the 1920s, is to be recited "like a quotation" (Brecht 1996, 101). The learning process envisaged by the learning play is based not so much on seeing the play as on exploring a part on stage by playing it: "If someone wants to commit treason then he will go to the theater in the morning and play a scene in which treason is committed" (Brecht, quoted in Steinweg 1972a, 18).What is being learned by such theatrical pedagogy are rules of political conduct and betrayal. By playacting one learns how to convince, undermine, gather intelligence, and stay unrecognized in the service of the revolution—in short, behaviors "executed in such a way that the state benefits" (Brecht 2003, 29), as Brecht notes in connection with another learning play, *Fatzer.* For Brecht, playacting is a training in political behavior. "Stances"—in the sense of political positions—can, as Benjamin noted with regard to Brecht's theater, "be learned" (Benjamin 1999, 366). To quote from the *Baden-Baden Lesson on Consent,* "just a stance, just a word of guidance / Can we give you" (Brecht 1997, 33; translation emended). The type of acting implied in the learning play is not just for professional actors; it is a technique of political action and analysis for everyone. Indeed, the most radical formulation of the *Lehrstück* theory eliminates the audience altogether (or at the very least considers it expendable):

> In principle the learning play does not require an audience, though it can of course be put to use. The learning play is based on the assumption that by acting out certain types of behavior, assuming certain positions, reproducing certain speeches, and so on, players can be socially influenced . . . The imitation of exemplary paradigms is as much a part of it as the critique of these paradigms by very deliberately playing them in a different ways. (Brecht, in Steinweg 1972a, 51)

Acting in a learning play can dispense with the audience because it is designed to train the thought and actions of the actors, not primarily the audience. The learning effect, however, arises not only from presenting or imitating exemplary behavior but also from acting out the reprehensible and "asocial." Acting, then, involves *taking* a position without necessarily *sharing* it; the goal is to explore and evaluate the internal logic of the position in question, its discourse and behavior, by means of acting (see also Horn 2006). The *Lehrstücke,* then, are "experimental setups" to promote "self-understanding" (Steinweg 1972b, 19).[17] However, in contrast to the "vulgar Marxism" of which Brecht was occasionally accused, the political instruction conveyed by this theatrical technique is anything but unequivocal. Brecht's texts do not transmit simple messages; they are a *practice* "to open the view on theory" (Nägele 1992, 30) or, to put it more broadly, to open a space for political reflection. The instructions of the *learning plays* thus have less to do with Marxist-Leninist doctrine than with acquiring a reflexive distance to an assumed position. It is this distance to one's own position as well as to that of others that ties the methods of the learning play to the ambiguities of the political, whose arcane side depends and thrives on this reflexive, theatrical distance.

The Measures Taken presents the aptitude for illegal work as an aptitude for acting. The effacement is represented by the agitators donning masks, and the "betrayal" of the Young Comrade consists in his removing the mask and divulging his origins: "We have come from Moscow" (Brecht 1977, 30). It is not only the plot but also its performance that turns this learning into a play about acting. After all, to reenact events for the benefit of the chorus the four young agitators have to play the part of the Young Comrade whom they killed.[18] Brecht had the idea that in the course of the drama each of the four actors playing the agitators should play the Young Comrade one time. "Each of them," he said shortly before his death, "has to take over one part after another: defendant, accuser, witness, judge. Under these conditions all of them will be part of the discussion and gain knowledge—practical knowledge—of what dialectics is" (Brecht, in Steinweg 1976, 197 and following). Parts, in other words, are positions that can be acted out, "experiments" (*Versuche,* as Brecht used to call his plays) or exercises that facilitate the dialectic reflection of political action because they demand that one assume contradictory positions: "exercises to increase suppleness, designed for mentally athletic good dialecticians" (ibid., 198). *The Measures Taken* demonstrates that only good dialecticians make good agitators. Dialectics is less a matter of Hegelian sublations than one of insisting on contradictions.[19] The Young Comrade shows that a lack of acting—which in Brecht's eyes equals a lack of dialectics—is fatal for a political praxis that demands subtle clandestine scheming, alliances with the enemy, furtive mobilizations, and stealthy progress rather than goodwill, confessions, convictions, and inflammatory rhetoric. What is at stake for the learning play, then, is not a politics of identity, of fixed positions that can be represented on stage, but the practice of shifting positions, of changing to—as Brecht liked to say—"change the world" (Brecht 1977, 25).

Taking Measures: The Ethics and Politics of Exception

Following his three mistakes involving the coolies, the strikers, and the rice merchant, the Young Comrade commits his gravest error: he attempts to stoke the scattered "hunger riots" into one armed insurrection. The agitators warn him that the masses are insufficiently armed and lack the necessary organization. To quote the 1931 version, his ultimate mistake is "betrayal" (Brecht 1977, 25). He renounces the "classics" of Marxism-Leninism, breaks with his comrades by going rogue and forcing an insurrection, and reveals the identity of the agitators. As a result, the group is persecuted and the insurgents face a bloodbath. In the final version of 1935–36 the Young Comrade's mistake is presented, more concretely, as an error of clandestine revolutionary work: he is fooled by one of the merchants' agents.

In his critique of the play the socialist author Alfred Kurella established a direct link between the play and the failed Hamburg insurrection of 1923.[20] Leaving aside Kurella's polemics against Brecht's so-called right opportunist point of view (Brecht 1965, 168), the reference serves to highlight a crucial aspect of revolutionary rationality: the timing or "readiness" of the revolution, or, more precisely, the vital issue of recognizing the right historical moment in which an insurrection is possible. Hamburg 1923 embodies the caveat all revolutionary action is subject to: namely, the question of whether "the time is ripe." Determining the latter involves observation and deferral, acceleration and retardation; it requires that one turn oneself into a both a seismograph and a willing instrument of the historical process. Wanting to bring about this historical moment on his own is the Young Comrade's gravest error. "Yours is an impetuous revolution," his comrades admonish him, "that will last a day / And be throttled tomorrow. / But our revolution begins tomorrow. / It will conquer and change the world. / Your revolution will end when you end." (Brecht 1977, 28). Rather than turning himself into a patient instrument, the Young Comrade aspires to be the revolution's impatient hero, thus violating the two fundamental commandments of revolutionary reason: the conspiratorial imperative and the submission to the historical advance of the party, the revolutionary subject:

> The individual has only two eyes
> The Party has a thousand eyes.
> The Party can see several lands
> The individual a single city.
> The individual has only his hour
> The Party has many hours.
> The individual can be annihilated
> But the Party cannot be annihilated
> For it is the vanguard of the masses

> And it lays out its battles
> According to the methods of our classics, which are derived from
> The recognition of reality. (Brecht 1977, 29)

The party transcends the knowledge and the will of the individual. It is a historic whole, while the individual is merely a part that lasts for no more than an "hour." The party is a mighty, indestructible entity, a force that focuses the will of many and advances the progress of history. Therefore only the party is able to decide on the right moment. Herein lies the specific sovereignty the party incorporates. As an antagonist to the sovereignty of the bourgeois state, the revolutionary party emerges as a countersovereignty, and the relationship of the revolutionary fighter to the party mirrors that of the subject to the state.

The state opposed by the revolutionary party, however, is conceived not so much as a sovereign structure but as a sphere of ruthless, implacable economic exploitation. Here is where Brecht's specific and very practical take on Marxism becomes most clearly visible. The world of *The Measures Taken* is one in which the workers are annihilated by underpayment and excessive work, as is evident both in the song of the rice merchant—"I don't know what Man is. / I only know his Price" (Brecht 1977, 24; translation emended)—and that of the barge haulers—"When . . . the children ask / Who pulled the heavy barge / The answer is: / It was pulled." This is classical Marxist theory: the commodity destroys and renders invisible the labor force that was necessary for its production; as a commodity that comes with a certain exchange value, the product obscures the producer as well as the labor behind objective exchange form. Marx refers to this process of destruction as a "mystery of commodities, [a] magic and necromancy that surrounds the products of labor as long as they take the form of commodities" (Marx and Engels 1975, 87). The exploitation of the coolies consists in the fact that the food they need to regenerate their physical strength is such an expensive commodity that they are unable to purchase it by selling their labor. They starve, in short, because the rice they are hauling is so much more expensive than their own labor. Surplus value is the degree to which labor is cheaper than the value of the commodity it produces. The rice barge haulers are pushed into death, as it were, by the economic conditions: they die from the surplus value they are producing. And there is no law to protect them from this extreme form of exploitation, they are "bare life"—Giorgio Agamben's term—exposed to the brutal mechanisms of the market (Agamben 1998). This gives rise to the revolutionary pathos eager to break the persistent economic annihilation. It is a world in which the law no longer protects humans but abandons them to economic destitution; and precisely this complete lack of rights legitimizes the party's revolutionary actions. Against the backdrop of this lawlessness and economic misery, the party's task and legitimation lies in its goal to bestow rights on those without rights, to bestow subsistence on those who are not killed but "pushed into death" by economic exploitation.[21]

By dissociating himself from the party as the ultimate instance of legitimation, the Young Comrade causes a "state of emergency" that requires the type of "measure" alluded to in the title of the play. He is injured and unable to flee, the agitators are on the run, and troops have been dispatched to deal with the insurgents. If Communist infiltrators are found among them, the agitators fear, the soldiers will massacre everybody. Such are the circumstances in which the agitators decide to take their "measure": to kill the Young Comrade and throw him into a lime pit to make every trace of him disappear. In doing so, they are following the command to "cover their tracks." They ask the Young Comrade whether he can think of a better solution to their problems, and he replies in the negative. But what exactly does it mean to take "a measure"? Why is Brecht using this term derived from legal theory?[22] The legal structure and implications of this particular term were at the center of an inquiry Carl Schmitt conducted around the same time that Brecht wrote his play. Schmitt contrasts the notion "measure" (*Maßnahme*) to the regular rule of law by describing it as a singular but necessary violent intervention in a state of emergency (Schmitt 1985c, 261). Indeed, the measure is justified only by the state of exception; it lacks any kind of regularity and falls outside the legitimacy of the law. The measure is not the application of a rule but an exception that cannot be generalized; its necessity arises from the singular circumstances of an "unprecedented, abnormal situation" (Schmitt 1985a, 333). According to Schmitt, to be able and entitled to take such measures is the mark and prerogative of sovereignty. The measure, he argues, is characterized by and tied to "singular circumstances," while the law is enacted on a sustained basis (and not just for a limited duration). Schmitt was aware of the proximity between his deliberations and Brecht's text: forty years later he noted on the margins of his copy of the Italian translation of *Legality and Legitimacy:* "cf. Bert Brecht. *The Measures Taken. Lehrstück,* first staged 10 December 1930 in Berlin" (see Sander 1979, 151).

The action of the agitators no doubt retains the status of a unique decision prompted by danger and lack of time. It is the result of an emergency, an expedient rather than "punitive measure," as years later the House Committee for Un-American Activities tried to insinuate when questioning Brecht (HUAC hearing, September 24–26, 1947, quoted in Steinweg 1972a, 256). Above all, it is no punishment in the legal sense.[23] Even though *The Measures Taken* assumes the shape of a trial by staging the agitators' self-justification to a party tribunal, the Young Comrade's "burial" (Brecht 1977, 32–34) does not constitute a juridical act; it is neither verdict nor punishment. The Moscow Version of 1934–35 clarifies: [The Control Chorus]: "So it was no sentence?" / [The four Agitators, very loud]: "No! A measure!" (Steinweg 1972a, 100). A measure is precisely the absence of a legal precedent or rule. Given that the events take place in an illegal, clandestine space, there is no law that applies to the case of the Young Comrade. The agitators act and reach their decisions in the extralegal sphere of the political secret and the secret war, a sphere marked by its constant exception from the law. In this sphere, actions are undertaken that are not covered by any legal order. But it nonetheless implies a sovereign entity—in this case, the party—that sees itself as the guarantor of law and justice. What Brecht is focusing on in this controversial turn of the play is the paradoxical entanglement of sovereignty and *arcanum*. The measure taken is both necessary and reprehensible; it is therefore not *justified* but *accepted* by the control chorus: "We agree with you" (Brecht 1977, 34). The measure is an act that cannot ever be generalized, neither politically (in the shape of a law or rule) nor ethically (as a moral imperative); instead it remains tied to a singular, exceptional situation. The secret opens the space of a politics of exception marked by a paradox: to do whatever may be necessary but to make it neither a rule nor an object of debate—precisely because any justification would be reprehensible.

The Measures Taken is a *Lehrstück* not only about politics but also about the ethics of clandestine operations. The revolutionary task requires more than techniques and tactics; it also demands a surrender of the self that goes beyond any submission to the party. The very moral integrity of the individual has to be sacrificed. Brecht spells out the monstrous implications of this sacrifice in the play's most famous and scandalous lines:

> THE CONTROL CHORUS:
>
> What vileness would you not commit
> To eradicate vileness?
> If at last you could change the world,
> What would be beneath you?
> Who are you?

Descend into filth
Embrace the butcher, but
Change the world: It needs it! (Brecht 1977, 25; translation emended)

The revolution demands of its agents nothing less than the surrender of their desire to do good. Agents may act in a tactical, unscrupulously "dirty" fashion, but according to Brecht this does not make them immoral. The paradox of doing evil for the sake of good is not, as Brecht was so frequently accused of, a type of opportunism for which the end justifies the means. What the "Descend into filth" lines attempt to formulate is at the core of what could be labeled "dirty ethics." It is the ethical paradox of betrayal—the drama of Judas, who does something as necessary as it is unforgivable. In an intricate reading of *The Measures Taken,* Slavoj Žižek notes that these dirty ethics contain an "inherent self-negation of ethics, that is, an ethical injunction which suspends ethical universality" (Žižek 1992a, 177). It denies the universality of a humanist ethics, whose ultima ratio consists in the well-being of an ultimately isolated "human" whose immediate sufferings are to be remedied. What is demanded instead—all the lies, cunning, deception, tactical alliances, and ultimately the killing of a comrade—does not follow any law, rule, or ethical commandment that anybody would wish to generalize. The dirt the individual brings down on himself is a self-violation (Žižek speaks of a "shooting at oneself," Žižek 2000, 150) that infringes on the revolution's humanism, its hope to end all "suffering." Ultimately, to do evil to achieve good means to harm good for its own sake, that is, to change the goal while one is heading toward it. Brecht adapts this "dirty" self-suspension of the ethical in favor of a radicalization of politics. However, this does not mean that the goal is abandoned. "Dirty ethics" aspires to a justice beyond all existing notions of goodness and justice—a justice which, as intimated by the eschatological undertones of the revolutionary project, is "not of this world." It can only be grasped negatively, as a utopian desire for a world that is completely "different": "Change the world: It needs it!" The "communism" Brecht speaks of, the revolution itself, is a project of pure change. The world is to be seen different and differently, as *changeable.* For Brecht, the revolution is the possibility of grasping and realizing the contingent and changeable within the given.

The agitators' most puzzling gesture serves to further emphasize this ethical paradox. Before they kill the Young Comrade and throw him into a lime pit, they ask for his consent—just as they later ask for that of the control chorus. At first glance the request seems absurd: the Young

Comrade is faced with a choice he does not have. How can he consent to something that he cannot refuse and that in any case will be brutally enforced? Nonetheless, as Žižek has emphasized, he is left with a choice, though it is not whether he is to live or die. The choice concerns his belonging to the fraternity of revolutionary fighters. If he did not consent, he would lose not only his life but also the community he was part of. With his final words he confirms his loyalty to the revolutionary community even beyond his death:

> And he said: In the interests of Communism
> In agreement with the progress of the proletarian masses
> Of all lands
> Consenting to the revolutionizing of the world. (Brecht 1977, 34)

Brecht's frequently quoted "consent," which was already at the center of his learning play *He Who Says Yes* (ibid., 62–69; see also Horn 2007), is the position that the subject may adopt in these particular circumstances—that is, to decide in favor of being part of a community even when the latter has decreed one's expulsion. He affirms it *ex negativo,* in much the same way that an exception confirms the rule. Žižek described this "paradox of forced choice" as one that involves the choice between pure force and necessity (of killing without consent) and the choice to have a choice (killing with consent):

> What is at stake in the situation of forced choice is that the subject freely *chooses* the community it *always already is* a member of . . . The paradox of the forced choice has nothing mad about it . . . On the contrary, the person is mad who behaves as though he had a free choice . . . The choice is always structured in such a way that it implies a meta-choice: if we make the wrong choice, we lose the very possibility of choosing. (Žižek 1991, 122–23)[24]

With the scene of the Young Comrade's consent (*Einverständnis*) Brecht seems to be eager to overstate this Žižekian ethico-political paradox. The agent's scandalous acquiescence to his moral and physical effacement highlights what is at stake in the relationship between agent and revolution: while the "whole" of the revolution comprises and surpasses the "individual," the individual remains, at least from Brecht's point of view, irreducibly a part of the whole, even in his very negation. By virtue of its emphasis on change Brecht's revolution is a source of potentiality in the realm of the political: it sees the world as one that can and must be changed. We have to keep the "whole" in mind when evaluating a measure taken, even and especially when it contradicts the "virtues" of the individual. But it is precisely this moment of contradiction which manifests the essence of affiliation:

> He who fights for Communism
> Must be able to fight and not to fight
> Must tell the truth and not tell the truth
> Render service and not render service
> Must keep promises and break promises
> Place himself in danger and avoid danger
> Be recognizable and be unrecognizable.
> He who fights for Communism
> Has of all virtues only one:
> That he fights for Communism. (Brecht 1977, 13; translation emended)

The flexibility of the good dialectician, the thespian skills of the actor trained in and by the learning plays, the *dissimulatio* of the agitator—they are the art of enduring and performing the inner paradox of a political project that arises first and foremost *as* a contradiction *in* contradiction to the existing order. Brecht reveals the irreducibly rhetorical and theatrical dimension of clandestine politics. The agent of the world revolution does something that is effectively impossible: the agent fights and does not fight, tells the truth and lies, serves and does not serve, reveals and conceals himself or herself. Brecht's envisaged revolution has no program (yet), no content, and no ideology. It is a pure struggle against a world of exploitation and annihilation, a suspension of the law in a world in which the lawful order is nothing but the order of injustice (see also Horn 2007). With all his or her moral and political contradictions the agent is a subject who embodies the degree zero of all political action, the pure potential of the political. The agent of the world revolution is literally capable of anything.

While *The Measures Taken* may amount to an analytics of illegal work, it is neither an apology nor a denunciation of that work. This reading argues that Brecht is primarily concerned with shedding light on the ethical and political *paradox* inherent to the revolutionary project and its *arcana:* "Descend into filth / Embrace the butcher, but / Change the world." This is neither an espousal of cynical ruthlessness nor, as Ruth Fischer claimed, a justification of terrorism. Fischer's anti-Stalinist furor nevertheless made her, next to Walter Benjamin, Brecht's most politically astute reader. While toward the late 1920s Comintern agents and chekists became suspected of being lackeys in the service of a cruel and perfidious politics, Brecht (who was personally acquainted with some of those Comintern emissaries) endeavored to illuminate the figures' innate political and ethical paradox. In doing so he saved what little was salvageable from the project of the world revolution and its clandestine program, before they succumbed to the paranoia and blunt brutality of Stalin's secret police. It is the pathos of changing the world at any price and by any means possible. Brecht's lyrical and theatrical school of revolutionary agents is neither a demonization nor a justification of this particular figure, but arguably the most revealing intensification of the fundamental contradictions that inevitably shape clandestine politics.

Part 6

Cold War

1 War and Peace

> We have no plans. We have games. We play games: What if? How many men? What would it take? Is there a cheaper way to stabilize a regime?—That's what we're paid to do.
>
> —Sydney Pollack and James Grady, *Three Days of the Condor* (1975)

One of the most apt emblems of the Cold War is a switch. By inserting a key and turning it 90 degrees you can switch from PEACE to WAR. The switch reduces war and peace to two states of a common machinal dispositive that goes by the name of "Cold War." No matter how clearly the switch may distinguish between the two, they are inextricably tied to each other as parts of the same apparatus. War is a latent possibility of peace; peace is guaranteed only by the constant threat of war. In the words of Herman Kahn, the most prominent theorist of thinking the unthinkable war, both are part of a continuum: "War is a terrible thing, but so is peace. The difference seems to be a *quantitative one of degree and standards*" (Kahn 1961, 28; emphasis added). The switch links war and peace and allows us to decide between the two, but also foregrounds the technical nature of this decision. It is a machine or weapon that, once released, can no longer be stopped—just like the hydrogen bombs and cruise missiles that have abolished all traditional concepts of war by posing the threat of total destruction. Even though the switch itself may still require a human hand, this new kind of war tends to render humans superfluous. As part of the setup that leads to total destruction, man is either the last, lonely decision maker or a dysfunctional, irrational element famously known as the "human factor." The possibility of total mutual destruction inverts the relationship between war and enmity: war is no longer grounded on enmity; enmity is structured by military technology. The entire population of a country or region becomes hostage to the political conflict. But precisely because a war can no longer be "won" in the traditional sense of the word, the Cold War can no longer be waged as war. The new weapons turn war into a merely hypothetical exercise. Waging war, in Kahn's frequently quoted formula, amounts to "thinking about the unthinkable" (Kahn 1962).

On/off, peace/war, 1/0: the binaries pinpoint the basic structure of the Cold War—a bivalent enmity that came to encompass the entire world. There was no region, no important country that was not caught up in this divisive global matrix. Everyone was forced to submit to this either/or structure by joining the alliances that, more or less willingly, supported one or the other of the two key players. As a result, the direct confrontation between the latter could be avoided by means of staging a series of proxy wars (Korea, Vietnam, Iran, Latin America, and last but not least the divided Berlin). In the face of total destruction the Cold War was "neither war nor peace" (Seton-Watson 1960)—a peace armed to the teeth and a frozen war. "The Cold War," Carl Schmitt wrote in 1963, "defies all established distinction between war, peace and neutrality, between politics and economics, military and civilian sphere, combatants and noncombatants—with the exception of the consistent distinction between friend and enemy which is both the source and the essence of this war" (Schmitt 1996, 13).

The logical and political impossibility of an all-out war between the superpowers entails a radical rethinking of the role and status of intelligence work. Intelligence is no longer a tool for the preparation of an armed conflict, and no longer a special military unit or auxiliary police force. Postwar intelligence services mutate into highly professionalized organizations that combine the power of the "state apparatus" and its administrative structure with the secrecy and violence of the "war machine" (Deleuze and Guattari 1987). Secret war *replaces actual combat.* Consequently, the real combatants of the Cold War are spies and traitors, while scientists and analysts are its intellectual fathers. Deeply enmeshed in the ambiguity of the political that is neither open conflict nor nonviolent peace, Cold War intelligence inhabits the gray zone between preventing and preparing war. "What is clear," Thomas Powers notes,

> is that the cold war was a war fought by other means. Principal among them was the arms race itself and the secret war of intel-

> ligence operatives and proxy armies. We may question whether this war-that-never-was could have been avoided, or might have been carried out more sensibly, or won more easily or cheaply . . . But there is now not much question that *the secret war and the cold war were the same thing.* (Powers 2002, 57)

Intelligence

The Cold War took place in people's heads, though less as a clash of ideologies and propaganda[1] than in the shape of a forty-year-long thought experiment. This thought experiment focused on turning the switch from peace to war by working out countless military scenarios under the conditions of nuclear war. The basic paradox was the existence of weapons "too effective to be used. This paradox is almost too much for the military mind . . . to bear" (Draper 1985, 27). Instead of waging war, parties prepare for and play out wars in constantly updated speculations based on the premise that a real conflict would entail the destruction of both parties. Nuclear war, the theoretically possible annihilation of large parts of the globe and its population, was, as Derrida claimed, a "fable" (Derrida 1984, 24), a phantasm that imbued the political with an apocalyptic formula. The Cold War is a war that projects itself as hypothesis and fiction: "What if?" Hovering on the threshold of possibility, it fuels an immense amount of research and speculation about the enemy. Its most important weapon was not the hydrogen bomb but knowledge of the enemy. Spying on the enemy's arsenals, defense capabilities, internal power structures, economy, and foreign alliances produced valuable knowledge that had to be processed in giant administrative structures and fed into the political decision-making process. Hence the history of U.S. foreign politics during that particular epoch can be summarized by looking at the changing relationship between the president and the director of central intelligence (Andrew 1995). At the same time, entire disciplines and areas of specialization, above all nuclear physics, were transformed, as it were, into "weapons-grade" arcane knowledge. Scientists became the bearers of secrets—and thus security risks. Classification and compartmentalization were supposed to prevent this knowledge from spreading, but as in the case of the Rosenbergs, fear (or mere suspicion) of leaks fueled hysterical witch hunts for "nuclear spies" (see the section titled "Classified Knowledge: Nuclear Secrets" in part 7, "State Paranoia"). The arms race was fundamentally a knowledge race.

The real Cold Warriors therefore were not men in uniform but civilians: secret agents, scientists, and all sorts of experts specializing in weapons, crisis management, and enemy resources—physicists, mathematicians, and computer scientists, as well as psychologists, ethnologists, and economists. University research, espionage, and military war games joined hands in the grand enterprise of speculating about the enemy. No longer out in the field, espionage was relegated to offices stuffed with files and model weapons (figure 21). The impressive list of names associated with think tanks like the Santa Monica–based RAND Corporation, financed by the U.S. Air Force, or the Hudson Institute in Washington, D.C., reveals the productive amalgamation of military and civilian knowledge: John von Neumann, Margaret Mead and Gregory Bateson, Herman Kahn, Albert Wohlstetter, and Herbert Goldhamer.[2] It was the task of this civilian military science to develop, analyze, and simulate possible military scenarios.[3] But since a real war was out of the question, all conjectures were limited to the virtual domain: a war that could not be waged had to be anticipated and investigated as a model. Neither knowledge of the enemy nor realistic models of the coming conflict could be derived from experience. When traditional military personnel attempted to resist input from civilians, Hermann Kahn used to ask them: "How many thermonuclear wars have you fought recently?" (quoted in Kostelanetz 1968, 105).

Not surprisingly, the fundamental difficulties involved in obtaining political-military knowledge led to the first epistemological self-reflection on the part of intelligence agencies. What kind of knowledge does intelligence represent? How is it gained? What methodological blind spots does it imply? Sherman Kent's *Strategic Intelligence for American World Policy* (1949), one of the most important postwar theories of intelligence, was the first attempt to describe intelligence as a specific type of knowledge and to analyze the issues that military-political intelligence work has to contend with: "What knowledge should the U.S. have about the future of other states to have the requisite foresight?" (Kent 1965, 40). A former professor of history at Yale and long-term head of the CIA's Office of National Estimates, Kent no longer conceives of intelligence as a state secret or military ruse but presents it as a commodity that is commissioned, produced, and received and that subsequently forms the basis for political and military decision making (figure 22). In Kent's view, intelligence is a type of research like any other. He civilizes intelligence by providing a theory of intelligence as a total, encyclopedic, and not necessarily secret type of knowledge. "Some of this knowledge," he notes, "can be acquired by clandestine means, but the bulk of it must be had through unromantic

Figure 21. Office of the Soviet Analysis Section of the CIA in the 1970s. Photograph by Roger Ressmeyer/Corbis Images.

open-and-above-board observation and research" (ibid., 3). Instead of deriving intelligence from police operations or military reconnaissance, Kent pioneers a distinction between different domains of intelligence gathering: people ("Who will be the director of the Pavlov Institute?"); geography (compilation and reconnaissance of terrains and regions, in-

Figure 22. Sherman Kent (1903–1986), a historian at Yale University and the spiritual father of intelligence analysis. Kent served in the Research and Analysis Branch of the Office of Strategic Services during the Second World War and was later appointed head of the CIA's Office of National Estimates. His study *Strategic Intelligence for American World Policy* (1949) is one of the most influential manuals for postwar intelligence evaluation.

cluding their changes); military data (from weapons technology to recruiting statistics and training procedures); political, economic, and social data ("What groups are emerging to social and economic eminence?"); mentalities and morality (attitudes toward the government, social conflicts, role of religion, and so on). He distinguishes between factual matters ("spot intelligence") and the targeted exploration of specific issues ("narrow-deep intelligence")—that is, between issues related to a concrete situation and those that concern the enemy's plans and potential. The epistemological self-reflection introduced by Kent not only gave rise to a quasi-academic self-understanding of the intelligence services but also had institutional consequences.[4] Improvised subsections attached to war ministries turned into autonomous administrative bodies that were fully equipped both financially and technologically. Now their image was shaped not by gun-toting field agents but by deskbound case officers: analysts, file clerks, specialists for war gaming or aerial reconnaissance. Among them were the protagonists of the era's espionage fiction, from John le Carré's George Smiley, the pudgy melancholic shuffling along the gray corridors of MI6, to Tom Clancy's experts for sonar acoustics, satellite imaging, and submarine technology and other such things. Secret service information was no longer made up of war secrets obtained out in the field; it was enigmatic raw material whose true significance must be carefully deciphered, evaluated, and processed in huge administrations.

Adventures of a Reader: *Three Days of the Condor*

It is therefore not a fancy idea but a succinct allegory of Kent's vision of intelligence work as quasi-academic research that Joe Turner, hero of Sydney Pollack's CIA thriller *Three Days of the Condor* (based on James Grady's novel *Six Days of the Condor*), is a professional reader (Grady 1974; Pollack 1975). His New York workplace, a CIA unit under the cover name "The American Literary Historical Society," is charged with scouring literally every text in the world (fiction or nonfiction) for useful or hidden information. *Three Days of the Condor* is one of the most incisive fables of the CIA because its (reluctant) hero is not a field agent but a bookish in-house analyst. It also displaces the methodological and epistemological self-reflection of the intelligence world that Kent had initiated from a peaceful academic setting into the violent world of contract killers, internal intrigues, and covert actions. But in the beginning, the protagonist agent Turner (Robert Redford) seems to take himself for exactly the quasi-academic researcher that Sherman Kent expected the new generation of intelligence officers to be: "I work for the CIA. I am not a spy. I just read books." Turner (code name Condor) is a professional reader and connoisseur of thrillers (he is able to solve the mystery of a vanished bullet by resorting to *Dick Tracy*) who peruses seemingly harmless texts in search of intelligence secrets without really knowing what he is looking for. He comes across an unsuccessful novel that has been translated into an unusual assortment of languages—a minor observation, it seems, but one that will result in his entire unit being wiped out by hired killers. Both the beginning of the film and its conclusion demonstrate that in the mid-1970s intelligence work amounts to textual processing. Machines scan and leaf through books, tickers disgorge endless tapes of text, and women with oversized glasses write reports and analyze entire books in half a day (figures 23 and 24). The secret Turner accidentally hits upon is revealed by the languages into which the novel has been translated: it concerns a covert, illegal operation launched by "a CIA inside the CIA" to secure U.S. access to Middle Eastern oil resources. Turner discovers that the mastermind behind the plan is a high-level CIA operative, the deputy director of operations, Middle Eastern section. The knowledge represented by Turner is archival knowledge, his gaze is that of a reader,

Figure 23. Sydney Pollack, *Three Days of the Condor* (U.S.A., 1975). Opening credits. Copyright © Paramount Pictures.

Figure 24. *Three Days of the Condor:* Agent Turner (Robert Redford) at his desk. Copyright © Paramount Pictures.

and his personal quirk is to predict the future (especially the weather)—which is exactly what analysts are supposed to be good at. A secondary character is given the illustrious name Heidegger, and the beginning of the film focuses on Chinese ideograms. All is text. Not coincidentally, in the end relief comes in the shape of a print medium: the *New York Times*, whose office building provides the backdrop for the final scenes. Turner hopes to save his own life by publishing the story for which his entire unit was killed. The public sphere is mobilized against the violence and secrecy of intelligence's world; for the upright operative fighting the "CIA inside the CIA," publicity is a last resort: words against bullets.

However, *Three Days of the Condor* also reveals the blind spot of Kent's academic vision of an intelligence work cleansed of all violence, deceit, and paranoia. Obviously, working for an intelligence agency involves more than quietly studying incoming data. It is, as Turner/Condor painfully must learn, also a matter of murder, treason, secrecy, and illegality. A "CIA inside the CIA" capable of eliminating one of its own sections embodies the agency's deeply paranoid and conspiratorial side; it represents a space of unbridled violence in the service of a power-hungry pragmatism whose credo is summarized by a CIA operative at the movie's conclusion: "We have no plans. We have games. We play games: '*What if? How many men? What would it take? Is there a cheaper way to stabilize a regime?*' That's what we're paid to do." War games and scenarios design a realpolitik that does not have concrete goals and plans but is eager to test what is politically possible: "What if . . . ?" The massacre of the American Literary Historical Society exposes the fury of a secret war that is bent on enforcing all that can be accomplished, whose secrecy is absolute, and whose paranoia is out of control. The CIA within the CIA embodies the unchecked violence and absurd mania for secrecy of those who won't shy away from murdering their own people to cover up a planned operation; in addition, it is the specter of an intelligence world with no political oversight that led to more and more public criticism and eventually to the creation of the Church Committee in 1975. Pollock's "CIA inside the CIA" embodies the internal paradox of a political-military institution which spends so much time speculating about the enemy that it turns into an enemy itself.

2 War Games: War as Hypothesis

The Enemy as Black Box

While postwar secret services differentiated into an array of highly specialized institutions (the American intelligence apparatus, for instance, is composed of more than fifteen different institutions), and while the process of assessing their own limits and potentials led to a permanent restructuring of internal organizations and screening strategies, fiction offers a second-order reflection of this self-reflective structure of intelligence. Political fictions of the Cold War mirror the occasionally delirious, at times stupid, and invariably hypothetical nature of the conflict. The dark side of the political may be removed from public deliberation and control, but spy thrillers shed light on the mechanisms of the secret war as the real venue of Cold War politics. As absurd as many of the plots and scenarios may be, and no matter how much they stress their own status as fiction (in the case of Stanley Kubrick's *Dr. Strangelove,* the disclaimer at the beginning was prescribed by the government), the Cold War fiction probes and elucidates the imaginary and phantasmal dimensions of the real-life conflict. It reflects on the fictional status of the hypothetical war.

Since the stability—the frozen status, as it were—of the Cold War depended on each side's ability to anticipate the other's every move, the superpowers faced each other as mysteries of monumental proportions. Obsessed by the idea of the enemy's unfathomability, Eastern and Western intelligence agencies tenaciously strove to pry into each other. Rarely did we gather so much knowledge about our enemy, and rarely did we feel so clueless. At the same time, there never was a time when we could less afford ignorance or errors of judgment. If, as military scenarios in the 1960s were eager to assert, war consists of a very small number of disastrous air strikes, then the whole war may be lost on account of one single error. The desire for total knowledge of the enemy, on the one hand, and the phantasm of the enemy's inscrutability, on the other, are the result of a war that is already over before it has begun. It cannot be waged in the open but has to be confined to the murky realm of secrecy.

The political epistemology of the Cold War hinges on the model of the "black box," a structure that is partially or completely unknown. As Philipp von Hilgers points out, it is by definition an epistemic thing that cannot be opened, conceived of as "the enemy's machine," an uncanny, dangerous object whose behavior (that is, its input and output) may, however, be observed or even tested. "The concept of the black box offers the chance to continuously and operatively determine anew the relation between knowing and not-knowing . . . With the constant displacement of the demarcation between knowing and not-knowing, the distinction between friend and enemy is converted from being absolute and imaginary to relative and operational" (von Hilgers 2011, 52–53). The question, however, is how to predict its future behavior when we do not know anything about the internal structure of the black box: "The only conceivable way of unveiling a black box," notes mathematician René Thom, "is to play with it" (Thom 1983, 289). Since war does not allow for experimentation, the "play" has to take place on a different, virtual level—the level of simulation. When it comes to the face-off between superpowers, "playing" entails the suspension of real war and its transfer into the Great Game of espionage and military scenarios. "To play" is to test, speculate, simulate, and project.

Cold War spy thrillers use a narrative format to reflect on the speculative nature of knowledge about the enemy.[5] No matter how diverse the scenes and settings, they all revolve around the central mystery of the enemy. What are the enemy's plans and internal structures? What does our antagonist know? How will the enemy react, and what is he or she capable of? Has the enemy subverted our side? How do we recognize him? Are we really observing the other side, or are we caught up in our own projections? Basically, we can distinguish two different strategies or poetics (which may on occasion overlap or complement each other): the *retrospective* reconstruction that reviews a case in hindsight to find out what *happened,* and the *prospective* conjecture of what *could happen* or what in all likelihood *will happen*. These two perspectives structure both real-world political-military intelligence analysis and associated fictional narratives. The retrospective reconstruction attempts to figure out a mysterious event in the past: take, for instance, the Warren Commission's report on the JFK assassination, or John le Carré's great novel about the MI6 mole Kim Philby. The retrospective is a classic ingredient of criminal investigations; it is as much part of police and intelligence work as it is of spy thrillers. Le Carré's George Smiley, the agent-detective responsible for uncovering the mole in the trilogy *The Quest for Karla,* refers to his investigative technique as "back-bearing." Methodically plowing through old files and conducting countless interviews with all the participants, Smiley tries to uncover the mole's identity. Uncovering the secret, here, is a process of reading and deciphering, both on the side of the detective figure and on the reader's. In this sense, both retrospective novel and police report are *fictions* in Borges's sense. In their search for the one truth they are compelled to constantly untangle the web of alternate versions.

Besides this criminalist *retrospective* model there is a second model that tries to *anticipate* what will or could be. The guiding question here is "What if?" In the context of the Cold War, political and military attempts to predict what is likely to occur *in the future* are at least as important as the retrospective analysis. What will the enemy do? What would make sense for him to do? What is he (technologically, politically, morally) capable of? This approach is concerned with multiple scenarios rather than with one uniform narrative. Its goal is to explore what is possible and probable by trying to find out what the enemy will, or could, do. If fiction—according to Borges—is a "garden of forking paths," the retrospective approach branches off into the past while the prospective approach is directed toward the various futures of possible outcomes. Both models are of fundamental importance to the ways in which Cold War knowledge is organized and narrated, yet the focus on scenarios is probably the most striking reflection of the global conflict's *virtual* character. Let us first concentrate on the future-oriented scenarios.

War Games and Scenarios

Both the Pentagon (especially its Cold War Division) and independent research institutes such as RAND, MIT, or the Hudson Institute started developing and exploring military scenarios in the late 1940s.[6] Based on comprehensive data covering regions, geographical features, armament, transportation systems, and the economic situation of the countries in question, the possible outcomes of political crises were explored by means of gaming. These games took a hypothetical situation as their starting point and then played through a number of possible developments. For instance: what could happen in the event of a Soviet takeover of Berlin or a U.S. intervention in the Far East? These scenarios have the advantage of simulating strategies and ideally pinpointing the most successful one without having to suffer the consequences of unsuccessful strategies in real life. Emerging problems such as logistical bottlenecks, interference of allies, or popular uprisings can be played through at leisure without the need to make decisions under pressure; enemy action may be anticipated by assessing the enemy's options for action.[7] The scenarios involve two very different levels: on the one hand, they require highly informed experts in possession of sufficient amounts of specific data able to guarantee that the game comes as close to reality as possible; on the other hand, the games are subject to formalized abstractions that analyze conflicts in terms of logical courses of action and rational strategies. The conceptual foundation of the latter is mathematical game theory or rational choice theory. These two levels indicate different "cultures" of war gaming: the Pentagon's Cold War division tended to prefer information-rich scenarios, while the RAND Corporation favored formalization and mathematical modeling. Especially at RAND, game theory—as a logical theory of rational decision making and courses of action—emerged as a political-military master science, a type of knowledge so intent on complex arithmetic operations that in due course human players had to be replaced by computers.[8]

It is worth taking a closer look at the epistemological form of such scenarios, some of which have been elaborated in great detail in military fiction and spy thrillers. Both—simulated crisis scenarios and Cold War political thrillers—employ a heuristic fiction of the enemy. Developing a scenario to simulate the possible outcomes of a given conflict first of all requires a formalization of this conflict to create an overview that is not possible in reality. As a second step, factors that might influence the situation must be determined—just as a novel determines its protagonists. The actual simulation will constitute the third step by playing through various versions in which the influencing factors are assigned varying importance, thereby developing a set of alternative narratives of the situation's possible outcomes. The main difference between the think tank's scenarios and the fictional plots is that the latter normally only come up with one version of events, not several.

These conflict scenarios can be read as an alternate history of the epoch's secret hopes and worst fears, fleshed out in fictional "What if?" plots: How could we devise a plan for an American invasion of Communist China? (Walter Herrmann, *Operation Intrigue* [1956].) Is it possible to dissuade the Chinese from pursuing their nuclear program by furnishing them with Western research? (Len Deighton, *An Expensive Place to Die* [1967].) What if a Soviet submarine captain in command of a new prototype defected to the United States? (Tom Clancy, *The Hunt for Red October* [1984].) What if the Soviet Union launched a conventional strike against NATO in a bid to secure Iranian oil resources? (Tom Clancy, *Red Storm Rising* [1986].) What if a psychotic general in charge of a fleet of B-52s gave an authorized command to attack the Soviet Union? (Stanley Kubrick's *Dr. Strangelove* [1964].) Clancy's novels in particular, which have established the techno-thriller genre, are renowned for a dazzling display of tactical and technological details that make them read like handbooks for Naval War College recruits. It is this particular feature that links them to expert-based war games staged at military academies and the Pentagon. Clancy's *Red Storm Rising,* a novel that takes place in the near future (of the year 1986) by playing through a conventional attack of the Warsaw Pact on NATO, congenially mimics the overall view, wealth of detail, and attention to the many different strategic moves that characterize the information-rich type of war game typical for the Pentagon's gaming culture (Clancy 1986). The ability of war games to integrate a wide variety of aspects and sideshows is re-created in Clancy's novels by means of a poetics of simultaneity. Countless narrative threads—from the inside of a stealth bomber and the debates of Soviet military cadres to the sleepless nights of American sonar experts—are arranged into a multifocal overall view of the war. As incomprehensible and badly written as they may appear, Clancy's novels offer the kind of war panorama typical of scientific war games. It is no coincidence that both *The Hunt for Red October* and *Red Storm Rising* were modeled as strategic computer games—indeed, Clancy is himself now shifting more and more into game development.[9] Ironically, in the face of these game-structured novels Clancy's most successful computer game *Splinter Cell,* featuring special agent Sam Fisher, seems like a throwback to the aesthetics and plot structure of a traditional spy thriller.

Clancy's scenariolike novels demonstrate the advantage war games have over traditional retrospective analyses of actual combat. Instead of getting lost in the heat of battle or the inscrutability of secret operations, it is possible to look at each individual aspect in isolation and analyze its impact on the overall events. In war gaming, we ideally arrive at a total view of the war and the enemy, similar to the global maps of the Cold War that depict incoming missiles and troops as illuminated dots. The first congenial aesthetic representation of this panoramic overview, now the basis for all strategic computer games, is the famous "war room" in Stanley Kubrick's *Dr. Strangelove* (figure 25). Such an overview, however, has to be complemented by formalization and selection of the truly relevant aspects. But what is even more important is the basic assumption that the enemy will pursue his goals in an orderly and rational fashion. The Cold War enemy, to be an object of speculation and prediction, must be calculable: that is, rational, cunning, perfidious, and implacable in the pursuit of his interests. What war gaming is unable to take into account is the enemy's stupid, irrational, or self-destructive behavior. Gaming and conflict simulation must always work with simplifying assumptions and projections—the most fundamental of which is the enemy's rationality.

Figure 25. The War Room in Stanley Kubrick's *Dr. Strangelove* (U.S.A., 1964).

Game Theory: *The Defection of A. J. Lewinter*

Where have all the Cold War games gone? Some are gathering dust in classified archives, others are obsolete, out-of-print publications of the RAND Corporation. What remains is fiction—for instance, Robert Littell's *The Defection of A. J. Lewinter* (1973), a novel that depicts the structural link between espionage, war gaming, and the phantasmatic construction of the enemy with astonishing precision. The point of departure for Littell's scenario is the Cold Warrior's wildest dream: having a defector coming in from the other side. Given the lack of insight into the enemy's black box, the defector promises a glimpse into this darkness. Littell's novel provides the Russians with such an unexpected opportunity: A. J. Lewinter, an American specialist for ceramic missile nosecones, turns up in the Soviet embassy in Tokyo and promises to deliver important data on U.S. missile trajectories. He is flown to the Soviet Union, but his hosts soon start to wonder whether the defector is trustworthy. Lewinter's information regarding the new American MIRVs (Multiple Independently Targetable Reentry Vehicles) would enable the Soviets to develop an efficient, though extremely expensive antimissile defense system, but knowing that the USSR has obtained this information could, in turn, force the Americans to reprogram their MIRVs—or maybe even scrap them, which would make the missile defense system obsolete. Consequently, both sides have a lot to gain (and lose), and both are faced with the same (though mirror-inverted) problem: The Russians are wondering whether Lewinter is a genuine defector or part of an American plan to lure them into setting up a new—and useless—defense system. The Americans are asking themselves whether Lewinter is in fact able to produce the data he promised the Russians. Moreover, will the Russians believe him? The mutual suspicion that unites the opponents brilliantly pinpoints the foundation on which all Cold War knowledge of the enemy is based: the conviction that the conduct of the enemy, invariably, is an act of deception. The enemy is a black box, but one whose output can never be taken at face value; it has to be decoded. Littell's American-Russian paradox of doubt zeros in on the specular as well as speculative framing of enmity: the enemy wants to deceive us and will inevitably do so—this is the underlying foundation of the Cold War's obsessive politics of distrust.[10]

But no matter how intricate the situation, the certainty of being fooled is, paradoxically, something you can work with. You can simulate it in a game. With this premise in mind, the intelligence experts of a Game Testing Center in Washington (modeled on the Pentagon's Cold War Division) in the novel assemble a group of experts called Committee 303 to conduct a role-play designed to simulate the Russian decision-making process. Each player is an expert on one of the Soviet officers, politicians, and intelligence agents dealing with Lewinter's case; and based on their extensive knowledge of the person they represent (known as "horse") they will take the position their "horse" is most likely to assume—a simulation game more akin to the Pentagon gaming culture based on expert information and role-play than to RAND's hyperrationalist type of scenario technique. What is most important for the Americans is to assess how the Russians, in turn, assess them. To play a part, then, is to simulate the thought processes of the enemy; it enables *us* to put ourselves in *their* place to find out how *they* put themselves in *our* place. One of the players offers this reflection (in the role of a Russian expert on American conflict simulation):

> The Americans are probably signaling us—but to what purpose? Everything depends, in the end, on what the Americans *want* us to believe. If they want us to believe he is real, he must be a fake. If they want us to believe he is a fake, he must be real. Here is where it gets complicated. I will raise the possibility that the Americans are signaling us that Lewinter is real in the expectation that we will discover they are signaling us that he is real and conclude he is a fraud. Ergo, they want us to believe he is a fraud. Ergo, he must be real. Do you follow me? (Littell 1973, 171)

What appears to resemble the dialectic imbroglio of Russian Marxism is in fact a succinct example of the logic of mutual enemy observation and its game-theoretical framing. As in the famous case of the Prisoner's Dilemma, game theory proceeds from the assumption that each player will logically deduce not only his own course of action but also those of the others.[11] My own decision depends on what I presume to be the other's decision; he, in turn, will try to anticipate my decision. The basic guideline of Cold War enmity is that every piece of data means the exact opposite of what it appears to mean. Contrary to the traditional understanding of enmity as a form of noncommunication, game theory appears to imply a kind of communication with other means, a code of paranoid distortion employed by both sides. Deception and disguise are part of a twisted and delirious yet nonetheless functional communication: "The Americans are signaling us." The defector is the medium of this bizarre understanding between enemies—and, naturally, its victim. At the end of the novel, the Russians consider him genuine but want to signal the opposite. Eventually he is sent back to America.

As dialectically convoluted as the results may appear, the logical premise of this simulation is very simple: each side assumes that the enemy will act exactly as oneself would do in the same situation. It is a form of projection that models the enemy on one's own image. We practice the art of deception and so does the enemy; the enemy does what we would do, and we do what the enemy would do. It took a while for intelligence theoreticians to fully understand that this presumption of structural identity is fraught with the methodological problem of "mirror-imaging" (Cohen 1980). Indeed, mirror-imaging is both the epistemological basis and the blind spot of the simulation and scenario culture of the 1960s. The RAND Corporation went so far as to construct a double of the Soviet Ministry of Economics in Santa Monica to better understand and anticipate Soviet economic development—as is well known, with limited success (Poundstone 1992, 94). The image reflected by this mirror, however, is not the "inverted" world alluded to in the title of John le Carré's *The Looking-Glass War* (see part 6, chapter 3,"The Human Factor") but one that tacitly obliges both players to follow common rules. These rules are informed by a rationalist universalism that presupposes that the enemy, no matter how hostile, is nonetheless a rational agent. Game theory as a form of modeling political conflicts (as well as economic behavior, negotiation tactics, and other civilian exchanges) is the most radical application of this mutual presumption of rationality. Defining itself as "a theory of rational decision in conflict situations" (Rapoport 1974, 1) game theory aims to illuminate the invisible enemy with the light of reason by assuming that the enemy, too, is a "player" who "can (i) assess outcomes; (ii) calculate paths to outcomes; and (iii) choose actions that yield their most-preferred outcomes, given the actions of the other players" (Ross 2010). If the game-theoretical conflict simulations are to make any sense, the enemy has to be equipped with freedom of choice, reasoning powers, and the ability to make calculated decisions. The Prisoner's Dilemma had assumed that each player is able to anticipate the other player's thinking; in the same way, game theoretical conflict modeling turns political secrets and invisible enemies into rationally predictable factors.

In the jargon of game theory, the role-game experiment carried out in Littell's novel is thus nothing but a "simulation of incomplete and incorrect information" (Herbert Goldhamer, quoted in Giffin 1965, 64). Both parties are rational agents striving for optimal payoff. The enemies—and this, too, is one of game theory's necessary assumptions—are structurally alike because they share the common goal of minimizing risk and maximizing profit (in this particular case, military strength). The Americans have the option to either spend a lot of money on redesigning the MIRVs or risk the danger of them becoming obsolete. The Soviet option: either spend a lot of money on a defense system based on false information or miss out on a chance to effectively counteract the American MIRVs. Both sides are in a position to mathematically calculate chances and risks. The rational options are valid regardless of the fact that what the enemy is *really* doing remains a secret (and is in all likelihood obscured by ongoing deception). Like espionage, simulations are a means of revealing enemy secrets, but they come with a decisive epistemological handicap: what game theorists figure out is not how the enemy *will* in fact act but how he—given the rules of logic—*should* act. During the Cuban Missile Crisis a U.S. intelligence expert acidly commented on a colleague's incorrect assessment of the situation: "His estimate on what was reasonable for the Soviet Union to do was a lot better than Khrushchev's and therefore he was correct in analyzing the situation *as it should have been seen by the Soviets.*"[12] Sometimes game theory is just more intelligent than the enemy. What if the enemy isn't that smart?

Worst-Case Scenario: *Dr. Strangelove*

Mad generals, base instincts, sheer stupidity, and petty internecine intelligence intrigues are baffling empirical phenomena that defy rational modeling. Stanley Kubrick's raucous World War III scenario *Dr. Strangelove or: How I Stopped Worrying and Learned to Love the Bomb* (1964) introduces all these elements into a system that was believed to be "fail-safe" exactly to the extent that it excludes human stupidity, fear, madness, or any other form of irrational behavior. Much like *Red Alert,* the novel it is based on (written by Peter George undet the pen name Peter Bryant), the film stages a military conflict scenario that spins out of control.[13] Kubrick/George's crisis scenario perfectly imitates the simulation technique's abstraction by limiting itself to three decisive scenes of action: Burpleson Air Force Base, the Pentagon War Room, and the inside of a B-52 bomber. The plot thus targets precisely those levels that are of interest to war games: political decision makers (the U.S. president, his staff, and the Soviet premier), the military (Generals Ripper and Turgidson), and the actual level of operations (the crew of the B-52 led by Major Kong). However, Kubrick's film is not just another scenario of just another United States–USSR confrontation. *Dr. Strangelove* is a brilliant and succinct version of the Cold War's worst-case scenario. It revolves around a military doctrine that came to dominate politics in the late 1950s and '60s—mutually assured destruction (MAD)—by tackling its unquestioned inherent rationalist assumptions. Kubrick/George's conflict scenario reads like a grim phenomenology of the multiple ways in which reason can be absent from political confrontation. A paranoid general (Ripper) issues an unauthorized order to a fleet of B-52s equipped with thermonuclear payloads to launch an attack on the Soviet Union ("Wing Attack Plan R"). Following emergency protocol the plane crews terminate all communication and head toward their Russian targets. While illuminated dots on the giant map of the War

Room show the bombers approaching Soviet airspace, the American president is left with no other option than to try to convince the Soviet premier that this is not a planned attack but an accident. The impressive triangular underground "war room" (designed by Ken Adam, who also worked on several James Bond movies) concisely stages the geographic matrix underlying strategic simulations (T. A. Nelson 1982, 88): a panoramic overview of the looming global confrontation. It represents the bird's-eye view on global conflicts that war games dream of: graphics depict the approach of the air fleet in real time by means of a computer-generated image.[14] Adam's war room aesthetically anticipates the computerization of war that only starts in the 1960s. Two decades later it is one and the same techno-political apparatus that represents, plans, and wages the conflict.

The world of *Dr. Strangelove* is a MAD world. Strictly speaking, the MAD doctrine implies that even after a devastating first strike combatants will still have the time and resources to launch a punishing counterstrike. MAD's "balance of terror" rests on the certainty of *mutual* destruction—more precisely, on the devastating impact of the *counter*strike. According to the doctrine, a power under attack will still be able to inflict devastating harm on the attacker, thereby making a first strike approach highly unattractive. This is the logic of deterrence: security can be guaranteed only if a first strike would not render the attacker unable to strike back. It was not coincidentally a RAND mathematician, Albert Wohlstetter, who developed this scenario and in 1953 proposed the strategy of "second strike capability" (Poundstone 1992, 91 and following). The notion that the ability to launch a retaliatory strike represents an assurance against a first strike breaks with the traditional military focus on offensive and defensive capabilities and instead takes its cue from the abstract logic of game theory, according to which both sides view a first attack as too risky.[15] However, this also implies that regardless of potential economic benefits it would also be too risky to disarm. It is exactly this logic that "freezes" the Cold War into an arms race that nevertheless forecloses the use of those arms. Kubrick's Dr. Strangelove, a Nazi scientist in a wheelchair and a caricature of RAND's mastermind, Herman Kahn, provides a succinct summary: "Deterrence is the art of producing in the mind of the enemy the fear to attack." But then again, from a strictly logical point of view MAD will work only if the counterstrike is automatized. For a leader whose land has been destroyed by a first strike, there no longer exists any rational motive (or, in the jargon of game theory, no "payoff") to lay waste to the enemy's territory. The human ability to reconsider matters, to veer off from preconceived plans and potentially relinquish vengeance, is the weak spot that may undermine the assurance of a counterstrike. The "Doomsday device," an automated mechanism for a globally devastating counterstrike installed by the Russians on Zhokhov Island, is therefore a highly appropriate measure. Ventriloquizing Kahn's "thinking the unthinkable," Dr. Strangelove explains the advantages of the device: it is an "automated and irrevocable decision-making process which rules out all human meddling. The doomsday machine is terrifying and simple to understand and completely credible and convincing." By removing any possibility of human interference the doomsday device is a decision to exclude all further decisions. It is the epitome of MAD's hyperrationalist logic, which aims to exclude any form of irrational "human factor." Only an enemy utterly convinced that he will be *inevitably* destroyed by a counterstrike will refrain from a first strike.

However, both Americans and Russians in *Dr. Strangelove* are forced to confront a serious problem: what happens if this highly rationalized setting, with its automated decisions, is punctured by a malfunction of reason? General Ripper is suffering from the delusion that the Communists are out to contaminate the water supply and poison our "precious bodily fluids"—a paranoid vision reminiscent of the "Reds under the beds" scare of the 1950s. The Russians, in turn, have not fully grasped the basic tenet of MAD that deterrence works only if the enemy *is aware of* the automated retaliatory strike. "The whole point is lost if you keep it a secret!" Dr. Strangelove angrily explains. Kubrick pointedly exposes the flaws of the game-theoretical modeling of enmity: in a world of logico-rational conflict simulations, an enemy who is either too stupid (the Russians) or too crazy (the Americans) to pursue the optimal strategy will bring about Armageddon—which is precisely how *Dr. Strangelove* ends.[16]

Littell's simulation experiment and the game-theoretical worst-case scenario of *Dr. Strangelove* reveal the complementary aspects of the Cold War's hyperrationalist showdown: secrecy and deception are at one and the same time both the opposite and the counterpart of the logic of deterrence that characterizes the Cold War's hypothetical conflicts. Public demonstrations of one's own military strength on the one hand and paranoid secrecy on the other are the two sides of the phantasmal paracommunication between enemies who despite their differences conceive of each other as mirror images. The anticipation of enemy plans, which is an indispensable part of scenarios and simulations, is based on the belief in rational and thus predictable strategies; it presupposes that both sides are pursuing the same goal in the same way. The enemy, then, is a black box—but an automated black box. Even the idea of the enemy's demonic will to deception implies a constancy that renders him predictable. In MAD's logic this predictability turns, however, into a self-fulfilling prophecy: final decisions are no longer left to humans because humans are the site of doubt, instability, and lack of reason. Both deterrence and secrecy are ingredients of an enmity that for the most part consists of projections. What the fictional re-creations and parodies of war game scenarios expose is "mirror-imaging" as the basis of these projections. From the point of view of the phantasm of predictability, humans—with all their inconsistencies, emotional ties, and psychological incentives—are the epitome of unpredictability. This is what makes them—despite all rational modeling—a decisive element: the human factor.

3 The Human Factor

> If love is whatever we can still betray, remember that I betrayed you a lot of days.
>
> —John le Carré, *A Perfect Spy* (1986)

As depicted *ex negativo* in Kubrick's *Dr. Strangelove,* humans are both the blind spot and the decisive factor of the rationalist conflict models in the Cold War. To the extent that human beings are excluded from attempts to think and wage war, they return as an imponderable element. During the Cold War espionage is the substitute for a war that can no longer be fought. However, unlike the heroes of the Great Game spies are no longer self-directed agents; unlike the glamorous courtesans à la Mata Hari they are no longer elegant seducers; and unlike the cunning and cosmopolitan Comintern agents they are no longer fervent ideologues who willingly submit to the "dirty ethics" of revolution. In the Cold War spies are no more than a means and medium in a war ideally devoid of humans. All the fictional portraits of the "human factor" in Cold War espionage will share the awareness that in this war humans do not count—unless as a site of unreliability, manipulability, or weakness.

The Wall

The story begins at one of the checkpoints of the Berlin Wall in the American sector, and it ends at this wall, north of Bernauer Strasse, in the floodlights of the border strip. It takes place during the first two years after the construction of the wall in 1961. On both occasions an agent of the British Secret Intelligence attempts to cross the border between the two

Germanys from East to West. In the beginning the exposed German agent Karl Riemeck tries to reach his British handler Alec Leamas in the American sector; in the end Leamas himself climbs the wall at an agreed-upon spot in an attempt to escape to the West. Neither Riemeck nor Leamas makes it across alive.

The spy on the border: these two emblematic frame scenes make John le Carré's *The Spy Who Came In from the Cold* (1963), arguably the most famous allegory of Cold War espionage. Martin Ritt's eponymous 1965 film starring Richard Burton provided the matching black-and-white footage, which for a long time shaped the visual image of the border between East and West (figures 26 and 27). Forty years later *Spy Games* (2001) would quote this imagery to conjure up the West Berlin of the 1980s. Between these two scenes a complicated plot unfolds that centers on Alec Leamas, a burned-out spy runner who, under orders from the British secret service, stages his own social demise to be recruited by the other side. While he effectively plays the role of a disgruntled ex-spy who lets himself slip into alcoholism, he dispassionately starts an affair with a young librarian who happens to be an idealistic member of the Communist Party—a seemingly marginal turn of the plot that in the end drags everybody into the abyss. The goal of Leamas's fake defection is to incriminate Hans-Dieter Mundt, a high-ranking member of the East German secret service, to discredit him in the eyes of his superiors. The emblematic site at the center of this complex operation is the border strip featuring the wall, watchtowers, barbed wire, and marksmen with orders to shoot on sight—a zone of death where the global enemies of the Cold War directly confront one another.

No other border embodied this clash of contrary ideologies and social systems as drastically as the German-German border, and no other city was as so ideally situated to become the scene of the secret war as "Berlin, the spy's eternal city" (le Carré 1991, 15)[17]—a closed-off metropolis, divided and insular, the perfect urban match to the paranoia of secret operations. The wall structures a space in which you are either here or there, in which you are either friend or enemy (see Horn, Bröckling, and Kaufmann 2002). Whatever happens on the other side of the wall, in enemy territory, is by definition unknown and menacing. The wall is the outer case of the black box. On this side of the border agents like Alec Leamas are able to observe events from the safety of American watchtowers; they are free to continue intelligence business as usual by collecting, interpreting, and drawing conclusions from the observed material. However, once you enter the border strip, once you are in the narrow zone of death, nothing but a few yards, the right papers, the correct pass-

Figure 26. Alec Leamas at Checkpoint Charlie waiting for agent Karl Riemeck (*The Spy Who Came In from the Cold,* 1965).

Figure 27. Alec Leamas on the Berlin Wall at the end of his escape.

word, the sentries' orders, or precut gaps in the barbed wire will determine whether you live or die.

The knowledge thus produced is a kind of information war games cannot anticipate and game theory cannot predict. HUMINT, intelligence gathered from human sources, is the necessary complement to the abstract, rationalist calculations. It involves smuggling agents into hostile territory and planting informers in enemy organizations, betraying and sounding out friends, colleagues, lovers. Employing human sources means having to deal with the unpredictable irrationality, occasional disloyalty, or plain unreliability of the human factor. Just as the border is not only a spatial demarcation but also a boundary of knowledge, the spy turns into an epistemological figure. Spies produce and convey information; they are media of secret knowledge, moving it across legal, geographical, institutional, scientific, and personal boundaries. But spies are also media in the sense that they are not (necessarily) the subject of this knowledge. Unlike the playfully self-directed agents of the Great Game, Cold War spies do not need to know or understand whatever they smuggle across the border. Once the goods are delivered, confessions made, and fake identities exposed, the spies themselves are empty, used up, and disposable. No matter how clever they may be, or how much power the secret temporarily may give them, the Cold War agents are never anything but instruments. Following in the footsteps of the Comintern agents, Western spies lucidly accept this status as a mere tool or "pawn," as John le Carré has it.

Behind the Border: *The Looking-Glass War*

No text of the Cold War has given such a grim account of the phantasm of the opaque, dangerous, and mysterious enemy territory as le Carré's novel *The Looking-Glass War* (1965). Its plot relocates and recycles the Cuban Missile Crisis of 1962: "a sort of Cuba situation all over again, only . . . more dangerous" (le Carré 1995, 63). This crisis, which had brought the superpowers to the brink of nuclear war, was set off when U.S. aerial reconnaissance, following up on evidence provided by CIA agents, determined that Soviet SS-4 rockets had been secretly stationed on Cuba. For the first time large parts of the United States were within range of Soviet medium-range missiles. When the review of the photographs revealed the full extent of the deployment, a tense period of threats and counterthreats began that came to end on October 28, 1962, when Khrushchev agreed to dismantle the Cuban rockets and the United States, in turn, agreed to remove its medium-range missiles from Turkey.

Le Carré's novel transfers the Cuban scenario to Europe, more precisely to East Germany. Its point of departure is the suspicion of the British secret service—based on dubious evidence including fuzzy photos taken by an East German refugee—that the Soviets are secretly stationing or assembling rockets close to the (fictitious) town of Kalkstadt in the northern province of Mecklenburg. As was the case in 1962, the authorities request aerial reconnaissance to verify matters. Using a navigational error as an excuse to fly over the area in question, a civilian plane en route from West Germany to Finland takes photos of Kalkstadt. The pilot recounts that he was pursued by two MIGs; the agent scheduled to pick up the photos in Finland is killed in a car crash on his way from the airport; the footage is lost. Matters remain unclear; nobody knows what is really going on, or whether anything is going on at all.

The novel details three missions in enemy territory—"Taylor's Run," "Avery's Run," and "Leiser's Run"—from which only one agent, young Avery, returns alive, though with the uncertain feeling that there was some suspicious nightly noise outside the door of his hotel room. In the end it remains unclear what is stored in the hangar at Kalkstadt, whether the population ever saw anything, and whether the death of the first agent was a murder or an accident. The only incontrovertible evidence is the intransparency of the unknown surroundings and the fear agents experience in enemy territory:

> There is no terror so consistent, so elusive to describe, as that which haunts a spy in a strange country. The glance of a taxi driver, the density of people in the street, the variety of official uniform—was he a policeman or a postman?—the obscurity of custom and language, and the very noises which comprised the world into which Avery had moved contributed to a state of constant anxiety, which, like a nervous pain, became virulent now he was alone. It was part of an effeminate dependence upon those whom he deceived. (Le Carré 1995, 105)

While Kim, the little agent of the big empire, is prone to treat strangers as potential allies and view unfamiliar customs as objects of curiosity and imitation, the agents of the Cold War are always at their breaking point: they are either nervous wrecks like Avery or stricken with the sad, suicidal courage of Leamas (*The Spy Who Came In from the Cold*), Leiser (*The Looking-Glass War*), or Jerry Westerby, the "honourable schoolboy" from le Carré's eponymous novel. The terrain behind the border is no colorful, thrilling unknown but is cloaked in darkness; it is not exotic but dreary, uninviting, and impenetrable.[18] Andrei Tarkovsky's film *Stalker* (1979) stages this nightmarish, inscrutable enemy territory as a "zone": a strange, forbidding terrain that following unknown rules constantly shifts from dangerous to harmless and back. It is a landscape composed less of geographical markers than of energies and power relations, risks and riddles, demanding familiarity with its rules to survive. It is the space *behind the wall* (see the section titled "Spatial Reconnaissance: Labyrinth, Wall, Pixel" in part 3, "The Great Game").

Pawn Sacrifice

It is "The Department," a minor and underfinanced section of British military intelligence, that eagerly dedicates itself to solving the mysteries of Mecklenburg. Nostalgic for the glory days of the Second World War when they were running agents against the Nazis, its members see this operation—ironically called Mayfly—as an opportunity for a grand reentry into the competitive intelligence world. Burning for action, they decide, "We may have to put a man in. It seems to be the only way" (le Carré 1995, 64). But rather than sending out one of their own people they recruit Fred Leiser, a Polish immigrant with a British passport whose greatest wish in life is to be accepted by the British as one of their own. Leiser receives superficial training, a twenty-five-year-old radio set weighing around fifty pounds, and no gun. Dressed in thin clothing and armed with no more than a knife, he sneaks across the border into East Germany and has to kill a guard. Panicking, he uses his obsolete equipment to communicate a first report; not surprisingly, his message is intercepted by East German counterintelligence, and he is hunted down and killed. The novel's motto, an erratic quotation from a handbook on Morse code, ironically sheds light on this fatal scene: "The carrying of a very heavy weight such as a large suitcase or trunk immediately before sending practice, renders the muscles of the forearm, wrist, and fingers too insensitive to produce good Morse" (ibid., 10). Given his unsuitable equipment and insufficient Morse skills, Leiser's mission was doomed from the start. While he is still "outside" trying to establish contact, the task force is recalled from its safe house behind the border in West Germany; no one will receive Leiser's second, and last, transmission. The mystery for which he risks his life is of no importance anymore.

The Looking-Glass War depicts the topography of an intelligence world that draws a clear line between inside and outside. The inside, the clannish world of administrative infighting, male bonding, and public school networks, justifies its existence by evoking threats that may be real or merely the misinterpretation of unlucky coincidences.[19] The field agents "outside" are the victims of "inside" intrigues and career plans. HUMINT turns out to be all too human: wishful thinking instead of rationality, administrative logic instead of relevant know-how, sentimental ties between agents and handlers instead of appropriate training, the callous use of other people's lives. Fueled by his desire for recognition in his adopted country, Leiser willingly becomes a pawn sacrifice for his superiors. For the novel's second motto, le Carré quotes Alice from Lewis Carroll's *Through the Looking-Glass* (1871):

"I wouldn't mind being a Pawn, if only I might join" (le Carré 1995, 6). Like Alice, Leiser desperately wants to join the life-sized chess game behind the mirror, even as just a pawn: that is, as one who is used, sacrificed, and forgotten. The "wasted," duped agent is nothing but a means to an end, an expendable figure lulled into believing that he or she is indispensable. They are the "Joes"—le Carré's jargon for the agents and sources used by a spy runner—who bear all the risk when they venture outside; they are pumped for information, met with distrust, and, if need be, dumped.[20] As Markus Wolf, the longtime head of the East German foreign intelligence division, frankly admits, they are usually kept in the dark about the nature of their contact and function: "Deception begins at the moment of recruitment, when the spy is chosen. In most cases he learns nothing about the true identity and intentions of his contact. It all starts with 'legends,' mock organizations, fake names and IDs" (Wolf 1998, 15).

Pawns deliver knowledge—they do not own it—and they are sacrificed whenever it seems opportune. The pawns disposed of in the Cold War are the Western variant of the chekists, the agents of the world revolution who have learned to efface and sacrifice themselves but who dirty their hands in the service of a higher goal (see part 5, chapter 1, " 'Bertolt Brecht, Minstrel of the GPU' "). But while chekists carry out their mission in the ardent belief that the revolution will "change the world" (Brecht), the pawns of Western intelligence services have little more than a vague conviction that the West is, somehow, the better system and must defend itself. Their deeds lack the ideological glamour that Brecht, much unlike le Carré, is still able to attribute to his figures. But that is precisely what makes courageous and laconic loser heroes like Leamas and Leiser the true embodiments of Cold War agents: they are unbelievers caught in a war of ideologies nobody truly believes in anymore.

Leiser is a means—but even those who use him have lost sight of the end. Pawns may help solve a problem, bring about a decision, or secure a victory, but they are never the ones who take these decisions. The pawn, not the enemy, is the dupe in this game. Why did he ever agree to this hopeless assignment? Le Carré answers this question in a dialogue of his handlers that succinctly expresses the cynicism of the Cold War agent world:

> "Why did he go, Avery?"
> "Jane Austen said money or love, those were the only things in the world. Leiser didn't go for money . . . Do you know what love is? I'll tell you: it is whatever you can still betray." (Le Carré 1995, 237)

Be it the desire for recognition, loyalty, friendship, as in Leiser's case, or the love for a woman and gratitude toward a friend (which turns Castle, hero of Graham Greene's *The Human Factor,* into a traitor) or the love of a daughter (the downfall of le Carré's Soviet spymaster Karla as well as Greene's Wormold from *Our Man in Havana*)—the "human factor" is the flaw that lures individuals into the web of the secret war. "Whatever you can still betray" is the dimension of human behavior that, defying all rationalist scrutiny, is marked as a specifically human vulnerability: emotional bonds, irrationality, affect. But "whatever you can still betray" also marks the private domain, the personal *secretum* that modernity has granted to the individual as a protective space beyond the reach of the political (see part 2, chapter 2, "Logics of Political Secrecy"). The protection of the individual's personal *secretum* has been, however, the West's ideological battle cry against the Communist belief in the sacrifice of the individual for the greater good of the collective. Fiedler, the upright Jewish agent in *The Spy Who Came In from the Cold,* defends this logic by appealing both to Stalin and the New Testament: "Some Roman said it, didn't he, in the Christian Bible—it is expedient that one man should die for the benefit of many" (le Carré 2001, 115). But Western intelligence services, according to le Carré, are engaged in perverting this very ideal. In an open letter to the *Moscow Literary Gazette* le Carré stated: "In espionage as I depicted it Western man sacrifices the individual to defend the individual's right against the collective. That is Western hypocrisy, and I condemned it because I felt it took us too far into the Communist camp" (le Carré 1966, 4). But once the West, for all its lip service to individual rights and freedom, grabs individuals to exploit and betray them, it is precisely this "humaneness" that becomes the worst of all weapons deployed by the netherworld of espionage.

Behind the Mirror: *The Spy Who Came In from the Cold*

Le Carré gives a dark twist to the old Great Game metaphor.[21] The games in his novels are the petty, manipulative "games people play," to quote the title of one of the most successful psychology books of the 1960s (Berne 1967).[22] Or they are games of fear and projection serving the phantasmal, imaginary side of politicking. In either case, they no longer have anything to do with the rationalism of war gaming. By quoting Lewis Carroll's *Through the Looking-Glass* in his title, le Carré is pointing at the political landscape that shapes his early novels. What determines the topography of the Cold War, le Carré suggests, is a mirror—a penetrable mirror like the one on Alice's house, allowing access to a strange realm of inverted rules and abstruse logic. The world behind Alice's mirror is not only a "reverse" world in which everything is similar but opposite (flowers can speak, you have to depart from a location to arrive there, you have to run to stay in one place, and so on); it is also a world of life-sized games. The landscape is a giant chessboard at the sight of which the enthused Alice voices her desire to be a pawn (Carroll 1939, 149). For le Carré, Carroll's dreamworld behind the mirror, with its strange rules, apparent absurdities, and good and bad kings and queens, epitomizes the imaginary construction of the enemy in the Cold War. Avery calls his section a "dream factory" made up of nothing but "rumors, a guess, a hunch one follows up; it's easy to forget what intelligence consists of: luck and speculation" (le Carré 1995, 121 and following). The reference to Carroll makes it clear that the knowledge of the enemy is not a knowledge but a *dream* of the enemy. Alice's question at the conclusion of her mirror dream—she asks whether it was her dream or whether she was dreamed by the Red King—illuminates the strange position occupied by the pawn. The pawn-agent is caught in a dream that is not his or her own. The agent is part of a fantasy—at the cost of his or her life.

This structure of a world behind the mirror also determines the highly complex plot of *The Spy Who Came In from the Cold.* Alec Leamas, the spy who—in one of le Carré's eponymous ironies—does *not* ever return from the cold, is just another pawn sacrificed in the Great Cold War Game. His assignment is a major disinformation task: he is to quit the service, pretend to be an embittered lush, be hired by the other side, and then use fabricated material to incriminate Hans-Dieter Mundt, a high-ranking member of the East German intelligence community. The only unplanned detail of this dramatically staged personal decline is a minor affair with Liz, a librarian—but exactly this turns out to be the "human factor" that the agency eventually employs to use Leamas in ways he had never expected. The East takes the bait: Leamas is brought to the GDR and questioned by Fiedler, Mundt's assistant and most determined antagonist. Fiedler is searching for evidence to incriminate his boss, whom he suspects of working for the West, and it appears to be Leamas's job to give him what he is looking for. Only in the course of a spectacular trial during which Fiedler aims to unmask Mundt does the real reason for Leamas's staged defection become clear: as the intelligent and upright Fiedler has come to suspect, Mundt is indeed a Western agent, but the true goal of Leamas's mission is not to incriminate him, only to make sure that he is cleared of Fiedler's justified accusations. The British secret service achieves the latter by smuggling the librarian into the GDR. Without the slightest knowledge of what is going on, she unwittingly turns into a witness against Leamas and undermines his credibility. With Leamas out of the picture, the case against Mundt collapses. In the end Leamas explains the hideous truth to Liz:

> I'll tell you what you were never, never to know, neither you nor I. Listen: Mundt is London's man, their agent; they bought him when he was in England. We are witnessing the lousy end to a filthy, lousy operation to save Mundt's skin. To save him from a clever little Jew in his own department who had begun to suspect the truth. They made us kill him, d'you see, kill the Jew. Now you know, and God help us both. (Le Carré 2001, 199)

Leamas is a different type of pawn than Leiser, more disillusioned and more intelligent, but together they embody the very ambiguity of secret intelligence consisting of both information gathering *and* disinformation (see part 2, chapter 3, "Secret Intelligence"). As an agent who only at the very end comes to understand his mission, Leamas is exactly what Sun Tzu labeled an expendable or doomed agent (Sun Tzu 1963, 146). The doomed agent's task is not reconnaissance but the communication of false information designed to confuse the enemy; he is expendable because—unlike the agent who is charged with gathering data—there is no need for him to return. And like Liz the librarian, his credibility is directly proportionate to his ignorance: the less he knows about his task, the more believable the story. He has no need for the professional arts of deception because he is exactly what he is supposed to be—an agent involved in a deception. In the case of Leamas, his ignorance of the real plan and his seemingly all too private affair with the librarian turn out to be tools used against him. "Oh God," Liz says at the end, when they have unraveled the deception and both start understanding that they are headed toward death rather than the West, "it's far more terrible, what they are doing; to find the humanity in people, in me and whoever else they use, to turn it like a weapon in their hands, and use it to hurt and kill" (le Carré 2001, 204).

After the overwhelming success of *The Spy Who Came In from the Cold,* John le Carré was able to withdraw from his work at the British secret service and retire to Cornwall as a full-time writer. Granted, le Carré's sober style and disillusioned view of the intelligence world struck a nerve of a Cold War audience used to the adventurous glamour of James Bond. But in the final analysis, the plot of *The Spy Who Came In from the Cold* is nothing less than ludicrous. The plan concocted by the British is reckless, its implementation riddled with inconsistencies. If Mundt is working for the British, why is he so ruthlessly efficient at decimating their agents in East Germany? Why does incriminating the defector automatically exonerate Mundt? Not to mention that Mundt is a bit too familiar with the internal workings of the British secret service, as both Leamas and Fiedler come to realize. And—the most important mistake—how can Mundt let Leamas and Liz escape from prison without once again incriminating himself? Günther Nollau, who in the early 1970s was the head of the German Verfassungsschutz (German domestic intelligence service), wrote a highly critical review in which he drew on his professional expertise to point out the many blunders committed by Leamas, his agents, his superiors, and the perfidious Mundt. When you are waiting for an agent to secretly cross the border, Nollau lectured Leamas, you do not sit around drinking coffee with American soldiers. The whole operation is much too twisted, conspicuous, and risky: "No head of an intelligence agency in full command of his mental faculties would ever come up with such a plan" (Nollau 1965).[23] So, what is the political gist of *The Spy Who Came In from the Cold*? Nollau's brief critique of the plot's technical defects manages to catch more of the novel's political structure than the cubic meters of research that time and again focus on the ethics and the sociology of British middle-class agents. Simply put, Nollau grasped that the story is both immensely complex and immensely abstruse—and that is exactly the *political* core of the story.

Enemies Are Friends

So radical is John le Carré's proposition regarding the Cold War that he never dared to clearly formulate it in an interview. It can only be told as a story. The true scandal of *The Spy Who Came In from the Cold* is the interlocking, if not identicalness, of friend and enemy. "You and Mundt are enemies, aren't you?" the incredulous Liz asks when she sees Leamas conversing with the hated Mundt (le Carré 2001, 199). For le Carré, friend and enemy are inextricably intertwined. The despicable ex-Nazi Mundt is "our man," while the bright and upright Fiedler, a Jew tortured by Mundt during the Third Reich, is vanquished and shot. Enmity and friendship are neither related to any real conflicts nor tied to any personal emotions like hatred or sympathy. Enmity is an abstract positing, a point le Carré later addressed by questioning the West's political means: "I tried to tickle the public conscience with the issue of raison d'état. I have posed this question: for how long can we defend ourselves—you and we [that is, East and West]—by methods of this kind, and still remain the kind of society that is worth defending?" (le Carré 1966, 3).

But the question of immoral means used to higher ends obscures the real point. What are the grounds for a war once friend and enemy mutually depend on each other to justify their existence? What is at stake? As Leamas explains to Liz, intelligence wars justify themselves by warding off the real war: "This is a war . . . It's graphic and unpleasant because it's fought on a tiny scale, at close range; fought with a wastage of innocent life sometimes, I admit. But it's nothing at all beside other wars—the last or the next" (le Carré 2001, 204). However, this miniature proxy war reflects the groundlessness of Cold War enmity. The world of intelligence is one and the same on both sides; the war they wage is nothing but a self-referential game. The gist of le Carré's argument is a deflation of the allegedly ineluctable enmity revealing the emptiness at the core of the Cold War.

The innovative brilliance of le Carré's books, then, is his erosion of the political—rather than the much-ballyhooed break with 007-style spy thrillers or his alleged "realism." Graham Greene's praise of *The Spy Who Came In from the Cold* as the best spy novel he had ever read is slightly misleading, for ultimately le Carré is closer to theorists like Schmitt, Schroers, and Boveri than to the spy novel genre. With his cold, disillusioning novels le Carré furnishes the literary pendant to the political reflections on treason of the era. In *Treason in the Twentieth Century,* Margret Boveri had analyzed treason as a crisis of political loyalty fueled by the unsolvable question of which community one belongs to, while Carl Schmitt, focusing on the issue of "real enmity," had diagnosed a blurring of discernible friend/enemy boundaries (see part 2, chapter 1, "The Age of Treason").

Following Schmitt's diagnosis, le Carré stages this crisis of the political in the world of intelligence, where friends and enemies are intertwined like the branches of a quarreling clan; apples of a kind, they fight with the same weapons and occasionally change sides. The enemies are substantially alike, not only because they—as has often been remarked—operate on the same "moral" plane and are equally manipulative, disloyal, and violent but also because they keep transforming into one another. The real difference is no longer between East and West but between the great masses peacefully asleep in bed and the netherworld of intelligence operations charged with protecting their collective slumber. Le Carré uses the emblematic image of the Berlin Wall to evoke the ideological boundary only to deconstruct it by pointing to the other, invisible line of demarcation between the public sphere and the sphere of the secret war. With its cruel yet aimless struggle, this netherworld is the "cold" from which agents like Leamas can never return.

Fall from Grace: Kim Philby

We should never forget the gaps.

—John le Carré, introduction to *Philby: The Spy Who Betrayed a Generation* (1968)

The "fall from grace," as le Carré later came to call it, took place on January 23, 1963.[24] Kim Philby, former head of MI6 Soviet counterespionage operations and subsequently a correspondent in Beirut, vanished on his way to a dinner party at the British Embassy. Months later he reappeared in Moscow, where he had asked for political asylum. The events confirmed the long-held suspicion circulating since the defection of Guy Burgess and Donald MacLean that Philby too had been a KGB mole. For years Philby had provided the Soviets with information on British counterespionage; for years he had exposed British agents and sabotaged potential Soviet defectors. He escaped to Moscow just when the evidence against him was about to result in an arrest. The Philby case was the trauma of Western intelligence: treason on the highest level committed by a civil servant whose loyalty was deemed unshakeable. Moreover, the case concerned a traitor who despite all suspicions had been protected by a network of friends in the British establishment. Philby was a product of English society and its secret service, both of which, as le Carré charged with untypical ire, identified "class with loyalty" (le Carré 1968, 17). Unlike nonestablishment traitors such as the Dutch-Jewish agent George Blake or the flamboyant, openly gay Guy Burgess, Philby was an epitome of British decorum. But he was also, as Hugh Trevor-Roper submitted to le Carré, a product of the secret service world, a recursion of the secret in the world of secrecy, covert operations, lies, and manipulations. Philby, Trevor-Roper writes, was "the effect of secrecy, of insulation, of immunity, of immediate circumstance—and perhaps also of a popular myth" (Trevor-Roper 1968, 75). But no matter how much Philby in the late 1950s may have posed as an English gentleman, he was—even when it came to his outward appearance—extremely adaptable: following his defection to the Soviet Union he donned the appropriate proletarian outfit, a flat cap and shapeless raincoat replacing the bourgeois English elegance of beret and trench coat (figures 28 and 29). From this point of view Philby is less an aberration of the system than a symptom of its innermost nature, the secret war taking on human shape, as it were.

Figure 28. Kim Philby (1912–1988) in London prior to his defection.

Figure 29. Kim Philby in Moscow after his defection.

My Silent War

If *Dr. Strangelove* staged the worst-case scenario of rationalist speculation, Philby was the worst-case scenario of HUMINT—and like any other worst case he sheds light on the structure whose failure he represents. The treachery of flamboyant or eccentric individuals such as Blake, Burgess, MacLean, or John Cairncross was ascribed to personal idiosyncrasies;

American moles like Aldrich Ames or Robert Hanssen, in turn, were seen as the result of failures of the CIA's internal warning system. Philby, however, and with him the subsequently uncovered Cambridge art historian Anthony Blunt have come to be regarded as symptoms of the pathology of the society they belonged to—a self-recruiting, self-protecting elite more interested in keeping the lower classes at bay than the enemy.

Philby embodies the very mystery of treason. Like Judas, man and case have remained a challenge both for the historiography of intelligence and the psychology of treason. Why did he work for the Soviet Union? Which secret operations was he involved in, and what was the extent of his involvement? Whom did he betray? What were his "real" allegiances? Amid the innumerable essays, investigative reconstructions, and novels based on the Philby case, Philby himself tried to make sense of his own story. Following his defection to Moscow in 1963 (and under the watchful eyes of the KGB), he penned a dry, irritatingly impersonal account of his activities as a Soviet double agent titled *My Silent War* (published 1968 in London; see Philby 1973). *My Silent War* does not qualify as an autobiography or exercise in introspective self-explanation; it is a rather tight-lipped account of some of the intelligence activities Philby was involved in as head of section V at MI6 and as an SIS representative in Washington, D.C. He dwells on the mysterious affair of the Russian diplomat Konstantin Volkov, vice consul at the Soviet Embassy in Istanbul, who would have exposed Philby and whose defection he was able to prevent at the last moment. And he offers a detailed account of the investigation launched in the wake of the disappearance of Burgess and MacLean. The most conspicuous feature of his text is the wavering between perspectives: for the main part, he sticks to the perspective of an SIS employee, but at times he casually adopts the perspective of an undercover agent who has to prevent his own exposure.

As an answer to the questions of motive, extent, technique, and background of his treason, Philby's account is more of a mystery than a solution. It is not a confession; it is what someone sitting in Moscow will allow the other side to know. It is a retrospective, yet it does not offer more than what the West—the addressee of the text—already knows or is allowed to know. There is no mention of any detail or name that is not already obsolete. Philby's text is, technically speaking, chicken feed, play stuff, a mixture of baits, gaps, trivia, all too transparent allusions, and a couple of downright lies.[25] And yet there is one confessional gesture: Philby insists that he was not a side-switching double agent but always loyal to the Soviets. "All through my career, I have been a straight penetration agent working in the Soviet interest. The fact that I joined the British Secret

Intelligence Service is neither here nor there; I regarded my SIS appointments purely in the light of cover-jobs" (Philby 1973, 14). This confession is the only part of *My Silent War* intended less for British readers than for Soviet KGB censors, who had long-standing doubts about Philby's loyalty. Indeed, who would fully trust such an accomplished liar?[26]

Philby's account is one of blinding emptiness: no personal information, no private comments, above all not the slightest trace of an explanation for his allegiance to the Soviet Union, which for over twenty years overruled all his personal ties. It sheds no light whatsoever on the person, motive, or circumstances of the traitor. Tackling the mystery of treason is, once again, up to the betrayed, in this case Philby's British readers. Innumerable texts written after 1963 inscribe themselves into this empty figure, trying to fill out the void left by Philby's own voice but also trying to explain the structure that enabled his treason. The friend who turns into an enemy becomes the symptom of the very community he betrays, the mirror in which society catches sight of itself. From now on, the phantasm that one's closest associates—boss, friend and colleague, wife—may be "the enemy" will haunt the political culture as well as its fictions.

A Question of Loyalty: Graham Greene

In a novel with the most appropriate of all possible titles—*The Human Factor* (1978)—Graham Greene, a personal friend of Philby's and highly sympathetic to him, took his chance to unravel the mystery of treason. To be sure, the issue of disloyalty had pervaded his oeuvre ever since *The Confidential Agent* (1939). Greene's heroes incur guilt for the sake of higher values: in *The Ministry of Fear* (1943), Arthur Rowe kills his first wife out of pity and proceeds to lie to his second wife—again, out of pity. Wormold, "our man in Havana," starts penning his fancy reports to MI6 because he needs money to support his beloved daughter's extravagant lifestyle. *The Human Factor,* in turn, turns treason into a balancing act between the protagonist's national loyalty, which in this particular case consists of membership in a stupid, rather thuggish intelligence service, and his personal ties to his family as well as to a friend who had once saved his wife's life. While on assignment in South Africa, Greene's hero and traitor, Maurice Castle, falls in love with a black African woman, Sarah, who with the help of Castle's Communist friend Carson was able to escape to Britain with her son. Out of gratitude for Carson Castle begins to provide the Soviets with material from MI6's boring South Africa section. Castle's mother illustrates this excessive need to thank—which persists even after the friend has died—with a childhood anecdote: in return for a chocolate-filled bun, her son gave his precious new pen to a friend. The touching absurdity of the image is Greene's metaphor for the impulse to betray: boundless gratitude. In turn, the betrayed in *The Human Factor* are not worthy of any loyalty: a coldhearted doctor poisons one of Castle's colleagues in the false belief that he is the leak; the rest are pathetic figures marred by broken marriages or excessive social ambitions. Greene, in other words, is highly apologetic of the motives that lead to treason: gratitude, love, personal loyalties. Time and again he emphatically invokes E. M. Forster's famous choice of personal over patriotic loyalties: "I hate the idea of causes, and if I had to choose between betraying my country and betraying my friend, I hope I should have the guts to betray my country" (Forster 1951, 78). What Forster describes as an act of courage, Greene turns into a humanist ethos. When Castle tells his wife, Sarah, about his betrayal she responds with a key axiom of Greene loyalty: "We have our own country. You and I and Sam. You've never betrayed that country, Maurice" (Greene 1978, 187). Betrayal thus becomes the affirmation of a *different* loyalty, which chooses the ethical over the political, intimacy over community, the individual over the whole. Greene presents the alternate options as a tragic conflict of values: two equally precious goods, one of which has to be sacrificed in favor of the other. In Greene's tragic theory of treason, however, the latter is then itself destroyed by this act of sacrifice. Consequently, Castle suffers the fate of a tragic hero. Following his exposure he flees to Moscow and waits for the arrival of Sarah and Sam, who were supposed to follow him. But the British have their revenge by denying Sarah an exit visa for her son. At the novel's drab end, there is nothing left but a last phone call in which the desperate Castle comes to realize that with his act of betrayal he has lost both—fatherland and family. In the middle of the conversation the line goes dead.

By betraying a fairly unsympathetic community—a nation made up of office intrigues and barely concealed racism—Castle performs Greene's ultimate ethical gesture: he demonstrates a true, unconventional form of loyalty. For Greene, there is loyalty in treason. Unlike le Carré, who described Philby as a born traitor and cynic (le Carré 1968, 12, 15), Greene has words of praise for him: "I think Philby genuinely believed in Communism . . . Oh yes, I did admire him—he did his job extremely well . . . He lived out of his belief and I admire him for that" (Greene 1988, 209). Betrayal, then, is a matter of sticking to one's faith. This link between betrayal and higher faith allows Greene in his introduction to *My Silent War* to compare Philby to a "kindly Catholic" who, had he lived in

Elizabethan England, would have stood up for the Catholic faith—and thus for Spain, the enemy (Philby 1973, 7). At its core Greene's theory of betrayal follows a profoundly Catholic logic of conversion: betrayal is less the turning away from an affiliation than the turning toward a higher, redemptive community. It reveals a faith that dissolves worldly and legal ties. Even though Castle may profess that he does not trust Marx and Engels more than Saint Paul, his act of betrayal is much closer in spirit to Saint Paul than to Marx (Greene 1978, 107). Saint Paul's conversion from Saul to Paul is the model of a fall from faith that gives rise to a new, higher faith. By alluding to Saint Paul rather than to Judas, Greene removes the paradox from the act of betrayal: disloyalty becomes a sign of integrity. The traitor embodies a form of loyalty greater and more steadfast than the civil servants' belief in the letter of the law. For Greene, the mystery of treason embodied by Judas and Philby is solved, or rather dissolved. Greene fills the emptiness at the center of Philby's decades-long treachery with a story of faith and loyalty, no matter, Greene adds, how misplaced that trust in Communism may have been. He thereby translates the political virulence of treason into the depoliticized sphere of personal ethics. "Friends" and "enemies" are no longer categories of groups or communities; they are nothing more than private choices. Greene, in short, solves the political mystery of treason by thoroughly depoliticizing it.

The Betrayed: *Tinker, Tailor, Soldier, Spy*

By contrast, John le Carré views the traitor—whose epitome, in his eyes, is Philby—as a symptom of a disease of the political itself. He is less interested in the traitor's personal ethics than in the phenomenology of secrecy. His trilogy *The Quest for Karla*—made up of *Tinker, Tailor, Soldier, Spy* (1974), *The Honourable Schoolboy* (1977), and *Smiley's People* (1979)—revolves around the quest for the "black grail," the head of Russian secret service code-named Karla, an enemy who represents the distant, intangible, and diabolical source of all the inner rot rendered visible by the Philby case. Karla, the Soviet handler who recruits and directs the mole in the SIS, embodies the nagging question of the source of treason, the evil genius who induced the traitor to commit his act. The trilogy stages the quest in search of the secret of treason as an attempt to unravel the secret of its originator. In his introduction to the biography of Kim Philby coauthored by Page, Leitch, and Knightley, le Carré poses the question in very technical terms: "This book is massively incomplete, as the authors are first to admit. *We should never forget the gaps.* In this most Marxian of novels . . . the principal character is still missing . . . He is the Soviet recruiter. For these men were recruited. By whom?" (le Carré 1968, 10; emphasis added).

The Soviet recruiter is the mysterious enemy that uses the idealism of well-bred Cambridge students to seduce them into a life of treachery. Le Carré's search for the originator of all evil starts with the fictional examination of the defector in the midst of an intelligence community that succumbs to the mole's deceptions with near-euphoric abandon.

The trilogy's first installment, *Tinker, Tailor, Soldier, Spy,* leads off with the words "The truth is . . . " (le Carré 2000b, 3). Well, the truth is that the novel's shrewd and inconsolable hero, the duped and lucid George Smiley, spends 418 pages on the trail of a mole without ever finding the entire truth. The retired agent Smiley is called back into service after the death of his boss, Control, with orders to investigate a suspicion harbored by the late Control: that there is a mole in his own unit who systematically scuttles all the unit's operations. The intrigue that Smiley begins to unravel started with a Russian agent called Irina whose defection to the British is thwarted at the very last minute—an incident that in many details recalls Philby's sabotage of Konstantin Volkov's planned defection. On her way to Hong Kong Irina approaches a minor SIS agent and asks him to organize her escape to London, though just like Volkov she urgently requests that only Control, the head of the secret service in London, be informed. In a further parallel to the Volkov case, Irina intimates the presence of a Soviet mole in the upper echelons of the SIS whom she could help expose provided that he is not able to foil her defection. As in the Volkov case, the mole intercepts the communication, warns the Soviet side, and kills enough time to enable the Russians to ship the prospective defector back to Moscow. The last we see of Irina/Volkov is a fully bandaged body on a stretcher being loaded onto a Russian plane headed to Moscow.

The mysterious last-minute failure triggers a far-reaching investigation of the upper echelons of the intelligence service. Smiley, who as a retired former employee is above suspicion, is reactivated to head the investigation. Its central phantasm, "the mole," is first mentioned in a report that Irina was able to pass on to the SIS agent in Hong Kong. The accompanying definition resonates with the strident class-consciousness of a Soviet operative:

> A mole is a deep-penetration agent so called because he burrows deep into the fabric of Western imperialism, in this case an Englishman. Moles are very precious to the Centre because of the many

> years it takes to place them, often fifteen or twenty. Most of the English moles were recruited by Karla before the war and came from the higher bourgeoisie, even aristocrats and nobles who were disgusted with their origins. (Le Carré 2000b, 67)

It takes half a lifetime to achieve the depth of penetration that will allow the mole to gradually rise in the enemy system, pursue a career, and make the right friends, all the while remaining inactive for years, maybe even decades. A silent outpost in the heart of enemy territory, he is both "one of them" and "one of us." Poring over files and interrogation protocols to identify the traitor by way of elimination (modeled on the counting rhyme "Tinker, tailor, soldier, spy . . ."), Smiley remains in the dark regarding the traitor's motivation. When the cool, brilliant, and erotically inscrutable Bill Haydon is finally revealed as the mole, Smiley describes him as a Russian puppet whose inner life was known only to Karla, his recruiter (le Carré 2000b, 416). Haydon is the epitome of the deceiver and seducer, a scoundrel who tries to protect himself from the investigation by compromising the investigator, Smiley. He begins an affair with Smiley's notoriously unfaithful wife, Lady Ann Sercombe, and lets himself be surprised by Smiley to tie the latter's hand: any attempt to expose Haydon will now be seen as the revenge of a cuckolded husband. While Greene used the entanglement of private and political to endow betrayal with an ethical motive, the exact opposite takes place here: Haydon seduces Ann for political purposes; sexual intimacy is subordinated to the logic of intelligence work. In addition, Haydon dupes the rest of the "Circus" with a ludicrous operation that has the SIS transfer huge sums of money to a supposed highly placed Soviet source known as Merlin, a source so secret that it is exempt from the usual review procedures. What the source delivers is, of course, nothing but chicken feed prepared by Moscow. Merlin and the mole embody the system's absurd self-referentiality: the Soviet secret service is supplying its enemy counterpart with allegedly precious information, and the British secret service is paying the enemy for its services. The two secret services are like two machines exclusively concerned with exploring and deceiving each other.

Nobody in le Carré's murky world escapes being deceived and betrayed—not even Smiley, the detective at the center of the novel. No matter how perspicacious he may be, he is also a pathetic cuckold; indeed, all of his subsequent insights arise from his initial blindness and humiliation. It is precisely this nuptial vulnerability that Karla had identified during his only encounter with Smiley; later on he will instruct Haydon to exploit "this last illusion of the illusionless man" (le Carré 2000b, 418). The investigator is the dupe, but this awareness of his own vulnerability makes him the one and only person able to expose the Merlin game. Smiley's acuity as a detective arises from his knowledge of his own blind spots.

Smiley is a melancholy brooder, as already indicated by his preference for German baroque literature. Like the baroque melancholic, he pores over the mysterious debris of failed operations and destroyed lives: Irina's failed defection, dubbed Operation Testify; the dead director Control; or the ruined life of Jim Prideaux, another victim of Haydon's game of seduction and betrayal. He is the one to look deep into the bottomless pit of intrigue that is the political of le Carré. In turn, Haydon, the Iago-type mole bent on fooling and manipulating everybody, is no less cheated and deceived, for he embodies the British mortification at the decline of the empire. The mole is one who has been cheated out of imperial dreams; he was supposed to carry on the Great Game in the footsteps of Kim. As Connie, the Soviet expert in the SIS, explains: "Poor loves. Trained to the Empire, trained to rule the waves. All gone, all taken away. You're the last, George, you and Bill" (le Carré 2000b, 128). This, precisely, is the gist of le Carré's theory of the mole: the traitor is a relic from another time, a creature of history deprived of present and future. Bill Haydon and Kim Philby are products of the glory days of empire: Philby's father—the famous Arabist St. John Philby, member of the Indian Civil Service, and later associate and competitor of T. E. Lawrence—gave him the nickname Kim. Philby is a fallen Kim, born and bred in India but then shipped off to rainy England and the stuffy corridors of MI6; a latter-day Kim who uses his protean adaptability to fool his own countrymen. The downward drop from Kim to Haydon—literary figures both related and distant—indicates the ultimate decline of the Great Game. The "little friend of all the world," as Kim is known, degenerates into a cunning manipulator of the cliques and coteries of the old boys' network. In *The Honourable Schoolboy* the figure of Kim is lamented as having "vanished for good" (le Carré 2000a, 28). Melancholy fools and scions of a long-lost empire, Smiley and Haydon are brothers.

Smiley's proclivity for German baroque literature is highly revealing. "The vain activity of the intriguer," Walter Benjamin writes on German baroque tragic drama, "was regarded as the undignified antithesis of passionate contemplation to which alone was attributed the power to release those in high places from the satanic ensnarement of history, in which the baroque recognized only the political aspect" (Benjamin 2003a, 141). A modern afterimage of the baroque intriguer, the scheming narcissist Haydon sets himself up as the secret maker of history, "standing at the middle of a secret stage, playing world against world, hero and playwright in one" (le Carré 2000b, 416). The traitor turns history into a drama tailor-made for himself. The supposed realities of power and enmity are turned into mere role-play. Or, even worse, he reveals the histrionic nature of the enmities. With his fake identities nested into one another, the traitor resembles a Russian matryoshka doll, but its center—like that of history—is empty. By contrast, Smiley is a figure that manages to perceive how agents and their enemies, including himself, are inextricably intertwined. No degree of contemplation will help him escape his entanglement. But he is, at least, able to identify rather than merely exploit the "baroque" feature of the Cold War: its completely secular, perfidious "vain activity" devoid of any illusions.

Taking Back Bearings

"The truth is . . . " The question remains how Smiley is able to track down the truth. Treason must be narrated, yet it confronts the act of narration with formidable obstacles. In Smiley's case, baroque contemplation yields to that classic technique of criminal investigation the retrospective process of establishing the truth often depends on: the art of listening. E. T. A. Hoffmann's famous first detective, Mademoiselle de Scuderi; Poe's sleuth Dupin and his positivist successor Sherlock Holmes; and even Joseph Vadassy, Eric Ambler's unwilling investigator in *Epitaph for a Spy* (1938) all share one outstanding quality: they are exceptionally gifted listeners. Smiley transforms this art into a technique that combines interrogation and psychoanalysis. Asked to head the search for the possible mole, he initiates a two-pronged procedure: he scrutinizes all available records and interviews all parties concerned. Smiley refers to this retrospective study of files, which in *The Honourable Schoolboy* will enable him to track a Chinese mole in the Soviet Union, as taking "back-bearings," a fishing in the muddy waters of money transfers, travel routes, debriefing protocols, and operational plans (le Carré 2000a, 68–69).[27] The goal is a thorough methodical scrutiny of coincidences and sequences of events, a kind of narrative X-ray, in search of whatever is omitted or covered up in these sequences: it's the operation's inconsistencies that betray an outside influence, the presence of the mole.

"We should never forget the gaps." Le Carré's reservations regarding the reconstruction of the Philby case also apply to Smiley's detective work—and, as Allan Hepburn has pointed out, to le Carré's poetology. Narrative—whether the tales told by le Carré's protagonists or the novel itself—is always made up of silences, gaps, vital truths that are being omitted (Hepburn 2005, 172–74). Smiley, too, is a reader and listener eager to fill in the gaps of the narrative: when he is not studying files in search of signs of an enemy presence he either talks to people or observes them talking to one another. Ultimately, conversations constitute the narrative core of le Carré's novels. Events unfold slowly and in fragmentary fashion along multiple story lines emerging from memories and interviews. The novel's conversations are characterized by the refusal of the queried to divulge the information Smiley is looking for. They evade, prevaricate, lose themselves in digressions, and fend off questions by invoking the need for secrecy or pleading ignorance. Of Tarr, the British agent to whom the would-be defector Irina had turned, Smiley says: "Tarr has not lied to us . . . Not in any material way. He has simply done what agents do the world over: he has failed to tell us the whole story" (le Carré 2000b, 213). Nobody ever tells the whole story. It takes shape only gradually in the head of a listener who prefers silence to asking questions and patiently waits for omissions and careless slips. The art consists in phrasing questions in such a way that they do not betray what the interrogator knows and, more importantly, *wants to know:* "Guillam had seen whole interrogations conducted that way: a laboured catechism swathed in deep coverings of routine; wearying pauses as each answer was written down in longhand and the suspect's brain besieged itself with a thousand questions to the interrogator's one; and his hold on his story weakened from day to day" (ibid., 217).

The art of examining and pumping for information that shapes le Carré's narrative poetics does not aim for a coherent story but for anything that disrupts narrative and causal connections: omissions, ellipses, vagueness, lies, self-serving declarations, or downright refusals to speak. Underneath the proffered tales are alternate versions, larger frames obscured and suppressed by the cover story. "Smiley was conscious all the while that even the little Haydon was telling him was selected with meticulous care from a greater and perhaps somewhat different truth" (le Carré 2000b, 408). The truths that emerge are fragments, maybe even cover stories for a "somewhat different truth" that is never entirely revealed. In the web of its many versions the one truth remains beyond reach; it is the negative foil that renders whatever may be grasped, every new insight and "fact," highly dubious.

In the final analysis, compared to authors like Graham Greene and Len Deighton, le Carré's higher political acuity and clear-sightedness rests in this narrative technique. Greene and Deighton—not to mention Fleming—stick to a narrative continuity that firmly ties the awareness of the reader to that of the protagonists: the duped Bernard Samson in

Len Deighton's trilogy (a simpler descendant of George Smiley afflicted by the double misfortune that his own wife is the mole), Greene's traitor Castle, or the kindhearted impostor Wormold from *Our Man in Havana* (Greene 1971). In Greene's and Deighton's novels, the identity of the enemy and the mystery of betrayal can be deduced in a linear fashion that moves parallel to the actual narrative. The solutions may be tragic, but they leave no question unanswered. By contrast, le Carré's complex back-bearing poetics are reminiscent of Borges's fiction. They are, in fact, fully aware that they may grasp only one of several *possible* versions—but never the one and only truth. While the Cold War's "what if?" scenarios unfold detailed and complex hypotheses as *pro*spective fictions, le Carré offers backward-oriented accounts made up of *retro*spective narratives. The framework of the scenarios is a rationalism that is said to apply to both sides, though on closer inspection it reveals itself to be a case of mirror-imaging, a projection designed to make the enemy resemble us. In turn, the narrative versions about hidden or unrecognizable enemies unfold in a tension between truth and lies, which will never reach a final version. Both are fictions in Borges's sense: contingent versions engaged in denouncing each other, versions that are neither innocent nor disinterested. The "human factor" conjured up by the bulk of the Cold War spy literature is the irrational flip side of game-theoretical rationalism, yet both sides are aware that this war is a fiction that is primarily concerned with maintaining itself.

PART 7

State Paranoia

Invisible Enemies

The mirror-imaging that marked Cold War enmity has a reverse side. When the combatants turn their suspicious gaze inward they discover the "enemy within." It now seems that the nooks and crannies of one's own society may harbor secret hostile forces, hence anything and anybody can be labeled an enemy. Richard Hofstadter famously attributed this notion of an omnipresent yet wholly indeterminable enemy to the "paranoid style of American politics" (Hofstadter 1965). The key term is *conspiracy:* "a vast and sinister conspiracy, a gigantic and yet subtle machinery of influence set in motion to undermine and destroy a way of life" (ibid., 29). Within the context of this political fantasy Hofstadter's term "paranoid" refers less to a psychological form of individual or collective delusion than to "a way of seeing the world and of expressing oneself" (ibid., 4). In essence, it is a matter of constructing a particular interpretation of reality and finding one's own place within that construct. The peculiarity of political paranoia is a view of the world as an omnipresent *secretum;* it shares with clinical notions of paranoia the impulse to be permanently wary of attacks emanating from that murky domain (Freud 1962; also see Horn and Rabinbach 2008). Given that the world is one big *effet de secret,* the paranoid style is bent on destroying its treacherous facade by calling into question all too obvious identities and antagonisms. Everything has to be read anew in different, distrustful ways: "Paranoia," Timothy Melley argues, "is an interpretive disorder that revolves around questions of control and manipulation" (Melley 2000, 16). This interpretive malaise—frequently dismissed as "conspiracism"—conjures up a global network of secret codes and symbols manipulated by hidden media; it searches for plans to establish new world orders and casts a suspicious eye at anything that smacks of governmental manipulation. The ubiquitous yet indeterminate enemy becomes the ideal projection surface for all conceivable sorts of social and cultural fears.

This distrust, which I will refer to as "state paranoia," has an epistemological as well as a political aspect. It is the expression of a twofold crisis: a crisis of control revolving around the exclusivity of secret state knowledge, and a crisis of perception triggered by the indeterminacy of the enemy. In the following section, the 1950s state paranoia in the United States will be examined by using two political phantasms of that period: "atom spies" (the case of Julius and Ethel Rosenberg) and "mind control" (as portrayed in *The Manchurian Candidate*). These phantasms mark the dark, inner side of the all too clear, all too rational enmity that characterizes the Cold War. If the enemy is, in fact, nothing but my mirror image, he may well be my friend and neighbor, a member of my society, maybe even part of my unconscious, rather than dwelling far away *beyond the wall.* This is the historical background to the discourse on "treason in the twentieth century" (Boveri 1956–60). However, there is more to "state paranoia" than the questions of shattered allegiances and ubiquitous treason as analyzed by authors from Boveri to Enzensberger (see part 2, chapter 1, "The Age of Treason"). The real—and, in the case of the Rosenbergs, lethal—fantasies of invisible enemies generated by the state paranoia of the 1950s represent a fundamental change in the figure of the enemy and a fundamentally new twist in the structure of modern *arcana imperii.*

"Paranoid style" and conspiracy theories are usually viewed as popular, if not populist ideologies, prompting critics to reveal their logical faults while analyzing their social, psychological, and cultural functions. Academic consensus has it that political conspiracy theories are totalizing explanations and narratives that, obsessing over the burning question why bad things happen to good people, reduce the complexities and negate the contingencies of modern society (see Groh 1987; Aaronovitch 2010). They give vent to nostalgic fantasies of an autonomous and self-reliant individual; they attempt to rationalize the loss of freedom of choice in modern mass culture by dreaming up an omnipotent, secret source of control and manipulation (Melley 2000). By contrast, they are also seen as symptoms of "the dissolution of social recognition, a paranoid form of non-knowledge caused by the rise of political ideologies, which foreground the rights of the individual at the expense of those of all others" (Featherstone 2001, 31). As Fredric Jameson would have it, political paranoia represents "the poor person's cognitive mapping in the postmodern age; it is a degraded figure of the total logic of late capital, a desperate attempt to represent the latter's system" (Jameson 1988, 356), hence conspiracy theory's affinity to populist political discourse (see also Fenster 2008). Jameson's patronizing account of the paranoid poor in spirit is characteristic of the treatment of conspiracy theories as *ideology,* that is, as a system of wrong answers to the right questions that result in a totalizing view of a nontotalizable world. This type of intellectual condescension toward conspiracy theory fails to recognize the intricate dialectic of blindness and insight that shapes the paranoid style. Its insight rests in the profound skepticism toward the authority of political claims and the recognizability of the enemy (see also Horn and Rabinbach 2008). Understood as a discourse on the modern *arcana imperii,* political paranoia is less an exaggerated system of explanations than a *challenging* of "official" explanations and appearances. It represents an attitude of profound distrust: distrust of the state against its citizens, of citizens against the state, of nonexperts against experts, of users of a certain technology against that technology, of media users against the media. In essence, conspiracy theory is nothing less than the distrust of all the indispensable technological and cultural foundations of society: for example, water, media, or signs on money bills (see Knight 2002, 1; Tanner 2008).

State paranoia is an epistemological crisis of secret state knowledge and its usage, a crisis that runs both ways: as a distrust of the state against its citizens, and as a distrust of the citizens against the state. On the one hand, it was triggered by the awareness that strategically important military knowledge could not be controlled and contained, as became clear in the case of secret atomic expertise. On the other hand, in the case of "mind control," it was the idea that media of communication could be used as media of manipulation. What triggered these suspicions was a fundamental practice of state secrecy: classification, the exclusion of certain data and types of knowledge from public circulation. At its center, state paranoia revolves around fantasies about the ability or *inability* to control the circulation and use of particular types of knowledge, whether nuclear science (in the case of the "atom spies") or experimental psychology (in the case of "mind control").

Thus state paranoia is not simply the paranoia of the state but an excessive distrust of both state and citizens toward each other. The arrest and conviction of the atom spies Julius and Ethel Rosenberg is the most revealing case in point for this mutual distrust as well as for its literary effects (see "The Public Burning"). While the state believes that it is hunting down a vast ring of Communist spies connected to Julius Rosenberg, the civil rights movement, American Jews, and liberal intellectuals see themselves at the mercy of a state-run conspiracy. But state paranoia is not limited to the "Red scare" of the 1950s. In much the same way the assassination of John F. Kennedy in 1963 would evoke both Communist-Cuban networks and speculations that the CIA itself organized, hushed up, or at least profited from the event (see part 8, "Invisible Government: JFK"). And last but not least the events of 9/11 would generate double-edged fantasies focusing either on an infinite terrorist network or, once again, on the government's alleged involvement (see part 9, chapter 1, "The Light of the Phantasm"). State paranoia is the symptom of a fundamental shift in the perceived shape of the enemy: while intelligence is—according to Michael Herman—"about 'them,' not 'us' " (Herman 1996, 34), political paranoia focuses on the *impossibility of distinguishing* between "them" and "us." The fictions state paranoia produces are about *us,* not them. Unable to tell friend from enemy, it becomes necessary to track down the enemy within society and, if need be, even inside our unconscious.

Classified Knowledge: Nuclear Secrets

Following his escape from Denmark to Sweden in September 1943, nuclear scientist and Nobel laureate Niels Bohr was flown out from Stockholm in a Mosquito bomber. He was placed inside the empty bomb bay, and the crew was given instructions to drop him into the sea in the case of a German attack (see Jungk 1958, 121; see also Blaedel 1988, 217). The scientist as bomb: nothing illustrates with greater clarity the importance of the military secret in the twentieth century. In the course of the Second World War, nuclear physics, hitherto based on international scientific cooperation, turned into a barracked, top-secret research project. The expertise of scientists like Bohr *was* the bomb before it was actually built and tested. The nexus of scientific research and secrecy was part of a modern research culture whose epistemological and political genesis is worth closer scrutiny. In the case of nuclear physics, scientific research, formerly dependent on competition and exchange within the scientific community, suddenly found itself restricted to a completely isolated, albeit international, group of experts pursuing one particular project (the atom bomb) in the service of one particular nation (the United States) without any possibility of publishing their work. Modern scientific knowledge, characterized by a high degree of specialization in combination with public accessibility of research results, turned into an arcane science. Driven by a constant fear of hidden leaks, the nuclear secret shaped a politico-epistemological structure bent on enforcing secrecy within the research apparatus by way of classification, compartmentalization, and nonpublication. The result was a massive transformation of areas of research classified as top secret—that is, the type of knowledge which would be one of the central phantasms of the McCarthy era. One of the most striking features of the Manhattan Project is how a motley group of international researchers with very different interests and working hypotheses was confined and homogenized into a research team working on one single goal: the bomb (for the political and military circumstances see Jungk 1958, 105–36). The barracking of the scientists at an isolated location in New Mexico under the leadership of J. Robert Oppenheimer and Major General Leslie Groves was a "safety measure" primarily designed to guarantee safety from possible indiscretions by the scientists.[1] One of the most important elements of these safety measures introduced by Groves, however, contradicted all usual research practice: compartmentalization. This meant that every scientist and engineer was only allowed to know what he needed to complete his particular task, and no more. Exchange or discussion about the overall context of everybody's work thus was reduced as far as possible. The compartmentalization imposed by Groves amounted to carving up knowledge into isolated, noncommunicating units, a reduction of complexity that did not sit well with the scientists (ibid., 115–17, 120–23) but marked a new technique of state secrecy cutting right into the flesh of science.

The practice of compartmentalizing researchers is part of the more comprehensive practice of classification.[2] As Peter Galison notes, classification essentially consists of withdrawing certain data from circulation. Even the author of a classified text no longer "owns" what she has written; strictly speaking, she is not even allowed to be in its possession and read it without proper clearance. Authorship, which according to Michel Foucault is one of the most important regulatory principles for the circulation of discourse, is suspended (Foucault 1987). The text can no longer be assigned or ascribed to anybody; it belongs to no one. What is of sole importance is the highly restricted group of potential addressees. However, while many data are only classified after thorough investigation, those related to atomic research are so from the very beginning. "Nuclear knowledge becomes classified the instant it is written down—even by someone who has no nuclear weapons (Q) clearance" (Galison 2004, 232). Classification of knowledge—indeed, the very idea of classifying—implies that we envision knowledge as a collection of discrete utterances, of which some may be plucked from the complex continuum of a given discipline or area of knowledge and removed from circulation. Conversely, declassified texts can be released to the public only after officials scar them with noticeable gaps (figure 30), a practice Galison refers to as "punctiform knowledge excision" (ibid., 243). But classification involves more than taking apart knowledge based on criteria completely external to this knowledge; it also entails that this knowledge be irreversibly nationalized. In the wake of the Manhattan Project and the postwar Atomic Energy Act every piece of data related to this area of research became top-secret U.S. property. After the war, this comprehensive classification, in turn, became the target of (ineffectual) objections by scientists who during the war had more or less willingly submitted to the demands of secrecy. Led by James Franck, seven scientists penned a memorandum suggesting that nuclear secrets be traded in exchange for an international nuclear treaty. Unlike the FBI and the government, the scientists were fully aware of the fact that long-term secrecy was out of the question. "Nuclear bombs," the Franck Report states, "cannot possibly remain a 'secret weapon' at the exclusive disposal of this country for more than a few years" (quoted in Jungk 1958, 359).

While some scientists hoped to exploit the knowledge gap for the benefit of future negotiations, others had already acted. The famous atom spies that haunted the political imaginary of the 1950s must be seen as the reverse side of this structure of secrecy. Ironically, the traitors are precisely those who had assisted in creating the dangerous secret in the first place: scientists such as Klaus Fuchs, Alan Nunn May, and Theodore Hall as well as engineers and technicians like David Greenglass, Harry Gold, and Julius Rosenberg. The most important was doubtless the physicist Klaus Fuchs, who had been passing on information to the Soviets since working in the British nuclear fission project and who had been part of the team of scientists at the Manhattan Project.[3] One of his temporary contacts, the chemist Harry Gold, led the FBI to the less important "spy ring" surrounding the Los Alamos technician David Greenglass and his brother-in-law Julius Rosenberg. Fuchs embodies the particular type of traitor that became the focus of the twentieth century's debate on treason: the rogue intellectual who goes it alone and insists on making his own decisions. Researchers like Fuchs and Nunn May were resolved to act in the spirit of scientific data circulation, as Nunn May declared in a written confession following his arrest: "I gave and had given very careful consideration to correctness of making sure that development of atomic energy was not confined to U.S.A. I took the very painful decision that it was necessary to convey general information on atomic energy and make sure it was taken seriously" (Hyde 1980, 78; quotation abridged). In other

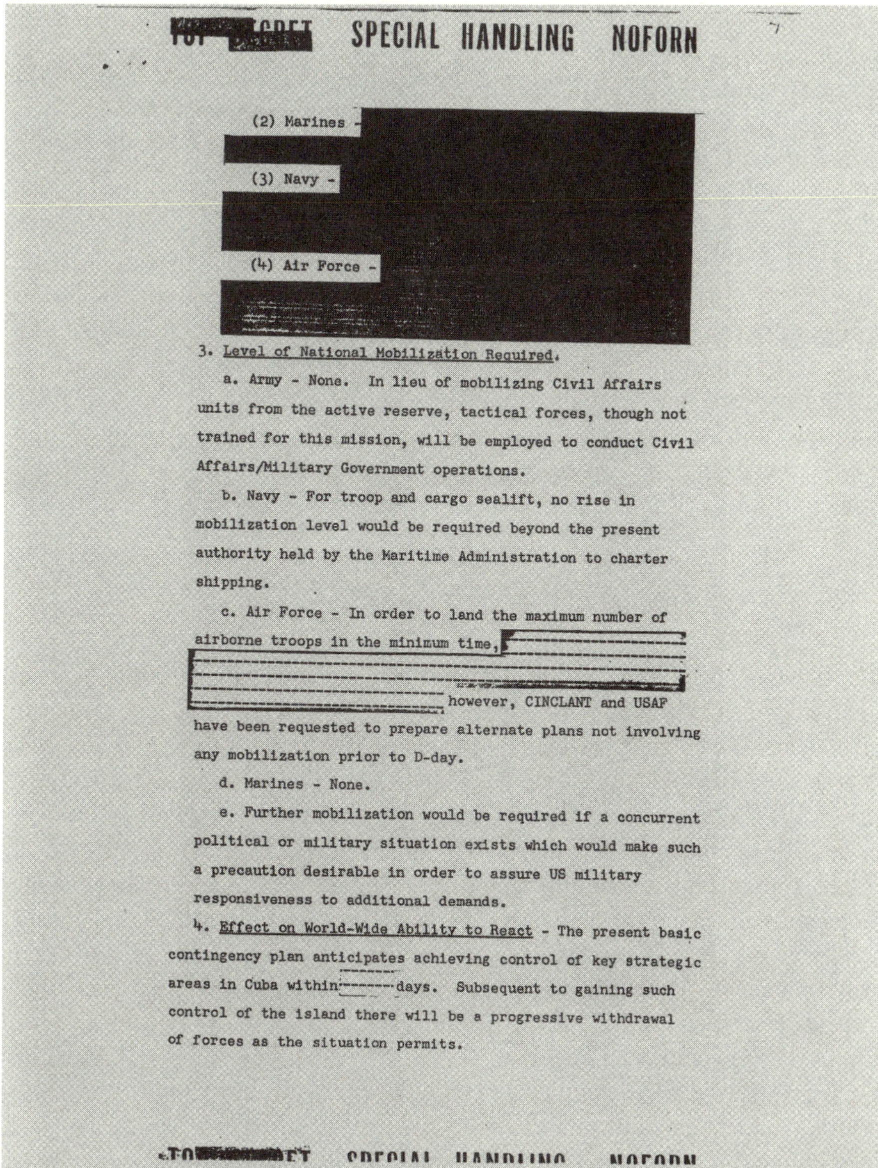

TOP SECRET SPECIAL HANDLING NOFORN

(2) Marines -

(3) Navy -

(4) Air Force -

3. Level of National Mobilization Required.

a. Army - None. In lieu of mobilizing Civil Affairs units from the active reserve, tactical forces, though not trained for this mission, will be employed to conduct Civil Affairs/Military Government operations.

b. Navy - For troop and cargo sealift, no rise in mobilization level would be required beyond the present authority held by the Maritime Administration to charter shipping.

c. Air Force - In order to land the maximum number of airborne troops in the minimum time, [...] however, CINCLANT and USAF have been requested to prepare alternate plans not involving any mobilization prior to D-day.

d. Marines - None.

e. Further mobilization would be required if a concurrent political or military situation exists which would make such a precaution desirable in order to assure US military responsiveness to additional demands.

4. Effect on World-Wide Ability to React - The present basic contingency plan anticipates achieving control of key strategic areas in Cuba within [...] days. Subsequent to gaining such control of the island there will be a progressive withdrawal of forces as the situation permits.

TOP SECRET SPECIAL HANDLING NOFORN

Figure 30. A declassified, blackened document titled "Consequences of U.S. Intervention in Cuba," Defense Department/Joint Chiefs of Staff, August 8, 1962. From Laurence Chang and Peter Kornbluh, eds., 1992, *The Cuban Missile Crisis, 1962: A National Security Archive Documents Reader* (New York: New Press).

words, they did what scientists normally do when they publish their findings to bring colleagues up to date. The great traitors of the twentieth century restitute science in the age of classification.

What heralded the state paranoia of the 1950s was thus not some irrational affect (neatly labeled "paranoid") but the inability to fully control military secrets. It began as a crisis of the *arcana imperii.* The atom spies who were so closely linked to the production of this dangerous knowledge offered what could be called "secrecy's counter-narrative" (Carmichael 1993, 58), that is, the appearance of an effective network of Soviet stooges breaking the Cold War's ban on communication. The fear of omnipresent Communists, which not coincidentally targets scientists, artists, emigrants, and intellectuals, must thus be understood as a fear of illicit contacts, harmful communications, and illegal avenues of knowledge. The Red-craze hysteria is fueled by the awareness that neither knowledge nor communication can be controlled, curtailed, or compartmentalized.

"The Public Burning": The Rosenberg Case

On August 29, 1949, the day of the first Soviet atomic test at Semipalatinsk-21, it became clear that the Americans had lost their nuclear lead. Given that the secret had once "belonged" to the Americans, it was logical to assume that the Soviets could have obtained it only by "theft." The "atom spy" thus became the phantasmatic missing link between the secret and the enemy. Nowadays historians estimate that U.S. nuclear research was roughly one to one and a half years ahead of the Soviet Union, a lead mainly due to the accelerated production of plutonium. Soviet research was in fact boosted by their analysis of the fallout from American tests. Nonetheless, Fuchs himself later asserted that the information provided by him saved the Russians at least one year (see Holloway 1994; Isaacs and Downing 1998, 145–47). In January 1950, Klaus Fuchs confessed to passing on material to the Soviets during the war; his contact had been Harry Gold, who in turn admitted to having worked as a courier and put the FBI on the trail of Los Alamos technician David Greenglass. The latter claimed to have been recruited by his brother-in-law Julius Rosenberg, who was said to have passed on material as well. As a result Julius Rosenberg and his wife, Ethel, found themselves at the center of a high-profile trial: they were accused of running a network of spies and were eventually sentenced to death.[4]

The 1951 Rosenberg trial and the couple's electrocution on June 19, 1953, were arguably the most spectacular events in the history of nuclear espionage—a "public burning," to quote Robert Coover's title. Treason turned classified knowledge into a fetish at the center of a grand theatrical spectacle. The trial itself was nothing less than a tragic drama bordering on the obscene: a brother, David Greenglass, accused his sister and brother-in-law of espionage to avoid prosecution; Ruth Greenglass spewed pointed lies to incriminate her sister-in-law Ethel; and Harry Gold, a key witness for the prosecution, had already been known to be a flamboyant raconteur long before the trial. Attempts to establish the truth degenerated into a web of clearly prefabricated lies (Harry Gold and David Greenglass were put in the same prison cell to ensure matching testimonies) and shaky pieces of evidence (for example, a mahogany console table from Macy's in which a witness claimed to have seen an apparatus for photographing material, or alleged drawings of a nuclear bomb that were never examined by experts). Even before the trial opened, the court appeared to have reached a verdict it was determined to impose at all cost; similarly, the public had already decided in advance which side it was on. As the authors of the most thorough study of the Rosenberg case point out, "Nearly all literature on the Rosenbergs is highly partisan. Either Julius and Ethel were the victims of a sinister government conspiracy or the case against them was flawless, an inspiring example of American justice in action" (Radosh and Milton 1997, 455).

This partisan polarity is paradigmatic for the structure of state paranoia. It consists of two contrary yet complementary narratives: on the one hand, the state's paranoid fear of its enemies; on the other, the citizens' paranoia in the face of state power. The former assumes that the enemies of the state—in the 1950s, "the Communists"—have infiltrated every nook and cranny of society and the governmental apparatus. While the roots of this "Red scare" may have been the fear of the Comintern (see part 5, "Agents of the World Revolution"),[5] the Cold War projected this fearful image onto the inner workings of society. Nobody embodied this state paranoia with greater vigor than J. Edgar Hoover, head of the FBI from 1924 to 1971. In *Masters of Deceit,* Hoover explains that the Communist Party of the United States (CPUSA) is the "Trojan horse" of world Communism; its tactics range from espionage and sabotage to "mass agitation," including demands for disarmament and civil rights protection (Hoover 1958, 198). The Rosenberg case provides this conspiracist mind-set with a case in point. Irving Saypol, chief prosecutor for the U.S. federal government, saw Julius Rosenberg as the main node in a wide net of Soviet spies: "Imagine a wheel. In the center of the wheel, Rosenberg, reaching out like the tentacles of an octopus" (quoted in Carmichael 1993, 101). The image of the tentacle reaching out for bits of secret knowledge beautifully illustrates the logic of state paranoia. Its reverse side, as Enzensberger has pointed out, is a form of distrust that takes the form of an infection: "The infectiousness of the secret taboo is unlimited. It is transferred onto each and every thing that comes into contact with it. The one who betrays the secret infects his 'contact persons' with it" (Enzensberger 1982, 89). Once the paranoid state starts to view its citizens as clandestine or potential enemies, it fixes its gaze on all the social affiliations and connections individuals are inevitably entangled in. Every social relation becomes suspect.

However, the Rosenberg case is also emblematic for the other side of state paranoia—that is, for citizens' conspiracist view of the state. The trial turned into a beacon of lawlessness, a spectacle in which the search for and administration of justice were pushed aside by public denunciations culminating in judicial murder. In the face of the pressure exerted on many witnesses, the delivery of prepared statements (as in the case of Ruth Greenglass), and the complicity between judge and prosecutor, not to mention the Rosenbergs' unflagging protestations of innocence, it was all too obvious that the defendants were not receiving a fair trial. The draconian verdict appeared to corroborate the observers' dim view of the proceedings. As a "sainted couple," the Rosenbergs became civil rights martyrs. "We are the first victims of American fascism," Ethel Rosenberg wrote to her lawyer on the day of her execution (quoted in Schneir and Schneir 1965, 130, 405). In the midst of the Korean War, and engulfed in the frenetic hunt for hidden Communist sympathizers, every form of opposition appeared to be life-threatening. Anson Rabinbach, witness and historian, describes the intimidating and divisive effect the events had on American Jews:

> Anyone who had been connected to or was in fact a member of the Communist Party was vulnerable. The innocence of the Rosenbergs proved that even the lowliest sympathizer could be murdered by the State. The paranoia among Jews was heightened by the fact that judge Kaufmann and Saypol's assistant Roy Cohn were themselves Jews. The implication was that Jews served two masters: the international Communist conspiracy and their own host state. The Jews who wanted to prove their patriotism fiercely defended the legality and justice of the trial; the campaign to save the Rosenbergs depicted them as innocent and arbitrary victims of state sanctioned violence. Behind the campaign (which the Communist Party only joined rather late in the game) was the widely sanctioned belief that the Rosenbergs were not only innocent but also innocent martyrs for the cause. (Rabinbach, email to the author June 19, 2003)

This sanctifying gesture is also found in many aesthetic re-creations. The most popular image of the "sainted couple" is the hasty kiss in handcuffs during the trial (figure 31). The couple's intimacy became an emblem of their innocence. Numerous images depict the execution in

Figure 31. Ethel (1915–1953) and Julius Rosenberg (1918–1953) on March 23, 1950, the day of their arraignment in New York Federal Court. The image of the kiss in handcuffs becomes widely distributed, with the affection of the couple seen as an indication of their innocence. Photograph from Corbis Images.

semirealistic or allegorical manner: Picasso drew poignantly pretty portraits of the couple; many artworks focused on the execution, sometimes in a sanctifying, sometimes in a rather grotesque aesthetic depicting the burning Ethel Rosenberg tied to the electric chair. Adrienne Rich, Louis Aragon, Allen Ginsberg, and many others have written poems about the Rosenbergs featuring either the destroyed family and the two orphans (Aragon), Ethel as mother, daughter, and wife "wanting to distinguish herself" (Rich 1981, 287), or the execution as a media event (Ginsberg): "Television was a baby crawling towards that death chamber" (see the collection of texts in Okun 1988).

This is the point at which state paranoia produces its very own literature, a "committed art" that emphatically sides with the victims of state injustice and that always already knows who the victims are. E. L. Doctorow's novel *The Book of Daniel* (1971) focuses on this very engagement by viewing events through the eyes of the Rosenbergs' (fictionalized) son Daniel. It is a perspective of innocence, impotence, and traumatization that merges the point of view of the child whose parents are arrested with that of the young adult protesting against the Vietnam War. It demonstrates that political commitment is rooted in radical empathy: empathy with the powerlessness of the individual, the fear of the parents, and the evil banality of the FBI agents. The child's point of view, both adopted and broken by the perspective of the distraught young adult, is nothing less than a narrative allegory of victimhood that serves to turn the Rosenbergs into the incarnation of a collective trauma. Doctorow moves the child's traumatic experiences forward in time to 1967 to connect the activities of the "Old Left," exemplified by the engagement on behalf of the Rosenbergs, with those of the "New Left," those protesting the Vietnam War.[6]

Both sides came to view the Rosenberg case as the crucial embodiment of a "paranoid style" of politics: on the one side, it fueled the frenzied persecution of hidden enemies; on the other, it gave rise to an aesthetic stylization of complete innocence and impotence (Neville 1995). But both the tale of irredeemable guilt and that of unsullied purity have proved to be wrong. In 1995 declassified files from the Venona Project, a secret Anglo-American joint intelligence venture dedicated to intercepting Soviet communications, contained references to an agent code-named "Antenna" and "Liberal," who in all likelihood was Julius Rosenberg (Radosh and Milton 1997, xv). The files support the claim that Julius Rosenberg was indeed a spy who had asked others to pass on technological information and who had himself stolen parts of the bomb (Feklisov 2001). However, the material also clearly proves that Ethel was not involved.[7] The FBI was

aware of the Venona files, that is, it knew about Julius's guilt and Ethel's innocence, but it could not use its knowledge in court without revealing its sources and jeopardizing the secret interception project. The Venona material is thus the uncanny, secret undercurrent in the cacophony of "fiction rivaling" in the Rosenberg case (Schneir and Schneir 1965, 365). It is, as it were, the skeleton in the case's closet—invisible, unnameable, but exerting a strange effect on the investigations. Given that the FBI was already aware of the truth, the manipulation of witnesses and statements can now be understood as the attempt to bring forth information that Venona already had revealed.

But if the Venona material proves the involvement of Julius Rosenberg, Greenglass, and Gold, the question remains why only the Rosenbergs were sentenced to death, amounting to judicial murder in the case of Ethel Rosenberg. The "Communist conspiracy" Hoover and Saypol were so keen to construct was the result of systematic smearing. For them, it was not a matter of guilt or innocence but of reeling in an entire net. But unlike Greenglass and Gold, the Rosenbergs had not denounced anybody, stubbornly refusing to submit to the logic of state paranoia and to its mechanism of smearing. Those who in the 1950s got caught up in the hunt for Communists—facing the FBI or the House Un-American Activities Committee—were coerced to name names, thus augmenting the number of potential suspects. State paranoia follows the logic of infection that Enzensberger associated with treason: it pursues social connections and hunts down the networks that constitute the very fabric of society to detect the traces of a secret and invisible force. The true enemy of state paranoia is society itself.

The Rosenberg trial reveals the new and paradoxical intertwinement of secrecy and the public sphere typical for the political imaginary of the McCarthy era. To be sure, the nuclear secret is no longer secret, but it is still endowed with the aura of dangerous knowledge.[8] The secret and its trivia—whether the Rosenberg's Macy console, a piece of cardboard from a Jell-O box, or the amateurish drawings of David Greenglass that served as evidence in the case—are publicly staged in a display of the traitor's trial and punishment. The secret is always already directed at its public exhibition.

It is precisely this entanglement of secrecy and public sphere that is addressed in Robert Coover's 1977 Rosenberg novel *The Public Burning*. In parodistic and lurid scenes, he depicts a society so infused with secret machinations and intrigue that it desperately needs a grand collective spectacle of punishing a scapegoat. Coover's text is remarkable for its refusal to submit to the logic of state paranoia by either decry-

ing the Rosenbergs as traitors or presenting them as the "first victims of American fascism." Instead it opts for a radically distanced view, a jarring narrative that revolves around the planned public execution of the Rosenbergs in Times Square. The idea of a "public burning" cites the frenzy of anti-Communist fervor and Korean War clichés, goaded by a press that represented this frenzy as the legitimate expression of the people's rage (figure 32). Uncle Sam, a repulsive allegory of all the pathologies of the American dream, haunts the scene, incessantly evoking the "Phantom," the Soviet archenemy. Coover's "art of excess" (Le Clair 1989) turns the Rosenberg case into a diffuse burlesque of crazy identifications (Nixon with the Rosenbergs), misguided desires (Nixon, eager to have sex with Ethel Rosenberg in jail, ends up with Hoover dressed up as Ethel), and perversions (in the end, Nixon is sodomized by Uncle Sam). The novel's crude aesthetic mirrors the political crudeness of the McCarthy era, showing how the case functioned as a sacrificial ritual intended to recoup the national community: "It ain't easy holdin' a community together," declares Uncle Sam in the wake of the execution, "order is not what comes natural . . . and a lotta people gotta get killt tryin' to pretend it is . . . but not many of em gets a chance to have it done to em on stage in Times Square!" (Coover 1998, 531). What separates Coover's approach from engaged literature, as well as from the polarized press coverage, is his choice not to tell the story from the victim's point of view but instead to opt for a highly unlikely narrator in the shape of "Tricky Dick" Nixon, the very incarnation of pragmatic cynicism. Of all people it is Nixon, the former HUAC Communist hunter, who comes to identify with the Rosenbergs because he suspects that the trial is rigged. He realizes that prosecutors and witnesses are lying and that the defendants are playing parts that will enable them to graduate from Lower East Side petty bourgeois to political heroes:

> And then what if, I wondered, there were no spy ring at all? What if all these characters believed there was and acted out their parts on this assumption, a whole courtroom full of fantasists? . . . They [the Rosenbergs] sink into a drab and scummy life, and then—BINGO!—the A-bomb trial, a chance to recover their pride and juice up their meaningless existence with real content. (Ibid., 135 and following)

Coover's text turns the trial itself into a gigantic fiction, a role-play in which everybody participates because they are either willing or forced to believe in the "spy ring." Even the victims are no longer victims but brilliant actors in the role of martyrs without which there would be no in-

Figure 32. An anti-Rosenberg demonstration in Washington, D.C., 1953. On June 19, 1953, Ethel and Julius Rosenberg were executed by electric chair in Sing-Sing. Photograph by Elliott Erwitt/Magnum Photos.

centive for engagement. Underneath the textual montage—which quotes, among others, the stilted letters the Rosenbergs wrote on death row—it becomes evident that there is no truth to be gained, least of all from the defendants' final confession. Coover's fiction is a piece of metafiction: it uses fictional means to fathom the *fictitious* character of the Rosenberg case (see MacCaffery 1982). He unveils political identity as a role-play in which both sides of state paranoia—victim and traitor—stick to their prescribed texts. History, Coover appears to say, is nothing but an invention, an unrestrained fabrication in which we all are so involved that none of us is able to recognize its fictional status.

Mind Control and Television: *The Manchurian Candidate*

One of the unresolved mysteries of the Rosenberg case is the question of motive. In Margaret Mead's words, "How could an American boy think that Communism was good?"[9] The question of the motive for treason, or, rather, the assumption that there can be no rational motive, frequently results in accounts highlighting the traitor's conspicuous psychological defects. Time and again observers have quoted Klaus Fuchs's self-description of his own "controlled schizophrenia," which allowed him to act as a valued member of a scientific community he betrayed at the same time. And while many observers were happy to adopt Fuchs's self-diagnosis, others were blind to the pathological mythomania of Harry Gold, who for years fed friends and colleagues with detailed accounts of a family life that did not exist. However, at no point during the Rosenberg trial did Gold's compulsion to fabulate trigger any distrust of his statements. Traitors, it appears, are psychologically disturbed; this is self-evident and has no impact on their guilt or truthfulness.

But if Margret Boveri is right to assert that sympathy for Communism—even worse, for treason itself—was a mass phenomenon, does this mean that all affected Americans were crazy? Or was it a form of *induced* madness that leads American boys to believe that Communism was something good? As in the case of the Rosenberg trial, the decisive background was the Korean War. Not only had a striking number of Americans collaborated with the enemy, but even after the armistice and the release of the POWs in 1953 twenty-one Americans (and one Briton) decided to remain in North Korea. "The belief in the American way of life had . . . failed" (Boveri 1960, 4:255). The attempts to rationalize this troubling phenomenon were labeled under the catchwords "mind control" and "brainwashing." China and the Soviet Union appeared to be in possession of miracle weapons or secret technologies that enabled them to "turn" people. Reports of such "brainwashing techniques" were first published by the CIA operative Edward Hunter, who had traveled Asia under a journalist cover (Hunter 1951; Hunter 1956). Allen Dulles, head of the CIA, spoke of "brain warfare" as the next great intelligence project. Even before attention focused on the "missile gap" he diagnosed a "mind-control gap" that prompted the CIA to initiate a number of research projects dedicated to researching behavioral manipulability (Marks 1979, 28; Killen and Andriopoulos 2011, 10). These projects saw themselves as a "tiny replica of the Manhattan Project" (Marks 1979, 131)—just as secret, just as interdisciplinary, and just as brutal.

Some of the most important (and infamous) research was conducted by the renowned psychiatrist Ewen Cameron at the Allan Memorial Institute at McGill University. Using electroshocks, drug-induced "sleep therapy," and sensory deprivation, Cameron attempted to "depattern" patients, that is, erase their usual behavior patterns to program new patterns by means of "psychic driving" (Cameron 1960; Cameron, Levy, and Rubinstein 1960).[10] In this context "behavior" encompasses all possible dimensions of human ability: memory, willpower, character disposition, and above all the possibility to incite humans to commit repulsive or self-endangering acts. The basic assumption was that special techniques or drugs could manipulate human behavior in any desired way, as succinctly expressed in a proposal submitted by Cornell researchers Harold Wolff and Lawrence Hinkle to investigate "how men can be made to think, 'feel' and behave according to the wishes of other men, and, conversely, how a man can avoid being influenced in this manner" (Marks 1979, 147). In the footsteps of nuclear research, behavioral science turned into one of the Cold War's fundamental research activities (see Lemov 2011). The possibility of nuclear mass extermination was joined by that of mass manipulation. But the latter posed not only a threat but also an opportunity. The threat was the possibility of a hostile manipulation of the consciousness, behavior, and opinions of each and every one, while the opportunity was the promise that hypnotized or psychically manipulated agents would be able to withstand any form of enemy torture.[11] The idea of "brainwashing" thus supersedes Hoover's vision of an omnipresent Communist network by conjuring up a hostile influence removed from sight and consciousness. What is striking about the type of knowledge generated by "brainwashing" and "mind-control" research, however, is its profound fictionality:

> Discussions of brainwashing frequently made recourse to fictional accounts. Given the absence of compelling proofs of the phenomenon, novels such as *1984* and *Brave New World* served a crucial role in authenticating allegations of Communist mind control. In a strange circularity, brainwashing discourse fell back on works of imagination to help document what had emerged as a "strategic fiction" in the first place. Rapidly assuming the status of a political axiom, a central "fact" of the Cold War, yet one lacking clear empirical basis, brainwashing inhabited a strange conceptual limbo. (Killen and Andriopoulos 2011, 10)

Brainwashing is not only state paranoia entering the unconscious; it is also the strategic fiction of a "knowledge of the enemy" that, again, is turned against both enemies and citizens.

It is not coincidentally a piece of popular or pulp fiction that offers the most striking mixture of pseudoscientific precision and political folly: Richard Condon's 1959 novel *The Manchurian Candidate*. The plot—and this, too, is no coincidence—originates in the Korean War. A group of ambushed U.S. soldiers is abducted to Manchuria and subjected to a brainwashing procedure administered by a Soviet-Chinese team of scientists. One of the soldiers, Raymond Shaw, scion of an influential political family, is "conditioned" to assassinate a presidential candidate (Condon 2003, 48). With meticulous attention to detail—including quotations from scientific publications on behavioral manipulation—the novel depicts the "reconstruction of the Sergeant's personality" (ibid., 48).[12] The point of departure is Pavlov's theory of conditioned reflex, its further elaboration in Andrew Salter's *Conditioned Reflex Theory* (1949), and a number of essays from the 1940s on behavioral control by hypnosis with menacing titles like "Experiments in the Hypnotic Production of Crime" (Condon 2003, 31).[13] Condon's descriptions of the assassin's conditioning resemble the experimental protocols published by researchers like Cameron; given how the actual research on "brainwashing" was infused with references to fiction, his novel can be seen as a narrative and fictional contribution to the research—while at the same time revealing the uncanny political foundations of the latter (see Marks 1979, 182–92; Orne 1961). Condon explicitly grounds his *science fiction* in the paranoid politics of the 1950s: on his return to the United States as a reputed war hero, Sergeant Shaw, the brainwashed Communist killer, is recruited by his mother to work for the vice-presidential campaign of Senator Iselin, her second husband. Iselin, obviously modeled on Joe McCarthy, profits not only from his stepson's martial glamour but also, ultimately, from the murder Shaw was programmed to commit. In a ludicrous plot twist Shaw's mother, the driving force behind Iselin's *anti*-Communist campaign, turns out to be her son's *Communist* handler. Condon does not shy away from yet another over-the-top twist by adding an oedipal subtext: Mother Shaw seduces her son to commit murder as well as incest. Pavlov and Freud perversely mate here just as mother and son do.

The political crux of Condon's plot is the merging of two types of paranoia: the paranoia of the Red witch hunters eager to expose all "card-carrying members of the Communist party" (Condon 2003, 128), and the scientific (as well as popular) paranoia triggered by the possibility of brainwashing. The most ardent anti-Communists are nothing but Communist puppets, *The Manchurian Candidate* proposes, and the most dangerous opponents of cherished all-American values are precisely those who most fervently support them. Condon elaborates a conspiracist variant of the typical Cold War collapse of friends into enemies also on display in le Carré, Greene, Grady, or Littell. Sergeant Shaw's case short-circuits the individual's desires and consciousness (in the shape of Shaw's erratic, highly ambiguous personality) and the sociopolitical state of exception of the McCarthy era. The incest involving mother and son is no titillating add-on but the very embodiment of this short circuit, which erodes both the political boundary between friends and enemies (Communists and anti-Communists) and psychic boundaries of the incest taboo. The parental bond is revealed as a relationship between agent and handler.

It is, however, John Frankenheimer's brilliant 1962 screen version that relates this intensification to its medial basis, thereby adding a media-theoretical dimension to Condon's novel. The aesthetics of the film, with its irritating disjunctions of spoken words and visible images, absurd dialogues, and embedding of television images, expose brainwashing as a media effect—or, more precisely, as a medial doubling of the visible and hence a splitting of reality into an actual event and its image. This becomes particularly clear in the film's arguably most bizarre scene, in which the conditioned U.S. soldiers are presented to a Soviet-Chinese scientific committee in the fictional Manchuria. While the soldiers believe that they are waiting out a storm in a New Jersey hotel listening to a tedious Garden Club lecture, they are in reality seated in an auditorium flanking Yen Lo, the mastermind in charge of the experiment.[14] Condon's novel stages the perceptive disjunction by using simple changes of perspective. In Frankenheimer's movie we see one long circular tracking shot in the course of which the cast irritatingly changes: the female Garden Club speaker, surrounded by yawning soldiers, suddenly turns into Yen Lo; the topic switches from "fun with hydrangeas" to conditioning and hypnosis; and the voice changes from feminine to masculine—all without a single cut. In addition, there is a confusing switching of positions when the hydrangea expert, taking her cue from Yen Lo, suddenly starts talking about brainwashing and hypnosis-induced murder (figures 33 and 34). While the uninterrupted gaze of the camera suggests a continuous space of reality, the switching of persons and decor shows a profound disruption of reality, a mental leap between irreconcilable realities, China and New Jersey. The scene succinctly confuses identities and realities by decoupling sound and image and disrupting the logical sequence of action—as does the entire film. What you see is not what you hear, and it does not follow from what you saw a few seconds earlier. The mental manipulation of the soldiers is, in effect, the manipulation of the viewer who—despite the fact that both images and dialogue are in themselves fully intelligible—loses track of reality.

Figures 33 and 34. John Frankenheimer, *The Manchurian Candidate* (U.S.A., 1962). The brainwashing experiment: without any cuts the scene changes from the Garden Club lecture (*top*) to the auditorium of the Communist research laboratory (*bottom*). Taking turns, the female speaker discusses hydrangeas while Yen Lo, center, talks about brainwashing. Copyright © MGM.

Underlying Frankenheimer's uniquely cinematic severing of what is seen and heard from what is said and done there is a reference to the specific entanglement of media and politics in the early 1950s. The film leaves no doubt that Iselin/McCarthy was a product of television. Indeed, McCarthy's rise and fall between 1950 and 1954 was a career acted out in front of TV cameras (Doherty 2003, 13–18, 232). He started as self-appointed public prosecutor (from 1953 to 1954 he was chairman of the Senate Permanent Subcommittee on Investigations), influential demagogue, and voluble interviewee, whose political impact was largely due to his skilled handling of the new medium. And even his downfall happened on air, during his questioning of Joseph Welch, who rebuffed him with the famous line "Have you no sense of decency?"

Frankenheimer's Iselin operates within an incessantly televised political arena in which everything is geared toward the cameras—including the planned assassination of the presidential candidate by the brainwashed Shaw, an act designed to provide Iselin with the opportunity to deliver a decisive televised speech. Time and again the film inserts television images as a doubling of screen events, for instance, in a scene in which Iselin—re-creating, it seems, McCarthy's Wheeling speech of 1950—uses a press conference to accuse the government of harboring Communists. While events on the movie screen come across as chaotic, the television close-ups that are embedded in the film turn Iselin into the embodiment of justified public anger. The doubling of screens illustrates that the demagogue's charisma is an effect of television (figure 35). McCarthyism—Frankenheimer's film argues and illustrates—is nothing but a camera effect or, as it were, a political culture dancing around the golden calf of TV. The

Figure 35. John Frankenheimer, *The Manchurian Candidate* (U.S.A., 1962). Scene of press conference held by Senator Iselin (modeled on Joseph McCarthy). The senator's wife (Angela Lansbury) follows the public impact of her husband on television. Copyright © MGM.

film is replete with television screens that enable protagonists to witness their own medial success. With the ubiquitous presence of television in American households, this camera effect is at the center of the collective political imaginary of the 1950s.

It is the film rather than the novel that establishes the conspiracist link between mind control and television. While Condon resorts to scientific quotations to give credence to the paranoia of manipulation, the film is able to perform and verify it by making self-reflexive use of its own medial qualities. This allows for a conspicuous media-theoretical intensification: television images are presented as an alternate reality, manipulated and manipulating, which makes them the structural equivalent of the conditioning of the brainwashed soldiers. While the film does not explicitly state that television engages in manipulation, it is part of an overall trend to move the paranoia of mind control onto a media-theoretical level. "Subliminal perception" became the key term expressing the fear that it may be possible to exert influence on viewers by flashing images on screen below the perception threshold. Not surprisingly, the advertising industry expressed considerable interest (Advertising Research Foundation 1958). But more important, the idea of subliminal behavioral control turned into the guiding metaphor for an essentially conspiracist cultural criticism, as offered, for instance, in Vance Packard's *The Hidden Persuaders* (Packard 1957). If the human psyche is in principle open to any kind of manipulation, then states and corporations will strive to fully exhaust human manipulability—whether to increase sales or control the electorate. New media, which in Marshall McLuhan's momentous formulation were seen as the "extensions of man" (McLuhan 1964), rendered the latter accessible to intrusions of any kind undertaken by the consumer society, the culture industry, or political enemies. It is no coincidence, therefore, that popular fantasies tended to connect media and manipulation fears: for instance, Walter Wager's 1975 novel *Telefon* (the basis of the 1977 Charles Bronson movie directed by Don Siegel), dealing with Soviet sleepers in the United States programmed to be reactivated by a phone call and a quotation from a Robert Frost poem; or J. G. Ballard's story "The Subliminal Man" (1963), which turns the idea of subliminal consumer manipulation into a nightmare of forced hyperconsumerism. The 2004 version of *The Manchurian Candidate* starring Denzel Washington updates the fantasy by replacing hypnosis and conditioning with implanted microchips, but it adds nothing conceptually new to the story.

Even though the conspiracist mind-control scenarios depend on the political imaginary of the anti-Communist witch hunts, they go a decisive step beyond it. The fantasy of mind control and brainwashing is, no doubt, an update of the anti-Communist paranoia, buttressed by psychological (pseudo)research and media theory. Politically, though, both are versions of the state paranoia that shaped political culture in the 1950s. Arcane nuclear science was complemented by psychology, that is, a hybrid mixture of psychiatry, behaviorism, psychoanalysis, drug experiments, and science fiction. The uncontrollable circulation and equally uncontrollable effects of scientific knowledge constituted the center of the political imaginary during the early stages of the American Cold War. While the secrets of nuclear research are of a purely technological nature, the knowledge behind brainwashing and mind control is derived from everyday life and individual psychology. Mind control implies actors that are not only invisible but also incapable of cracking under pressure because they know nothing about their mission. The unconscious—both the cultural and its individual counterpart—provides a political target. If nuclear state paranoia is directed against social networks and the very idea of sociality, mind control sets its sights on the innermost sanctuaries of the individual—an individual that in the worst case turns into his own enemy.

Part 8

Invisible Government: JFK

> Powerful events breed their own network of inconsistencies. Loose ends, dead ends, small mysteries of time and space.
>
> —Don DeLillo, "American Blood" (1983)

The assassination of U.S. President John F. Kennedy in November 1963 in Dallas was dreamed of long before it became reality. Just one year earlier, *The Manchurian Candidate* had depicted the killing of the president as the worst of the many nefarious plots hatched by Communists and remote-controlled psychopaths. Yet when the fatal event occurred, it was not the realization of the dark fantasies of 1950s state paranoia but, rather, a break with them. JFK marks the arrival of a different set of political fantasies obsessed with state secrets and hidden enemies—but also of a new type of knowledge involved in and produced by secrecy. The 1950s state paranoia—both the state's fear of invisible enemies and the citizens' fear of manipulation and violence—generated images that despite their hysterical (J. Edgar Hoover), hallucinatory (*Manchurian Candidate*), or pathos-ridden (Rosenberg case) overtones aimed to reveal a "truth" behind all treacherous appearances. By contrast, JFK raises the fundamental question of whether political "reality" can be grasped at all. In light of the unfathomable assassination, the political suffers a loss of reality and the state secret turns into a theology of a secret, an investigation into the "holy" remainders of the enigmatic catastrophe (DeLillo 1991, 15). Fiction here is left with two options: it may either construct a narrative that heroically "unveils" the secret (for example, Oliver Stone's *JFK*) or self-reflexively ponder the epistemic abyss of an inscrutable secret that resists all attempts at narration or reconstruction (as in Don DeLillo's unsurpassed *Libra*).

The assassination of John F. Kennedy was not a unique occurrence; it heralded a veritable era of political murder. Malcolm X was killed in February 1965 in Harlem, Martin Luther King in April 1968 in Memphis, and Robert Kennedy in June 1968 in Los Angeles. The 1960s are a decade of great unsolved American assassinations, featuring dead perpetrators (Oswald), assassins who either never confessed or retracted their confessions (Sirhan Sirhan and James Earl Ray, respectively), too many wounds and bullet holes for too few shots (Robert Kennedy), lost evidence, pressured witnesses, insufficient motives. What is new in this succession of political assassinations starting in Dallas is that they are no longer part of the accustomed juridical-criminal order of crime and punishment, cause and effect, perpetrator and deed. Instead, they unsettle this very order. One crime, numerous motives, one perpetrator—but there is no logically coherent plot able to fit perpetrator, motives, and deed into a plausible frame. Thus there is, in most of these cases, no judicial process: no trial, no sentence, no penance.

This epistemic, legal, and political inaccessibility of the Dallas shooting has been the point of departure for countless narratives—from the Warren Report's forensic scrutiny, with its many supplements and conspiracist rebuttals, to the slew of literary and cinematic reconstructions that either claim to uncover the "hidden truth" or cunningly hide behind fictionality disclaimers. Unlike the *prospective* bias of the political paranoia of the 1950s—that is, its focus on everything that *could* happen—it is now a matter of examining what *did* happen. Indulging in worst-case scenarios and anticipating the future is replaced by attempts to look back and reconstruct the past. McCarthyist state paranoia may have succumbed to the fearful impression that reality is opaque and threatened from all sides, yet it still saw that reality as a *given;* the Dallas assassination, however, creates a *deprivation* of reality. As Don DeLillo put it in a 1988 interview: "What's been missing over these past twenty-five years is a sense of manageable reality. Much of that feeling can be traced to that one moment in Dallas. We seem much more aware of elements like randomness and ambiguity and chaos since then" (DeCurtis and DeLillo 1988, 56).

This growing feeling of randomness, ambiguity, and chaos, all of which stand at the center of DeLillo's arguably best text, the Dallas-inspired novel *Libra* (1988), is the flip side of the suspicion that nothing is random but everything has become ambiguous and chaotic (see the section "Coincidences: Don DeLillo's *Libra*"). Reality eludes all attempts to render it lucid and plausible. The greatest possible crime may be committed but never solved and avenged. As DeLillo argues, randomness and the hidden manipulation of events, conspiracy and contingency, appear to be complementary appearances of a fundamental loss of reality: "Beyond this confusion of data, people have developed a sense that history has been secretly manipulated . . . So from the initial impact of the visceral shock, I think we've developed a much more deeply unsettled feeling about our grip on reality" (DeCurtis and DeLillo 1988, 56).

What happened in Dallas has all the ingredients of a trauma—an event that must be reconstructed and retold after the fact because it wasn't properly experienced in the first place. To bring order to chaos, assassination narratives seek to infuse the collective political confusion with some kind of meaning. The event gains a measure of reality only in reconstructive fictions. Unlike with le Carré's and Greene's reconstructions of the Philby case, however, the goal here is not to furnish psychologically or socially plausible explanations but, more fundamentally, to inquire into the very nature of the event. What on earth happened? Narratives aim to get a grip on the chaotic, murky reality to resolve the *secretum* of the event: Norman Mailer's retelling of Oswald's story in the shape of a tragedy (Mailer 1995), the government report designed to close the case, the uncovering of the secret machinations at the heart of American politics, the exposure of an "invisible government," and so on. Without fail, the reconstructions' titles reveal the claim to have uncovered everything there is to know: for example, *Final Disclosure: The Full Truth About the Assassination of President Kennedy* (Belin 1988) or *Case Closed: Lee Harvey Oswald and the Assassination of JFK* (Posner 1993). But in this cacophony of "final disclosures" the "full truth" is, inevitably, just another version, another fiction in a web made up of all possible versions. In the case of JFK, such fictions become the medium of national self-reflection. The "disclosures" that keep quoting, reinterpreting, and contradicting one another are every bit as fictional as the novelistic and cinematic re-creations of the event: they are all variations of a "case" that can only be told as a *story* but can no longer be reintegrated into *history*. With JFK, the fictionality of the political becomes self-reflexive. This is why novels and films, in particular Oliver Stone's *JFK* (1991), tend to cause more political furor than forensic or political nonfiction accounts. With the JFK case, fictions become politically indispensable because they offer a degree of plausibility that thousands of pieces of evidence no longer provide—whether by presenting the pathetic loser Oswald as a lone gun or by exposing a vast conspiracy inside the U.S. government. Self-reflexive fictions remain the only medium capable of telling the "truth."

Paradigm of Clues: The Warren Report and Conspiracy Theories

At first, things moved incredibly fast. At 12:30 P.M., immediately after the presidential limousine turned from Dealey Plaza into Elm Street, shots were fired, one of which shattered the right side of Kennedy's head. One and a half hours later Lee Harvey Oswald was arrested at the Texas Theater movie house and charged with the murder of police officer J. D. Tippet, who had been shot thirty minutes earlier. That same night Oswald was also charged with assassinating the president; two days later, while being transferred from Dallas Police Headquarters to the county jail, he was shot by nightclub owner Jack Ruby. After the shots came the experts, and from then on time ground almost to a halt. The 5.6 seconds of the shots and the minutes and hours following the assassination, in which police and FBI questioned witnesses, secured the crime scene, and arrested and interrogated Oswald; and doctors at Parkland Hospital released Kennedy's body to the Secret Service to be flown back to Washington on Air Force One—all of these crowded, confused moments have been meticulously dissected countless times in attempts to arrive at a coherent, reliable version of events.

Abraham Zapruder's Kodachrome film has become the true measure of time for what happened in Dallas: each frame received a number and was turned into a temporal "location" of the event. According to the official version, the shots were fired over a total of 5.6 seconds between frames Z-210 and Z-313. Each sixteenth of a second turns into a clue; each single frame becomes a chapter in the progression of events (figure 36). The frame-by-frame analysis of time is complemented by an equally painstaking dissection of space into strategically advantageous locations (who can shoot from where?), fields of vision (what can be seen from where?), shooting angles, and escape routes. Based on Kennedy's and Governor Connally's bullet wounds, experts devise a cone-shaped area in which gunmen could have been positioned; based on statements of eyewitnesses who saw Oswald immediately after the shooting in the Texas Schoolbook Depository, the latter's three-minute escape route is meticulously reconstructed.[1] Reality—a reality so fleeting and incredible that nobody "experienced" it—is decomposed into eyewitness reports, reconstructions, pieces of evidence, visual and auditory recordings, the body of the president, and, last but not least, a surprisingly swiftly apprehended main suspect, who is denied legal counsel, questioned without any recording devices present, and then silenced by Jack Ruby.

Lee Harvey Oswald was left with too little time to confess or present

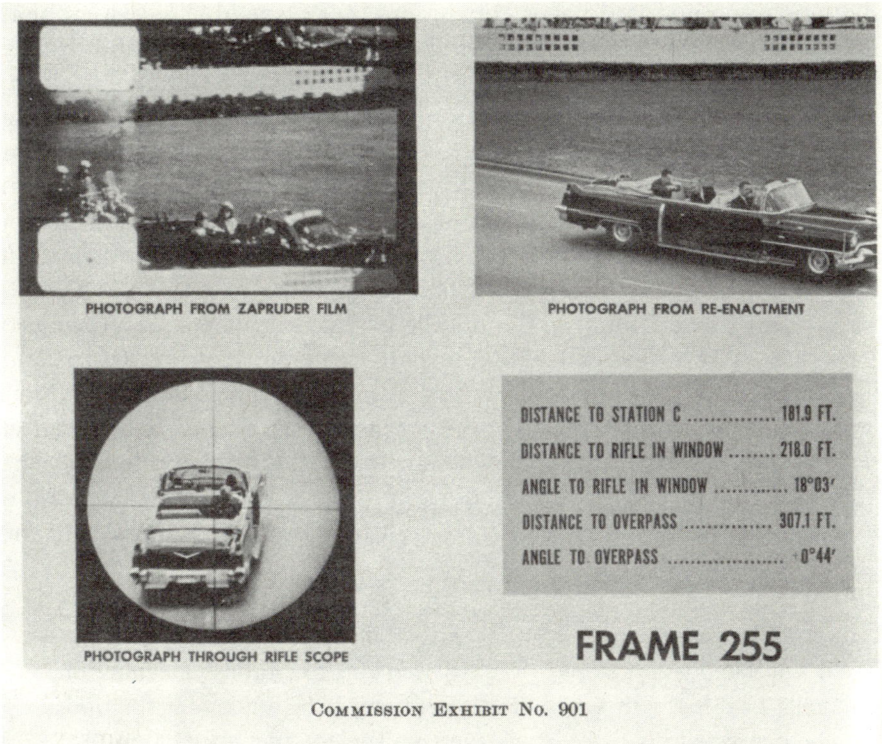

Figure 36. Image 225 from the Zapruder film with additional material from the *Report of the President's Commission on the Assassination of President John F. Kennedy* (Warren Report), Washington, D.C.: Government Printing Office, 1964.

a convincing defense. After his death he became the defendant in a posthumous trial based, for obvious reasons, on nothing but circumstantial evidence. Inevitably, the proceedings focus on the question of whether Oswald (who eventually found a lot of defenders convinced of his innocence) was a lone gun or a manipulated scapegoat. Regardless of the fact that the defendant could not be questioned and sentenced, the principal goal of the report submitted by the Warren Commission, appointed by Lyndon Johnson one week after Kennedy's assassination, was to either affirm or rule out Oswald's guilt.[2] No more than forty-eight hours after the shooting, the Dallas Police and the FBI presented evidence indicating that Oswald acted on his own: agents found his finger- and handprints as well as his Carcano rifle with attached telescopic sight and three spent shells in his hiding place on the sixth floor of the Schoolbook Depository. In September 1964 the Warren Commission submitted its famous report of almost nine hundred pages concluding that Oswald acted alone, that there was no connection whatsoever between him and Ruby, and that he had no links to U.S. and Soviet intelligence agencies or the Mafia. In short, there was no conspiracy, just two lone gunmen, and the only remaining mystery was the question of motive. The Warren Report is the first of several fictions dealing with the JFK assassination whose epistemological difficulties arise from its judicial underpinning: it is, in effect, pursuing a lawsuit against Oswald. Since there is no confession, attention focuses on Oswald's puzzling biography. How had a man in his twenties managed to move to the Soviet Union in the middle of the Cold War and return two years later with a Russian wife and daughter? Between his return and the assassination he held down several jobs, proclaimed himself a Communist, and founded the local chapter of the Castro-friendly organization Fair Play for Cuba, all the while consorting with anti-Communists. The numerous biographical contradictions and about-faces render Oswald a mystery, but for the Warren Commission they are nothing less than the key to solving the riddle:

> Oswald was motivated by an overriding hostility to his environment. He does not appear to have been able to establish meaningful relationships with other people . . . Long before the assassination he expressed his hatred for American society and acted in protest against it . . . He sought for himself a place in history . . . Out of these and the many other factors which may have molded the character of Lee Harvey Oswald there emerged a man capable of assassinating President Kennedy. (Warren 1964, 423)

There is nothing dishonest about the Warren Commission's procedure. It is simply trying to verify or falsify a hypothesis—Oswald's guilt. The "verdict" (both supporters and critics referred to the findings as a "verdict")[3] is based on an accumulation of incriminating evidence: motives like "hatred for American society" and "Communism," fingerprints and witness reports, and an alleged photo of Oswald holding his Carcano, not to mention his suspicious behavior immediately after the shooting. The pattern of a trial by evidence defines and limits the commission's epistemological perspective. According to this logic, any hypotheses pursuing the idea that Oswald was *not* at the center of events would have resulted in a deviation from the topic at hand. In other words, the Warren Report is subject to an inductive bias that arranges facts in line with an initial hypothesis. This methodological narrowing of the narrative renders this first of many JFK fictions so vulnerable. It is misleading, therefore, when critics accuse the Warren Commission of deliberate deception or irresponsible sloppiness. The ignorance with which the commission dismissed alternative versions—the report snidely refers to them as "rumors"—is a result of the basic epistemological decision to structure the investigation as a *trial against Oswald*.[4]

By contrast, the report's numerous critics have come to demand an investigation that resembles a *police investigation* rather than a trial. In other words, what the critics of the Warren Report required was a different type of narrative: a detective story featuring an *unknown* perpetrator. This, precisely, is the point of departure for Oliver Stone's *JFK,* a cinematic counterdraft to the Warren Report. By focusing on the investigation conducted by New Orleans District Attorney Jim Garrison (Garrison 1988), who remains the only official to ever have filed charges in the JFK assassination case, Stone nevertheless adheres to the judicial procedure of the Warren Commission—but only to subject it to withering criticism (see the section "Invisible Government: Oliver Stone's *JFK*"). No matter how critical Garrison/Stone and the immense flood of conspiracy theories around JFK may be of the Warren Commission, they are forced to deal with the evidence presented in the report. Twenty-six volumes of evidence, including the 486 individual frames of the Zapruder film, witness statements, ballistic reconstructions, photo analyses, autopsy X-rays—an infinite number of clues and tiny fragments of reality—are recruited to support alternate versions of the event.

Every detective story is based on what Carlo Ginzburg has called the "paradigm of clues." Securing evidence and interpreting clues is part of a semiotic attempt to "read" the arbitrary signs of an opaque reality. By insisting that these signs do not refer to general laws but to the contingencies of an individual case (Ginzburg 1988), Ginzburg emphasized the "textual" nature of a semiotically apprehended world: the floor is a carrier of footsteps, the body is a texture of symptoms, and the scene of the crime is the "text" of the crime in need of deciphering. But if signs are discrete units that in significant ways stick out from the amorphous continuum of reality, then the forensic reading of these signs amounts to a segmentation of reality into "signlike" units. This could, for example, be the focus (or lack thereof) of a film image, the striations of a bullet, the size of a bullet wound, or the question of whether a wound is an entry or exit wound. Ultimately, however, it is the reader of clues and traces who determines whether something constitutes a piece of evidence and, if so, what it points to. Given that the FBI conducted the first and most important investigation in the Kennedy case, and given that the bureau always assumed Oswald acted alone, all of the clues submitted to the Warren

Commission were subject to this selection criterion. Whatever clue appeared to have no bearing on the question of Oswald's delinquency could not be seen as a clue at all. If traces are read as signs and reality amounts to a "text," then these traces are not only part of a "context"; there also has to be a "code" that constitutes the meaningfulness of a trace. You need a hypothesis to read a clue. This is the crux of the matter when it comes to reconstructing a crime: the question is whether something constitutes a clue and, if so, for what. The traditional remedy is to seek help from experts. Established in the mid-nineteenth century, criminalistics is a science that draws on the skill and experience of specialists: for example, medical doctors familiar with strangulation marks and bullet wounds, chemists who can prove the presence of toxic substances, ballistics experts able to match guns and bullets or derive trajectories from bullet marks. In the Kennedy case all of this highly specialized knowledge became critical. After the Warren Commission three government commissions continued the investigation with additional documentary material and new techniques for analyzing the evidence. The Warren Commission's emphasis on eyewitness testimony was later replaced by "hard scientific data," that is, ever more refined technological analysis of documentary material "such as autopsy, ballistics, handwriting, fingerprint, photographic and acoustic analysis" (House Select Committee on Assassinations [HSCA] 1979, 19). But rather than facilitating a final conclusion, the increasingly scientific methods of investigation rendered it impossible.

The arguably most widely discussed question concerns the number and trajectory of the shots fired. The lone gunman theory holds that there were no more than three: the first missed its target; the second traveled through Kennedy's neck, entered Governor Connally's back, exited at his chest, shattered his wrist, and finally lodged in his thigh. This second bullet, which according to the Warren Report caused four serious injuries to two men, has gone down in history as the "magic bullet." The third, final shot, allegedly also fired from behind (that is, from the Schoolbook Depository the motorcade had just passed), caused a fatal injury by shattering Kennedy's skull. In short, there were injuries, trajectories, and entry and exit wounds, and there are hypotheses as to how many shots were fired from which direction—but despite all this meticulously reconstructed knowledge there is hardly any consensus when it comes to determining what these injuries "tell" us.[5]

These inconsistencies have a devastating impact on the paradigm of clues. Since every trace can be described and interpreted differently, every trace must be constantly reexamined. No witness statement can be taken at face value; no photo, no scrap of film is trustworthy; everything has to be scrutinized over and over and, if need be, dismissed as a forgery. The clue paradigm, so instrumental for the development of criminalistics and forensic pathology, gets entangled in the aporia of its own semiotic structure. Rather than resulting in a better, more plausible, or more "realistic" theory with greater explanatory power than the tale of the lone gunman and magic bullet, the incessant reexamination and reinterpretation of the evidence suggests than one can no longer trust any investigative work. The probative force seemingly guaranteed by the body of evidence flips over into a pervasive distrust of every single piece of evidence. The autopsy report? A forgery. Even worse: Kennedy's corpse was exchanged for another during the flight to Washington (Lifton 1981). The Zapruder film? A shoddy piece with missing frames, maybe even a fake from start to finish (White 1988; Fetzer 2003). Oswald? A scapegoat, obviously, whose weird CV looks as if it had been concocted just for this purpose (Eddowes 1977). Most likely he was a CIA agent, which would explain the ease with which he commuted between the United States and the Soviet Union. The expert knowledge mobilized by the trial of evidence is caught between the aporias of a judicial procedure exclusively focused on a dead defendant and a forensic investigation no longer able to trust its own clues. While the approach taken by the Warren Commission had restricted the processing of clues to one specific hypothesis, the (obvious and necessary) attempt at a more extensive forensic investigation resulted in the destruction of the clue paradigm. It is literally impossible to think of any piece of evidence that could put a stop to this development.

Invisible Government: Oliver Stone's *JFK*

Matters got even worse. While the collapse of the clue paradigm produced the unsatisfactory result that there is a high probability of a conspiracy (HSCA 1979, 95), it did not touch on the issue of the assassination's political significance. Even after sealing the evidence for the next fifty years, the House Select Committee on Assassinations' Final Report did not manage to assuage the cacophony of suspicions and conspiracy theories claiming that the solution was hidden somewhere in the bulk of evidence and thus had to be withheld from the public. Oliver Stone's highly controversial *JFK* (1991) was neither the first nor the only attempt to deal with the political implications of the event. Stone both followed and opposed the judicial approach of the Warren Commission by focusing on the only real trial ever held in connection with JFK: Garrison's indictment of a businessman allegedly involved in the assassination.[6] With inimitable irony Stone cast Garrison himself as Earl Warren: his film is an anti–Warren Report. While the Warren Commission had falsely understood its investigation to be a trial, Garrison—depicted as an upright patriot—conducts the real legal investigation. Stone's pathos derives from the fact that he takes the judicial paradigm more seriously than the Warren Commission ever did. The "wrong" trial is to be amended by the "right" one.

Stone's point of departure is deeply nostalgic: a glossy revue of the bygone Kennedy glamour and the lost age of American political integrity. President Eisenhower's famous farewell warning of the might of the "military-industrial complex," quoted at the outset of the movie, becomes a prelude to the assassination. For Stone, Kennedy's death marks the point at which American postwar politics veers off into a criminalization of the political with the unbroken chain of assassinations of politicians and civil rights leaders, CIA interventions in Africa and Central America, and the domestic scandals ranging from Watergate to the Iran-Contra affair under Ronald Reagan. By making a district attorney his central protagonist, Stone appeals to the authority of the legal sphere and its juridical mechanism to scrutinize the new epoch of uncontrollable *arcana imperii.* The film presents itself as a trial-based attempt to solve an unpunished crime that ushered in a historical period of political depravation in U.S. foreign and domestic policy.

Tracing Oswald's contacts in New Orleans, Garrison (Kevin Costner) slowly and painstakingly works his way through a network of anti-Castro militias, ex-FBI agents, gays, and mobsters. His choice to file charges against respected businessman Clay Shaw (Tommy Lee Jones), who had some ties to this network, is born out of desperation. The sleazy demimonde to which both Oswald and Jack Ruby belonged is not the ultimate goal of Garrison's investigation (though it is the only thing he arrives at). What is at stake is a political dimension that may well lie beyond the reach of legal procedures. This dimension briefly flashes up when Garrison is contacted by an anonymous Pentagon insider. In a detailed monologue, "Mr. X" (Donald Sutherland), an ominous Pentagon informer based on retired Air Force Colonel L. Fletcher Prouty (who did indeed meet Garrison in person and later published a book on the Kennedy assassination), fills Garrison in on the political background of the assassination. A network of high-ranking military and CIA personnel that saw their politics threatened and foiled by Kennedy planned and carried out the killing. Mr. X is not willing to appear in court—all he can do is nudge Garrison to lay charges: "Don't take my word for it. Do your work, your own thinking . . . I can give you the background, you find the foreground, the little things. Keep digging, remember you're the only one to bring a trial in the murder of John Kennedy." To which Garrison responds: "I don't have much of a case." Garrison is well aware of the failure of his attempt to bring matters to a close by staging a trial based on circumstantial evidence. Mr. X, however, is aiming for a political effect: "Your only chance is to come up with a case. Something. Anything. Make arrests. Stir the shitstorm."

Clearly, Clay Shaw is neither Garrison's nor Stone's real target. What is at stake is a political suspicion shared by Stone, Garrison, Prouty, and many others that reaches far beyond corruption in the Big Easy. The ultimate goal is to reopen an investigation that will not limit itself to questions of What and How but will also address the Why and Wherefore. This is, at one and the same time, the juridical *and* antijuridical thrust of the film: on the one hand *JFK* asserts that only the law can rein in the *arcana imperii,* while on the other hand it signals that any such attempt is futile. Adopting a legal demeanor, the film stages a prosecutorial investigation culminating in a lengthy trial to make the point that the blinkered focus on clues and circumstantial evidence should yield to altogether different questions. Neither Garrison nor Stone is interested in convicting a defendant; their goal is to ask the right—that is to say, political—questions:

> The how and the who is just scenery for the public. Oswald, Ruby, Cuba, the Mafia keeps them guessing, like some kind of game. But that prevents them from asking the most important question: Why? Why was Kennedy killed? Who benefited? Who has the power to cover it up? Who? . . . The organizing principle of any society, Mr. Garrison, is for war. The authority of the state over its people resides in its war powers. And Kennedy wanted to end the Cold War in his second term. (Stone 1991)

From the aporias of the clue paradigm the film leads into the depths of a *political* conspiracy. The key question is cui bono? Is it possible that the government is involved in, of all things, the attack on its very top? Mr. X points to the true guilty party: a coterie of senior generals, CIA department heads, and high-ranking civil servants sidelined by the Kennedy administration—in other words, precisely the "military-industrial complex" Eisenhower had warned against. Garrison refers to the power of this network as "the ascendancy of invisible government."

Stone's Garrison is quoting from the political best seller *The Invisible Government,* published by journalists David Wise and Thomas B. Ross one year after the assassination. "Invisible government" is a formula for the monstrous proliferation of the *arcana imperii* of the Cold War. The "invisible government" is not elected; far from being a "formal body," it is a "loose, amorphous grouping of individuals and agencies drawn from many parts of the visible government. It is not limited to the Central Intelligence Agency, although the CIA is at its heart" (Wise and Ross 1964, 3). According to Wise and Ross it is an uncontrollable network spreading its tentacles across administration, military, police, secret services, and maybe even trade unions and the mafia, conducting its own foreign policy, launching covert actions in other countries, and manipulating elected governments by means of a subtle mix of cover-ups, misinformation, and inscrutable shadow administrations. In the wake of the Bay of Pigs disaster Kennedy had adopted an increasingly hostile attitude toward this apparatus, whose innermost core is described by Prouty as a "secret team" (Prouty 1973)—a structure that Kennedy, relying more on family ties and political coteries than on military and intelligence networks, simply did not understand and subsequently curtailed. Stone adopts the theory of the "secret team" directly from Prouty: at the very center of the *arcana imperii* we find a nexus of power no longer dedicated to preserving state power but instead following a logic of self-preservation and discreet hegemony. More than ten years after the assassination, Sydney Pollack's *Three Days of the Condor* (1975) will refer to this structure as "a CIA inside the CIA" (see the section titled "Adventures of a Reader" in part 6, "Cold War")—a structure that was first investigated in 1975 by a U.S. Senate Committee, the Church Committee. In Stone's view, Kennedy's death provides evidence of the unlimited power of this shadow government. Not only is it able to manipulate and deceive the legitimate government; if the need arises, it will get rid of the latter altogether. With the shooting of the president the invisible government devours its visible, legitimate counterpart. Ultimately, the *arcana imperii* are all that remain of the state. The power of the official government, Stone argues, has been fissured to such a degree that it is no longer possible to draw a clear distinction between servants and enemies of the state, between the president who is a representative of the people and—as Watergate demonstrated—the one who is a criminal.

Stone's revelatory gesture falls back on a well-tried model of the relationship between fiction and politics. It is no coincidence that a teary-eyed Garrison makes reference to *Hamlet* in his closing statement. *Hamlet,* after all, presents a political world completely out of joint, with the hero acting in protest against the most grievous *arcanum:* the unpunished murder of the ruler.[7] But Stone is ahead of Garrison. His film does what *The Murder of Gonzago,* the play-within-a-play staged by Hamlet, attempts to do: to present, in accusatory fashion, a real crime in the guise of fiction. Garrison's trial is a failure, but a failure that ensures the success of Stone's film. Fiction is the medium for charges against the political, for objections whose power arises from their bitterness of failure and pathos of impotence. Stone's film thus delivers a far more effective statement than the historical Jim Garrison ever did. Reacting to the movie, in 1992 the U.S. Congress passed the John F. Kennedy Assassination Records Collection Act, paving the way for the disclosure of all documents related to the case in 1998 (see Assassinations Records Review Board 1998).[8] With its questions and its *version* of the truth, Stone's film poses the politically momentous challenge that justice return to the lawless sphere of the *arcana imperii:* "A patriot," the film Garrison urges with a pathos that is also Oliver Stone's, "must always be ready to defend his country against its government."

Coincidences: Don DeLillo's *Libra*

A few years before Stone's *JFK,* Don DeLillo also resorts to the paradigm of clues. He too diagnoses a submersion of the event in the flood of evidence and theories—but rather than reenacting the juridical search for justice and ultimate truth, he concludes that there can never be anything more than alternate versions: in other words, more fictions. In his 1983 article "American Blood" he had described Kennedy's assassination as "a *natural disaster* in the heartland of the real, the comprehensible, the plausible" (DeLillo 1983, 23). Five years later his novel *Libra* recycled this diagnosis, addressing the documentary relics produced by the disaster: "There is much here that is holy, an *aberration* in the heartland of the real." And later: "Let's regain our grip on things" (DeLillo 1991, 15). The overwhelming "natural disaster," which according to DeLillo turned him into a writer (DeCurtis and DeLillo 1988, 56), changes into a man-made "aberration," an auratic withdrawal of things that renders "our grip" on reality both necessary and impossible. DeLillo questions the transformation of the "real" by and into an event, thereby exposing the divergence between the event as a natural catastrophe and all the clues, discourses, and interpretations whose "aberrations" make it impossible to pin down what they refer to. But unlike the myriad of conspiracy theorists, DeLillo, celebrated and castigated by critics as "the chief shaman of the paranoid school of American fiction" (Towers 1988), is not out to reconstruct yet another semiplausible version. Authors like Oliver Stone or Norman Mailer had responded to the withdrawal of the event by offering either *one* incriminating version of the real (Stone) or an individual's tragedy constructed from the quagmire of countless subjective narratives (Mailer

1995).[9] DeLillo instead focuses on the *analytics* of this withdrawal by trying to break through to a "reality" behind the historical accumulation of evidence. He takes the diverse and contradictory theories and narratives generated by the paradigm of clues not as his conclusion but as his poetic starting point.[10] Contrary to frequent claims, paranoia—the will to impose significance and connections on the world—is neither DeLillo's medium nor his narrative method but his object of study. What is at stake is a narrative epistemology of the paranoid style as an *effet de secret* deeply rooted in the American political imaginary.[11]

The crux of this fictional reflection on paranoia is already evident in the basic construction of the text: DeLillo combines two mutually exclusive theories, the lone gunman scenario and the anti-Kennedy conspiracy, into one comprehensive (historical and narrative) plot (see Melley 2000, 133–60). *Libra* contains two separate yet intertwined narratives. On the one hand, we have the story of Lee Harvey Oswald, a disoriented loner driven by half-baked Marxism and a craving for recognition, who at age twenty-one immigrates to the Soviet Union, marries a Russian, and returns to America with wife and child in tow. He drifts from job to job, founds pro-Castro groups, and entertains sporadic contacts with various intelligence agencies. On the other hand, there is the story of a discharged CIA black-ops expert who, to redirect the public's attention toward Castro following the disastrous Bay of Pigs invasion, hatches the (by no means unpatriotic or subversive) plan to *simulate* a Cuban plot to assassinate Kennedy. However, the staged attack, prepared in great detail by Win Everett, retired head of two of the CIA's covert action units, is in need of a presentable guilty party, a "perpetrator" who will not only indicate a Cuban connection but also serve to shield the real gunman. "They wanted a name, a face, a bodily frame they might use to extend their fiction into the world" (DeLillo 1991, 50). The forensic detection of future traces, the paradigm of clues, is thus already part of the planning of the plot. While still immersed in manufacturing a fitting perpetrator, the team discovers that he really exists: Oswald is a culprit of such overdrawn features that, as DeLillo remarked in 1983, he appears to have been invented:

> "Lee Harvey Oswald" often seems a secret design worked out by men who will never surface—a procedural diagram, a course in fabricated biography. Who put him together? He is not an actor so much as he is a character, a fictional character who first emerges as such in the year 1957 . . . Oswald seems scripted out of doctored photos, tourist cards, mail-order forms, altered signatures, pseudonyms. (DeLillo 1983, 24)

Cadigan Exhibit No. 21

Face and reverse sides of the Oswald Selective Service System Registration Certificate and the Oswald Certificate of Service in the U.S. Marine Corps.

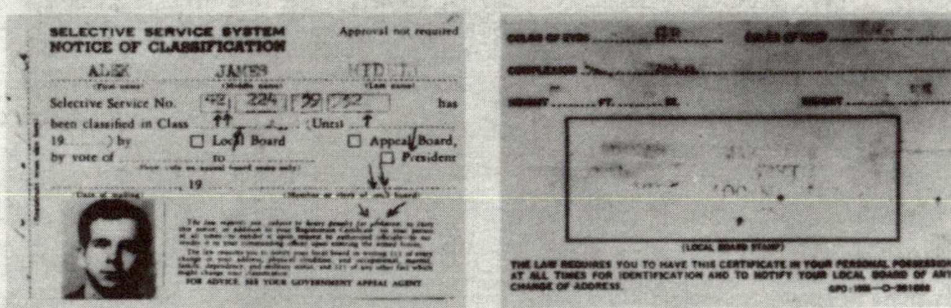

Face and reverse sides of the Hidell Selective Service System Notice of Classification.

Cadigan Exhibits Nos. 15 and 16

Face and reverse sides of the Hidell Certificate of Service in the U.S. Marine Corps.

Figure 37. Oswald's various IDs as Lee Harvey Oswald and Alek James Hidell, from the *Report of the President's Commission on the Assassination of President John F. Kennedy* (Warren Report), Washington, D.C.: Government Printing Office, 1964.

But DeLillo does not simply invent the invention of his protagonist; he refers directly to the Warren Report's meticulous documentation of Oswald's fake identities (figure 37). In the novel, Oswald turns into the real referent of an initially fake identity, thereby highlighting something the Warren Commission eagerly latched on to without ever questioning it: the fact that (the historical) Oswald's strange vita looks like a caricature of a 1950s Communist state enemy. Fiction exposes the fictionality of political identities that are taken for real by attempts to shed light on the shooting in Dallas. Oswald's artificiality, as it were, also applies to DeLillo's conspirators and their plot. The CIA veterans are planning not to assassinate the president but to fake an attempt; the shots are designed to miss the ostensible target and to hit Castro instead. It is a stage production, an "assassination theatre" (Lentricchia 1991, 201) in the guise of a covert operation aimed at providing the government with a pretext to attack Cuba and remove Castro from power.

The operation is a classic example of how the "invisible government" conducts foreign policy; it contains all the elements that characterize U.S. covert actions from Guatemala (1954) to Iran-Contra (1987). The hearings prompted by Iran-Contra left no doubt that it was still possible in the 1980s to conduct with impunity intelligence activities removed from congressional oversight. Secret planning—which enabled President Ronald Reagan to invoke "plausible deniability"—remained a viable foreign policy option, as did U.S.-controlled coups that the media celebrated as struggles for liberation or legitimate acts of reprisal.[12] DeLillo provides a meticulous account of the administrative work that goes into CIA-directed black ops, including the measures to shield responsible decision makers from knowing too much about the details of the operations. Nonetheless, the conspiracy—just like real-life black ops—aims to realize Kennedy's own secret desires: "They all knew that Kennedy wanted Castro cooling on a slab but they weren't allowed to let on to him that his guilty yearning was the business they'd charged themselves to carry out. The White House was to be the summit of unknowing" (DeLillo 1991, 20 and following; quotation on 21–22).

Libra elaborates a complex social profile of the professional covert action experts whom the CIA has been training since the 1950s. The team includes high-ranking planners like Win Everett and Larry Parminter, members of the "Yale-OSS network of so-called gentlemen-spies" (DeLillo 1991, 30); organizers and combat instructors like T. J. Mackey, who meanders from assignment to assignment; and outright killers such as Vásquez, Raymo, and Elko. Instead of conducting regular intelligence work the conspirators are engaged in a vengeful overfulfillment of the (supposed) presidential will. Once "plausible deniability" has become an integral part of intelligence operations, there is no longer any central responsibility and no executive order. As Gregory Treverton points out, this is precisely what marks the political culture of covert actions: "Subordinates were in the position of interpreting what the president wanted without asking directly for authorization" (Treverton 1987, 5). By unfolding the plot in painstaking detail, DeLillo offers a trenchant analysis of the secret structure of the black ops world that forms the core of the invisible government. This secret structure does away with chains of command and control mechanisms; instead it generates its own, informal networks (DeLillo 1991, 22). All of the shadowy figures that subsequently get caught up in the investigation of the assassination (that is, the novel's cast of characters) are part of this mixed, corrupt network: embittered Communist haters like ex–FBI agent Guy Banister; gay ex-pilot David Ferrie, who spends his time training paramilitary units; inscrutable businessman George de Mohrenschildt; mafiosi like Carmine Latta, who will order the murder of Oswald; and, last but not least, Oswald himself.

DeLillo's conspiracy isn't something cooked up by a few initiates. It is a complex enterprise that follows its own logic: "Plots carry their own logic. There is a tendency of plots to move toward death. He [Win Everett] believed that the idea of death is woven into the nature of every plot. A narrative plot no less than a conspiracy of armed men" (DeLillo 1991, 221). We tend to think of conspiracies as the very essence of a controlled intervention by invisible, cunning actors, but this conspiracy is one in which everything gets out of control. At one point one of the planners, T. J. Mackey, has the "revelation" (ibid., 220) to carry things through to the bitter end by *not* missing Kennedy. DeLillo's text insists that the course of events obeys the inherent logic of the plot rather than the planning of individual agents. Every narrative gravitates toward death, the absolute zero point and end of all stories.[13] For DeLillo, political conspiracies are determined by the "poetic" principles of a *narrative* logic that weaves events into a plot.

While the conspiracy is carried away by its own narrative logic, Oswald, too, is nothing but a fictitious part of this "plot." He is already shaped by a conspiracist view of the world long before the conspirators catch sight of him. Inspired by readings of Marx, he adopts the fundamental axiom of all conspiracy theories: "There is a world inside the world" (DeLillo 1991, 13, and passim). Oswald's world—as well as that of the black ops—is one of omnipresent mysteries and hidden forces. It is significant that Oswald, who grew up in the 1940s and '50s, latches on to the state paranoia of those decades. The Rosenbergs are mentioned three times (ibid., 12, 38 and following, 160), figuring as symbols for the U.S. government's conspiracy against its own citizens: "It was Eisenhower and Nixon who killed the Rosenbergs" (ibid., 39, 160). But the 1950s, when it was at least clear who was plotting against whom, are long gone. Oswald's world is opaque. The only way he can acquire an identity is to invent himself as a bearer of secrets—yet he "knows" that his secret is empty: "Nobody knew that he knew. The whirl of time, the true life inside him. This was his leverage, his only control" (ibid., 46). He invents cover names, forges documents, purchases a Minox, and reads James Bond novels (ibid., 180). His Marxism is less an ideology than a way of ferreting out connections behind seemingly contingent events.[14] His move to the Soviet Union, his random contacts with pro-Cuban groups, and his desire to immigrate to Cuba are attempts to carve out a space for himself in the secret class struggle: "He thought the only end to isolation was to reach the point where he was no longer separated from the true struggles that went on around him. The name we give this point is history" (ibid., 248). To overcome isolation and aimlessness, Oswald is searching for his place in a narrative, a (hi)story of struggles and secret meanings made up of a texture of invisible connections—a history that is always already a *secret* history, a hidden plot whose unfolding he is trying to understand.

Libra narrates Oswald's life as a sequence but not as a biography; his life is marked as a peregrination through space. While the chapters dealing with the preparations for the assassination plot are headed by dates, a countdown to November 22, Oswald's life is referred to by locations used as chapter headings: New Orleans, Atsugi, Moscow, Minsk, Dallas. The two narrative threads remain unconnected until they finally merge: "[DeLillo has] given us one perfectly shaped, intention-driven narrative while folding within it, every other chapter, a second narrative, his imagined biography of Oswald, a plotless tale of an aimless life" (Lentricchia 1991, 201). The question remains how exactly the novel connects "plot" and "plotlessness," conspiracy and contingency, intentionality and randomness.

After years of research, this conflagration of opposites will also be at the heart of the reconstruction undertaken by ex–CIA analyst Nicholas Branch, whose painstaking yet furtive collecting and researching of the facts forms a third narrative thread within the novel:

> He has learned enough about the days and months preceding November 22, and enough about the twenty seconds itself, to reach

> a determination *that the conspiracy against the President was a rambling affair that succeeded in the short term due mainly to chance.* Deft men and fools, ambivalence and fixed will and what the weather was like. (DeLillo 1991, 441; emphasis added)

Chance and planning, conspiracy and contingency make up both Oswald's story and the plot[15]—and precisely this inability to distinguish between (intended) connections and (random) simultaneities constitutes the strange character of a "history" which the novel itself does not so much reconstruct as decompose. *Libra* carves out the indeterminacy and ambivalence of the coincidences marking the historical event (see Herbert 2010, 310). The character that offers the most radical take on these coincidences is crazy and paranoid David Ferrie, who trains young men for missions in Cuba, conducts his own cancer research on mice, organizes arms deliveries, and, last but not least, brings together Oswald and the conspirators. Apart from being an expert in all kinds of esoteric sciences (he says he believes in everything), Ferrie is also the resident theorist of coincidence, planned chance, astrology, and secret messages: "I have studied patterns of coincidence . . . Coincidence is a science waiting to be discovered" (DeLillo 1991, 44). He teaches Oswald to decipher the existence and the plans of the plotters from a slew of strange coincidences: from the affinities between Kennedy and Oswald (both are dyslexic and share a passion for James Bond, and they have wives who are pregnant at the same time), from the fact that two guns ordered at different times arrive on one and the same day, from television movies, and even from the stars (both Kennedy and Oswald were born under the sign Libra). Oswald can enter the plot only because he has been taught by Ferrie to see himself—more precisely, to *decipher* himself—as a part of the narrative. Toward the end, just before Mackey hands him the directions for how to shoot Kennedy, Oswald has attained a state of paranoid world interpretation in which "everything revolves around him" (ibid., 385) and which enables him to take his part in the grand scheme. Nonetheless, Ferrie remains vague when it comes to explaining the nature of the connection between Oswald and the CIA. Apparently it is a matter not of cause and effect, common interests, guided control or manipulation, but, again, of an intertwining of narrative threads:

> Think of two parallel lines. One is the life of Lee H. Oswald. One is the conspiracy to kill the President. What bridges the space between them? What makes a connection inevitable? There is a third line. It comes out of *dreams, visions, intuitions, prayers,* out of the

> deepest levels. It's not generated by cause and effect like the other two lines. It's a line that cuts across causality, cuts across time. It has no history that we can recognize or understand. But it forces a connection. It puts a man on the path of his destiny. (DeLillo 1991, 339; emphasis added)

This is DeLillo's metapoetics of conspiracy. Traditionally envisaged as an ultimate act of covert manipulation, an *invisible hand* of history, conspiracy here emerges as the outcome of much more complex connections. The parallel, contingent, and wholly unconnected lines of an individual life and a political plan are brought together by a dimension of the *imaginary:* "dreams, visions, intuitions, prayers." It is the unconscious of society and politics, a web of desires and phantasms rather than rational decisions or vested political interests. This central dimension also explains the novel's title, the astrological sign of the scales. Astrology, a type of hybrid knowledge lodged somewhere between popular culture and esoteric teachings, is an emblem of the will to decipher patterns and discover the deeper meanings of coincidences and simultaneities—such as the connection between the two Libra men, Oswald and Kennedy. What remains unclear, however, is the nature of the connection. Ferrie can do no more than announce a future theory of coincidences (DeLillo 1991, 44). In fact, the only "meaning" of the coincidences between the two men's lives is the *desire for a connection—and the connection of two desires.* The third line, which connects Oswald's life to the political desires and plans, is nothing but a line of desires: the desire to play a part in the great script of history, and the president's "guilty yearning" for Castro's demise—or at least the interpretation of his desire by the CIA veterans. The narrative teleology of the plot connects the two lines, thus bringing about a wish-fulfillment in the deepest, most secretive domains of the political unconscious.

But *Libra* would not be so brilliant a novel if it only dealt with the *effets de secret* of the political unconscious that are crystallized in a traumatic historical event. It is also a paradigmatic book about the relationship between the political unconscious and fiction. *Libra* abounds with references to narrating and inventing: Oswald sees himself as a writer of short stories, even though he is orthographically challenged and a pathetically inept author.[16] Eventually his shots come, literally, from a world of books, the Texas Schoolbook Depository. And the arguably most important figure in the novel is a reader: Nicholas Branch, the archivist commissioned by the CIA to write a secret—and thus ultimately "true"—history of the assassination. Branch's insights, written in the present tense, are the novel's third narrative thread. He embodies the paradigm of clues and evidence: every year, a "curator" hands over new files, pieces of evidence, documents, and samples to Branch, who desperately tries to avoid getting entangled in the growing web of "endless suggestiveness": "He is writing a history, not a study of the ways in which people succumb to paranoia" (DeLillo 1991, 57). Branch is Ferrie's secret antipode. While Ferrie believes in everything, Branch believes in nothing—neither in any detail-oriented speculation nor in any comprehensive theory claiming to explain everything about the assassination. Branch's role as a reader of clues has from the very beginning been part of the plot—much like the historian's role in Borges's "The Theme of the Traitor and the Hero" (see part 1, "Borges—A Poetics of Treason"). Branch is paralyzed by that knowledge; he senses that solving the plot is part of the plot. "Create coincidences so bizarre they have to believe it . . . An arrest, a false name, a stolen credit card" (ibid., 147). Branch is adrift in a sea of relevant and irrelevant material (the dental records of Ruby's mother, microphotos of Oswald's pubic hair) and baffled by the many untimely and unnatural deaths: Banister, Frank Vásquez, de Mohrenschildt, Ferrie. "It is impossible to stop assembling data" (ibid., 59). At the same time he harbors the suspicion that the CIA curator is unwilling to present all the evidence: "There are worrisome omissions, occasional gaps in the record . . . Why are they withholding material from him as well?" (ibid., 442). Branch has good reason to distrust both the abundance of evidence and its gaps. Shannon Herbert has shown that Branch's confusion directly reflects the new attitude of the HSCA, with its more "scientific" approach toward the evidence, an attitude that leads to less rather than more clarity:

> Branch's relation to material mirrors that of the three government commissions that investigated the assassination after the Warren commission. In a climate of conspiracy, any narrative interpretation appears conspiratorial, and to allay such concerns, the commissions gradually began to decline to draw conclusions from the evidence they gathered. (Herbert 2010, 294)

Branch too learns that working with clues and traces is a never-ending affair. Is the material authentic? Is it complete? What is the meaning and relevance of a document or piece of evidence? The desire for meaning erodes the reality of the examined item: "A fact is innocent until someone wants it" (DeLillo 1991, 227).

Branch reflects DeLillo's ideas about the event's lack of reality that he first expressed in his 1983 essay "American Blood." Not so much a symptom of "postmodern impotence" (Hutchinson 2001, 118), Branch is rather an incarnation of "epistemological self-control, a self-policing against interpretation and speculation" (Herbert 2010, 296) that threatens not just the fictional accounts of the assassination but also the attempts to reconstruct it as a historical event. Branch is an "authorial fiction," though a wholly paradoxical one, since his doubts unsettle the coherence of the other two narrative threads (Johnston 1998, 191). Even more, he is a cryptic self-inscription of the author into the text, a figure who quotes DeLillo verbatim (especially his 1983 article). Just as DeLillo burrowed through the documents (mainly the Warren Report) to write *Libra,* Branch collects and evaluates documents—but, unlike his author, *does not write.* The "true story" of the assassination is something he cannot produce. Branch is DeLillo's canceled signature, an "author" who like the wannabe story-writer Oswald does not write but embodies the impossibility of writing and narrating.[17] In a 1988 interview DeLillo distanced himself from his 1983 claims by attributing them to Branch and other "people who have developed a sense that history has been secretly manipulated" (DeCurtis and DeLillo 1988, 56). DeLillo, then, is using the figure of Nicholas Branch to mock attempts to turn the illegible traces of the shooting into a historical narrative capable of satisfying a desire for the "whole truth." Branch realizes that this truth, which would always have to remain a secret, is part of the intelligence service's knowledge structure: a structure upheld by a "vast theology, a formal coded body of knowledge that was basically play material, secret-keeping" (DeLillo 1991, 442). An integral part of this knowledge structure is the ongoing suspicion that material has been withheld as well as the no less incessant urge to come up with theories that offer no conclusive answers.

But while Branch fails to write his "secret history," his author DeLillo no longer claims to do so. Instead he writes a "work of imagination" which clearly states that it will not "furnish factual answers to any questions raised by the assassination" (DeLillo 1991, 458). The fact that Branch quotes what DeLillo had expressed five years prior to the novel's publication shows that the *novel* has progressed beyond Branch/DeLillo of 1983. Branch's problem provides the novel's point of departure, not its conclusion. *Libra* ventures beyond the aporias unfolded in the essay. As a piece of self-reflexive fiction, as a "plot" of a "plot," the novel overcomes the "aberration in the heartland of the real" (DeLillo 1991, 15), with its concomitant loss of reality. This, however, serves to revise the relationship between historical event and fiction, as DeLillo points out in his brief afterword: "A novel about a major unresolved event would aspire to fill some of the blank spaces in the known record. To do this, I've altered and embellished reality, extended real people into imagined space and time, invented incidents, dialogues and characters" (ibid., 458).

DeLillo invents and transforms historical figures, but this transformation provides a coherence and inner structure of meaning the real event lacks. Gaps are filled and reality attains a certain plausibility only *as fiction. Libra* is not only an analysis of the paranoid style as an unquenchable, ever prolific desire for connection and meaning; it also traces how this desire turns into "history." In the midst of a confusing jumble of theories that all proclaim the "truth," the novel offers a salutary—or, to quote DeLillo, "consoling"[18]—and fully self-conscious *effet de réalité* because it does not aspire to be anything else than *fiction*—a fiction, however, that both reflects and satisfies the desires of the political unconscious. Unlike Stone's film (which amounts to yet another plea to reveal the "whole truth"), *Libra* wants to be a piece of literature, yet its narrative reveals that the "reality effects" of the political—all the talk about dark secrets hidden from the public in inaccessible archives—are based on nothing but a "theology" of the secret. This "theology" concocts politics out of a system of beliefs, desires, dreams, and suspicions and even devises its own exposure as an effect that is fully intended yet constantly deferred.

Unlike the specular enmity of war games and espionage plots from the Cold War era, and unlike the McCarthyist state paranoia, the notion of the "invisible government" moves treason into the innermost recesses of power. To speak of an invisible government is to collapse power and conspiracy to such a degree that they become coextensive. Within the invisible core of power there is a suspension of all legal instances of sovereignty: to ensure plausible deniability, the president must neither know nor decide. And he may even be killed as the result of a plot that can neither be uncovered nor brought to trial. In the era of the invisible government, the all-encompassing distrust of the "paranoid style" (Hofstadter 1965), which in the 1950s was directed at an object (a dangerous form of knowledge, an invisible enemy), comes to entail the collapse of friend/enemy distinctions as well as of sovereignty and the judicial apparatus. The paranoid style leads to a distrust of reality itself, of all the traces and documents that—as bodies of evidence—once guaranteed a sense of reality. Fiction, in turn, has several options: it may abjure its status as fiction (that is, as a possible but contingent version of reality) and appeal to an "ultimate truth," which is what the many conspiracy theories have in common with the Warren Report they contest. Or it can use the space of the fictional to either provide plausible accounts of incomprehensible events (Mailer 1995) or raise charges and pose questions to gesture at a hidden truth that may be still be accessed and revealed (Stone 1991).

Fiction is a recourse to reality; it is the medium in which political truth, the unraveling of a mystery, can at least be referred to. In this way, stories can heal the wounds inflicted by history's secrets. With DeLillo, however, we find an altogether different strategy. Fiction no longer points toward the possibility of accessing a hidden truth behind state secrets. Instead it reflects on the intransigence of these secrets and a structure of history that follows a narrative logic fueled by the political *unconscious*. Fiction thus not only changes the discourse of the secret but also alters the very notion of the political itself, which is now revealed to be a matter of beliefs, wishes, dreams, and desires.

Part 9

After 9/11

1 The Light of the Phantasm

The name under which an event enters history books says something about its character. "9/11," the strangely emaciated date that now stands for the notorious attacks on the World Trade Center and the Pentagon, denotes nothing but the date itself. Unlike "the outbreak of the First World War" or "JFK," its secret is linked to a specific point in time: more precisely, to the improbable coincidence of four almost simultaneous airplane crashes, destroyed buildings, some three thousand deaths, and a global media transmission in real time. But its importance also resides in the rupture that separates the years before 2001 from its aftermath, as well as in the greatest overhaul of the intelligence apparatus since the Second World War. Whatever happened on 9/11 has always been part of the discussion of what this rupture signifies. What future began on September 11 (see Derrida 2003)? Was it the beginning of a new form of warfare? Did it reveal a new type of enemy? A clash of cultures? A disappearance of the real in the medial's persistence of images?

To assess the political trauma of 9/11 it is helpful to briefly compare it to the events in Dallas. All the questions and mysteries connected to "JFK" point toward a dark past that culminated in the deaths of Kennedy and Oswald. At the time nobody viewed Kennedy's murder as a beginning; only in hindsight did it turn out to be the first in a series of assassinations, a symptom of deep-seated political corruption and, as DeLillo remarked twenty years later, "a natural disaster in the heartland of the real" (DeLillo 1983, 23). In the case of 9/11, however, the question of the "real" is present right from the very beginning—and with it the questions of what kind of what future awaits us. Already in the immediate aftermath of the event, 9/11 was not seen as an end but as a departure into new wars, new crises, new enemies, new rules for domestic security, and new threats. And from the very beginning the repeatability of the event was invoked: 9/11 is seen as the beginning of a series. The riddle posed by 9/11, then, points to the future rather than the past. The question is not *What happened?* but *What will happen from now on?* This concerns not only the event's many interpretations and consequences but also the ways it relates to fiction. It is as if 9/11 could only be presented as part of a scenario (both present and future) that suggests, introduces, and ultimately justifies possible new threats and types of warfare.

This doubling of the event into present and future, facticity and virtuality, has less to do with the inevitably invoked "postmodern" regime of derealization than with the epistemic and rhetorical structure of a political discourse that turns 9/11 into a date marking a rupture between a *before* and a *from now on.* As the Bush government proclaimed in the fall of 2002:

> Enemies *in the past* needed great armies and great industrial capabilities to endanger America. *Now,* shadowy networks of individuals can bring great chaos and suffering to our shores for less than it costs to purchase a single tank. Terrorists *are organized* to penetrate open societies and to turn the power of modern technologies against us. (National Security Strategy 2002; emphasis added)

The dissolution of clearly identifiable enemies into "shadowy networks," which are discussed in later segments, appears to indicate a transition from "the past" to the *now,* heralding a future replete with terrorists "organized" to "penetrate open societies." 9/11 becomes an epistemologically operative moment, an event whose historical significance resides in the fact that it sheds light on a political landscape hitherto shrouded in darkness. The event produces an *effet de secret:* it is seen as the emergence of something hidden—hidden in the future, that is, but also obscured by the "open societies" in which we live.

Joseph Joffe has provided a more precise, less agitated account of the *before/from now on* binary invoked by the U.S. government:

> What has really changed since last September 11? Not very much. Cataclysmic as it was that event was more like a bolt of lightning that illuminated the essential contours of the international landscape than like an earthquake that reconfigured it. It dramatized,

> but did not shape, some profound transformations of world politics in the making for at least a decade. (Joffe 2002)

Joffe's lucid metaphor highlights the paradoxical structure of the historic impact of 9/11—a structure that involves more than a switch from conventional, cost-intensive wars to irregular, scandalously low-cost terrorism. It implies a different epistemology of political knowledge. In new and unique fashion, 9/11 reveals what was neither new nor unique: the political landscape of the post–Cold War, with its low-intensity conflicts, revivals of ethnic and religious forms of enmity, and an increasingly blurred distinction between citizens and enemies. In terms of target and intention, the 2001 attack on the World Trade Center was a repetition of the 1993 bombing, just a great deal more devastating. To describe 9/11 as a bolt of lightning that renders the political landscape visible—or at least conjecturable—implies that something hitherto obscured has moved out into the open. More precisely, it implies a political latency period in which the "actual" event is not yet manifest but may be imagined in the shape of deferrals and screen memories. During this phase the relationship between politics and fiction is once again transformed: it is neither (as in times of the Cold War) a matter of exploring the secret undergrowth of the political, nor of imagining worst-case scenarios or (as in DeLillo's metafictional rendition of JFK) experiencing a removal of reality. 9/11 inverts the relationship between fiction and politics by having the latter turn into a reflection and interpretation of the former. 9/11 is metafiction.

If 9/11 was an event that illuminated already existing yet invisible cultural and political formations, this explains why so many fictional scenarios depicted 9/11 long *before* it happened. Popular renditions of the destruction of major Western cities (with a special preference for New York), from *Independence Day* (1996) and *Godzilla* (1998) to *Fight Club* (1999) and the eerily precise *The Siege* (1998), are phantasmal displacements of something the Cold War mentality was not able to fully decipher. This displacement had less to do with depicting different actors, different locations, or different goals (aliens, mutated monsters, male aggression fantasies) than with the simple fact that these scenarios were presented *as fiction*. As a result, the televised images of a New York under attack invoke Hollywood images from the 1990s. According to Jean Baudrillard, this uncanny recognition is related to the fulfillment of unacknowledged (and unacknowledgeable) dreams: "The fact that we have dreamt of this event, that everyone without exception has dreamt of it—because no one can avoid dreaming of the destruction of any power that has become hegemonic to this degree—is unacceptable to the Western moral conscience" (Baudrillard 2002, 5). In other words, Baudrillard insinuates that the illegitimate dreams and desires of the West and the rest share fantasies of destruction centered on "Western" symbols. Without a doubt 9/11 represents a new tactics of terrorist violence aware of its own media effects, choosing targets with a symbolic dimension most forcefully revealed in their moment of destruction. But Baudrillard's notion of illegitimate desires is based on a relatively simple structure of desire and representation: the goal is the exhilarating annihilation of symbols and centers of power, a liberating desire reputedly shared with differing degrees of conviction by Hollywood directors, television viewers, and Islamic fundamentalists.

But the relationship between the images, fictions, and scenarios that act out "9/11" years before the fact may be more complex. Rather than joining the chorus which insists that the images of destruction repeat our fictions of destruction, resulting in an irruption of the "real" into a world of fictions, Slavoj Žižek suggested we view 9/11 as the irruption of a phantasm. From a psychoanalytic perspective, the phantasm implies the notion of latency; it is a "screen" that both hides and indicates an unbearable and nonrepresentable "real," an *effet de secret* that is both evidence and concealment of the "real." Much like Joffe's image of the lightning bolt illuminating a darkness of unacknowledged realities, the phantasm represents and disfigures this "real":

> It was before the WTC collapse that we lived in our reality, perceiving Third World horrors as something which was actually not part of our social reality . . . and what happened on September 11 was that this phantasmatic screen apparition entered our reality. It is not that reality entered our image: the image entered and shattered our reality. (Žižek 2002, 16)

For Žižek 9/11 is the realization of a structure that, familiar as it may be to us, we do not accept as part of our reality. Yet by referring to it in terms of "Third World horrors," Žižek instinctively repeats the common gesture of rendering this reality less real by moving it as far away as possible—into the third world or into a future ransacked by aliens. Fictions that depict the destruction of Western cities—that is, of our social reality—are a formation of symptoms, the phantasmic avoidance of something that cannot be recognized as real. The work carried out by fiction consists of a condensation and hybridization that projects "foreign" fears straight into the center of everyday Western life.

Anticipations: Edward Zwick's *The Siege*

Edward Zwick's *The Siege* (1998) is a particularly striking example of the strange anticipatory force of phantasms that seem like disconcertingly realistic early stagings of 9/11. In hindsight, many of the film's details look like a cinematic adaptation of the attack on New York: explosions in the street, New Yorkers covered in blood, a network of Islamic terrorists eager to exploit media presence, and last but not least the collapse of a tall administrative building, the New York FBI headquarters. Because of the eerie similarity to scenes that took place three years later—fleeing masses, scraps of paper filling the air, policemen taking cover from blast waves behind cars—the film's DVD was the most popular DVD right after 9/11. The film's screenwriter, Lawrence Wright, later turned to journalism and wrote an award-winning book on Bin Laden and al-Qaeda (Wright 2009).

The similarities, however, are not limited to the images. The terrorists turn out to be anti-Saddam partisans trained by the CIA who were abandoned when the Americans left Iraq after the first Iraq War. The shadowy CIA agent Bridger who grew up in Lebanon (Annette Bening) embodies the prehistory of an aborted, hushed-up covert operation in the Middle East. In the end she pays the price for the bad conscience of the CIA by dying at the hands of the last remaining terrorist. Clearly, the plot refers to the American training and support of the Afghan mujahideen. The message is: we raised our enemies ourselves. And indeed, this is precisely the prehistory of al-Qaeda, whose struggle against the Soviet Union received material, financial, and weapons support from the United States (already noted in Alexander and Swetnam 2001).

But the terror scenario—which combines the domestic terrorism of Oklahoma City with Hamas suicide bombings in Israel—is only one half of the prophetic phantasm. The other half is the government's response: as the president declares martial law in New York, a general—played by Bruce Willis (who looks the part)—has all young men of Arab descent detained in Yankee Stadium and orders the torture of a prisoner suspected of having knowledge of future attacks. In a scene in which members of the CIA, FBI, and the military discuss whether or not exigent circumstances justify the use of torture, Žižek's "Third World" is clearly named: in Israel, CIA agent Bridger notes dryly, torture works, but only after thirty-six hours of sleep deprivation. The phantasm operates by way of a relocation: the intifada moves to New York, Midtown turns into Tel Aviv, and Brooklyn becomes the West Bank. Not coincidentally, Samir (Sami Bouajila), the key terrorist and lover of CIA agent Bridger, is a Palestinian.

The terror scenario of *The Siege* is, in the words of its director, a "sum of all fears" (Zwick, in Bay 1998)—more precisely, a condensation of two catastrophes: that of terror and that of a paranoid state bent on suspending all civil rights and revealing its true face in the state of exception. Linking conservative, security-conscious fears of foreign terrorism to liberal fears of governmental repression, the film updates the phantasm of state paranoia. It revolves around a center of fear containing nothing other than the manifestation of the repressed, an emergence of the secret side of the political. If the terrorists are nothing but former allies gone rogue, the "measures" taken by the military—in the exact judicial sense of the word—are the return of the political repressed: the extralegal sphere of the *arcana imperii*. The latency of the political, which (in the word's double meaning) "contains" the phantasm, is a war that has been geographically and politically marginalized—it has been pushed to the outer boundaries of the "West" ("Israel") and down into the shadowy world of uncontrollable terror, shameful alliances, dirty interventions, secret torture, and violated civil rights.

Granted, in 1998 all this amounted to little more than an average thriller that wasn't a big success (and that caused controversy due to its perceived anti-Muslim discrimination; see Zwick 2001). But what happens to the phantasm in the moment of its irruption into reality? What does it mean to catch sight of the fantasies of Islamic terror networks and a brutal state machinery in the glaring flash of 9/11? If 9/11 is less an irruption of the real than an irruption of a phantasm into our "social reality," a realization of political fictions, then the question arises to what extent the phantasm is subject to a new psychic economy. Instead of structuring a subtle economy of repression and displacement, the phantasm of 9/11 presents itself *as reality itself*. Following Lacan, Žižek calls it "traversing the phantasy":

> In our daily existence, we are immersed in "reality" (structured and supported by the fantasy), and this immersion is disturbed by symptoms which bear witness to the fact that another, repressed, level of our psyche resists this immersion. To "traverse the phantasy" therefore, paradoxically, means *fully identifying oneself with the fantasy*—namely with the phantasy which structures the excess that resists our immersion in daily reality. (Žižek 2002, 17)

If this is correct, then 9/11—the event itself, not the fictions and image that "presage" it—fundamentally changes the relationship between politics (with its repressed *arcana* underside), phantasm, and fiction. Politics now involves "traversing the phantasy," acting it out, and on all levels *identifying* with it. With this in mind *The Siege* is a film "about" 9/11. It showcases the Islamic terror networks that above and beyond all religious and cultural rhetoric have an account to settle with the United States; but it also shows the domestic consequences of this kind of terrorism, including the suspension of civil rights, with its attendant rhetoric of "legitimate" means of defense. Some of this surfaced in the aftermath of 9/11, such as comprehensive security checks on all Arab Americans (as took place in spring and summer of 2002), arrests that violated the legal process including the Habeas Corpus Act (Guantánamo), and the torture of prisoners (Abu Ghraib in 2004). In hindsight Bruce Willis's General Devereaux is a walking embodiment of the Patriot Act. In other words, U.S. politics has started to treat the playful and ominous fictions that before 9/11 did not rise above the level of "entertainment" as "real" imperatives of political action that need to be implemented with all necessary rigor.

But this also means that the phantasms of politics have crossed over from fictions into politics. More precisely, they have strayed into political notions of the real. In his attempt to elucidate the mechanisms underlying the self-realization of phantasms, Philipp Sarasin used "bioterror" fantasies that link the biohazard thrillers of the Clinton era (for example, Richard Preston's *Cobra* or films like *Outbreak* and *Twelve Monkeys*) to the anthrax letters of October 2001 and Iraq's alleged biological weapons program (Sarasin 2006). Much as *The Siege* anticipates the attacks carried out by so-called Islamic networks, "bioterror" is the dream dreamed by postmodern society in the throes of a self-determined state of war, and "anthrax" its wish-fulfillment (Sarasin 2006, 11). To be sure, this does not mean that there are no Islamic terrorists or anthrax spores; neither does it reduce them to the status of ideological constructions or mere Hollywood fictions. What we are dealing with is a new discourse on terror and enmity that takes recourse to notions of infections, nets, and swarms (more of which later), a discourse marked by a phantasmic drift from the *possible* or *conceivable* straight into the *factual* and hence *necessary,* thereby eroding the boundary between the virtual and the factual.

The relationship between fictions and political phantasms has changed. For most of the twentieth century, literary and cinematic explorations of wars and state secrets were attempts to illuminate the secret in the guise of fiction. Now what has opened up is a space in which the political and the fictional have become indistinguishable. This not only means that Hollywood directors and thriller writers have been called upon for political advice, imagining possible and conceivable scenarios of attack. It also means that the political—that is to say, the determination of the enemy, the decisions regarding military campaigns, and the initiatives to prevent disasters—takes place in a space marked off by fictions like *The Siege* or *Cobra,* Steven Spielberg's *War of the Worlds,* or Frank Schätzing's *The Swarm.* In the twenty-first century the space of the *arcana imperii* is no longer just illuminated by fictions. Today, fictions are responsible for creating and structuring that space in the first place—and for raising the questions that the intelligence world will have to answer.

World Trade Center Conspiracy

The fact that the images from New York repeated a phantasm that had been put on screen countless times before reveals the degree to which fictions constitute the space of the political. The attacks immediately became the focus of intensive discussion about the "reality" of the event. What is its real background, who masterminded the attack, what is the exact sequence of events, and how credible are the official accounts? 9/11 is infected with fictionality: nothing is at it seems. Nonetheless, the notion of a "World Trade Center conspiracy" differs from the fifty-year-old debate surrounding the death of John F. Kennedy at the hands of an invisible government. To be sure, in both cases we encounter self-appointed experts who subject every single aspect of the event—from the passenger list of the hijacked planes and the architecture of the WTC to the Pentagon crash site, the reaction of NORAD, and the many intelligence blunders—to meticulous scrutiny to reveal the inconsistencies hidden in the official investigations. But what distinguishes 9/11 from JFK is the fact that from day one the U.S. government was locked in a struggle over the prerogative of interpretation. Just a few hours after the event officials presented perpetrators and evidence of such obvious convenience that they appeared to be blatant diversions, such as the "testament" of Mohammed Atta found in a misdirected suitcase and the almost undamaged passport of one of the hijackers in the debris only a few blocks from the World Trade Center.[1] Nine days after the attacks President Bush declared: "On September 11, enemies of freedom committed an act of war against our country" (Bush 2001a). Speaking to the General Assembly of the United Nations one month later, Bush further corroborated the claim to interpret what had happened by determining, once and for all, both the identity of the perpetrators as well as the political significance of the attacks: "We must speak the truth about terror. Let us never tolerate outrageous conspiracy theories concerning the attacks of September 11th, malicious lies that attempt to shift the blame away from the terrorists themselves, away from the guilty" (Bush 2001b). But the events of 9/11 are far from obvious; they cry out for examination and interpretation. Not surprisingly, even after the publication of the 9/11 Commission Report in 2004, the meaning and significance of the attacks remained hotly contested for years.

No sooner had the U.S. government presented its evidence, named perpetrators, and identified Osama bin Laden as the powerful exotic mastermind than journalists, political groups, and private individuals began to question the official version. One of the very first was the German journalist Mathias Bröckers, who happened to be working on the translation of Robert A. Wilson's *Everything Is Under Control: Conspiracies, Cults and Cover-Ups* (R. A. Wilson 1998). Presenting himself as a "conspiracy theorist" (and thus ironically anticipating inevitable objections), he immediately began to cast doubt on the official statements in his weblog *World Trade Center Conspiracy:*

> [Blog of September 13, 2001] How is it possible . . . the conspiracy theorist asks, to pull off the logistical masterpiece of simultaneously hijacking four airliners and approaching the targets undetected just three months after warnings of a massive attack had come in from Egypt? The abducted passengers were able to phone friends and relatives—while air traffic controllers and military personnel, whose global snooping systems are normally able to pick up every fart by an Indian rice farmer, were all left in the dark? And this even in the Pentagon itself? . . . Strangely, nobody talks about this scandal. (Bröckers 2002, 1:73)

Bröckers's conspiracy diary blog—which appeared daily from September 13, 2001, to March 22, 2002, and then continued on a weekly basis—was at the vanguard of a very heterogeneous movement that sought to either question specific details of 9/11 or prove that it was an inside job (or, at the very least, that the U.S. government had known about the impending attacks and let them happen).[2] As in the case of the Kennedy assassination, European observers were the first to contribute their share of conspiracy theories, followed by a surge of American publications a few years later (see, for example, Fetzer 2007; Zwicker 2006; Marrs 2006, 2011; Griffin 2007, 2008). In 2002 Thierry Meyssan published his "Pentagate" thesis, according to which it was a rocket or a military jet rather than a passenger plane that crashed into the Pentagon (Meyssan 2002). Bröckers's sources were the online editions of international newspapers and news agencies, information services specializing in intelligence and security issues, and websites maintained by political activists or interested private individuals. His goal was to present connections indicating an alternative history of the attacks, and he wanted his readers to follow these connections by clicking on the links provided on his blog. The official version of a centrally organized, ideologically fully committed secret terror network, Bröckers charged, was no less of a conspiracy theory, albeit one that conformed to firmly established models. In turn, he offered a "counter-conspiracy-conspiracy" that would "free conspirology from its association with messy thinking and transform it into a serious science of perception" (Bröckers 2002, 1:10). Despite its logical bootstrapping conspiracy theory turns into a heuristic method, a way of posing questions (rather than providing answers), making connections (rather than sticking to entrenched friend/enemy distinctions), and perceiving causalities (rather than coincidences). What is at stake is to question the prerogative of interpretation, offering an unofficial or independent interpretation—and, at the same time, a critique of affirmative media. Bröckers's was one of the first takes on 9/11 determined to restructure political knowledge by means of the "supermedium," the Internet, which "contains all previous media: the established major broadcasters and newspapers as well as the marginalized alternative media and specialized publications" (Bröckers 2002, 1:19).

In contrast to slow print media (with their locally confined access restrictions) and television (a medium which since its inception has been suspected of consumer manipulation), the Internet facilitates rapid and global access to all possible sources. The importance, however, resides less in speed and breadth than in the simple access. Unlike unidirectional print and broadcast media, the Internet enables readers to check references by following the links leading to the sources quoted. If you post something online, you are informing and affirming yourself online; in addition, you are reacting to a medium that contains all other media (print, television, film, images, and so on). Writing in the Internet is always already a dialogical "writing-back." This, however, creates a fundamentally different form of political knowledge and discourse: dialogical and plural, self-organizing and decentralized. Post–9/11 conspiracy theories highlight these qualities by exploring the possibilities of critical discourse and alternative epistemological structures within a medium that is no longer hierarchical, monological, or based on clearly defined criteria of truth. Ultimately, this is why 9/11 fundamentally differs from the JFK assassination (see also Knight 2008).

Bröckers was not only among the first to connect the new online forms of knowledge circulation with a new type of political event; he was also one of the first to reflect on this connection. The suspicious or embarrassing connections highlighted in his blog (such as those between the Bush and Bin Laden families) aim to reveal a corrupt global power elite behind 9/11 and other events. But unlike the official accounts and those furnished by investigative journalism, both of which explicitly claim to present the ultimate truth, Bröckers eludes such claims by insisting on the fundamentally fictitious character of all political information:

> It's all nothing but "inventions." Don't believe anything I say, even though I claim to have researched matters to the best of my ability. And should this or that passage really add up to something and convince you that "this is true" . . . then activate your inner observer and refer to conspiracist question #1: "And what's behind it?" (Bröckers 2002, 1:16)

It was only with a certain delay (and lacking Bröckers's self-irony) that the questioning of the official version also gained ascendance in the United States, first on websites and in various publications, and more recently in a number of documentaries. The most important platform is the 9/11 Truth Movement, which combines countless questions and hypotheses, from alternative forensic reconstructions of the event and the examination of neglected aspects (such as the environmental impact for Lower Manhattan or the recycling of the debris) all the way to extremely detailed reconstructions of what occurred before and after 9/11. The most comprehensive accessible collection of data is the Complete 9/11 Timeline, managed as an open-content database by a Californian calling himself Paul Thompson. The Timeline offers brief summaries of media reports (complete with sources) and draws connections to related topics grouped under headings such as "Before 9/11," "Warning Signs: Specific Cases," "The Alleged 9/11 Hijackers," "Day of 9/11," and "The Post–9/11 World." Unlike Bröckers, the partisan 9/11 documentaries, or the various angry "debunking" books from Meyssan to Marrs, the Timeline adopts a neutral demeanor devoid of speculation and personal comments. It not only allows us to break down events into countless parallel fragments but also, above all, gestures at the interconnectedness of this one event with others: The Complete 9/11 Timeline (which according to its own premise can never be "complete") is not only counterhistoriography; it is also historiography under the conditions of Web 2.0—a history that for the sake of comprehensibility still contains some traces of linear chronology but is in fact net-shaped, synchronous, and hypercomplex.

The year 2006 saw the premiere of two documentary films about 9/11. One, *9/11: Press for Truth,* draws on material from the Complete 9/11

Timeline to highlight the unresolved inconsistencies of the attack and accuse the United States of exploiting the disaster for political purposes (Nowosielsky and Duffy 2006). An even more controversial feature is Dylan Avery's *Loose Change,* which in the summer of 2006 was the most frequently downloaded video from Google Video, even though it contains no new footage or new hypotheses (it is a mash-up of material from CNN, NBC, Fox News, and other sources equipped with commentary and sound track) and restricts itself to once again voicing doubts about the official account—doubts that for the most part have long since been rebutted. Among these are the suspicion that the hole in the Pentagon is much too small to have been caused by a Boeing 757; that the FBI incorrectly identified the hijackers (because some of them were seen alive following 9/11); that the Twin Towers and the building WT7 were blown up by explosives from within (the so-called controlled demolition thesis); or that the inability of NORAD to organize efficient countermeasures indicates a willingness on the part of the authorities to let the attack happen. *Loose Change* especially highlights the first three suspicions and adds that WT7 housed large amounts of gold reserves that subsequently disappeared. In its initial version, the film further speculates that United Airlines flight 93 did not crash in Pennsylvania (the aircraft wreckage, so the argument goes, was too small) and that the passengers were evacuated to an abandoned NASA research site. Compared to many other WTC conspiracy theories, *Loose Change* adopts an extreme, if not ludicrous, position by claiming that the attacks were an inside job, a theory known as MIHOP (make it happen on purpose). The film has since been changed various times; certain claims have been attenuated or dropped, others added. As of 2007, a "final cut" is available online. Other positions, including those adopted by Bröckers, Timeline, or the 9/11 Truth Movement, focus on unsolved details, demand new investigations, and criticize the political exploitation of the events by the U.S. government. They represent the moderate conspiracist perspective that the government did little to stop the attacks—the position known as LIHOP (let it happen on purpose).

Despite the many patently absurd claims, conspiracy theories in the age of the Internet have little in common with the "paranoid style" that Richard Hofstadter attributed to the Kennedy era. It is no longer a matter of a "vast and sinister conspiracy, a gigantic and yet subtle machinery of influence set in motion to undermine and destroy a way of life" (Hofstadter 1965, 29). Neither is it a matter of media manipulating their users (contrary to the opinion of Zwicker 2006). Rather, what has emerged is the use of a new metamedium as a tool for counterinformation and counterhistoriography that eludes the monological structure and monolithic truth claims of the old media. Neither Bröckers nor Thompson is interested in following in the heroic footsteps of investigative journalism to reveal the truth and nothing but. They merely want to raise questions and shed light on hidden interests and obscured or embarrassing connections—like the far-ranging business connections of the Carlyle Group, which appears to have profited from virtually every political decision since 9/11. By detailing decades of Middle Eastern intelligence history up to 9/11 as well as providing a wealth of information on terrorists, important political decisions, arrests, and business deals, the Complete 9/11 Timeline arrives at an image of the political in which "everything is connected" (Pynchon 1995, 703 and passim). Pynchon's famous mantra, however, no longer implies that there is an invisible all-manipulating hand at work or that every seeming coincidence is grounded in a hidden causality, but that we are dealing with an almost inextricable mesh of connections of powerful and influential (though by no means omnipotent) interests and unseemly alliances. Such a view serves to retire the insufficiently complex traditional friend/enemy rhetoric, but it does not provide any clear answers in return. Instead, it evokes the image of a decentralized, plural intelligence very different from the *central* or centralized type of intelligence which the CIA programmatically enshrined in its name. These reflexive forms of conspiracism are aware of their uncertainty, opacity, and hypercomplexity. They affirm a bewildering interconnectedness of political, economic, social, and media conditions and attempt to shed light on the event by reproducing this complexity. They insist that everything is connected to everything and that we are always already part of this web—as members of social groups, data networks, markets, and financial transactions. Their goal is not to transform their questions into certainties but to bring awareness to our connectedness and the impalpability of political "truths."

2 The Future of Enmity: Nets, Swarms, Viruses

The enemy is the figure of our own question.

—Carl Schmitt, *Theory of the Partisan* (2007; translation emended)

It takes networks to fight networks.

—John Arquilla and David Ronfeldt, "Networks, Netwars, and the Fight of the Future" (2001)

Networks

If the event called "9/11" and the structure of the political that gave rise to it are marked by a doubling of facticity and virtuality that can only be grasped as a phantasm or fiction, then one might wonder what exactly constitutes the "content" of this phantasm. How is the friend/enemy relationship structured? Once again, the blinding light of the event reveals how far removed it is from the Cold War. Faceless yet located, abstract but predictable, the Cold War enemy was a black box whose moves and reactions could be anticipated by mirror-imaging one's own rationality (see part 6, chapter 2, "War Games"). The new enemy, however, appears to lack any common rationality. The first televised images of Osama bin Laden presented the new adversary as an exotic, though still recognizable face. "Lily-white are the garments of the tall, self-absorbed savior of the mountain caves, soft and graceful the gestures of his beautiful hands, sensuous the lips from which hatred pours. His flowing beard recalls the old prophets, his voice is soft and melancholy, and the fragility of his body endows him with a peculiar dignity" (Widmann 2001, 160). The venerable props of the Great Game are on display: we are faced with the nomad, the religious fanatic displaying all the charismatic ascetism of the Muslim propagated by T. E. Lawrence (see part 3, "The Great Game"). But the exotic enemy that initially embodies the "clash of cultures" soon vanishes from political and military analyses. A new form of enmity emerges to erase the enemy faces and grimaces drawn in the sands of the twentieth century. The enemy no longer has a face, not because he has become "faceless" but because he has assumed a shape that no longer has a head.

The central metaphor was around long before 9/11, but in the wake of the attacks it started to crop up in handbooks of the RAND Corporation, position papers of the Naval Institute, and defense-oriented research articles by sociologists and media experts: "shadowy networks" are the enemy of the future.[3] The National Security Strategy issued in 2002 outlines this new form of enmity:

> Enemies in the past needed great armies and great industrial capabilities to endanger America. Now, shadowy networks of individuals can bring great chaos and suffering to our shores for less than it costs to purchase a single tank. Terrorists are organized to penetrate open societies and to turn the power of modern technologies against us. (National Security Strategy of the United States of America, 2002)

The brief quotation succinctly contains all the main characteristics of the new enemy: the networks are clandestine and criminal; they operate in the obscure regions of the "open societies" they attack; and they are "networks of individuals," dispersed structures oriented less toward nations and central high-profile symbolic figures than individuals. Little more than criminal organizations, these networks have nothing in common with the centrally controlled cohorts of "Reds under the beds" conjured up by J. Edgar Hoover. They are, seemingly, unpolitical, but precisely this depoliticization implies a completely new way of thinking about the enemy: it demands first and foremost an analysis of the enemy's *organizational structure*.

In the 1990s networks became a hotly debated topic in social and media theory, but it was 9/11 that moved the metaphor into the vacuum left by the Cold War. However, it is not a matter of simply replacing old Cold War enemies with tech-savvy bearded jihadists; the proliferation of the network metaphor (and its metamorphosis into *swarms* and *infections*) indicates a profound change in the way the enemy is researched and categorized. Is it nothing less than a fundamental transformation of the knowledge of an enemy who is now conceived of in terms of his organizational and communication structure? If Cold War practices of guessing at the enemy's plans and capabilities involved a focus on the upper echelons of his military and intelligence command apparatus, it is now a matter of getting inside unstable structures that lack centralized leadership and clear chains of command. If the enemy is a network, intelligence turns into organizational analysis. What enables the network to operate? What are its internal dynamics? What holds it together? How does it communicate?

Animal Models: Spielberg's *War of the Worlds*

Swarms and networks are—according to RAND Corporation analysts John Arquilla and David Ronfeldt—the "future of conflict" (Arquilla and Ronfeldt 2000). Strikingly, the "net" and "swarm" models refer to animal rather than human forms of guidance and communication. If talking about "nets" still implies a cultural achievement, terms like "swarming" point toward natural forms of collective organization that delegate guidance and coordination processes to life itself. What is a swarm? Why do swarms and packs; the colonies of bees, ants, and termites; and last but not least viruses, bacteria, and antibodies turn into models for future forms of coordination, cooperation, and conflict? And what kind of "future" does this imply?

Demonic wolves, hordes of rats and insects, mass infections—all these belong to the long and dubious tradition of depicting the enemy as an animal onto whom we project fear and disgust. Now, however, we are dealing with a metaphoric transfer that projects imaginary animal qualities onto humans. Philipp Sarasin has analyzed how this worked in the case of 9/11: starting on the day of the attacks and continuing into the planning of the Iraq War, talk about terrorist infiltration resorted to metaphors of infection, which then were "incarnated" in the discourse of bioterror—from the anthrax letters in October 2001 to the justification of the invasion of Iraq as a preliminary strike against Saddam Hussein's bioweapons. The metaphor or phantasm of the unchecked spread of a virus implies a form of intense biopolitical defense: a defense against foreigners, against circulation, against communication, against any kind of intermixture. Politics becomes a form of containing epidemics; it involves a gesture of immunization against something so foreign that it categorically precludes any form of coexistence, communication, or exchange (Sarasin 2006).

Spielberg's *War of the Worlds* (2005), based on H. G. Wells's 1895 novel, stages this fantasy on multiple levels. The blockbuster features Martian invaders who venture from their increasingly uninhabitable home planet toward Earth in search of new living space, wreaking havoc among the humans whom they start exterminating with the help of giant killing machines. While the alien-as-enemy figure evokes a more than classical political image, there is a disconcerting detail about the killing machines used by the aliens: they were not brought from the outside but were already lying in wait underneath our streets. In a way, the enemies are "sleepers"; they use (or they *are*) what has always been lurking beneath and among us. In one of the many chase sequences there is a short exchange in which a father (Tom Cruise), responding to his child's question, denies that these enemies are "terrorists." What they are fleeing from, however, clearly corresponds to the fantasy of terrorists living in our midst. Just like the terrorists who turned planes into weapons, the aliens are strange composites of technology (titanic killing machines) and exotic organic life-forms (pathetic extraterrestrial bodies eventually defeated by a common cold). Like so many other monsters originating in outer space, they are indebted to concepts of classical modernism: gigantic hybrids of life and technology engaged in the "struggle for survival" that informs Wells's original tale. If this were all, it could easily be a movie from the 1940s. But by zooming in on a drop of water during the opening and closing credits Spielberg adds a new, biological dimension: the camera turns into a microscope and travels from the level of DNA and the world of microorganisms upward into the domain of macroorganisms. The struggle against the aliens, the film points out, is decided on the microbiological level. What is post–9/11 about this scenario? The simultaneous attack from the inside and the outside, in combination with the reference to microbes, implicitly stages politics as a form of pest control. Spielberg's film is a first attempt to explore the real terrain of the "enmity of the future." This terrain is nothing less than "life itself": the organic domain, the organizational forms and "technologies" of animal biosystems rather than human society and its classic wars. With *War of the Worlds* the thinking of enmity moves into the realm of biology: the problem now is how to define the enemy, within the domain of the living, as a "form of life" (that is, as a structure, a form of organization and communication) opposed to our form of life. There is more at stake in this transformation than going beyond established enemy stereotypes, crisis scenarios, or standard notions of political control; we are faced with a fundamental alteration of the political that nonetheless still refers to the structuring principles of hierarchy and control, inclusion and exclusion, containment and delineation.

The notion of swarming exhibits this transformation with particular clarity. If the phantasm of organic infection acts as an appeal to immunization and systemic closure, swarming turns the animal into an epistemological paradigm. It becomes a model of a knowledge that transcends the animal but that nonetheless can only be deciphered with its help. It is a model of life as a network of mutually interdependent organisms. Colonies or swarms of insects are the paradigmatic example of social organization in nature. But what is the particular fascination of swarms as an epistemological and political model? Ever since antiquity bees have been seen as the emblematic, quintessential animal collective. For a long time it was assumed that the queen was in charge of reproduction as well as of governance and control; she decided where the swarm settles and how it organizes itself. It was only in the twentieth century that insects were discovered to be a *leaderless* aggregation of individual creatures following a "swarm instinct." A hundred years ago William Morton Wheeler described the swarm (referred to as the "state" of the ants) as a "superorganism," that is, as a unit made up of a multitude of coordinated, yet nonetheless uncontrolled individual elements—an intelligent and complex unity composed of relatively "stupid" individual beings (Wheeler 1928). More recent research has focused on the communication of social insects that allows for the emergence of complex behavior. This communication arises from the movement of individual animals rather than from the exchange of signs.[4] In similar ways, flocks of birds and schools of fish coordinate their behavior based on a small number of behavioral rules (for example, stay close to your neighbor, avoid collisions, adapt to speed). The coordination of individual members is based on the combination of interaction, communication, and environmental adaptation. The simple set of rudimentary behavioral rules enables a complex overall behavior. It is a structure that can only be understood as a system of *relations,* not as a top-down coordination. In other words, self-organization is the emergence of an overall pattern from a multiplicity of local interactions; it can be explained neither by analyzing the pattern nor by focusing on the individual actors, but only by looking at the relations themselves. Swarms point toward the complex entanglement of everything with everything without referring it back to any one single source.

Paradoxically, swarms and networks are both the Holy Grail and the nightmare of control. In contrast to traditional hierarchical, linear "clockwork" solutions (technology), they are better able to adapt to environmental change and compensate for the failure of individual units. On the other hand they are fairly clumsy: their redundancy (many unsupervised individual bodies performing the same task) reduces their efficiency (ants foraging for food tend to run off in all directions). But above all they cannot be controlled; you cannot simply redirect or "turn off" swarms, and their inner dynamics are extremely difficult to predict (see K. Kelly 1994, 21–25). Exploiting their internal logic is the only way to fight or at least influence them. Grasping the structure of swarms demands that we go beyond the traditional understanding of "control" or "development" as linear processes. But if swarms and networks are models for a decentralized social structure, then this transformation of thought implies a far-reaching transformation of the political. As Eugene Thacker notes in his overview of network theories and their political implications:

> A political ontology of networks, swarms and multitudes will necessitate a reconsideration of many terms that are central to political thought—power, right, and democracy. These terms are in turn related to philosophical issues—individuation, multiplicity, and materiality. This might be as simple as thinking about instances of distributed dissent (politics) in terms of the concepts of living systems (biology), or it might be finding ways to set political concepts (such as "the people") into a dialogue with techno-scientific concepts (such as "the pack" or "the network"). (Thacker 2004)

Precisely because the field of the political—that is, the organization of consensus and dissent, the question of representation and its denial, and last but not least the modeling of enmity—has to be conceptualized in new and different ways, the theory of networks and swarms is in the final analysis a matter of *intelligence*. As a form of knowledge of the enemy that is involved in warfare itself, as a part of the *arcana imperii* devoted to control, defense, and guidance, and finally as an institution that is both researching and itself structured by networks, *intelligence always already implies an epistemology of the network*. This network and its epistemology, however, have come to undermine classical concepts of the political. If the very same think tanks that during the Cold War explored possible scenarios for the U.S. intelligence apparatus are now investigating nets and swarms, if former Middle Eastern CIA agents now author lengthy sociological treatises on "terror networks" (for example, Sageman 2004), the theory of networks and the reflection of their political consequences may represent the most fundamental post–9/11 transformation of intelligence. As event *and* phantasm 9/11 requires an understanding of interconnectedness, of a global wiring on all levels of our existence—the politics of ecology, economy, or communication. Above all, it calls for an understanding of the fact that we are always already connected with what we describe as our "enemy." The enemy becomes a network by being part of our network.

The Ultimate Enemy: Frank Schätzing's *Swarm*

Significantly, those popular fictions that leave the old Cold War paradigm behind and instead shed light on this new "global" perspective no longer belong to the spy genre. There are exceptions such as *Syriana* (Gaghan 2005), a brilliant thriller that offers a complex snapshot of the global entanglement of (geo)politics, economic interests, and the anger of those on the losing side of globalization. But to find more informed perspectives we have to turn to seemingly less political genres, namely "ecological" fictions. They are able to present interconnectedness and its consequences, that is, the emergence of unpredictable phenomena. For instance, weather: Roland Emmerich's *The Day After Tomorrow* (2004) depicts a cataclysmic climate change resulting in tsunamis and a sudden global cooling that buries New York under meters of ice. In contrast to Spielberg's apocalypse this scenario features neither an "enemy" nor any clearly identifiable perpetrators, though it does hint that the "cause" is an interruption of the Gulf Stream brought about by global warming. One of the most explicit and detailed unfoldings of a vision of global connectedness, however, is Frank Schätzing's blockbuster novel *The Swarm* (2006). Beneath its highly conventional, run-of-the-mill narrative is one of the most meticulously researched fictions to address the area of interdisciplinary scientific exploration that over the last thirty years has devoted itself to phenomena such as *emergence, self-organization,* and *swarm intelligence.*

The book depicts a global catastrophe emerging from the sea. Out of the blue, fish and whales start attacking ships and humans, a sudden change of behavior accompanied by the equally sudden appearance of strange mutations: deep-sea worms with enormous jaws that threaten to destabilize the methane hydrate on the continental slopes, lobsters containing toxic microalgae, tsunamis caused by methane deflagrations. Following standard procedure a team of scientists and intelligence officers first suspects that everything is caused by Arab terrorists intent on manipulating the crude oil market, yet eventually they realize that they are dealing with animals rather than insurgents: all kinds of animals, that is, big and small, from blue whales capable of capsizing ships to methane-consuming bacteria that can dislocate entire continental slopes to rid themselves of humans. In this threatening scenario environmental activists and marine biologists no longer stand out because they embody humanity's ecological consciousness; they are simply the better experts because they understand the concept of biological emergence. What they discover is a highly evolved marine intelligence composed of a giant mass of amoebas, a swarm the clueless experts call the *yrr* (resonating the German word for animal, *Tier,* as well as the word *irr,* which denotes crazy, unpredictable behavior). This intelligence is able to wage war as an ecological catastrophe—a type of warfare that exceeds the accustomed dimensions of biowarfare by virtue of its ability to directly interfere in ecological processes. The hostile bio-intelligence is making use of the most advanced form of biotechnology: it "produces" its own weapons in the shape of living beings, but in stark contrast to humans it is "aware" of the ecological impact of these mutations (for example, the planned erosion of the continental slope brought about by mutated bacteria that results in the flooding of northern Europe). Unlike humans, who depend on techno-human hybrids for their martial exploits (and who remain ignorant of the impact of biological weapons), organic intelligence works with what it knows best—itself: that is, organic life. The removal of humans polluting and overfishing the seas is nothing but an ecological measure, a minor rectification of one particular part of the network that threatens to destroy the entire system.

As ludicrous as it may sound (a German newspaper scathingly headlined its review "The Revenge of the Killer Slime"), the research behind the story is impeccable. Schätzing's intelligent swarm takes its cue from a new field of research into organizational and communication structures, swarm intelligence (see the seminal work of Bonabeau, Dorigo, and Théraulaz 1999; Bonabeau and Théraulaz 2000). Swarm intelligence took its start from the observation of self-organized behavior in animal collectives and transferred the "solutions" thus found to technological or computational problems. The key question posed in swarm intelligence research is how highly complex and dynamic behavioral patterns can emerge from relatively simple individual agents and algorithms. Swarm intelligence systems typically consist of a population of simple agents (animals, or—by transferring the animal model to a computer—computer agents) interacting with one another and with their environment. Biology here serves not only as a model for technological solutions but also as a criticism of centralized models of control and organization (Horn and Gisi 2009). But Schätzing's swarm is not just an epitome of applied swarm intelligence; it has the special ability to split up, recombine itself, and assume all kinds of shapes. This capability of the *yrr* refers to pioneering research into self-organization carried out by Evelyn Fox Keller and Lee A. Segel in the early 1970s. Their principal object of investigation was the slime mold *Dictyostelium discoideum* (figure 38), which in the course of its life cycle transforms from an amoeba into a multicellular organism and finally enters a stage of reproduction by forming a fruiting body (Fox Keller and Segel 1970). More recent research has revealed that these amoebas are "intelligent" enough to find the shortest route through a maze in search of food (see Nakagaki, Yamada, and Tóth 2000). Schätzing's novel adds a further stage by imagining how the aggregation of the simplest organisms may result in the emergence of an intelligence capable of solving complex problems. The *yrr* form an amorphous mass that constantly assumes new shapes; that, like slime molds, "communicates" by way of cAMP (cyclic adenosine monophosphate) waves; and that—like bee swarms, which "have" a longer memory than any individual bee (see K. Kelly 1994, 12)—is able to think and remember. Highly complex cognitive abilities in combination with a virtually infinite memory arise from the equally infinite aggregation of single organisms. In other words, the intelligence of the *yrr* is a classic case of emergence, the appearance of a complex structure from the mere quantity of relatively primitive single elements. The qualities of such a structure cannot be deduced by observing any individual organism because it is more than the sum of its parts and only arises by being combined into a system (see S. Johnson 2001). The *yrr* are the fictional perfection of swarm intelligence and smart network solutions: they are a system and think as a system, and this is the basis of their profound difference from—and superiority over—humans.

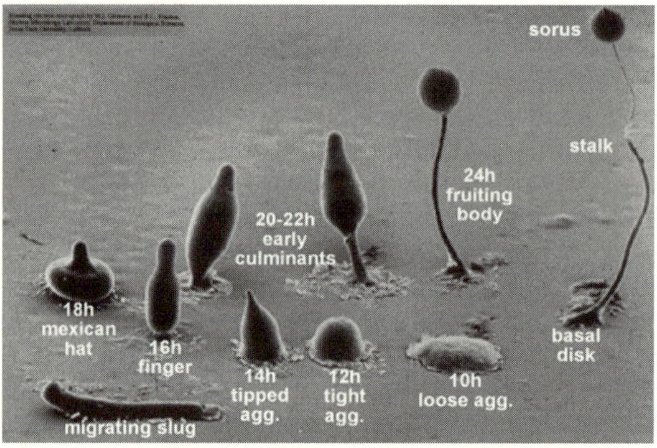

Figure 38. The transformation cycle of the slime mold *Dictyostelium discoideum* from the unicellular to the slug phase and on to the fruiting body—the basis for Schätzing's swarm. Copyright © M. J. Grimson and R. L. Blanton, Biological Sciences Electron Microscopy Laboratory, Texas Tech University.

Schätzing, then, creates a different type of enemy and a different form of *intelligence*. To recognize the enemy and understand how he operates not only requires that you grasp his structure; you also have to think using the enemy's own logic. The *yrr* embody the (nonhuman) net humans are always already entangled in, which is why this particular form of enmity cannot be directed toward the annihilation of the enemy (which is the solution proposed by the novel's all too traditional intelligence experts). The *yrr* cannot be targeted for destruction because this would entail the destruction of every living being, including humanity. The *yrr are* life itself, they *are* the ocean, they *are* the lifeworld and environment of their human antagonists. In short, they are the impossible—that is to say, the *ultimate*—enemy of mankind. To understand the *yrr* means to understand oneself as part of a system composed of the most heterogeneous elements imaginable: humans and *yrr*.

Schätzing's novel is science fiction, but in a sense that goes beyond all merely literary classifications: ultimately, it is a thought experiment that examines and reflects a scientific problem in the mode of fiction (see Macho and Wunschel 2004). *The Swarm* explores the consequences of an epistemological transformation whose far-reaching consequences may be beyond our grasp. Swarm intelligence is a type of knowledge that transforms the very structures of knowledge and thus changes *the way we know.* By introducing this new type of knowledge into a scenario of enmity, which serves to define the *yrr* as something that is both radically different and superior to man, the novel demonstrates the dramatic necessity to think in and about swarms—to think "life itself"—and to see oneself as part of a system that comprises both friends and enemies. The swarm is the uncanny and horrifying embodiment of "life itself" (Horn 2009b). The swarm is both a single and multiple animal lacking any technological construction or anthropomorphous intelligence (unlike the many generic aliens), an incorporation of "multitude" (Hardt and Negri 2004). With lots of pathos, the novel's epilogue expresses the necessity for humanity to behave in conformity with the system. But the global form and shapelessness of the swarm also points toward the ambivalent nature of a new form of enmity. In the swarm model, we are dealing with an enemy that—as an animal—represents a very different form of life devoid of intentions, hierarchies, political organizations, or subjectivity; yet it is also an enemy that—as an animal—shares the human lifeworld and is (in systems-theoretical terms) as much part of the human environment as humans are part of the animals' environment. Swarm theory has a special (though not exclusive) preference for animal models (ants, bees, or the notorious slime mold) because they enable a suspension of "human" categories like intentionality, self-guidance, control, and hierarchy of command. Animal swarms are collectives that function very differently from human collectives, which is precisely why they are so useful when it comes to modeling complex human phenomena like economic markets, communication networks, transportation flows, or social change.

But what does it mean to think of the enmities of the future in terms of swarms and networks? If the latter represent the other of contemporary political structures, they challenge the political to transform itself. Arquilla and Ronfeldt conclude that "it takes networks to fight networks" (Arquilla and Ronfeldt 2001). But again, what does this mean? If the enemy has no clearly discernible identity, if he, she, or they are no longer an identifiable group but a swarm or network, then the very concept of enmity is put into question. If, to return to Carl Schmitt's famous dictum, "the enemy is the figure of our question," we have to ask ourselves what figure underlies all the talk about "terror networks" and imaginary swarms. Swarms and networks are not only the other of our social, political, and media lifeworld (insofar as it involves identities, intentions, subjectivities, boundaries, hierarchies, and so on); they also represent that which fundamentally shapes them: communication, self-organization. Terror networks are held together—and this is their perplexing irony—by the very ties we value most: trust, dependability, and belief in a common cause (see Sageman 2004). Whether we talk about markets, logistics, data transfers, energy supplies, or even our health, global interconnectedness is a source of support as it is one of concern. Phantasms of infection, for instance, now pervade our linked data systems; they shape logistics, travel experiences, and maybe our future social conduct. Interconnectedness means that the failure of one part of the system can be absorbed by other parts, yet it may also facilitate the global escalation of a local problem.[5] If everything is connected with everything else, a minor disturbance can result in a cascading failure, a catastrophic chain reaction: that is the disastrous appearance of emergence. Networks are enemies as much as they are the form of our own social life; swarms embody both our worst fears and our brightest dreams (Horn 2009b). What fascinates us about networks is the end of outdated notions of power and control—but also the fear of losing control over the systems in which we exist. If intelligence is knowledge of the enemy that always already presupposes a knowledge of our strengths and weaknesses, then above all we have to remain aware of the inescapable interrelatedness of friend and enemy. We must recognize *our* question when we profess to recognize the shape of the enemy.

Conclusion

Our Man in Havana, arguably Graham Greene's best and certainly his most entertaining novel, tells the story of James Wormold, a vacuum cleaner salesman who, to supplement his meager income, agrees to become an MI6 agent. Lacking both sources and agents, he decides to invent them. He presents MI6 with a roster of imaginary agents in need of financial support and hands over intriguing plans for secret weapons that are, in fact, sketches of vacuum cleaners. Just as the intelligence world stands in for a world of literary imagination, Wormold, the presumptive spy and creator of make-believe reports and fake sources, is a figuration of Graham Greene, his own creator. His agents are characters in a novel who for reasons of plausibility and literary economy must on occasion be withdrawn from circulation. "Just as in real life," Wormold muses, "accidents could happen; a character might take control" (Greene 1971, 106). But while Wormold is pondering the literary fate that may befall his heroes, his creations take on a life of their own: London sends him a secretary and an assistant—and attempts are made to poison him. This sudden, crucial flip from make-believe into reality marks the relationship between intelligence work and fiction. The world of secret services—a world of fabrications, lies, and speculations—suddenly irrupts into real life: fictions unleash their violence with the result that both fictitious agents and real people end up dead. No matter how far they may stray from reality, fictions bring about their own realization; in the shadowy domain of intelligence work, fabrications and hypotheses give rise to surreal but no less brutal events.

This recursion of fiction into reality and reality into fiction highlights the epistemological structure of the secret. The secret produces reality as a fiction, yet it also requires fiction to track down reality. For it is fiction rather than investigative journalism and historical research that discloses the operative structure of the secret, and it does so precisely because it does not claim to uncover any "ultimate truth." Fictions explore how the secret operates: from agents' clandestine tactics and ethics to the inevitable dialectic of blindness and insight that marks the production of intelligence, and eventually to the figurations and disfigurations of the enemy. Last but not least, fictions often are the only way the practices and failures of intelligence agencies may be elucidated without violating the secrecy clause employees have to sign before they enter the service. The most revealing and incisive insights into the shady world of intelligence have been presented as "fiction" from the hands of insiders such as Graham Greene and John le Carré, or more recently Richard A. Clarke or Robert Baer. Clarke wrote *The Scorpion's Gate,* a novel broadly drawing on his experiences as member of the United States National Security Council and counterterrorism expert (Clarke 2005), while Robert Baer's memoir *See No Evil: The True Story of a Ground Soldier in the CIA's War on Terrorism* (the basis for the movie *Syriana*) (Gaghan 2005) draws extensively on novelistic narrative techniques (Baer 2002). Fictional and nonfictional forms of writing increasingly tend to merge when it comes to political "revelations" in the realm of intelligence.

Exempt from secrecy clauses or libel suits, fictions are able to shed light on the basic paradox of the political secret in the modern age: the conflict between the political idea of transparency and democratic control on the one hand and the necessary, or at least inevitable, use of covert actions and secret intelligence on the other. It is in modern democracies, more than in any other political system, that the *arcana imperii* come to embody the inherent self-contradiction of politics by opening up a shadowy, uncontrollable domain of illegality marked by lies, deception, cover-ups, theft, disinformation, blackmail, and, in the worst case, murder. It is a gray zone of secret plans and hidden operations that, as the assassination of John F. Kennedy appears to imply, will ultimately even turn on the government itself—a zone that blurs the boundaries between state apparatus and war machine. Only democracies manifest this paradox in all its fearful clarity, as may be glimpsed from the dramas and tragedies of the secret war all the way from the Great Game to the Cold War and the newest scenarios of corruption and networked terrorism. Because this paradox of secrecy is central to our investigation, this book is not about the Stasi and the HVA (the foreign intelligence service of the GDR), the NKVD and the KGB, or the National Socialist Gestapo and the Abwehr. Neither is it a comprehensive history of political secrecy and its associated institutions. Instead it focuses only on those political and historical moments where the use of secrecy resulted in a dramatic, even tragic contradiction within democratic political culture.

In light of constantly changing political scenarios, with their many different political institutions, configurations of knowledge, and historical fears and phantasms (such as the anxieties arising from the comedy of the sexes in the First World War or the urge to hunt down moles and traitors in the Cold War), it should be clear that there is no continuity, no set of unchanging rules or "tricks" underlying the political secret. To speak of spying as the "world's second oldest profession" (a catchphrase that crops up in virtually all histories of espionage) appears to imply an anthropological constant that comes into play whenever war and politics take on a secret dimension. I hope I have shown that this is not the case. The secret war cannot be reduced to one unchanging "human factor." We have to take into account the historically variable forms of knowledge that are at stake in matters of treason and secrecy. If the First World War still believed, as it were, in the sexual transmission of governmental and military secrets, the Cold War produced a wide array of highly specialized research projects that were off-limits even to the scientists involved. To understand the secret war without the usual lapse into paranoid depiction of the alleged omnipotence of secret services (and without the customary ridiculing of their incompetence) requires that we attempt to understand the operative and epistemological structure of state secrecy. It also requires that we understand the structure of enmity shaping a historic conflict. Accustomed, as we were, to a rational enemy in the shape of another prodigiously armed state, the end of the Cold War abandoned us in a wasteland of bewildering connections and improbable alliances: among them, a "military-industrial complex" able to forge its own intelligence and start a war on the basis of the latter (as seen in the Bush administration's path to the Iraq War), the interweaving of economic and (geo) political interests in the oil market, and the new, all too inconspicuous jihadists who on 9/11 demonstrated to the West their ideological commitment and ruthlessness. Intelligence agencies are charged with knowing and understanding the enemy—but it is also the duty of informed citizens and critical readers who are not willing to succumb to knee-jerk fears and populist calls for more homeland security. Yet we must also understand the common denominator that unites friend and enemy: they may oppose each other, but their conflict shares a common logic, a blind spot in need of adjustment.

No matter how secrecy and treason may have changed throughout the many historical contexts of the last century, the figure of the agent—defector, mole, traitor, seducer, bearer of secrets, hidden agitator, sleeper, partisan—remains a fixture of modern political anthropology. It is this thoroughly solitary figure, acting under orders and yet without ties, disloyal but frequently idealistic, a survival artist left to die, sacrificed and yet deprived of all heroism, that allows us to explore the extremes of going it alone in the modern structure of loyalty. From Judas to Kim Philby and Maurice Castle, betraying one's own community is a moment of both absolute freedom and tragic entanglement. Invariably, treason only allows you to decide *against* a community, never *in favor of* a new one. The agent embodies—often in tragic ways—the very basis of life and survival in modern societies: the role-play, the crossover between mutually exclusive groups, the difficulty, if not impossibility of straightforward loyalty, and the seductive power of social paranoia. With his survival skills, his ability to recognize social subtexts before they turn dangerous, his cold gaze and solitary state, the agent is an epitome of autonomy—an autonomy, however, that is constantly thwarted. The playful, open-air metaphors from the Great Game to war gaming cast the agents as actors in a virtual ludic space: they are masked actors (like Mata Hari and Brecht's agitators), gamblers (like Fleming's Bond and, no doubt about it, Mata Hari), athletes (Baden-Powell), and, like Greene's and le Carré's pathetic heroes, sacrificed pawns in a game that is no longer theirs.

With the passing of the twentieth century it has become increasingly anachronistic to speak of the secret war in terms of *gaming*. The intensity of new cultural and religious clashes and the cool pragmatism of current struggles over resources and economic hegemony have banished all ludic overtones from politics. But as the novels and films under discussion here have revealed time and again, a strong fictional component remains. Indeed, the fictional appears to be an indispensable ingredient of politics: it surfaces in the imaginary delineations of the enemy, the techniques of disinformation and clandestine operations, in virtual war and crises scenarios, or in the phantasms depicted in popular culture from Hollywood movies to 9/11 online conspiracy theories. The fictional is not the opposite of a truth to be extricated from lies, deceptions, or ideological constructs; it is a crucial part of that which in the space of war and politics is presented as necessary decision, immutable fact, or iron necessity. Fictions such as the Cold War conflict scenarios, assassination plots, or visions of a New York in ruins are not simply inventions but heuristic devices designed to explore what is possible, conceivable, and maybe even probable. They guide and shape what we perceive as "political reality." This does not mean that we once and for all should rid ourselves of these fictions, even if we could; it means first and foremost that we should recognize them for what they are. To achieve such an understanding, literary and cinematographic fictions are so illuminating because they show that the narratives that politics and history necessarily fall back on are only *one possible* story. By foregrounding biased versions and unsaid narrative intentions, these fictions emphasize that the claims to truth mobilized in support of political decisions are maybe just one contingent narrative that could just as well be told otherwise. Revealing the vested interests, concealed agendas, and blind spots at the base of any political discourse serves to unsettle the customary appeals to political emergencies and incontrovertible facts. Fiction teaches us to understand politics as a domain of contingent decisions and highly variable conditions. Stories open up a new space of political thought: a space of suspicion, but also of necessary information and analysis. Just as every individual story is confronted by countless alternate versions, so the political space always harbors a different truth, a different, more complex story that points toward a different solution. Such stories are at the center of this book.

NOTES

Introduction

1. For a new survey of the most important aspects see Klassen 1999.

2. According to Kautsky, these "true events" are the peaceful subjugation of Christianity to Rome in combination with the enforced dissociation from Jewish culture and tradition, on the one hand, and the concealment of the class struggle, on the other (Kautsky 1953).

3. The two words have the same root. See also Klauck 1987, 45.

4. In the words of Karl Barth, "God has acted as Judas acted" (Barth 1957, 488): that is, Judas repeats and doubles God's act of giving away his son.

5. In the Gnostic tradition Barbelo is the divine mother of all things, that is, the annunciation (*pronoia*) of the infinite father. The Gospel of Judas is part of the Codex Tchacos, which was found in the 1970s in Middle Egypt. The text is written in Coptic but appears to be a translation from the Greek. Since Irenaeus in 180 C.E. refers to the belief in Judas as a confidant of Jesus, it can be assumed that the text was written before 180 C.E. (Kasser, Meyer, and Wurst 2006).

6. This "frightful community" (Bonhoeffer 1998, 36) is emphasized in a sermon by Dietrich Bonhoeffer from March 14, 1937. Bonhoeffer's emphasis on the bond between Jesus and Judas covertly refers to that between Jews and Christians, which he evokes as the origin of Christianity—an extremely courageous gesture, given the political circumstances in 1937 Germany.

7. This is how Irenaeus summarizes the belief of the Cainites (*Adversus Haereses,* book 2, section 6), that Judas, as if to speed up the redemption of man, betrayed Jesus for the sake of man but not in accordance with the will of Jesus. The quotation in the section epigraph comes from Saint Irenaeus 1992, 102–3. The Latin original is "Et haec Judam proditorem diligenter cognovisse dicunt, et solum prae caeteris cognoscentem veritatem, perficisse proditionis mysterium: per quem et terrena et coelestia omnia dissoluta dicunt. Et confinctionem adferunt huiusmodi, Iudae Evangelium illud vocantes" (quoted from Irenaeus von Lyon 1993, 350).

Part One

1. On the publication history of *Ficciones,* see Woodall 1996, 111–34.

2. Borges's concept of fiction has been repeatedly analyzed with a pronounced emphasis on its antirealism and intertextuality. Ronald Christ describes Borgesian fiction as a narrative or explicative unfolding of a metaphor or conceit that removes the "as if" in much the same way that a metaphor eliminates the "like" (Christ 1969, 15). This reference to the displacement contained in the "as if" and "like" comes close to my emphasis on fiction as

"bifurcation," that is, as the divergence of equally possible yet contradictory versions of an event. For a general theory of fiction as a structure of "as if," see Vaihinger 1968.

3. Ana María Barrenechea's influential study *La expresión de la irrealidad en la obra de Jorge Luis Borges* (1967) started the analysis of Borges as an author who dissolves the "world" into texts and whose texts celebrate this dissolution of the real into unreality. This way of locating Borges's narratives within the tradition of fantastic literature, however, tends to ignore the complex references to history in Borges's work that cannot be reduced to a "fictitious history." For example, see Sosnowski: "The primary purpose of all his motifs is to provide joy for the 'fiction maker' and the selected group of seers who will recognize a fictitious web in the no less fictitious history recorded by man" (Sosnowski 1973, 381).

4. See Bell-Villada 1999, who in essence equates fictionality with nonreality.

5. By contrast, numerous interpreters use Borges's alleged trivializations of historical research to argue in favor of his unfettered "pure" fictionalism (for example, Franco 1981).

6. Floyd Merrell establishes a convincing connection between Borges's notion of fiction and modern scientific theories which stress that scientific data, models, and concepts are themselves nothing but heuristic fictions. When it comes to elaborating models and hypotheses, it is evident that each hypothesis also reflects the possibility of alternative hypotheses and deductions (see Merrell 1991, 166 and following).

7. Treason and betrayal are not, as Bell-Villada (1999, 79 and following) notes, simply a theme characterized by a particular "handiness" but one that sharply questions conventional understandings of Borges's allegedly worldless, unreal writings.

8. John Irwin notes the model-like character of Quain's fictions for the other *Ficciones* (Irwin 1994, 78 and following).

9. Paul, 2 Thessalonians 2:7; 1 Timothy 3:16. In his comprehensive monograph on the Protestant approach to Judas, Kurt Lüthi refers to the latter's deed as the prototype of the *mysterium iniquitatis* (Lüthi 1955, 5).

10. Borges 1998, 165. For the allusion to Robertson, see *Jesus and Judas: A Textual and Historical Investigation* (Robertson 1927). A further candidate for a radical reinterpretation of Judas would be the German poet Friedrich Gottlieb Klopstock (1724–1803), who in the fourth canto of his *Messias* goes beyond the depiction of Judas as a straightforward villain and instead psychologizes him as a tormented person challenging Jesus. Kautsky's investigation was not published until 1908, that is, four years after Runeberg's first (fictitious) book, *Kristus och Judas*.

11. Victoria Ocampo, *338171 T.E. (Lawrence d'Arabie)* (Ocampo 1947), first published in 1947 with an English translation in 1963.

12. The allusion to William Butler Yeats's "Platonic Year" quoted at the outset is part of a theme that keeps recurring in Borges: the doctrine of the eternal recurrence or cyclical time. However, Borges does not, as many interpreters would have it, subscribe to this doctrine; he tends to treat it ironically.

Concerning the Platonic year he notes in "Circular Time" ("El tiempo circular"): "If the planetary periods are cyclical, so must be the history of the universe; at the end of each Platonic year the same individuals will be born again and will live out the same destinies" (Borges 2000, 225). "The Theme of the Traitor and Hero" explicitly refers to this doctrine as an erroneous hypothesis that Ryan must discard to arrive at the truth.

13. *New York Times,* Tuesday, January 4, 1944.

14. This passage, among others, shows that the idea of the circularity of history, which large portions of Borges scholarship present as one of the key features of the master's oeuvre, is in fact presented in highly ironic fashion.

15. In his complex study *The Mystery to a Solution,* Irwin focuses on the affinity between Poe, Borges, Lacan, and Lewis Carroll, especially with regard to the question (discussed by Lacan and Derrida) whether it contains three or four positions. In the case of Borges, however, we are, it seems, dealing with a minimal structure: the shifting figure of hero/traitor and, in addition, the observer or reader (Irwin 1994), of great interest to Derrida in his critique of Lacan.

16. Following several other readers, Daniel Balderston notes that neither the Liddell Hart page reference nor the month of the British attack (June 24) provided by the narrator is correct (Balderston 1993, 41; see also Irwin 1994, 85). Balderston interprets the distortions as a reference to the nonrepresentability of the traumatic realities of trench war (Balderston 1993, 55). For a similar reading see Millington 1988, 185.

17. In fact the British offensive at the Somme began (as Liddell Hart notes) on July 1, 1916, following a shelling of the German lines that commenced on June 24. The town of Albert served as an organization center for the offensive; its fame rests on the fact that in 1915 a statue of the Virgin Mary on the top of the church had been toppled by a shell but did not fall to the ground and remained in a horizontal position (known to soldiers as the "Leaning Virgin"). The town, which had been under constant German bombardment since 1915, housed the general staff and field hospitals during the Battle of the Somme.

18. I am indebted to Wolfgang Schäffner for pointing out this implausibility.

Part Two

1. I am using the notion of the "irregular" as developed by Carl Schmitt in his *Theory of the Partisan* (Schmitt 2007), which employs the term to designate not only a type of military tactic but also an overall form of political conduct.

2. *Translator's note:* In English scholarship Jünger's text is sometimes referred to as *Treatise of the Rebel,* which may be in deference to the French and Italian translations (*Le traité du rebelle ou le recours aux forêts* and *Trattato del ribelle,* respectively). To date only a short excerpt has been translated into English. Interestingly enough, it was the first paper of a three-issue *Confluence* special (edited by Henry Kissinger) titled "The Ethics of Loyalty." See Jünger 1954.

3. Etymologically, *decidere* derives from *caedere* (to cut, separate).

4. Jünger 1960, 339. *Translator's note:* Jünger uses the word *heimlich,*

which usually translates as secretive or *covert,* but which like the more famous *unheimlich* (uncanny) contains *Heim* (home).

5. *Translator's note:* Horn is referencing a famous poem by Joseph von Eichendorff: "Schläft ein Lied in allen Dingen / die da träumen fort und fort / und die Welt hebt an zu singen / trifftst du nur das Zauberwort" ("There's a song asleep in everything / that dreams in silence and unheard / but the world will start to sing / once you find the magic word").

6. Shocked by this highly contradictory collection of names, the historian Golo Mann (son of Thomas Mann) accused Boveri of using a "day-night-lamp" that obscured the differences between highly diverse situations and motivations by exposing them all to the unifying twilight of treason (further see Mann 1956).

7. Boveri 1963, 17; translation emended. *Translator's note: Treason in the Twentieth Century* (Boveri 1963), the single-volume English version of *Der Verrat im 20. Jahrhundert* (Boveri 1956–60), covers roughly one-third of the four-volume German original; moreover, the translation is at times somewhat irregular, if not treacherous.

8. Despite her wanderlust and multilingual skills, Boveri, herself of German-American descent and perfectly bilingual, liked to present herself as an embodiment of this highly localized principle of belonging. Not only did she remain in Berlin after the Nazis took power, but during the war she also kept returning from her postings in Stockholm, New York, Lisbon, and Madrid. Explaining her behavior to the perplexed East German writer Uwe Johnson after the war, she remained adamant that staying at home had been the right thing to do. In fact, she blamed the lack of understanding of those who had remained in Germany for the postwar German-American misunderstandings that she aimed to ameliorate in her *Amerika-Fibel* (Boveri 1946; further see Breslau 2000).

9. See the famous opening line of Schmitt's *Political Theology:* "Sovereign is he who decides on the exception" (Schmitt 1985b, 5).

10. Schroers had first developed the concept of the "interested third party" (Schroers 1961b, 247–98); Schmitt, in turn, picks up Schroers's term to underscore the new structure of enmity brought about by the partisan.

11. See Samuel Griffith's introduction to his translation of Sun Tzu's *Art of War* (Sun Tzu 1963, 45–56). All of the following quotations are to this edition.

12. See, for example, *The Acme of Skill,* a CIA handbook, which borrows its title from Sun Tzu (quoted in Der Derian 1992, 22).

13. By contrast, McNeilly emphasizes Sun Tzu's "holistic approach," which is said to unite the arts of war and government. Compared to European concepts of sovereignty, however, Sun Tzu's wise leader appears to be a variant of the skillful commander (see McNeilly 2001, 14).

14. The comparison of Clausewitz and Sun Tzu is a well-established trope in current military theory, yet despite certain parallels it is necessary to emphasize the fundamental difference between Clausewitz's notion of war as a duel and the modern doctrine of a "people in arms," on the one hand, and Sun Tzu's tactics of a cost-efficient war of spies and subterfuges, on the other. See Handel 2001, 22–31, 215–51.

15. Virilio describes these aspects of war—"psychological warfare," the restructuring of perception, and the representation of war in images and texts—as the "immateriality of war." Sun Tzu deals with some of these aspects as well, but he restricts himself to the space of war, while Virilio is concerned with the ways in which war takes hold of civil space (see Virilio 1989, 5 and following).

Part Three

1. "Smooth" as opposed to "striated," as described by Deleuze and Guattari in chapter 12 of *A Thousand Plateaus* (Deleuze and Guattari 1987).

2. For an introduction to the history of military IMINT, see the documentation of the Federation of American Scientists, "U.S. Army Intelligence School: IMINT 101. Introduction to Imagery Intelligence" (February 1996, http://www.fas.org/irp/imint/imint_101.htm). For an update on more recent technological developments see James Bloom, "Way up There—and Personal," *Guardian,* January 28, 2009, http://www.guardian.co.uk/technology/2009/jan/28/satellite-photography-privacy; and the GeoEye home page, http://www.geoeye.com/GeoEye101/satellite-imagery/high-resolution-imagery.aspx.

3. On the general connection between geography and colonialism see Said 1994, 216–19.

4. Research on the British spy novels generally tends to work within the confines of genre theory and to limit itself to discussing plots, protagonists, and national stereotypes. This approach sometimes involves a comparison between fiction and the "realities" of the secret service, often emphasizing the novels' lack of "realism." What it mainly ignores is the fact that literature, far from simply mirroring intelligence work, is actually deeply enmeshed in it. See Masters 1987; Panek 1981; Hindersmann 1995; Becker 1973; Atkins 1984; Lenz 1987. For a criticism of this approach and a more sophisticated take on the poetic structure of espionage novels, see Hepburn 2005.

5. Childers, himself a passionate sailor who drew on his own 1897 sailing experiences in the North Sea while writing *The Riddle of the Sands,* produced sketches to complement his maps. They are reprinted in Erskine Childers, *A Unique Edition of the Riddle of the Sands, with Historical Postscript by R. M. Bowker* (Old Bosham, U.K.: Bowker and Bertram, 1976).

6. For an excellent analysis of this tension between local and global knowledge see Thomas Richards's chapter on *The Riddle of the Sands* 131.

7. For a good survey of English invasion fears in the context of the conflicts with France and Russia (Germany enters the picture with a slight delay), see Matin (1999), who argues that the fear of an attack on the mother country is rivaled by the fear of losing India, the most important colony. The Great Game, then, is a variation of the general fear of an attack on the British Empire.

8. Seed 1992, 71; Andrew 1985, 81. Andrew emphasizes the "gentlemanly tradition of espionage" that informed the German trial.

9. For an encyclopedic overview of the heroes, martyrs, and adventurers of this conflict see Hopkirk 1990.

10. See Bayly 1996, whose important study covers the period until shortly after the 1857 uprising.

11. See Bucher 1998, 11. Like the majority of postcolonial Kipling research undertaken in the wake of Said, Bucher's reconstruction of visuality in Kim aims to reveal that a "Napoleonic" gaze at Indian culture and the orientalizing essentialization of the native are expressions of Kipling's imperialist attitude. However, she thereby misses out on the exact poetic structure of this visuality as well as on its political function to train the observational skills of the colonial subject. Older positions lauded Kipling's intimate knowledge of India and the novel's picturesque quality as its main strengths: see Kinkead-Weekes 1964; Renouard 1994.

12. In the novel an old soldier recalls the uprising thus: "A madness ate into all the Army, and they turned against their officers" (Kipling 1987, 100).

13. On the Survey of India see Edney 1997.

14. Some of the pundits were considered valued collaborators by the geographers. See, e.g., Edmund Smyth's obituary for the pundit Nain Singh (Smyth 1882).

15. In his report "Journey to Shigatze," Montgomerie recounts how "Native Explorer No. 9" received support from a village after curing a sick woman. Kim accomplishes the same several times. See Montgomerie 1875, 331.

16. Postcolonial readings of Kim focusing on cartography tend to argue that cartography amounts to a mimetic and totalizing representation of the world to prove that Kipling is caught up in this complicity of exploration and colonial spatial control. The analysis, regrettably, is unnecessary given that the novel explicitly states the connection (e.g., see Huggan 1990).

17. In his insightful analysis Baucom insists that this hybridity has a tragic component insofar as Creighton's education of Kim effectively erases the Indian Irish "Little Friend of All the World" in favor of a new identity as a loyal and useful servant of the empire (Baucom 2002, 353).

18. See Conolly 2002. In 1829 Conolly was sent on a mission to explore the region between the Caucasus and the Khyber Pass, which was a possible route for a Russian invasion. Conolly, in Hopkirk's judgment "the archetypal Great Game player," fell victim to the game when in 1839 he traveled to the emir of Bokhara to negotiate the release of the captured agent and diplomat Colonel Charles Stoddart. Like Stoddart, Conolly was imprisoned, tortured, and executed in June 1842.

19. Edward Ingram views the early phase of the Great Game as a defense of the important colonies rather than an aggressive striving for hegemony. Although he rejects Mackinder's geopolitical interpretation of the Anglo-Russian conflict, he employs the categories developed by Mackinder (see Ingram 1984, especially 7–19).

20. The tension between mapping large spaces and detailed microgeography also characterized the Survey of India while it was still under the rule of the East India Company. Matthew Edney has shown that although detailed local maps would have better served administrative and economic objectives, the Survey of India initially preferred large-format trigonometric charts (Edney 1993).

21. On the implementation of the public school boyhood ideal in the colonies, see Mangan 1986.

22. For detailed biographical information, see the scholarly biography by Jeremy Wilson, *Lawrence of Arabia: The Authorized Biography of T. E. Lawrence* (J. Wilson 1989), which was authorized and based on material provided by T. E. Lawrence's brother A. W. Lawrence. For a recent, more narrative description of Lawrence's life, see Michael Korda's *Hero: The Life and Legend of Lawrence of Arabia* (Korda 2010).

23. *Revolt in the Desert,* the abridged, highly successful version of *Seven Pillars of Wisdom,* was not published until 1927.

24. On the reconstruction of Lawrence's original mission based on declassified archival material, see Morsey 1976 and 1984.

25. The Sykes-Picot Agreement is part of the highly contradictory and internally divisive colonial policy pursued by the British Empire in the Near and Middle East. While His Majesty's High Commissioner in Cairo, Sir Henry MacMahon, was negotiating with the Arabs over possible British support for their war of liberation, Sykes-Picot was already being negotiated by another section of the Foreign Office.

26. The Sykes-Picot Agreement remained secret until it was revealed by the Bolsheviks in the wake of the October Revolution. See Liddell Hart 1937, 48 and following.

27. Given the conspicuous similarities between Sun Tzu's deliberate avoidance of large-scale confrontations and Lawrence's theory of partisan warfare, it is quite possible that Lawrence was familiar with *The Art of War.* A first English edition, translated by Lionel Giles and subtitled *The Oldest Military Treatise in the World,* appeared in 1910.

28. Lawrence's "Twenty-Seven Articles," first published in the *Arab Bulletin* (1917), serves as a short manual and summarizes the recommended behavior of British agents toward the Arabs (quoted in Liddell Hart 1937, 110–17).

29. This point is further developed in Silverman 1992, one of the most insightful texts on the Lawrence phenomenon.

30. The traumatic episode of Dera'a also reveals the dangers of disguise (not to mention the illusion that it makes one invisible). In a foolhardy attempt to scout the surroundings of the city, Lawrence is arrested; mistaken for a young, blond, and seductively pale-skinned Circassian; and tortured and raped by the Turkish bey.

31. Further see Morsey 1976, who discusses the many—and many passionate—accusations of fraud against Lawrence.

32. Aldama (2000) convincingly links the heterogeneity and the narrative incoherence of the text to Lawrence's partisan tactics rather than to the complexities of a poetics of treason. The very structure of this partisan text is shaped by decentered, fleeting combat operations that are almost impossible to perceive and just as difficult to depict.

Part Four

1. Kim may be an adolescent, but he is uninterested in sex. Though he understands the advances by the "woman of Shamlegh," he explicitly rejects them. Sexual restraint, no doubt, marks the conduct of the gentleman spy.

2. Schirmann argues that at this point in time such an admission would have been tantamount to suicide.

3. According to Schirmann's analysis of the code employed by Major Kalle, the goal of the telegrams was to incriminate Mata Hari in the eyes of the French. They contained so many details concerning the travels and circumstances of "H 21" that it was easily apparent who "H 21" was. While these details were of no relevance to Kalle's superiors in Berlin, they were of interest to the French, since they enabled them to identify Mata Hari's code name. The encryption used by Kalle had been broken by the French and was used only for communications of little importance—or for those the Germans *wanted* the French to decode. Even the fact that the French were intercepting messages between Spain and Berlin was known to German intelligence. It seems very likely, therefore, that Kalle was not sending these telegrams to provide Berlin with information about Mata Hari. Her reports, though characterized as "very thorough," were completely useless, as Berlin was quick to point out in its response: "Services are insufficient" (quoted in Schirmann 1994, 146). It was evidently more a matter of delivering Mata Hari to the other side (ibid., 81–92). Schirmann treats the inability or unwillingness of the court and the presiding judge to take note of this obvious trap as proof of their prejudice (ibid., 145 and following).

4. French politics in 1917 was obsessed with traitors. The failure of the Nivelle offensive targeting the Chemin des Dames ridge was attributed to treason. Louis Malvy, the minister of the interior, was forced to resign on August 30, 1917, because he stood accused of having handed over French deployment plans to the enemy and—naturally—of having had an affair with Mata Hari. George Ladoux, head of counterespionage, was arrested in the fall and spent the remainder of the war in prison. Years later the Gempp report noted that the overwhelming majority of those accused of treason never had any contact with German intelligence (Gempp 1939–43, 19).

5. Actually, the two female spy legends met in March 1916 in Cologne when Schragmüller trained and instructed Mata Hari for espionage services she promised to perform for the Germans. Not surprisingly, Schragmüller was taken aback by Mata Hari's lack of professional skills and discipline: "The behavior of Mata Hari at the hotel, at lunch and at the theatre is that of a 'Grande Dame,' although her eccentric personality and exquisite elegance attracts general attention. It is an effort for her to obey to the restrictions to her freedom of movement which have to be imposed for her new role. Yet, she is unable to stick to prescribed regulations" (quoted after Hieber 2005, 106).

Part Five

1. Karl Löwith revealed—not without polemical intent—this eschatological tendency to be at work in Marx's conceptualization of Communism as a historical movement (Löwith 1949).

2. Trotsky later vigorously denied Malaparte's account of his role in the "Bolshevist coup."

3. For the various Soviet networks and infiltration practices, see Dallin's

exhaustive study of the early Soviet state security organizations (Dallin 1955). The Cheka (Chrezvychaynaya Komissiya, or Extraordinary Commission) was dissolved in 1922 and replaced by the GPU (later OGPU), which in 1934 was replaced by the NKVD, the principal instrument of Stalin's purges.

4. In *Armed Insurrection* by A. Neuberg, Kippenberger provided valuable insights for future insurrections based on the experience of the aborted Hamburg uprising (Neuberg 1970, 81–104). As Erich Wollenberg (see note 5), one of the coauthors of the collection, which appeared illegally in Germany, explains in his introduction to the English translation, "A. Neuberg" was a collective pseudonym: "Since it was to be published first in German, and since it was a new book on the subject of armed insurrection, we chose the name '*Neu*berg.' We added an 'A' before this surname; a 'B' would have served equally well" (ibid., 10). The pseudonym was a security measure; it would allow those found in possession of the book to claim that they had bought it from an unknown seller in the belief that it was a legal publication. Kippenberger himself wrote the chapter on the Hamburg uprising (see ibid., 101–4).

5. The KPD agent and Red Army officer Erich Wollenberg gives one of the best-informed accounts of the development of the secret "apparatuses" of the German Communist Party (KPD). Ousted from the party by the International Control Commission of the Comintern in 1933, Wollenberg fled to Prague and became active as an anti-Bolshevik publicist. His report *Der Apparat: Stalins fünfte Kolonne* (*The Apparatus: Stalin's Fifth Column*) was published in 1952 by the West German Ministry of All-German Affairs.

6. For the best depiction of the German-Russian Berlin and its conspiratorial underground see Schlögel 1998, especially the chapters "Global Village Komintern" and "In einer Landschaft des Verrats" ("In a Landscape of Treason").

7. I shall refer to all agents of this type as "chekist" regardless of the changing names of the Soviet intelligence organizations (CK, VCK, GPU, OGPU).

8. In 1930, following the removal of Mikhail Trilisser, his superior, Agabekov fled from Constantinople to France. He published two books detailing his experiences and the organizational structure of the Cheka/GPU. He shared the fate of many other Soviet defectors: following a long pursuit he was assassinated by the NKVD in Belgium (see Orlov 1954, 333).

9. Agabekov 1933, 18–28. It was said of Trilisser's assistant Styrné that he had his own parents killed (see Agabekov 1931, 12 and following). Ruth Fischer claimed that her brother Gerhart Eisler, who worked for the Comintern in China and was acquainted with Bertolt Brecht, had betrayed his mentor and friend Nikolai Bukharin (see Hering and Schilde 1995, 277).

10. Schlögel 1998, 244. Schlögel provides an excellent overview of the chekist agents' fate in the 1930s: most, including Hans Kippenberger, fell victim to the *Yezhovshchina,* the most intense period of Stalin's great purge (1936–38).

11. In particular, see Manès Sperber's *Burned Bramble* (Sperber 1987), the first volume of his trilogy *Like a Tear in the Ocean,* which depicts the tragedy of the underground Communist fighters during the party infighting after 1930. See also Arthur Koestler's *Darkness at Noon* (Koestler 1940), in which the

fate of the protagonist Rubashov, culminating in his annihilation by the party apparatus, serves to analyze the cruel quandaries of revolutionary ethics.

12. On the tactics and organization of conspiratorial subversion by the so-called Zer-Divisions, see Kaufmann et al. 1993, 142–47.

13. Walter Benjamin credited Heinrich Blücher with helping him understand "that certain passages in *A Reader for Those Who Live in Cities* are no more than formulations of the methods of the GPU." Brecht "poetically transfigures" the conduct and tactics of Communist secret services, whether part of the KPD or the GPU. Looking back at his earlier reading of Brecht's poem, Benjamin was unflinching in his self-criticism: "The commentary, in the form I gave it, is a pious falsification which obscures the extent to which Brecht is implicated in the development in question" (Benjamin 2003b, 159). In 1980 Franco Buono read the poem as a primer for the urban guerrilla (Buono 1980, 153).

14. *Translator's note:* Bertolt Brecht's play *Die Maßnahme,* a text of central importance for this section and indeed for Horn's entire book, is a translator's nightmare. There are five German versions and almost as many competing English translations. In the following I will be quoting from Carl Mueller's version (Brecht 1977, 7–34), primarily because it is the most literal rendition and thus best equipped to support Horn's close reading of the text. However, readers are recommended to also consult the translations by Eric Bentley (Brecht 1965, 75–108) and John Willett (Brecht 1997).

15. Ruth Fischer provides an extensive summary of *The Measures Taken* (in her book the title is rendered as *The Punitive Measure*), which she reads as "a mirror of the totalitarian party and its elite guard, the NKVD" (Fischer 1948, 618). Fischer, who had turned from a radical Communist into a fervent anti-Communist, was the sister of Brecht's collaborator Hanns Eisler (who wrote the music for the songs in *The Measures Taken*) and Gerhard Eisler, who had been sent to China by the Comintern in 1929 to organize the local Communist cells. Fischer claims that he had been sent there "to liquidate the opposition to the Russian Politburo" (Fischer 1948, 618).

16. For example, see the critique by Kurella 1931 (see note 20) and Kaiser 1983.

17. Roland Jost locates this open experimental structure within the context of the aesthetic discourse of modernity (see Jost 1998).

18. Emphasizing the "ex post" quality of the events on stage, Nikolaus Müller-Schöll and Susanne Winnacker have described the play as virtually unplayable. Such an interpretation, however, remains in the innocent domain of the "poetical" without exploring the play's political implications. From this point of view literature is in the final analysis merely a *commentary* on rather than intervention in politics (Winnacker 1997; further see Müller-Schöll and Winnacker in Gellert, Koch, and Vaßen 1998).

19. Burckhardt Lindner rightly emphasizes that Brecht's notion of dialectics has nothing to do with sublating syntheses (Lindner 1993, 51).

20. *Translator's note:* Alfred Kurella (1895–1975) was later a leading cultural functionary in the German Democratic Republic. An English translation of the

full text of his critique of *The Measures Taken* is reprinted in Brecht 1965, 163–72.

21. The inherent "thanatopolitical" tendency in *The Measures Taken,* that is, the fact that for Brecht the ultimate political act consists in killing or dying, is also present in his other *Lehrstücke* (see Horn 2007).

22. For the relation of *The Measures Taken* to legal theory, especially the concept of "measure" (*Maßnahme*) and its role in the state of exception, see in greater detail Horn 2001.

23. At his hearing at the House Committee on Un-American Activities on September 24–26, 1947, Brecht and his translator pointed out (for transparent reasons) that the "measure" alluded to in the title of the play did not constitute a "disciplinary measure."

24. Throughout Žižek's work there are recurring references to Brecht's learning plays, especially *The Measures Taken* and *He Who Says Yes,* some of which are only present in the German translations of Žižek's writings. His *Liebe dein Symptom wie dich selbst!* (Žižek 1991), from which this quotation is taken, is not identical with *Enjoy Your Symptom* (Žižek 1992a).

Part Six

1. In hindsight historians have expressed growing doubt about the "ideological" description of the Cold War (for example, Stephenson 2000).

2. For the history of the RAND Corporation, with special emphasis on its use of game theory for military simulation, see Poundstone 1992.

3. Next to well-known civilian and academic institutions (for example, MIT, RAND, and the Hudson Institute founded by Herman Kahn) it was above all the Pentagon's Cold War division in the Joint War Games Agency that was heavily engaged in the design and staging of military simulations.

4. This self-reflection (both in the footsteps of and in direct opposition to Sherman Kent) left its mark on most of the comprehensive theories of secret intelligence. For the most important contributions see Herman 1996; Shulsky and Schmitt 1991; Godson 1980, 1989.

5. Attempts to dismiss Cold War spy thrillers as political escapism "seeking to allay the fear and anxiety of nuclear annihilation and national security" (Der Derian 1992, 51) miss out on how these novels participate in the knowledge structure of the intelligence business (frequently with incredible informedness) as well as on their reflexive relationship to the world of the political secret. In addition, they ignore the structural diversity of the textual and cinematic engagements in favor of an all too simplistic ideological verdict on the "popular genre" allegedly culminating, not coincidentally, in the wholly apolitical James Bond novels.

6. On the history of crises and war-gaming scenarios see A. Wilson 1968. For a more detailed account of the change of conflict modeling from Pearl Harbor to the Cold War, see Allen 1987.

7. For a general theory of the function of war games in political decision-making processes, see Brewer and Shubik 1979.

8. On the gradual mathematization and subsequent computerization of war games, see the excellent chapters 5 and 6 in Pias 2002.

9. In the preface to *Red Storm Rising,* a novel written in collaboration with war game designer Larry Bond, Clancy calls the novel a "scenario" that remediates a "macro war game" in the Northern Atlantic. Clancy, a conservative army groupie and himself the author of complex and successful war games, is concerned with anticipating possible conflicts and providing the right military and technological means to master them. Ronald Reagan was one of his most enthusiastic readers. On Clancy, further see Carson 1996.

10. See the study by Deborah Welch Larson on the political psychology of the Cold War and the missed opportunities for détente caused by the pervasive culture of distrust (Larson 1997).

11. The so-called Prisoner's Dilemma is an experimental thought model fundamental to game theory. It involves two players who independently of each other have to reach a decision that takes into account what the other may decide: Two prisoners are being interrogated in isolation. Together they committed a theft, but it cannot be proved. If both deny the crime, they will both be imprisoned for one year on lesser charges. If both confess, they will both end up in jail for five years. If one offers a confession and the other continues to deny any involvement, the former will receive immunity as a crown witness and be released, while the latter will be sentenced to fifteen years. The model is based on the premise that, though unable to communicate with each other, both prisoners are very much aware of the possibility that the other could confess. A strategy of minimal risk is for both to confess (the so-called Nash equilibrium). Though not the optimal solution, it is the most probable outcome. For a critical take on the application of the Prisoner's Dilemma to international conflicts, see Rapoport 1974.

12. This was Ray S. Cline's comment on the incorrect assessment that the Soviets would not station missiles in Cuba (quoted in Cohen 1980, 78; emphasis added).

13. *Red Alert* was first published in 1958. Unlike Kubrick's apocalyptic scenario, the novel ends with the American president saving the world from annihilation. Herman Kahn, incidentally, addresses the *Red Alert* scenario in his infamous *Thinking the Unthinkable.* Displaying his hallmark laconic detachment in depicting and calculating doomsday scenarios, he argues that the probability for such an unintended war is 1:10. Statistically, Kahn claims, it is reasonable to assume that this will not take place before the year 2000 (Kahn 1962, 44).

14. The film *WarGames* (Badham 1983) updates *Dr. Strangelove,* though it opts for a much more comforting ending. As in the case of Kubrick's movie, the principal problem arises from the recursivity of a military computer that both simulates and wages a war. Instead of an out-of-control general, the film features a juvenile hacker, who—believing it is only a simulation—starts a game of "Global Thermonuclear War" with the central computer at NORAD, the U.S. Air Force headquarters, by launching a "Red" attack on North America. This prompts the computer to launch a real, massive retaliatory strike against the Soviet Union. Like *Dr. Strangelove, WarGames* deals with the question of

an unintended war that is so difficult to stop precisely because the automatized processes involved exclude human interventions. The accidental war is the figure of the hypothetical becoming reality (further see Horn 2007).

15. The first-strike strategy is an attempt to escape the MAD dilemma that a counterstrike, while it may satisfy a desire for revenge, no longer amounts to a successful defense (see Aldridge 1983).

16. *WarGames* offers a more comforting solution. While the computer—a gigantic Doomsday Machine that has achieved a certain level of self-awareness—puts itself at the highest state of alert (Defcon 1) and starts computing ICBM launch codes, the hacker engages it in a game of tic-tac-toe with itself. The latter is, of course, a game you cannot win once you have grasped the essential moves, but the computer is forced to expend so much power on learning this that it eventually shuts down.

17. On the Berlin Wall as a site in spy thrillers of the 1960s and 1970s, see the contributions by Siegfried Mews ("The Spies Are Coming In from the Cold War") and Jürgen Kamm ("The Berlin Wall and Cold War Espionage: Visions of Divided Germany in the Novels of Len Deighton") in Schürer et al. 1996.

18. For an allegorical reading of the Berlin Wall (and the novel altogether), see Hepburn, who contends that "in the allegory of the novel [*The Spy Who Came In from the Cold*], the Berlin Wall contains information that the West cannot assimilate, namely, that within an ethos of individualism, such as the West adheres to, individuals are dispensible" (Hepburn 2005, 180).

19. Le Carré scholarship tends to focus on the interpersonal relationships between the protagonists. His novels are mostly seen less as political literature than as a sociology of the British middle class, embodied by the malicious, philistine intelligence community (e.g, Hindersmann 1995; Aronoff 1999).

20. The sentimental yet nonetheless suspicious relationship between handler and agent shapes le Carré's late Cold War collection *The Secret Pilgrim.* One of the most interesting and refreshingly factual studies is *Le Carré's Landscape* (2001) by former Canadian intelligence operative Tod Hoffman, who offers an informed account of the handler-agent relationship.

21. For an elaboration of the game metaphor in espionage fiction and history, see the chapter "The Great Game" in Atkins's study of the British spy novel (Atkins 1984, 131–39).

22. Eric Berne's theory of interpersonal psychology, *Games People Play,* published one year before *The Looking-Glass War,* was highly influential. Its traces can be found in the psychology of many spy thrillers of the 1960s and 1970s. Tony Barley correctly points out that the games played by the spy novel's protagonists primarily involve their spouses (Barley 1986, 48–65).

23. Other experts—among them, Kim Philby, who escaped to Moscow in the year of the novel's publication, and Richard Helms, head of the CIA—have voiced similar misgivings: the plot is implausible (Philby) or darkly defeatist (Helms). See Stafford 1988, 200.

24. This is a phrase used by le Carré in *The Honourable Schoolboy* to refer to the exposure of the mole Bill Haydon, a fictional version of Kim Philby (le Carré 2000b, 59).

25. A cautious assessment of the half-truths and "gaps" in *My Silent War* and Philby's later statements can be found in Knightley 1988. The book contains subsequently confirmed details concerning the fact that to avoid a scandal the SIS let Philby escape after he had offered a part confession to the head of SIS in Beirut, Nicholas Elliott. For Philby's work for the KGB, see Borovik 1994.

26. Andrew Boyle reports that as late as 1954 the Soviets kidnapped and extensively interrogated a former agent of the German Abwehr to find out whether Philby was leading them on (Boyle 1979, 409). Tod Hoffman, in turn, speculates that Philby may have tried to contact the SIS while in Moscow (Hoffman 2001, 120).

27. The method is first explicitly mentioned in *The Honourable Schoolboy,* but it already determines Fiedler's actions toward Mundt and Smiley's investigation of Haydon.

Part Seven

1. On the construction of the atom bomb as the first and most important U.S. "big science" project, see Hughes 2002, 45–63. Jungk describes the many security measures installed by the FBI in Los Alamos, Oak Ridge, and Hanford, including the usual loyalty tests, the bugging of phones and apartments, postal censorship, eavesdropping, and garbage inspection (Jungk 1958, 116).

2. While the Atomic Energy Acts of 1946 and 1954 finalized the classification of all nuclear research, all research conducted in Britain and the United States during the war had been subject to military secrecy protocols. On the history and logic of classification see Quist 2004; for an epistemological analysis of classification see Galison 2004.

3. Even in his prison notes, Fuchs scrupulously adhered to the dictate of classification (that is, no reproduction of technological details for those lacking proper clearance), describing the material he had passed on to the Soviets as "classified data dealing with the whole problem of making an atom bomb from fissionable material as I then knew the problem; information as to the principle of the method of detonating an atom bomb" (quoted in Moss 1987, 73).

4. The other defendants were either sentenced to jail or acquitted as FBI collaborators. Serving time in Britain, Fuchs was released in 1959 and moved to East Germany; Greenglass and Gold were released in 1960 and 1966, respectively. Morton Sobell, codefendant of the Rosenbergs, was sentenced to thirty years and released in 1969.

5. On the prehistory of the "Red scare" from the First World War to 1945, see Murray 1955.

6. Further see Carmichael (1993, 131–56), who reads Doctorow's version as yet another distortion of the Rosenberg case by turning the children (in the novel, the siblings Daniel and Susan) into the deeply distraught, incurable martyrs of the Rosenberg cult (Carmichael 1993, 145 and following).

7. During the trial the Greenglass couple claimed that Ethel had copied secret material and had on one occasion communicated a message from Julius to David Greenglass—reason enough to sentence her to death.

8. In an act of stageworthy patriotism, Rosenberg's lawyer Emanuel Bloch

refrained from submitting to closer examination the sketches Greenglass allegedly prepared for the Soviets. Obeying the logic of classification, he missed out on the opportunity to have experts publicly debunk the sketches as completely useless (see Radosh and Milton 1997, 188 and following).

9. Thus Mead's pithy summary of the perplexing question, raised at the third Macy Conference, of how Communist manipulation techniques function (see Schaffner 1957, 251).

10. Marks (1979) refers to these papers as the published (that is, nonclassified) results of the MKULTRA subproject 68. MKULTRA was the code name for all the CIA-initiated projects dedicated to researching behavioral change. For a more detailed appraisal of Cameron's role in the "brainwash" research, see Lemov 2011.

11. Marks describes CIA experiments designed to employ hypnotized agents as possible assassins. This research project—whose failure was, no doubt, related to the fact that experimental assassinations are difficult to organize—is not without a certain comedic potential; it is already present in the premise that the agents involved were not allowed to know anything about their mission (further see Marks 1979, 182–92).

12. For an excellent reading of the novel as a symptom of the "brainwash furor" of the 1950s, and of Sergeant Shaw as what David Riesman calls an "other-directed personality," see Hahn 2004; for the scientific context alluded to in Condon's novel and the film, see Andriopoulos 2011; and for the links between Pavlov and the mind-control research, Killen 2011.

13. For an explanation of the theoretical basis for conditioning, see Condon 2003, 40 and following. The literature quoted by Condon does indeed exist.

14. For an extensive commentary on the nightmarish qualities of the scene and its cultural associations, see Marcus 2002, 19–32; Andriopoulos 2011.

Part Eight

1. See the diagrams in Posner 1993, 473–82. Posner provides the latest and most detailed attempt to corroborate the Warren Commission's lone gunman theory.

2. Presenting Oswald as a lone gun had the advantage of being a politically opportune theory. One of the reasons for establishing the commission in the first place was to silence emerging rumors of a Communist conspiracy, which, one year after the Cuban missile crisis, could have had a catastrophic impact on the relationship between the superpowers.

3. Observers have noted the conspicuous amount of judicial vocabulary spread throughout the Warren Report. For criticism of the Warren Report, see Lane 1966; Epstein 1966; and (endorsing the report) Ford and Stiles 1965.

4. See the excellent account of the various JFK conspiracy theories in Knight 2007.

5. While the number of injuries caused by the "magic bullet" appears to indicate several shooters, Kennedy's head injury poses even more of a quandary. The presumed entry wound is the size of an exit wound, which would indicate that the shot was fired from the front and would thus imply at

least one more gunman. Strangely enough, on this point there are discrepancies between the report filed by the doctors at Parkland Hospital, who took care of Kennedy immediately after the shooting, and that of the Bethesda Hospital in Washington, which conducted a hasty autopsy that merely established the cause of death (head injury) but did not examine the circumstances more closely. Depending on vested interests, traces are decoded as supporting either one or the other hypothesis: a shot from the front points to a conspiracy, while a shot from the back buttresses the lone gunman theory. Supporters of the latter explain the backward motion of Kennedy's head as a muscle spasm typical for head wounds—a hypothesis nobody is eager to experimentally verify. For the best summary of the lone gunman theory, see chapters 1 through 9 in Posner 1993; for the conspiracy hypothesis positing several shooters, see Marrs 1990.

6. On the development of the film, for which Stone conducted his own research, see Simpson 2003.

7. Peter Knight in his otherwise outstanding book is wrong to suggest that the film stages an oedipal drama (Knight 2000, 104) shaped by the plot of Sophocles's play *Oedipus Rex*. In my opinion, the principal reference is not *Oedipus Rex* but *Hamlet*.

8. On the history of this far-reaching declassifying initiative undertaken during the Clinton administration, see Nelson 1998.

9. See Mailer 1995. For Mailer, the casting of Oswald as a lone, tragic gunman emerging from American postwar culture is the only bearable version of the story. Initially he planned to name the novel *An American Tragedy*. Interestingly, Mailer is not able to fully sustain the tale of Oswald as a self-inflicted downfall. After six hundred pages of narrative, interviews with family members, and reworked transcripts, the narrator comes to a stop and ponders whether his initial hypothesis that Oswald was a self-directed "prime mover" is in need of revision: "Tragedy is vastly preferable to absurdity. Such is the vested interest that adheres to perceiving Oswald as a tragic and infuriating hero (or, if you will, antihero) rather than as a snarling little wife abuser or a patsy" (Mailer 1995, 607).

10. Many scholars miss out on the historical precision with which DeLillo reworks the material because they are more interested in highlighting his postmodern "derealization" of reality. For a criticism of the postmodernist approaches to *Libra,* see Hutchinson 2001.

11. For this reason critics appreciate DeLillo not only for giving a fictional voice to paranoia but also for deconstructing the classic American ideology of the self-fashioning, solitary, and free individual (with Oswald as the latter's weird embodiment). Further see Mott 2000, esp. 237.

12. On the theory of covert actions see Nutter 2000, 74–93. Nutter emphasizes that the most important feature of covert actions, the feature that separates them from other forms of indirect influence, is the obscuring of actors and political responsibility.

13. Bill Millard offers an alternate reading based on the convergence of different, noncoordinated, and myopic individual actions (Millard 2000). His reading refrains from indulging in the long-standing discussion of whether or

not conspiracy theories and conspiracy narratives (including *Libra*) still allow for some kind of individual agency (for example, Melley 2000; Knight 2003).

14. Following the Warren Commission's assessment that Oswald's Marxist conviction was nothing but an "overriding hostility to his environment," researchers have paid little attention to the depiction of Oswald's Marxism in *Libra*. But as Skip Willman convincingly points out, it is an integral part of the way the novel constructs "history" (Willman 1999).

15. Skip Willman reads the two principles, the "conspiracy theory" and the "contingency theory," as the novel's two basic elements and tries to explain their underlying social functions. While conspiracy theory assumes that all social actions are controlled by a single invisible actor, the no less deluded contingency theory claims that there are no structural social mechanisms whatsoever, only a sequence of random events. Radical distrust of the social is opposed by radical affirmation (Willman 1998).

16. John Johnston and José Liste Noya interpret Oswald's troubled relationship to language (dyslexia, anagrammatic transformations of his name, unconscious quoting of literary cliches) as marking the secret's emblematic inscription into the novel (Johnston 1998, 200 and following; Noya 2004).

17. It is particularly ironic that the cunning "curator" starts sending Branch literary accounts of the assassination (DeLillo 1991, 442).

18. In unsurpassed irony, DeLillo calls fiction "one of the consolation prizes for having lived in the world" (Connolly and DeLillo 2005, 31).

Part Nine

1. The terrorists' "spiritual guidance" found in Mohammed Atta's bag has since been thoroughly analyzed and declared authentic by noted Arabists and religious scholars (see Kippenberg and Seidensticker 2006).

2. In 2002, Bröckers published the bulk of his blogs as a book (Bröckers 2002).

3. Since 9/11 was the manifestation of a latent structure present long before 2001, it comes as no surprise that the most important publications on terrorist networks, net wars, and the networked society appeared in the 1990s but did not garner a lot of attention until 9/11 (see especially Cebrowski and Garstka 1998). The important study by Arquilla and Ronfeldt had already been published in 1996. In 2001 it was reissued with an added chapter on 9/11 and given a new title. On the basics of the information society, see Castells 1996.

4. Searching out food sources, ants leave a pheromone trail; if they have found food, they leave another trail heading back, which will entice their fellow foragers to follow along the same path. The trail "broadens" with the growing number of individual ants using it (see Bonabeau and Théraulaz 2000).

5. The best examples are financial markets that may suffer crashes due to local turbulence. One technical example is the power outage in Canada and the northeastern United States on August 14, 2003, caused by a cascading failure set off after a generating plant in Parma, Ohio, had shut down because of a falling tree.

WORKS CITED

Aaronovitch, David. 2010. *Voodoo Histories: The Role of the Conspiracy Theory in Shaping Modern History.* New York: Riverhead.

Advertising Research Foundation. 1958. *The Application of Subliminal Perception in Advertising.* New York: Advertising Research Foundation, Inc.

Agabekov, G. S. 1931. *OGPU: The Russian Secret Terror.* Translated by Henry S. Bunn. New York: Brentano's.

———. 1933. *Die Tscheka bei der Arbeit.* Stuttgart: Union Deutsche Verlagsgesellschaft.

Agamben, Giorgio. 1998. *Homo Sacer: Sovereign Power and Bare Life.* Translated by Daniel Heller-Roazen. Chicago: University of Chicago Press.

———. 2005. *State of Exception.* Translated by Kevin Attell. Chicago: University of Chicago Press.

Aldama, Juan Alonso. 2000. "El desierto del sentido." *Revista de Occidente* 232 (September): 60–72.

Aldridge, Robert C. 1983. *First Strike! The Pentagon's Strategy for Nuclear War.* Boston: South End Press.

Alexander, Yonah, and Michael S. Swetnam. 2001. *Usama bin Laden's al-Qaida: Profile of a Terrorist Network.* Ardsley, N.Y.: Transnational.

Allen, Thomas B. 1987. *War Games: The Secret World of the Creators, Players, and Policy Makers Rehearsing World War III Today.* New York: McGraw.

Altenhöner, Florian. 2001. " 'Spionitis'—reale Korrelate, Imaginationen und Deutungsmuster der Angst vor Spionen 1900–1914." In *Kollektive Identitäten und kulturelle Innovationen: Ethnologische, soziologische und historische Studien,* edited by Werner Rammert et al., 77–91. Leipzig: Leipziger Universitätsverlag.

Ambler, Eric. 1938. *Epitaph for a Spy.* London: Hodder and Stoughton.

Andreyev, Leonid. 1947. *Judas Iscariot, the Christians, the Phantoms.* Translated by Walter Morison. London: John Westhouse.

Andrew, Christopher. 1985. *Her Majesty's Secret Service: The Making of the British Intelligence Community.* New York: Viking.

———. 1995. *For the President's Eyes Only: Secret Intelligence and the American Presidency from Washington to Bush.* New York: HarperCollins.

———. 2009. *The Defence of the Realm: The Authorized History of MI5.* London: Allen Lane.

Andrew, Christopher, and David Dilks, eds. 1984. *The Missing Dimension: Governments and Intelligence Communities in the Twentieth Century.* London: Macmillan.

Andriopoulos, Stefan. 2011. "The Sleeper Effect: Hypnotism, Mind Control, Terrorism." *Grey Room,* no. 45 (Fall): 88–105.

Arendt, Hannah. 1951. *The Burden of Our Time.* London: Secker and Warburg.

———. 2004. *Origins of Totalitarianism.* New York: Schocken.

Aronoff, Myron. 1999. *The Spy Novels of John le Carré.* New York: St. Martin's.

Arquilla, John, and David Ronfeldt. 2000. *Swarming and the Future of Conflict.* Santa Monica, Calif.: RAND. http://www.rand.org/publications/DB/DB311/.

———. 2001. "Networks, Netwars, and the Fight for the Future." *First Monday* 6, no. 10 (October). http://www.firstmonday.dk/issues/issue6_10/ronfeldt.

Assange, Julian. 2006. "Conspiracy as Governance." http://cryptome.org/0002/ja-conspiracies.pdf.

Assassination Records Review Board. 1998. *Final Report of the Assassination Records Review Board.* Washington, D.C.: United States Government Printing Office.

Atkins, John. 1984. *The British Spy Novel: Styles in Treachery.* London: Calder.

Avery, Dylan. 2006. *Loose Change.* http://www.loosechange911.com.

Baden-Powell, Robert Stephenson Smyth. 1899. *Aids to Scouting for N.-C.Os & Men.* London: Galde and Polden.

———. 1915. *My Adventures as a Spy.* London: Arthur Pearson.

Badham, Sidney. 1983. *WarGames.* Directed by James Badham, written by Lawrence Lasker and Walter F. Parkes. United Artists.

Baer, Robert. 2002. *See No Evil: The True Story of a Ground Soldier in the CIA's War on Terrorism.* New York: Crown.

Balderston, Daniel. 1993. *Out of Context: Historical Reference and the Representation of Reality in Borges.* Durham, N.C.: Duke University Press.

Ballard, James Graham. 1969. "The Subliminal Man." In *The Disaster Area,* 55–76. London: Panther.

Barley, Tony. 1986. *Taking Sides: The Fiction of John le Carré.* Philadelphia: Open University Press.

Barrenecheas, Ana María. 1967. *La expresión de la irrealidad en la obra de Jorge Luis Borges.* Buenos Aires: Editorial Paidos. First published 1957.

Barth, Karl. 1957. *Church Dogmatics.* Vol. 2, *The Doctrine of God.* Edinburgh: T. and T. Clark.

Baucom, Ian. 2002. "The Survey of India." In *Rudyard Kipling: Kim. Authoritative Text, Backgrounds, Criticism,* edited by Zohreh T. Sullivan, 351–58. New York: Norton.

Baudrillard, Jean. 2002. *The Spirit of Terrorism.* London: Verso.

Bay, Willow. 1998. "Director Ed Zwick Defends 'The Siege.'" *CNN Entertainment Weekly,* November 10. http://edition.cnn.com/SHOWBIZ/Movies/9811/10/siege/.

Bayly, Christopher Alan. 1996. *Empire and Information: Intelligence Gathering and Social Communication in India, 1780–1870.* Cambridge: Cambridge University Press.

Becker, Jens Peter. 1973. *Der englische Spionageroman: Historische Entwicklung, Thematik, literarische Form*. Munich: Goldmann.

Belin, David W. [counsel to the Warren Commission]. 1988. *Final Disclosure: The Full Truth About the Assassination of President Kennedy*. New York: Scribner.

Bell-Villada, Gene H. 1999. *Borges and His Fiction: A Guide to His Mind and Art*. Austin: University of Texas Press.

Ben-Israel, Isaac. 1989. "Philosophy and Methodology of Intelligence: The Logic of Estimate Process." *Intelligence and National Security* 4, no. 4 (October): 660–718.

Benjamin, Walter. 1999. *Selected Writings*. Vol. 2, *1927–1934*. Edited by Michael W. Jennings et al. Cambridge, Mass.: Harvard University Press.

———. 2003a. *The Origin of German Tragic Drama*. Translated by John Osborne. London: Verso.

———. 2003b. *Selected Writings*. Vol. 4, *1938–1940*. Edited by Howard Eiland and Michael W. Jennings. Cambridge, Mass.: Harvard University Press.

Benn, Gottfried. 1981. "Wie Miss Cavell erschossen wurde." In *Gesammelte Werke*, vol. 4, edited by Dieter Wellershoff, 194–201. Stuttgart: Klett-Cotta.

Berndorff, Hans Rudolf [Rudolf van Wehrt]. 1927. *Spionage!* Stuttgart: Dieck.

Berne, Eric. 1967. *Games People Play*. New York: Grove Press. First published 1964.

Besson, Luc. 1990. *Nikita*. Directed by Luc Besson. Written by Luc Besson, from a novel by Gérard de Villiers. Starring Anne Parillaud, Tchéky Karyo, Jeanne Moreau, and Jean-Hugues Anglade. Gaumont.

Birchall, Clare. 2011. " 'There's Been Too Much Secrecy in This City': The False Choice Between Secrecy and Transparency in US Politics." *Cultural Politics* 7, no. 1: 133–56.

Bizard, Léon. 1925. *Souvenirs d'un médecin de la Préfecture de police et des prisons de Paris*. Paris: Grasset.

Blaedel, Niels. 1988. *Harmony and Unity: The Life of Niels Bohr*. Madison, Wis.: Science Tech.

Blei, Franz. 1927. "Die Kurtisanin." In *Glanz und Elend berühmter Frauen*, 267–80. Berlin: Rowohlt.

Bley, Hauptmann a. D. Wulf. 1931. "Spionage und anomale Veranlagung." In *Die Weltkriegsspionage*, edited by Paul von Lettow-Vorbeck, 378–83. Munich: Justin Moser.

Bloom, James. 2009. "Way up There—and Personal." *Guardian*, January 28, http://www.guardian.co.uk/technology/2009/jan/28/satellite-photography-privacy.

Bonabeau, Eric, Marco Dorigo, and Guy Théraulaz. 1999. *Swarm Intelligence: From Natural to Artificial Systems*. New York: Oxford University Press.

Bonabeau, Eric, and Guy Théraulaz. 2000. "Swarm Smarts." *Scientific American* (March): 72–79.

Bonhoeffer, Dietrich. 1998. *Meditations on the Cross*. Translated by Douglas W. Scott. Louisville, Ky.: Westminster John Knox Press.

Borges, Jorge Luis. 1964. *Other Inquisitions 1937–1952.* Austin: University of Texas Press.

———. 1998. *Collected Fictions.* Translated by Andrew Hurley. New York: Viking.

———. 2000. *The Total Library: Non-Fiction 1922–1986.* Edited by Eliot Weinberger. London: Allen Lane.

Borovik, Genrikh. 1994. *The Philby Files: The Secret Life of the Master Spy—KGB Archives Revealed.* London: Little, Brown.

Botero, Giovanni. 1997. *Della Ragion di Stato libri dieci, con tre libri delle cause della grandezza, e magnificenza delle cittá.* Reprint edited by C. Continisio. Rome: Donzelli. First published in Venice: Gioliti 1589.

Bouchardon, Pierre. 1953. *Souvenirs.* Paris: Albin Michel.

Boveri, Margret. 1946. *Amerika-Fibel für erwachsene Deutsche: Ein Versuch Unverstandenes zu erklären.* Freiburg im Breisgau, Ger.: Badischer Verlag.

———. 1956–60. *Der Verrat im XX. Jahrhundert.* 4 volumes. Reinbek, Ger.: Rowohlt.

———. 1960. *Der Verrat im XX. Jahrhundert.* Vol. 4, *Verrat als Epidemie: Amerika.* Reinbek, Ger.: Rowohlt.

———. 1963. *Treason in the Twentieth Century.* Translated by Jonathan Steinberg. New York: Putnam.

Boyle, Andrew. 1979. *The Climate of Treason: Five Who Spied for Russia.* London: Hutchinson.

Brack, Walter. 1931. "Frauen und Krankheiten als Kampfmittel." In *Die Weltkriegsspionage,* edited by Paul von Lettow-Vorbeck, 413–18. Munich: Justin Moser.

Brandstetter, Gabriele. 1995. *Tanz-Lektüren.* Frankfurt am Main: Fischer Taschenbuch.

Brecht, Bertolt. 1965. *The Jewish Wife and Other Short Plays.* Translated by Eric Bentley. New York: Grove.

———. 1976. *Poems 1913–1956: Part One 1913–1928.* Edited by John Willett and Ralph Manheim. London: Methuen.

———. 1977. *"The Measures Taken" and Other Lehrstücke.* Translated by Carl R. Mueller. London: Methuen.

———. 1996. "Short Description of a New Technique of Acting Which Produces an Alienation Effect." Edited by Michael Huxley and Noel Witts. *The Twentieth-Century Performance Reader,* 99–111. London: Routledge.

———. 1997. *The Decision.* In *Collected Plays: Three,* edited and translated by John Willett, 61–91. London: Methuen.

———. 2003. "Theory of Pedagogies." In *Brecht on Art and Politics,* edited by Tom Kuhn and Steve Giles, 28–29. London: Methuen.

Breslau, Ralf. 2000. *"Ich möchte schreiben und schreiben": Margret Boveri—eine deutsche Journalistin. Ein Ausstellungskatalog (Ausstellung in der Staatsbibliothek zu Berlin anlässlich des 100. Geburtstags).* Berlin: Staatbibliothek zu Berlin.

Brewer, Garry D., and Martin Shubik. 1979. *The War Game: A Critique of Military Problem Solving.* Cambridge, Mass.: Harvard University Press.

Bröckers, Mathias. 2002. *Verschwörungen, Verschwörungstheorien und die Geheimnisse des 11.9.* Frankfurt am Main: Zweitausendeins.

Bryant, Peter [Peter Bryan George]. 1958. *Red Alert.* New York: Ace Books.

Bucher, Christine. 1998. "Envisioning the Imperial Nation in Kipling's *Kim.*" *Journal of Commonwealth and Postcolonial Studies* 5, no. 2 (Fall): 7–17.

Buono, Franco. 1980. "Nachwort." In Bertolt Brecht, *Gedichte für Städtebewohner,* edited by Franco Buono. Frankfurt am Main: Suhrkamp.

Bush, George W. 2001a. Address to the Nation, September 20. Full text at http://www.washingtonpost.com/wp-srv/nation/specials/attacked/transcripts/bushaddress_092001.html.

———. 2001b. Statement by H. E. Mr. George W. Bush President at 56th Session of the United Nations General Assembly, November 10, New York. Full text at http://www.un.org/webcast/ga/56/statements/011110usaE.htm.

Cambrelin, Alfred Léon. 1874. *Conférences sur les reconnaissances militaires.* Brussels: Bruylant-Christophe.

Cameron, Ewen D. 1960. "Production of Differential Amnesia as a Factor in the Treatment of Schizophrenia." *Comprehensive Psychiatry* 1: 26–34.

Cameron, Ewen, Leonard Levy, and Leonard Rubenstein. 1960. "Effects of Repetition of Verbal Signals upon Behaviour of Chronic Psychoneurotic Patients." *Journal of Mental Science* 106: 742–54.

Carmichael, Virginia. 1993. *Framing History: The Rosenberg Story and the Cold War.* Minneapolis: University of Minnesota Press.

Carroll, Lewis. 1939. "Through the Looking-Glass." In *The Complete Works of Lewis Carroll,* 126–250. London: Nonesuch Press. First published 1871.

Carson, Helen S. 1996. *Tom Clancy. A Critical Companion.* Westport, Conn.: Greenwood.

Castells, Manuel. 1996. *The Information Age.* Vol. 1, *The Rise of the Network Society.* Oxford: Blackwell.

Cebrowski, Arthur K., and John J. Garstka. 1998. "Network-Centric Warfare." *Proceedings of the United States Naval Institute* 24, no. 1: 28–35.

Chesterton, Gilbert Keith. 1908. *The Man Who Was Thursday: A Nightmare.* Bristol, U.K.: J. W. Arrowsmith.

Childers, Erskine. 1976. *A Unique Edition of "The Riddle of the Sands" with Historical Postscript by R. M. Bowker.* Old Bosham, U.K.: Bowker and Bertram.

———. 1978. *The Riddle of the Sands: A Record of Secret Service.* Reprint of 2nd ed. London: Penguin. First published 1903.

Christ, Ronald. 1969. *The Narrow Act: Borges' Art of Allusion.* New York: New York University Press.

———. 1974. "Borges at NYU." In *Prose for Borges,* edited by Charles Newman and Mary Kinzie, 396–411. Evanston, Ill.: Northwestern University Press.

Clancy, Tom. 1984. *The Hunt for Red October.* Annapolis, Md.: Naval Institute Press.

———. 1986. *Red Storm Rising.* New York: Putnam.

Clapmarius, Arnold. 1602. *Disputatio de iure publico excerpta ex C. Cornelio Tacito.* Altdorf, Switz.

———. [2009]. *De arcanis rerum publicarum libri sex.* Bremen, Ger.; repr., edited by Ursula Wehner, Stuttgart: Frommann-Holzboog. First published posthumously 1605.

Clarke, Richard A. 2005. *The Scorpion's Gate.* New York: Putnam.

Clausewitz, Carl von. 1976. *On War.* Edited by and translated by Michael Howard and Peter Paret. Princeton, N.J.: Princeton University Press.

Cohen, Eliot. 1980. "The 'No Fault' View in Intelligence." In *Intelligence Requirements for the 1980s: Analysis and Estimates,* edited by Roy Godson, 71–96. Washington, D.C.: National Strategy Information Center.

Colette, Sidonie-Gabrielle. 1957. *My Apprenticeships.* Translated by Helen Beauclerk. New York: Farrar, Straus and Giroux.

Condon, Richard. 2003. *The Manchurian Candidate.* Preface by Louis Menand. New York: Four Walls Eight Windows. First published 1959.

Connolly, K., and DeLillo, D. 2005. "An Interview with Don DeLillo." In *Conversations with Don DeLillo,* edited by Thomas DePietro, 25–39. Jackson: University Press of Mississippi.

Conolly, Arthur. 2002. *Journey to the North of India Through Russia, Persia and Afghanistan.* 2 vols. London: Richard Bentley; repr., New York: Elibron Classics. First published 1834.

Coover, Robert. 1998. *The Public Burning.* New York: Grove Press. First published 1977.

Cunningham, Karen. 2002. *Imaginary Betrayals: Subjectivity and the Discourses of Treason in Early Modern England.* Philadelphia: University of Pennsylvania Press.

Cuttler, S. H. 1981. *The Law of Treason and Treason Trials in Later Medieval France.* Cambridge: Cambridge University Press.

Dallin, David J. 1955. *Soviet Espionage.* New Haven, Conn.: Yale University Press.

Daub, Carl. 1816–18. *Judas Iskarioth oder das Böse im Verhältnis zum Guten.* 2 vols. Heidelberg: Mohr und Winter.

Dean, Jodi. 2002. *Publicity's Secret: How Technoculture Capitalizes in Democracy.* Ithaca, N.Y.: Cornell University Press.

DeCurtis, Anthony, and Don DeLillo. 1988. " 'An Outsider in This Society': An Interview with Don DeLillo." In *Conversations with Don DeLillo,* edited by Thomas DePietro, 52–68. Jackson: University Press of Mississippi.

Deighton, Len. 1967. *An Expensive Place to Die.* London: Jonathan Cape.

———. 1986. *Berlin Game—Mexico Set—London Match.* London: Grafton Books. First published 1983, 1984, and 1985, respectively.

Deleuze, Gilles. 1997. "Shame and Glory: T. E. Lawrence." In *Essays Critical and Clinical,* 115–25. Minneapolis: University of Minnesota Press.

Deleuze, Gilles, and Félix Guattari. 1987. *A Thousand Plateaus.* Translated by Brian Massumi. Minneapolis: University of Minnesota Press.

DeLillo, Don. 1983. "American Blood: A Journey Through the Labyrinth of Dallas and JFK." *Rolling Stone* 8 (December): 22–28.

———. 1991. *Libra.* New York: Penguin. First published 1988.

DePietro, Thomas, ed. 2005. *Conversations with Don DeLillo.* Jackson: University Press of Mississippi.

De Quincey, Thomas. 1873. "Judas Iscariot." In *Theological Essays and Other Papers,* 115–53. Boston: James R. Osgood.

Der Derian, James. 1992. *Antidiplomacy: Spies, Terror, Speed, and War.* Cambridge, Mass.: Blackwell.

Derrida, Jacques. 1984. "No Apocalypse, Not Now (Full Speed Ahead, Seven Missiles, Seven Missives)." *Diacritics* 14, no. 2: 20–31.

———. 1994. "To Do Justice to Freud: The History of Madness in the Age of Psychoanalysis." *Critical Inquiry* 20, no. 2: 227–66.

———. 2003. "Autoimmunity: Real and Symbolic Suicides—A Dialogue with Jacques Derrida." In Giovanna Borradori, *Philosophy in a Time of Terror,* 85–136. Chicago: University of Chicago Press.

Descartes, René. 2006. *Meditations, Objections, and Replies.* Edited and translated by Roger Ariew and Donald Cress. Indianapolis: Hackett.

Dewerpe, Alain. 1994. *Espion: Pour une anthropologie du secret d'État contemporain.* Paris: Gallimard.

Didi-Huberman, Georges. 2004. *Invention of Hysteria: Charcot and the Photographic Iconography of the Salpêtrière.* Translated by Alisa Hartz. Cambridge, Mass.: MIT Press.

Doherty, Thomas. 2003. *Cold War, Cool Medium: Television, McCarthyism, and American Culture.* New York: Columbia University Press.

Draper, Theodore. 1985. "Nuclear Temptations." In *The Nuclear Reader: Strategy, Weapons, War,* edited by Charles W. Kegley and Eugene R. Wittkopf, 21–37. New York: St. Martin's.

Drummond, Maldwin. 1985. *The Riddle.* London: Nautical Books.

Eddowes, Michael. 1977. *The Oswald File.* New York: Clarkson N. Potter.

Edney, Matthew H. 1993. "The Patronage of Science and the Creation of Imperial Space: The British Mapping of India, 1799–1843." *Cartographica* 30, no. 1: 61–67.

———. 1997. *Mapping an Empire: The Geographical Construction of British India, 1765–1843.* Chicago: University of Chicago Press.

Enzensberger, Hans Magnus. 1982. "Toward a Theory of Treason." In *Critical Essays.* Edited by Reinhold Grimm and Bruce Armstrong, 79–93. New York: Continuum.

Epstein, Edward J. 1966. *Inquest: The Warren Commission and the Establishment of the Truth.* London: Hutchinson.

Featherstone, Mark. 2001. "The Obscure Politics of Conspiracy Theory." In *The Age of Anxiety: Conspiracy Theory and the Human Sciences,* edited by Jane Parish and Mark Parker, 31–45. Oxford: Blackwell.

Feklisov, Alexander. 2001. *The Man Behind the Rosenbergs.* New York: Enigma.

Felger, Friedrich, and Walter Jost, eds. 1936. *Was wir vom Weltkrieg nicht wissen.* Leipzig: Fikentscher.

Fenster, Mark. 2008. *Conspiracy Theories: Secrecy and Power in American Culture.* Minneapolis: University of Minnesota Press.

Ferguson, Niall. 2002. *Empire: The Rise and Demise of the British World Order and Lessons for Global Power.* London: Penguin.

Fetzer, James H. 2003. *The Great Zapruder Film Hoax: Deceit and Deception in the Death of JFK.* Chicago: Catfeet Press.

———. 2007. *The 9/11 Conspiracy. The Scamming of America.* Chicago: Catfeet Press.

Fischer, Ruth. 1948. *Stalin and German Communism: A Study in the Origin of the State Party.* Introduction by Sidney B. Fay. Cambridge, Mass.: Harvard University Press.

Ford, Gerald R., and John Stiles. 1965. *Portrait of the Assassin.* New York: Ballantine.

Forster, E. M. 1951. *Two Cheers for Democracy.* London: Edward Arnold.

Foucault, Michel. 1977. *Discipline and Punish.* Translated by Alan Sheridan. New York: Vintage.

———. 1980. *The History of Sexuality.* Vol. 1, *An Introduction.* Translated by Robert Hurley. New York: Vintage.

———. 1987. "What Is an Author?" In *Twentieth-Century Literary Theory,* edited by Vassilis Lambropoulos and David Neal Miller, 124–42. Albany: State University of New York Press.

Fox Keller, Evelyn, and Lee A. Segel. 1970. "Initiation of Slime Mold Aggregation Viewed as an Instability." *Journal of Theoretical Biology* 26, no. 3 (March): 399–415.

Franco, Jean. 1981. "The Utopia of a Tired Man: Jorge Luis Borges." *Social Text* 2, no. 1: 52–78.

Frankenheimer, John. 1962. *The Manchurian Candidate.* Directed by John Frankenheimer. Written by George Axelrod from the novel by Richard Condon. Starring Frank Sinatra, Lawrence Harvey, and Angela Lansbury. United Artists.

Freud, Sigmund. 1962. "Analysis of a Case of Chronic Paranoia." In *The Standard Edition of the Complete Psychological Works of Sigmund Freud, Volume 3 (1893–1899): Early Psycho-Analytic Publications.* Edited by James Strachey, 174–88. London: Hogarth Press.

———. 1982. "Über den psychischen Mechanismus hysterischer Phänomene." *Studienausgabe,* vol. 6, 9–24. Frankfurt am Main: Fischer Taschenbuch. First published 1893.

Friedrich, Carl Joachim. 1957. *Constitutional Reason of State: The Survival of the Constitutional Order.* Providence, R.I.: Brown University Press.

———. 1972. *The Pathology of Politics: Violence, Betrayal, Corruption, Secrecy, and Propaganda.* New York: Harper and Row.

Gaghan, Stephen. 2005. *Syriana.* Directed by Stephen Gaghan. Written by Stephen Gaghan, based on the memoir of Robert Baer, *See No Evil.* Starring George Clooney, Matt Damon, Amanda Peet, and Alexander Siddig. Warner Bros.

Galison, Peter. 2004. "Removing Knowledge." *Critical Inquiry* 31 (Fall): 229–43.

Garrison, Jim. 1988. *On the Trail of the Assassins: My Investigation and Prosecution of the Murder of President Kennedy.* New York: Sheridan.

Gellert, Inge, Gerd Koch, and Florian Vaßen, eds. 1998. *Maßnehmen: Die Maßnahme*. Berlin: Theater der Zeit, Recherchen 1.

Gempp, Friedrich. 1939–43. Geheimer Nachrichtendienst und Spionageabwehr des Heeres, Typoskript für den internen Dienstgebrauch, today at Bundesarchiv/Militärarchiv Potsdam.

GeoEye home page, http://www.geoeye.com/GeoEye101/satellite-imagery/high-resolution-imagery.aspx.

George, Stefan, and Friedrich Gundolf. 1962. *Briefwechsel*. Edited by Robert Böhringer and Georg Landmann. Munich: Küpper.

Gerecht, Reuel Marc. 2001. "The Counterterrorist Myth." *Atlantic Monthly* (July/August 2001). http://www.theatlantic.com/magazine/archive/2001/07/the-counterterrorist-myth/302263/.

Gibson, William. 2012. *Distrust That Particular Flavor*. New York: Putnam.

Giffin, Sidney F. 1965. *The Crisis Game: Simulating International Conflict*. New York: Doubleday.

Giles, Lionel. 1910. *On the Art of War: The Oldest Military Treatise in the World*. London: Luzac.

Ginzburg, Carlo. 1988. "Clues: Morelli, Freud and Sherlock Holmes." In *The Sign of Three*, edited by Umberto Eco and Thomas A. Sebeok, 81–118. Bloomington: Indiana University Press.

Godson, Roy, ed. 1980. *Intelligence Requirements for the 1980s: Analysis and Estimates*. Washington, D.C.: National Strategy Information Center.

———. 1989. *Intelligence Requirements for the 1990s: Collection, Analysis, Counterintelligence, and Covert Action*. Lexington, Mass.: Lexington Books.

Grady, James. 1974. *Six Days of the Condor*. New York: Putnam.

Greene, Graham. 1939. *The Confidential Agent*. London: Heinemann.

———. 1971. *Our Man in Havana*. Harmondsworth, U.K.: Penguin. First published 1958.

———. 1978. *The Ministry of Fear*. Harmondsworth, U.K.: Penguin. First published 1943.

———. 1988. "Interview with Maria Couto." In *Graham Greene: On the Frontier—Politics and Religion in the Novels*, 209. Basingstoke, U.K.: Macmillan.

———. 1999. *The Human Factor*. London: Vintage. First published 1978.

Griffin, David Ray. 2007. *Debunking 9/11 Debunking: An Answer to "Popular Mechanics" and Other Defenders of the Official Conspiracy Theory*. Northampton, Mass.: Olive Branch Press.

———. 2008. *9/11 Contradictions: An Open Letter to Congress and the Press*. Northampton, Mass.: Olive Branch Press.

Groh, Dieter. 1987. "The Temptations of Conspiracy Theory, or: Why Do Bad Things Happen to Good People?" In *Changing Conceptions of Conspiracy*, edited by Carl F. Graumann and Serge Moscovici, 1–37. New York: Springer.

Habermas, Jürgen. 1956. "Der Verrat und die Maßstäbe: Wenn Jungkonservative alt werden." *Deutsche Universitätszeitung* 11, no. 19: 8–11.

Hahn, Torsten. 2004. "Z wie Zombie oder V wie Verräter? Manchurian Candidate—Sleeper—Subliminal Man: Mind Control und Literatur." In *Freund,*

Feind und Verrat: Das politische Feld der Medien, edited by Cornelia Epping-Jäger, Torsten Hahn, and Erhard Schüttpelz, 118–37. Cologne: Dumont.

Handel, Michael I. 2001. *Masters of War: Classical Strategic Thought.* 3rd ed. London: Frank Cass.

Hardt, Michael, and Antonio Negri. 2004. *Multitude: War and Democracy in the Age of Empire.* New York: Penguin.

Harries, Jill. 2007. *Law and Crime in the Roman World.* Cambridge: Cambridge University Press.

Haverkamp, Anselm. 1991. "Kryptische Subjektivität: Archäologie des Lyrisch-Individuellen." In *Laub voll Trauer: Hölderlins späte Allegorie,* 15–29. Munich: Fink.

———. 1993. "Lichtbild: Das Bildgedächtnis der Photographie." In *Memoria—vergessen und erinnern: Poetik und Hermeneutik XV,* edited by Anselm Haverkamp and Renate Lachmann, 47–66. Munich: Fink.

———. 2004. "Das Ende politischer Theologie." In *Hamlet: Hypothek der Macht,* 2nd ed., 93–108. Berlin: Kadmos.

Hecht, Werner. 1997. *Brecht-Chronik.* Frankfurt am Main: Suhrkamp.

Henderson, David. 1915. *The Art of Reconnaissance.* London: Murray.

Hepburn, Allan. 2005. *Intrigue: Espionage and Culture.* New Haven, Conn.: Yale University Press.

Herbert, Shannon. 2010. "Playing the Historical Record: DeLillo's 'Libra' and the Kennedy Archive." *Twentieth Century Literature* 56, no. 3 (Fall): 287–317.

Hering, Sabine, and Kurt Schilde. 1995. *Kampfname Ruth Fischer: Wandlungen einer deutschen Kommunistin.* Frankfurt am Main: Dipa.

Herman, Michael. 1996. *Intelligence Power in Peace and War.* Cambridge: Cambridge University Press.

Herrmann, Walter. 1956. *Operation Intrigue.* New York: Avon.

Hewitt, Steve. 2010. *Snitch: A History of the Modern Intelligence Informer.* New York: Continuum.

Hieber, Hanne. 2005. "'Mademoiselle Docteur': The Life and Service of Imperial Germany's Only Female Intelligence Officer." *Journal of Intelligence History* 5 (Winter): 91–108.

Hindersmann, Jost. 1995. *Der britische Spionageroman: Vom Imperialismus bis zum Ende des Kalten Krieges.* Darmstadt, Ger.: Wissenschaftliche Buchgesellschaft.

Hirschfeld, Magnus, ed. 1930. *Sittengeschichte des Weltkriegs.* Leipzig: Verlag für Sexualwissenschaft Schneider.

———. 1941. *The Sexual History of the World War.* New York: Cadillac Publishing.

Hitz, Frederick. 2004. *The Great Game: The Myth and Reality of Espionage.* New York: Knopf.

Hobbes, Thomas. 1976. *Leviathan.* Harmondsworth, U.K.: Penguin Books.

Hoffman, Tod. 2001. *Le Carré's Landscape.* Montréal: McGill-Queens University Press.

Hofstadter, Richard. 1965. *The Paranoid Style in American Politics and Other Essays.* New York: Knopf.

Holloway, David. 1994. *Stalin and the Bomb.* New Haven, Conn.: Yale University Press.
Hoover, J. Edgar. 1958. *Masters of Deceit: The Story of Communism in America and How to Fight It.* New York: Holt, Rinehart and Winston.
Hopkirk, Peter. 1990. *The Great Game: On Secret Service in High Asia.* London: Murray.
———. 1997. *Quest for Kim: In Search of Kipling's Great Game.* Ann Arbor: University of Michigan Press.
Horn, Eva. 2001. "Die Regel der Ausnahme: Revolutionäre Souveränität und bloßes Leben in Brechts Maßnahme." *Deutsche Vierteljahrsschrift* 4: 680–709.
———. 2003a. "Knowing the Enemy: The Epistemology of Secret Intelligence." *Grey Room,* no. 11 (May): 59–85.
———. 2003b. "Politische Störungen: Streik, Sabotage, Staatsstreich." In *Signale der Störung,* edited by Albert Kümmel and Erhard Schüttpelz, 321–34. Munich: Fink.
———. 2004. "'Waldgänger,' Traitor, Partisan: Figures of Political Irregularity in West German Postwar Thought." *New Centennial Review* 4, no. 3 (special issue titled "Carl Schmitt: Theory of the Partisan," edited by David Johnson): 125–43.
———. 2006. "Actors/Agents: Brecht and the Politics of Secrecy." *Grey Room,* no. 24, Special Issue (Summer 2006): 38–55.
———. 2007. "'Sterbt, aber lernt': Thanatopolitik in Brechts Lehrstücken." In *Das Totalitäre der Klassischen Moderne: Politische Souveränität der Literatur 1900–1933,* edited by Uwe Hebekus and Ingo Stöckmann, 311–36. Munich: Fink.
———. 2008a. "'Like Actors on a Foreign Theatre': Kulturelle Mimikry im Great Game." In *Mimikry: Gefährlicher Luxus zwischen Kultur und Natur,* edited by Andreas Becker, Martin Doll, Serjoscha Wiemer, and Anke Zechner, 110–19. Schliengen, Ger.: Edition Argus.
———. 2008b. "Media of Conspiracy: Love and Surveillance in Fritz Lang and Florian Henkel von Donnersmarcks." In *Dark Powers: Conspiracies and Conspiracy Theory in History and Fiction,* edited by Eva Horn and Anson Rabinbach, 127–44. Special edition of *New German Critique* 103, February 2008.
———. 2009a. "Borges' Duels: Friends, Enemies and the Fictions of History." In *Reading with Borges,* edited by David Johnson and William Egginton, 175–200. Aurora, Colo.: Davies Group.
———. 2009b. "Das Leben ein Schwarm: Emergenz und Evolution in moderner Science Fiction." In *Schwärme—Kollektive ohne Zentrum. Eine Wissensgeschichte zwischen Leben und Information,* edited by Eva Horn and Lucas M. Gisi, 101–24. Bielefeld, Ger.: Transcript.
———. 2011. "Experts or Impostors? Blindness and Insight in Secret Intelligence." In *Expert Cultures in Central Eastern Europe: The Internationalization of Knowledge and the Transformation of Nation States Since World War I,* edited by Martin Kohlrausch, Katrin Steffen, and Stefan Wiederkehr, 23–31. Osnabrück, Ger.: Fibre.
Horn, Eva, Ulrich Bröckling, and Stefan Kaufmann, eds. 2002. *Grenzverletzer.* Berlin: Kadmos Kulturverlag.
Horn, Eva, and Lucas M. Gisi, eds. 2009. *Schwärme-Kollektive ohne Zentrum: Eine Wissensgeschichte zwischen Leben und Information.* Bielefeld, Ger.: Transcript.

Horn, Eva, and Anson Rabinbach. 2008. "Introduction." In *Dark Powers: Conspiracies and Conspiracy Theory in History and Fiction,* edited by Eva Horn and Anson Rabinbach, 1–8. *New German Critique* 103, February.

House Select Committee on Assassinations [HSCA]. 1979. *Final Report of the Select Committee on Assassinations.* Washington, D.C.: United States Government Printing Office.

Howard, Michael. 1976. *War in European History.* Oxford: Oxford University Press.

Huggan, Graham. 1990. "Decolonizing the Map: Post-Colonialism, Post-Structuralism and the Cartographic Connection." In *Past the Last Post: Theorizing Post-Colonialism and Post-Modernism,* edited by Ian Adam and Helen Tiffin, 125–38. Calgary, Alta: University of Calgary Press.

Hughes, Jeff. 2002. *The Manhattan Project: Big Science and the Atom Bomb.* Cambridge, U.K.: Icon Books.

Hunter, Edward. 1951. *Brainwashing in Red China.* New York: Vanguard Press.

———. 1956. *Brainwashing: The Story of the Men Who Defied It.* New York: Farrar, Straus and Cudahy.

Hutchinson, Stuart. 2001. "Don DeLillo's *Libra* and the Real." *Cambridge Quarterly* 30, no. 2: 117–31.

Hyde, H. Montgomery. 1980. *The Atom Bomb Spies.* New York: Atheneum.

Ingram, Edward. 1984. *In Defence of British India: Great Britain in the Middle East, 1775–1842.* London: Frank Cass.

Irenaeus, Saint. 1992. *Against the Heresies.* Translated and annotated by Dominic Unger and John Dillon. Mahwah, N.J.: Newman Press.

Irenaeus von Lyon. 1993. *Epideixis/Adversus Haereses.* Bilingual edition in Latin and German. Translated by Norbert Brox. Freiburg im Breisgau, Ger.: Herder.

Irwin, John T. 1994. *A Mystery to a Solution: Poe, Borges, and the Analytic Detective Story.* Baltimore: Johns Hopkins University Press.

Isaacs, Jeremy, and Taylor Downing. 1998. *Cold War: An Illustrated History, 1945–1991.* Boston: Little, Brown.

Jameson, Fredric. 1988. "Cognitive Mapping." In *Marxism and the Interpretation of Culture,* edited by Cary Nelson and Lawrence Grossberg, 347–60. London: Macmillan.

Joffe, Joseph. 2002. "Hubs, Spokes, and Public Goods." *National Interest,* no. 69 (Fall): 17–20. Full text at http://belfercenter.ksg.harvard.edu/files/joffe.pdf.

Johnson, Loch. 2007. "Lawmakers and Spies: Congressional Oversight of Intelligence in the United States." In *Geheimhaltung und Transparenz: Demokratische Kontrolle der Geheimdienste im internationalen Vergleich,* edited by Wolbert K. Schmidt, Ulrike Poppe, Wolfgang Krieger, and Helmut Müller-Enberg, 173–92. Münster, Ger.: Lit Verlag.

Johnson, Stephen. 2001. *Emergence: The Connected Lives of Ants, Brains, Cities, and Software.* New York: Scribner.

Johnston, John. 1998. *Information Multiplicity: American Fiction in the Age of Media Saturation.* Baltimore: Johns Hopkins University Press.

Jost, Roland. 1998. "Experiment und Fragment: Die Maßnahme im Kontext der literarischen Moderne." In *Maßnehmen: Die Maßnahme,* edited by Inge Gellert, Gerd Koch, and Florian Vaßen, 72–82. Berlin: Theater der Zeit, Recherchen 1.

Jünger, Ernst. 1954. "The Retreat into the Forest." *Confluence* 3, no. 2: 127–42.
———. 1960. "Der Waldgang." In *Werke,* vol. 5, *Essays I,* 291–388. Stuttgart: Klett.
Jungk, Robert. 1958. *Brighter Than a Thousand Suns: A Personal History of the Atomic Scientists.* Translated by James Cleugh. San Diego: Harcourt Brace.
Jussawalla, Feroza. 1998. "(Re)reading *Kim:* Defining Kipling's Masterpiece as Postcolonial." *Journal of Commonwealth and Postcolonial Studies* 5, no. 2 (Fall): 122–30.
Kahn, Herman. 1961. *On Thermonuclear War.* Princeton, N.J.: Princeton University Press.
———. 1962. *Thinking About the Unthinkable.* New York: Horizon Press.
Kaiser, Joachim. 1983. "Brechts *Maßnahme.*" In *Drama und Theater im 20. Jahrhundert,* edited by Hans Dietrich Irmscher and Werner Keller, 169–76. Göttigen, Ger.: Vandenhoeck.
Kantorowicz, Ernst H. 1965. "Mysteries of State: An Absolutist Concept and Its Late Medieval Origins." In *Selected Studies,* 381–98. New York: J. J. Augustin.
Kaplan, Carola M. 1995. "Conquest as Literature, Literature as Conquest: T. E. Lawrence's Artistic Campaign in *Seven Pillars of Wisdom.*" *Texas Studies in Literature and Language* 37, no. 1 (Spring): 72–97.
Kasser, Rodolphe, Marvin Meyer, and Gregor Wurst, eds. 2006. *The Gospel of Judas: From Codex Tchacos.* Washington, D.C.: National Geographic.
Kaufmann, Bernd, Eckart Reisener, Dieter Schwips, and Walter Henri. 1993. *Der Nachrichtendienst der KPD 1919–1937.* Berlin: Dietz.
Kautsky, Karl. 1953. *The Foundations of Christianity.* Translated by Henry F. Mins. New York: Russell and Russell.
Kazantzakis, Nikos. 1960. *The Last Temptation of Christ.* Translated by P. A. Bien. New York: Simon and Schuster.
Kelly, Kevin. 1994. *Out of Control: The Rise of Neo-Biological Civilization.* Reading, Mass.: Addison-Wesley.
Kelly, Tobias, and Sharika Thiranagama. 2010. "Introduction: Specters of Treason." In *Traitors: Suspicion, Intimacy, and the Ethics of State-Building,* 1–23. Philadelphia: University of Pennsylvania Press.
Kennan, George F. 1979. *The Decline of Bismarck's European Order: Franco-Russian Relations, 1875–1890.* Princeton, N.J.: Princeton University Press.
Kent, Sherman. 1965. *Strategic Intelligence for American World Policy.* Hamden, Conn.: Archon Books. First published 1949.
Killen, Andreas. 2011. "*Homo pavlovius:* Cinema, Conditioning, and the Cold War Subject." *Grey Room,* no. 45 (Fall): 42–59.
Killen, Andreas, and Stefan Andriopoulos. 2011. "Editor's Introduction: On Brainwashing. Mind Control, Media, and Warfare." *Grey Room,* no. 45 (Fall): 7–17.
Kinkead-Weekes, Mark. 1964. "Vision in Kipling's Novels." In *Kipling's Mind and Art,* edited by Andrew Rutherford, 197–234. Stanford, Calif.: Stanford University Press.
Kipling, Rudyard. 1987. *Kim.* Edited and with an introduction by Edward Said. London: Penguin. First published 1901.
Kippenberg, Hans G., and Tilman Seidensticker. 2006. *The 9/11 Handbook: Annotated Translation and Interpretation of the Attacker's Spiritual Manual.* London: Equinox.

Kittler, Friedrich A. 1986. "Über die Kunst, mit Vögeln zu jagen: The Maltese Falcon von Dashiell Hammett." In *Phantasie und Deutung: Psychologisches Verstehen von Literatur und Film,* edited by Wolfram Mauser, 299–314. Würzburg, Ger.: Königshausen und Neumann.

———. 1993. "Draculas Vermächtnis." In *Draculas Vermächtnis: Technische Schriften,* 11–57. Leipzig: Reclam.

———. 1999. *Gramophone, Film, Typewriter.* Translated with an introduction by Geoffrey Winthrop-Young and Michael Wutz. Stanford, Calif.: Stanford University Press.

Klassen, William. 1999. *Judas: Betrayer or Friend of Jesus?* Minneapolis, Minn.: Fortress Press.

Klauck, Hans-Josef. 1987. *Judas—ein Jünger des Herrn.* Freiburg im Breisgau, Ger.: Herder.

Klopstock, Friedrich Gottlieb. 1981. *Ausgewählte Werke.* Vol. 1. Edited by Karl August Schleiden. Munich: Hanser.

Kloth, Michael. 2004. "Wieder einer, wieder einer!" In *Der Erste Weltkrieg: Die Urkatastrophe des 20. Jahrhunderts,* edited by Stephan Burgdorff and Klaus Wiegrefe Klaus, 162–66. Munich: DVA.

Knight, Peter. 2000. *Conspiracy Culture.* London: Routledge.

———. 2002. "Introduction." In *Conspiracy Nation: The Politics of Paranoia in Postwar America,* edited by Peter Knight, 1–77. New York: New York University Press.

———, ed. 2003. *Conspiracy Theories in American History: An Encyclopedia.* Santa Barbara, Calif.: ABC Clio.

———. 2007. *The Kennedy Assassination.* Edinburgh: Edinburgh University Press.

———. 2008. "'Outrageous Conspiracy Theories': Popular and Official Responses to 9/11 in Germany and the United States." In *Dark Powers: Conspiracies and Conspiracy Theory in History and Fiction,* edited by Eva Horn and Anson Rabinbach, 165–93. *New German Critique* 103, February 2008.

Knightley, Philipp. 1988. *Philby: The Life and Views of the KGB Masterspy.* London: Deutsch.

Koestler, Arthur. 1940. *Darkness at Noon.* London: Jonathan Cape, Macmillan.

Korda, Michael. 2010. *Hero: The Life and Legend of Lawrence of Arabia.* New York: HarperCollins.

Koselleck, Reinhart. 1988. *Critique and Crisis: Enlightenment and the Pathogenesis of Modern Society.* Oxford: Berg.

Kostelanetz, Richard. 1968. "One-Man Think Tank." *New York Times Sunday Magazine,* December 1.

Kraus, Karl. 1906. "Der Schmock und die Bajadere." *Die Fackel,* nos. 214–15, December 22.

Krivitsky, Walter. 1985. *In Stalin's Secret Service.* Frederick, Md.: University Publications of America.

Kubrick, Stanley. 1964. *Dr. Strangelove: or How I Learned to Stop Worrying and Love the Bomb.* Directed by Stanley Kubrick. Written by Stanley Kubrick, Terry Southern, and Peter George. Columbia Pictures.

Kupferman, Fred. 1992. *Mata Hari: Träume und Lügen.* Berlin: Aufbau.

Kurella, Alfred. 1931. "Ein Versuch mit nicht ganz tauglichen Mitteln." *Literatur der Weltrevolution,* no. 4: 100–109.

Lacan, Jacques. 2006. *Écrits: The First Complete Edition in English*. Translated by Bruce Fink et al. New York: W. W. Norton.

Ladoux, Georges. 1937. *Mes souvenirs (Contre-espionnage), receullis et mis au point par Michel Berger*. Paris: Editions de la France.

Lane, Mark. 1966. *Rush to Judgment: A Critique of the Warren Commission's Inquiry into the Murders of President John F. Kennedy, Officer J. D. Tippit, and Lee Harvey Oswald*. Introduction by Hugh Trevor-Roper. New York: Holt, Rinehart and Winston.

Laqueur, Walter. *A World of Secrets: The Uses and Limits of Intelligence*. New York: Basic Books.

Larson, Deborah Welch. 1997. *Anatomy of Mistrust: U.S.-Soviet Relations During the Cold War*. Ithaca, N.Y.: Cornell University Press.

Lawrence, Arnold Walter. 1962. *Letters to T. E. Lawrence*. London: Jonathan Cape.

Lawrence, Thomas Edward. 1991. *Seven Pillars of Wisdom: A Triumph*. New York: Anchor Books. First published 1926.

Le Carré, John. 1966. "To Russia, with Greetings: An Open Letter to the *Moscow Literary Gazette*." *Encounter* 26: 3–6.

———. 1968. "Introduction." In Bruce Page, Davis Leitch, and Philipp Knightley, *Philby: The Spy Who Betrayed a Generation*, 9–24. London: Deutsch.

———. 1983. *The Little Drummer Girl*. New York: Simon and Schuster.

———. 1986. *A Perfect Spy*. London: Hodder and Stoughton.

———. 1991. *The Secret Pilgrim*. London: Hodder and Stoughton.

———. 1992. *Smiley's People*. London: Hodder and Stoughton. First published 1979.

———. 1995. *The Looking-Glass War*. London: Hodder and Stoughton. First published 1965.

———. 1996. *The Tailor of Panama*. New York: Viking.

———. 2000a. *The Honourable Schoolboy*. New York: Pocket Books. First published 1977.

———. 2000b. *Tinker, Tailor, Soldier, Spy*. New York: Pocket Books. First published 1974.

———. 2001. *The Spy Who Came In from the Cold*. New York: Pocket Books. First published 1963.

———. 2010. *Our Kind of Traitor*. New York: Viking.

Le Clair, Tom. 1989. *The Art of Excess: Masters in Contemporary Fiction*. Urbana: University of Illinois Press.

Lemon, Rebecca. 2006. *Treason by Words: Literature, Law, and Rebellion in Shakespeare's England*. Ithaca, N.Y.: Cornell University Press.

Lemov, Rebecca. 2011. "Brainwashing's Avatar: The Curious Career of Dr. Ewen Cameron." *Grey Room*, no. 45 (Fall): 61–87.

Lenin, Vladimir Ilich. 1966. *Collected Works*. Vol. 31 (April–December 1920). Translated by Julius Katzer. Moscow: Progress.

Lentricchia, Frank. 1991. "Libra as Postmodern Critique." In *Introducing Don DeLillo*, edited by Frank Lentricchia, 192–215. Durham, N.C.: Duke University Press.

Lenz, Bernd. 1987. *Factifiction: Agentenspiele wie in der Realität. Wirklichkeitsanspruch und Wirklichkeitsgehalt des Agentenromans*. Heidelberg: Universitätsverlag Carl Winter.

Lethen, Helmut. 1992. "Brechts Hand-Orakel." *Brecht-Jahrbuch* no. 17, *The Other Brecht I:* 77–99.

———. 2002. *Cool Conduct: The Culture of Distance in Weimar Germany.* Translated by Don Reneau. Berkeley: University of California Press.

Lettow-Vorbeck, Paul von, ed. 1931. *Die Weltkriegsspionage.* Munich: Justin Moser.

Lewal, Jules-Louis. 1876. *Études de guerre: Tactique de marche.* Paris: J. Dumaine.

Liddell Hart, Basil. 1937. *Lawrence of Arabia.* New York: Halcyon House. First published 1934.

Lifton, David S. 1981. *Best Evidence: Disguise and Deception in the Assassination of John F. Kennedy.* New York: Macmillan.

Lindner, Burkhardt. 1993. "Das Messer und die Schrift: Für eine Revision der 'Lehrstückperiode.'" *Brecht-Jahrbuch* no. 18, *The Other Brecht II:* 43–57.

Littell, Robert. 1973. *The Defection of A. J. Lewinter.* Boston: Houghton Mifflin.

Löwith, Karl. 1949. *Meaning of History.* Chicago: University of Chicago Press.

Lüders, Christine. 1997. *Apropos Mata Hari.* Frankfurt am Main: Verlag Neue Kritik.

Luhmann, Niklas. 1997. "Geheimnis, Zeit und Ewigkeit." In Niklas Luhmann and Peter Fuchs, *Reden und Schweigen,* 101–37. Frankfurt am Main: Suhrkamp.

Lüthi, Kurt. 1955. *Judas Iskarioth.* Zürich: Zwingli-Verlag.

MacCaffery, Larry. 1982. *The Metafictional Muse: The Works of Robert Coover, Donald Barthelme, and William H. Gass.* Pittsburgh: University of Pittsburgh Press.

Macho, Thomas, and Annette Wunschel. 2004. *Science and Fiction: Über Gedankenexperimente in Wissenschaft, Philosophie und Literatur.* Frankfurt am Main: Fischer Taschenbuch.

Mackinder, Halford. 1904. "The Geographical Pivot of History." *Geographical Journal,* no. 23: 421–37.

Mahan, Alfred Thayer. 1918. *The Influence of Sea Power upon History, 1660–1783.* Boston: Little, Brown.

Mahle, Melissa Boyle. 2005. *Denial and Deception: An Insider's View of the CIA.* New York: Nation Books.

Mailer, Norman. 1995. *Oswald's Tale: An American Mystery.* New York: Random House.

Malaparte, Curzio. 1932. *Coup d'État: The Technique of Revolution.* Translated by Sylvia Saunders. New York: Dutton.

Mangan, James Anthony. 1986. *The Games Ethic and Imperialism.* Middlesex, U.K.: Viking.

Mann, Golo. 1956. "Mit der Tagnachtlampe: Zu Margret Boveris Buch über Verrat und Verräter." *Der Monat* (November): 63–65.

Marcus, Greil. 2002. *The Manchurian Candidate.* London: British Film Institute.

Marin, Louis. 1998. "The Logic of Secrecy." In *Cross-Readings,* translated by Jane Maria Todd, 195–204. Atlantic Highlands, N.J.: Humanities Press.

Marks, John. 1979. *The Search for the "Manchurian Candidate": The CIA and Mind Control.* New York: New York Times Books.

Marrs, Jim. 1990. *Crossfire: The Plot That Killed Kennedy.* New York: Carroll and Graf.

———. 2006. *The Terror Conspiracy: Deception, 9/11, and the Loss of Liberty.* New York: Disinformation.

———. 2011. *The Terror Conspiracy Revisited: What Really Happened on 9/11 and Why We Are Still Paying the Price.* New York: Disinformation.

Marx, Karl, and Frederick Engels. 1975. *Collected Works.* Vol. 35, *Capital,* vol. 1. London: Lawrence and Wishart.

Masters, Anthony. 1987. *Literary Agents: The Novelist as Spy.* Oxford: Blackwell.

Matin, A. Michael. 1999. "'The Hun Is at the Gate!': Historicizing Kipling's Militaristic Rhetoric, from the Imperial Periphery to the National Center." *Studies in the Novel,* no. 31.3 (Fall): 317–56 and no. 31.4 (Winter): 432–70.

Maugham, William Somerset. 1967. *Ashenden.* London: Heineman.

McLuhan, Marshall. 1964. *Understanding Media: The Extensions of Man.* New York: McGraw-Hill.

McNeilly, Mark. 2001. *Sun Tzu and the Art of Modern Warfare.* New York: Oxford University Press.

Meinecke, Friedrich. 1957. *Machiavellism: The Doctrine of Raison d'État and Its Place in Modern History.* Translated by Douglas Scott. London: Routledge and Paul.

Melley, Timothy. 2000. *Empire of Conspiracy: The Culture of Paranoia in Postwar America.* Ithaca, N.Y.: Cornell University Press.

Merrell, Floyd. 1991. *Unthinking Thinking: Jorge Luis Borges, Mathematics, and the New Physics.* West Lafayette, Ind.: Purdue University Press.

Meyssan, Thierry. 2002. *9/11: The Big Lie.* London: Carnot.

Millard, Bill. 2000. "The Fable of the Ants: Myopic Interactions in DeLillo's *Libra.*" In *Critical Essays on Don DeLillo,* edited by Hugh Ruppersburg and Tim Engels, 213–28. New York: G. K. Hall.

Millington, Mark. 1988. "The Importance of Being Albert or the Borgesian Alternative to History." *Ibero-Amerikanisches Archiv* 14, no. 2: 173–86.

Montgomerie, Thomas G. 1866. "On the Geographical Position of Yarkund, and Some Other Places in Central Asia." *Journal of the Royal Geographical Society* 36: 157–72.

———. 1875. "Journey to Shigatze, in Tibet, and Return by Dingri-Maidan into Nepaul, in 1871, by the Native Explorer Nr. 9." *Journal of the Royal Geographical Society* 45: 330–49.

Montgomerie, Thomas G., and Pundit. 1868. "Report of a Route-Survey Made by Pundit, from Nepal to Lhasa, and Thence Through the Upper Valley of the Brahmaputra to Its Source." *Journal of the Royal Geographical Society* 38: 129–219.

Morgan, Gerald. 1973. "Myth and Reality in the Great Game." *Asian Affairs* 60 (February): 55–66.

Morsey, Konrad. 1976. *T. E. Lawrence und der arabische Aufstand 1916/18.* Osnabrück, Ger.: Biblio.

———. 1984. "T. E. Lawrence: Strategist." In *The T. E. Lawrence Puzzle,* edited by Stephen E. Tabachnick, 185–203. Athens: University of Georgia Press.

Moss, Norman. 1987. *Klaus Fuchs: The Man Who Stole the Atom Bomb.* London: Grafton.

Mott, Christopher. 2000. "*Libra* and the Subject of History." In *Critical Essays on Don DeLillo,* edited by Hugh Ruppersburg and Tim Engels, 229–44. New York: G. K. Hall.

Mühr, Alfred. 1931. "Koste es was es wolle." In *Die Weltkriegsspionage,* edited by Paul von Lettow-Vorbeck, 405–12. Munich: Justin Moser.

Mühsam, Erich. 1994. *Tagebücher 1910–1924.* Edited by Chris Hirte. Munich: dtv.

Müller, Jan-Dirk. 2007. *Rules for the Endgame: The World of the "Nibelungenlied."* Translated by William Whobrey. Baltimore: Johns Hopkins University Press.

Murray, Robert K. 1955. *Red Scare: A Study in National Hysteria, 1919–1920.* Minneapolis: University of Minnesota Press.

Nägele, Rainer. 1992. "Augenblicke: Eingriffe—Brechts Ästhetik der Wahrnehmung." *Brecht Jahrbuch* no. 17, *The Other Brecht I:* 29–52.

Nakagaki, Toshiyuki, Hiroyasu Yamada, and Ágota Tóth. 2000. "Intelligence: Maze-Solving by an Amoeboid Organism." *Nature* 407 (September 28): 493–96.

National Security Strategy of the United States of America. 2002. September. Online at http://www.state.gov/documents/organization/63562.pdf.

Nelson, Anna Kasten. 1998. "The John F. Kennedy Assassination Records Review Board." In *A Culture of Secrecy: The Government Versus the People's Right to Know,* edited by Athan G. Theoharis, 211–31. Lawrence: University of Kansas Press.

Nelson, Thomas Allen. 1982. *Kubrick: Inside an Artist's Maze.* Bloomington: Indiana University Press.

Neuberg, A. [pseudonym]. 1928. *Der bewaffnete Aufstand: Versuch einer theoretischen Darstellung.* Zürich: Otto Meyer.

———. 1970. *Armed Insurrection.* Translated by Quintin Hoare. London: NLB.

Neville, John F. 1995. *The Press, the Rosenbergs, and the Cold War.* Westport, Conn.: Praeger.

Nollau, Günther. 1965. "Nichts ist authentisch. Rezension zu John le Carré: *Der Spion, der aus der Kälte kam.*" *Der Spiegel* no. 4 (no pages given).

Nowosielsky, Ray, and John Duffy. 2006. *9/11: Press for Truth,* documentary based on the Complete 9/11 Timeline by Paul Thompson, DVD. Online at http://www.911press-fortruth.com/.

Noya, José Liste. 2004. "Naming the Secret: Don DeLillo's *Libra.*" *Contemporary Literature* 45, no. 2: 239–75.

Nutter, John Jacob. 2000. *The CIA's Black Ops: Covert Action, Foreign Policy, and Democracy.* Amherst: Prometheus Books.

Ó Tuathail, Geraóid, Simon Dalby, and Paul Routledge, eds. 1998. *The Geopolitics Reader.* London: Routledge.

Ocampo, Victoria. 1947. *338171 T.E. (Lawrence d'Arabie).* Paris: Gallimard.

Okun, Rob A., ed. 1988. *The Rosenbergs: Collected Visions of Artists and Writers.* New York: Universe Books.

Orlov, Aleksandr. 1954. *The Secret History of Stalin's Crimes.* London: Jarrolds.

Orne, Martin T. 1961. "The Potential Uses of Hypnosis in Interrogation." In *The Manipulation of Human Behavior,* edited by Albert Biderman and Herbert Zimmer, 169–215. New York: Wiley.

Packard, Vance. 1957. *The Hidden Persuaders.* New York: David McKay.

Page, Bruce, David Leitch, and Philipp Knightley. 1968. *Philby: The Spy Who Betrayed a Generation.* London: Deutsch.

Panek, Leroy L. 1981. *The Special Branch: The British Spy Novel, 1890–1980.* Bowling Green, Ohio: Bowling Green University Popular Press.

Parker, E. D. 1898. *An Outline of Reconnaissance.* London: E. Stanford.

Pfaffenroth, Kim 2001. *Judas: Images of the Lost Disciple.* Louisville, Ky.: Westminster John Knox Press.

Philby, Kim. 1973. *My Silent War.* Frogmore, U.K.: Panther Books. First published 1968.

Pias, Claus. 2002. *Computer Spiel Welten.* Munich: Sequenzia.

Piekalkiewicz, Janusz. 1988. *Weltgeschichte der Spionage.* Munich: Südwestverlag.

Piper, Leonard. 2003. *Dangerous Waters: The Life and Death of Erskine Childers.* London: Hambledon.

Poe, Edgar Allan. 1850. "The Purloined Letter." In *The Works of the Late Edgar Allan Poe,* edited by Nathaniel Parker Willis, James Russell Lowell, and Rufus Wilmot Griswold, 1:262–80. New York: J. S. Redfield.

Pollack, Sydney. 1975. *Three Days of the Condor.* Directed by Sydney Pollack. Written by Lorenzo Semple and David Rayfiel, based on a novel by James Grady. Starring Robert Redford, Faye Dunaway, and Max von Sydow. Paramount Pictures.

Popplewell, Richard J. 1995. *Intelligence and Imperial Defense: British Intelligence and the Defense of the British Empire, 1904–1924.* London: Frank Cass.

Posner, Gerald. 1993. *Case Closed: Lee Harvey Oswald and the Assassination of JFK.* New York: Random House.

Poundstone, William. 1992. *Prisoner's Dilemma.* New York: Doubleday.

Powers, Thomas. 2002. *Intelligence Wars: American Secret History from Hitler to Al-Qaeda.* New York: New York Review of Books.

Prouty, Fletcher. 1973. *The Secret Team: The CIA and Its Allies in Control of the United States and the World.* Englewood Cliffs, N.J.: Prentice Hall.

Pynchon, Thomas. 1995. *Gravity's Rainbow.* New York: Penguin. First published 1973.

Quist, Arvin S. 2004. *Security Classification of Information.* Full text at http://www.fas.org/sgp/library/quist/.

Rabinbach, Anson. 2003. Email to the author, June 19.

Radosh, Ronald, and Joyce Milton. 1997. *The Rosenberg File.* 2nd ed. New Haven, Conn.: Yale University Press.

Rapoport, Anatol. 1974. "Prisoner's Dilemma—Recollections and Observations." In Anatol Rapoport and Albert M. Chammah, *Game Theory as a Theory of Conflict Resolution,* 17–34. Boston: Reidel.

Renouard, Michel. 1994. "L'odeur de l'Inde dans Kim." *QWERTY,* no. 4 (October): 197–201.

Rich, Adrienne. 1981. "For Ethel Rosenberg." *Iowa Review* 12, nos. 2–3: 286–90.

Richards, Thomas. 1993. *The Imperial Archive: Knowledge and the Fantasy of Empire.* London: Verso.

Richer, Marthe. 1935. *I Spied for France.* Translated by Gerald Griffin. London: John Long.

Ritt, Martin. 1965. *The Spy Who Came In from the Cold.* Directed by Martin Ritt. Written by Paul Dehn. Starring Richard Burton, Claire Bloom, and Oskar Werner. Paramount Pictures.

Robertson, John Mackinnon. 1927. *Jesus and Judas: A Textual and Historical Investigation*. London: Watts.

Rosenberg, Ethel. 1951. "Open Letter." *National Guardian* (United States), May 16.

Ross, Don. 2010. "Games Theory." *Stanford Encyclopedia of Philosophy*, May 5. Full text online at http://plato.stanford.edu/entries/game-theory/.

Sageman, Mark. 2004. *Understanding Terror Networks*. Philadelphia: University of Pennsylvania Press.

Said, Edward. 1994. *Orientalism*. New York: Vintage. First published 1978.

Salter, Andrew. 1949. *Conditioned Reflex Therapy: The Direct Approach to the Reconstruction of Personality*. New York: Creative Age Press.

Sander, Hans-Dietrich. 1979. "Die Maßnahme, rechtsphilosophisch betrachtet." *Deutsche Studien* 17 (June): 135–54.

Sarasin, Philipp. 2006. *Anthrax: Bioterror as Fact and Fantasy*. Cambridge, Mass.: Harvard University Press.

Sauerland, Karol. 1992. "Hebbel als Schlüsselfigur für Irzykowski und Lukácz zu Beginn des 20. Jahrhunderts." *Hebbel-Jahrbuch*, no. 47, 105–15.

———. 2000. *Dreißig Silberlinge: Denunziation. Gegenwart und Geschichte*. Berlin: Volk und Welt.

Schaffner, Bertram, ed. 1957. *Group Processes: Transactions of the Third Conference October 7, 8, 9, and 10, 1956, Princeton, N.J.* New York: Josiah Macy Jr. Foundation.

Schätzing, Frank. 2006. *The Swarm*. Translated by Sally-Ann Spencer. New York: William Morrow.

Schirmann, Léon. 1994. *L'affaire Mata Hari: Enquête sur une machination*. Paris: Tallandier.

Schlögel, Karl. 1998. *Berlin Ostbahnhof Europas*. Berlin: Siedler.

Schmitt, Carl. 1985a. "Legalität und Legitimität." *Verfassungsrechtliche Aufsätze*, 263–350. Berlin: Duncker und Humblot. First published 1932.

———. 1985b. *Political Theology*. Chicago: University of Chicago Press.

———. 1985c. "Die staatsrechtliche Bedeutung der Notverordnung." In *Verfassungsrechtliche Aufsätze*, 235–62. Berlin: Duncker und Humblot. First published 1931.

———. 1995. *Die Diktatur: Von den Anfängen des modernen Souveränitätsgedankens bis zum proletarischen Klassenkampf*. Berlin: Duncker und Humblot. First published 1921.

———. 1996. *The Concept of the Political*. Translated and with an introduction by George Schwab. Chicago: University of Chicago Press.

———. 2007. *Theory of the Partisan*. Translated by G. L. Ulmen. New York: Telos.

Schneider, Manfred. 1994. "Die Allegorie der Hysterie und das tête-à-tête der Wahrheit." In *Allegorien und Geschlechterdifferenz*, edited by Sigrid Schade, Monika Wagner, and Sigrid Weigel, 137–55. Cologne: Böhlau.

Schneir, Walter, and Miriam Schneir. 1965. *Invitation to an Inquest*. Garden City, N.Y.: Doubleday.

Schoonover, Thomas. 2008. *Hitler's Man in Havana: Heinz Lüning and Nazi Espionage in Latin America*. Lexington: University Press of Kentucky.

Schragmüller, Elsbeth. 1914. *Die Bruderschaft der Borer und Balierer von Freiburg und Waldkirch*. Karlsruhe, Ger.: Braun.

———. 1936. "Aus dem deutschen Nachrichtendienst." In *Was wir vom Welt-*

krieg nicht wissen, edited by Friedrich Felger and Walter Jost, 124–38. Leipzig: Fikentscher. Volume first published 1920.

Schroers, Rolf. 1961a. "Maschinist und Partisan." *Frankfurter Hefte* 16: 149–56.

———. 1961b. *Der Partisan.* Cologne: Kiepenheuer und Witsch.

Schürer, Ernst, Manfred Keune, and Philipp Jenkins, eds. 1996. *The Berlin Wall: Representations and Perspectives.* New York: Peter Lang.

Schweitzer, Albert. 2001. *The Quest of the Historical Jesus.* Edited by John Bowden. Minneapolis, Minn.: Fortress Press.

Scorsese, Martin. 1988. *The Last Temptation of Christ.* Directed by Martin Scorsese. Written by Paul Schrader. Starring Willem Dafoe, Harvey Keitel, Barbara Hershey, Harry Dean Stanton, and David Bowie. Universal Pictures.

Seed, David. 1992. "Erskine Childers and the German Peril." *German Life and Letters* 45, no. 1 (January): 66–73.

Semprún, Jorge. 1973. *The Second Death of Ramón Mercader.* Translated by Len Ortzen. New York: Grove Press.

Serres, Michel. 2007. *The Parasite.* Translated by Lawrence R. Schehr, with an introduction by Cary Wolfe. Minneapolis: University of Minnesota Press. First published 1980.

Seton-Watson, Hugh. 1960. *Neither War nor Peace: The Struggle for Power in the Postwar World.* New York: Praeger.

Shakespeare, William. 1967. *Macbeth.* Edited by George Kirkpatrick Hunter. Harmondsworth, U.K.: Penguin.

Shipman, Pat. 2007. *Femme Fatale: Love, Lies, and the Unknown Life of Mata Hari.* New York: HarperCollins.

Shulsky, Abram, and Gary Schmitt. 1991. *Silent Warfare: Understanding the World of Intelligence.* Washington, D.C.: Brassey's.

Siegel, Don. 1977. *Telefon.* Directed by Don Siegel. Written by Peter Hyams and Stirling Silliphant. Starring Charles Bronson and Lee Remick. MGM.

Silverman, Kaja. 1992. "White Skins, Brown Masks: The Double Mimesis, or With Lawrence in Arabia." In *Male Subjectivity at the Margins,* 299–338. London: Routledge.

Simmel, Georg. 1906. "The Sociology of Secrecy and of Secret Societies." *American Journal of Sociology* 11: 441–98.

———. 1917. *Der Krieg und die geistigen Entscheidungen.* Munich: Duncker und Humblot.

———. 2009. *Sociology: Inquiries into the Construction of Social Forms.* 2 vols. Translated and edited by Anthony J. Blasi et al. Boston: Brill.

Simpson, Philip L. 2003. "Stone, Oliver." In *Conspiracy Theories in America: An Encyclopedia,* edited by Peter Knight, 175–79. Santa Barbara, Calif.: ABC-Clio.

Sloterdijk, Peter. 1987. *Critique of Cynical Reason.* Translated by Michael Eldred, with an introduction by Andreas Huyssen. Minneapolis: University of Minnesota Press.

Smyth, Edmund. 1882. "Obituary: The Pundit Nain Singh." *Proceedings of the Royal Geographical Society of London,* n.s., 4, no. 5 (May): 315–17.

Sosnowski, Saúl. 1973. "The God's Script—A Kabbalistic Quest." *Modern Fiction Studies* 19, no. 3: 381–94.

Sperber, Manès. 1987. *Like a Tear in the Ocean: A Trilogy.* Teaneck, N.J.: Holmes and Meier.

Spielberg, Steven. 2005. *War of the Worlds*. Directed by Steven Spielberg. Written by Josh Friedman and David Koepp, from the novel *War of the Worlds* by H. G. Wells (1898). Starring Tom Cruise, Dakota Fanning, and Tim Robbins. Paramount Pictures and DreamWorks Pictures.

Stafford, David. 1988. *The Silent Game: The Real World of Imaginary Spies*. Toronto: Lester and Orpen Dennis.

Starobinski, Jean. 1988. *Jean-Jacques Rousseau: Transparency and Obstruction*. Translated by A. Goldhammer. Chicago: University of Chicago Press.

Steinweg, Reiner. 1972a. *Bertolt Brecht: "Die Maßnahme." Kritische Ausgabe mit einer Spielanleitung von Reiner Steinweg*. Frankfurt am Main: Suhrkamp, Text D 30/3 Brecht.

———. 1972b. *Das Lehrstück: Brechts Theorie einer politisch-ästhetischen Erziehung*. Stuttgart: Metzlersche Verlagsbuchhandlung.

———, ed. 1976. *Brechts Modell der Lehrstücke: Zeug, Diskussion, Erfahrungen*. Frankfurt am Main: Suhrkamp.

Stephenson, Anders. 2000. "Liberty or Death: The Cold War as U.S. Ideology." In *Reviewing the Cold War: Approaches, Interpretations, Theory*, edited by Odd Arne Westar, 81–100. London: Frank Cass.

Stolleis, Michael. 1980. *Arcana imperii und ratio status: Bemerkungen zur politischen Theorie des frühen 17. Jahrhunderts*. Göttingen, Ger.: Vandenhoeck und Ruprecht.

Stone, Oliver. 1991. *JFK* (director's cut). Directed by Oliver Stone. Written by Oliver Stone and Zachary Sklar. Starring Kevin Costner, Tommy Lee Jones, Sissy Spacek, Gary Oldman, and Jim Garrison. Warner Bros.

Sun Tzu. 1963. *The Art of War*. Edited and translated by Samuel B. Griffith, with a preface by Basil Liddell Hart. Oxford: Clarendon.

Tacitus, P. Cornelius. 1996. *The Annals of Imperial Rome*. Translated by Michael Grant. Harmondsworth, U.K.: Penguin.

Tanner, Jakob. 2008. "The Conspiracy of the Invisible Hand: Anonymous Market Mechanisms and Dark Powers." In *Dark Powers: Conspiracies and Conspiracy Theory in History and Fiction*, edited by Eva Horn and Anson Rabinbach, 51–64. *New German Critique* 103, February 2008.

Tarkovsky, Andrei. 1979. *Stalker*. Directed by Andrei Tarkovsky. Written by Arkadi Strugatsky and Boris Strugatsky. Starring Alexander Kaidanovsky, Alisa Freindlich, Natasha Abramova, Anatoli Solonitsyn, and Nikolai Grinko. Mosfilm.

Taussig, Michael. 1999. *Defacement: Public Secrecy and the Labor of the Negative*. Stanford, Calif.: Stanford University Press.

Thacker, Eugene. 2004. *Networks, Swarms, Multitudes*. Two parts. Online at CTheory, http://www.ctheory.net/articles.aspx?id=422 and =423.

Thérive, André. 1951. *Essai sur les trahisons*. Preface by Raymond Aron. Paris: Calman-Lévy.

Theweleit, Klaus. 1987. *Male Fantasies*. 2 vols. Translated by Stephen Conway in collaboration with Erica Carter and Chris Turner. Minneapolis: University of Minnesota Press.

Thom, René. 1983. *Mathematical Models of Morphogenesis*. Chichester, U.K.: Horwood. First published Bring Thompson, Paul from p. 382. 1968.

Thompson, Paul. Complete 9/11 Timeline. http://www.historycommons.org/project.jsp?project=911_project.

Tolstoy, Aleksey. 1949. *Selected Stories.* Moscow: Foreign Languages Publishing House.
Towers, Robert. 1988. "From the Grassy Knoll." *New York Review of Books* 35, no. 13, August 18. http://www.nybooks.com/articles/article-preview?article_id=4350.
Treverton, Gregory F. 1987. *Covert Action: The Limits of Intervention in the Postwar World.* New York: Basic Books.
Trevor-Roper, Hugh. 1968. *The Philby Affair.* London: William Kimbler.
Trotter, David. 1991. "The Politics of Adventure in the Early British Spy Novel." In *Spy Fiction, Spy Film and Real Intelligence,* edited by Wesley K. Wark, 30–54. London: Frank Cass.
U.S. Army Intelligence School. 1996. IMINT 101. Introduction to Imagery Intelligence, February. http://www.fas.org/irp/imint/imint_101.htm.
Vaihinger, Hans. 1968. *The Philosophy of "As If."* Translated by Charles Kay Ogden. London: Routledge and Kegan Paul.
Virilio, Paul. 1989. *War and Cinema: The Logistics of Perception.* Translated by Patrick Camiller. London: Verso.
Von Hilgers, Philipp. 2011. "The History of the Black Box: The Clash of a Thing and Its Concept." *Cultural Politics* 7, no. 1: 41–58.
Wager, Walter. 1975. *Telefon.* New York: Macmillan.
Warren, Earl. 1964. *Report of the President's Commission on the Assassination of President John F. Kennedy* [Warren Report]. 1964. Washington, D.C.: United States Government Printing Office.
Watlin, Alexander. 1993. *Die Komintern 1919–1929: Historische Studien.* Mainz, Ger.: Decaton.
Weingart, Brigitte, and Ruth Meyer, eds. 2004. *Virus! Mutationen einer Metapher.* Bielefeld, Ger.: Transkript.
West, Nigel. 2004. "Fiction, Faction and Intelligence." In *Understanding Intelligence in the Twenty-First Century,* edited by L. V. Scott and P. D. Jackson, 122–34. London: Routledge.
West, Rebecca. 1947. *The Meaning of Treason.* New York: Viking.
Wheeler, William Morton. 1928. *Emergent Evolution and the Development of Societies.* New York: W. W. Norton.
Wheelright, Julie. 1992. *The Fatal Lover: Mata Hari and the Myth of Women in Espionage.* London: Collins and Brown.
White, Jack. 1998. "Evidence . . . or Not? The Zapruder Film: Can It Be Trusted?" In *Assassination Science: Experts Speak Out on the Death of JFK,* edited by James H. Fetzer, 211–20. Chicago: Catfeet Press.
Whymant, Robert. 1996. *Stalin's Spy: Richard Sorge and the Tokyo Espionage Ring.* London: I. B. Tauris.
Widmann, Carlos. 2001. "Der Che des Propheten." *Der Spiegel* no. 43, October 22: 160–62.
Wilds Craft, Brigette. 1998. "Apprentice to the Empire, or 'What Is Kim?' " *Journal of Commonwealth and Postcolonial Studies* 5, no. 2 (Fall): 18–35.
Willman, Skip. 1998. "Traversing the Fantasies of the JFK Assassination: Conspiracy and Contingency in Don DeLillo's *Libra.*" *Contemporary Literature* 39, no. 3: 405–33.
———. 1999. "Art After Dealey Plaza: Don DeLillo's *Libra.*" *Modern Fiction Studies* 45, no. 3 (Fall): 621–40.

Wilson, Andrew. 1968. *The Bomb and the Computer: Wargaming from Ancient Chinese Mapboard to Atomic Computer.* New York: Delacorte.

Wilson, Jeremy. 1989. *Lawrence of Arabia: The Authorized Biography of T. E. Lawrence.* London: Heinemann.

Wilson, Robert A. 1998. *Everything Is Under Control: Conspiracies, Cults, and Cover-Ups.* In collaboration with Miriam Joan Hill. New York: HarperCollins.

Winnacker, Susanne. 1997. *"Wer immer es ist, den ihr hier sucht, ich bin es nicht": Zur Dramaturgie der Abwesenheit in Bertolt Brechts Lehrstück "Die Maßnahme."* Frankfurt am Main: Lang.

Wise, David, and Thomas B. Ross. 1964. *The Invisible Government.* New York: Random House.

Wolf, Markus. 1997. *Man Without a Face: The Autobiography of Communism's Greatest Spymaster.* London: Jonathan Cape.

———. 1998. "L'arte della simulazione: Thesen für ein Podiumsgespräch der Accademia KOS in Mailand, März 1998." In *Die Kunst der Verstellung, Dokumente, Gespräche, Interviews,* edited by Markus Wolf, 8–18. Berlin: Schwarzkopf und Schwarzkopf.

Wollenberg, Erich. 1952. *Der Apparat.* Bonn: Bundesministerium für gesamtdeutsche Fragen.

Woodall, James. 1996. *The Man in the Mirror of the Book: A Life of Jorge Luis Borges.* London: Hodder and Stoughton.

Wright, Lawrence. 2009. *The Looming Tower: Al Qaeda and the Road to 9/11.* New York: Vintage.

Žižek, Slavoj. 1991. *Liebe dein Symptom wie dich selbst! Jacques Lacans Psychoanalyse und die Medien.* Berlin: Merve.

———. 1992a. *Enjoy Your Symptom: Jacques Lacan in Hollywood and Out.* New York: Routledge.

———. 1992b. "Symptom." In *Feminism and Psychoanalysis: A Critical Dictionary,* edited by Elisabeth Wright, Dianne Chisholm, Juliet Flower MacCannell, and Margaret Whitford, 423–27. Oxford: Blackwell.

———. 2000. *The Fragile Absolute: Or, Why Is the Christian Legacy Worth Fighting For?* London: Verso.

———. 2002. *Welcome to the Desert of the Real! Five Essays on September 11 and Related Dates.* London: Verso.

Zwick, Edward. 1998. *The Siege.* Directed by Edward Zwick. Written by Lawrence Wright, Menno Meyjes, and Edward Zwick. 20th Century Fox.

———. 2001. Interview with Val Zavala, September 19. http://www.thescreamonline.com/commentary/comment2-1/.

Zwicker, Barry. 2006. *Towers of Deception: The Media Cover-Up of 9/11.* Gabriola Island, B.C.: New Society Press.

INDEX